RURAL REFLECTIONS

A Brief History
of Traps, Trapmakers
and Gamekeeping
in Britain

Stuart Haddon-Riddoch

ARGYLL✠PUBLISHING
Glendaruel Argyll Scotland

© Stuart Haddon-Riddoch

This second edition 2006

First published 2001
Argyll Publishing
Glendaruel
Argyll PA22 3AE

British Library Cataloguing-in-Publication Data.
A catalogue record for this book is available from
the British Library.

ISBN 1 902831 96 9

Printing & Binding
Cromwell Press Ltd, Wiltshire

This book is dedicated
to the two most important 'traps' in my life.
The first 'trap' is my own 'little nipper',
my son and only child, Stewart.
The second 'trap' is my loving 'mantrap',
my wife, Lucy McInnes,
who over many years has listened patiently
to conversation after conversation about traps,
traps and more traps.
When things were not going right
it was her often well-timed humour
and never-failing encouragement for me
to finish this book and finally 'shut my trap'
that has made this book possible.

RURAL REFLECTIONS

The Advantage of a Wooden leg. upon a Pinch

The Poacher's Prayer

Keep me from the clutches of the trap
that they have laid for me,
And from the snares of those practising what is hurtful.
The wicked will fall into their own nets all together,
while I, for my part, pass by.

Psalm 141 (9-10)

ACKNOWLEDGEMENTS

I should like to acknowledge, firstly, my cousin, Trevor J. Dowson of Sheffield, with whom I have spent many long, enjoyable hours, searching through libraries and flea markets as we pursued our own separate hobbies. Secondly, the contribution of many librarians and trap collectors should be mentioned, and many other people too numerous to thank individually who have kindly supplied me with information or items of interest over the years and helped me to preserve this neglected subject.

Stuart Haddon-Riddoch
Inveraray, Argyll
February 2006

Highland Gamekeeper

IN THE EARLY 1800S, BEFORE THE INTRODUCTION OF INTENSIVE GAME
REARING OF PHEASANTS ETC IN SCOTLAND, MANY HIGHLAND MEN WERE
EMPLOYED AS GENERAL VERMIN KILLERS. MANY LAIRDS HAD LARGE ESTATES
WITH VAST NUMBERS OF SHEEP. THESE SKILLED HIGHLAND MEN WHO
SPECIALISED IN FOX CONTROL OFFERED THEIR SERVICES TO THESE
LANDOWNERS AND WERE PAID AN ANNUAL RETAINER FEE TO KEEP FOX
NUMBERS DOWN. THEY WOULD ALSO OFFER THEIR SERVICES TO ANY
FARMERS WITH SMALLER ACREAGES WHO WERE HAVING TROUBLE WITH FOXES
DURING LAMBING TIME, FOR A FEE PAYABLE FOR EVERY FOX DESTROYED.
LATER, WITH THE INTRODUCTION OF HIGHLAND SPORTING ESTATES AND
ESPECIALLY THE NEWLY FORMED DEER FORESTS, THESE MEN BECAME
HIGHLAND GAMEKEEPERS AND WOULD ALSO CONTROL THE NUMBERS OF
EAGLES, BOTH GOLDEN AND SEA EAGLES, AND SUCH PREDATORS AS THE
WILD CAT. ALL OF THESE PREDATORS WERE CAPABLE OF TAKING YOUNG
DEER, AS WELL AS THE LAMBS. DUE TO THESE MEN BEING ORIGINALLY
EMPLOYED TO SEEK OUT AND KILL FOXES, THEY WERE MORE COMMONLY
KNOWN AS TOD HUNTERS, THE REASON FOR THIS BEING THAT THE FOX IS
KNOWN, IN VARIOUS PARTS OF SCOTLAND, BY THE NAME OF TOD.

CONTENTS

THE RABBIT SUPPLY IN THE NORTH (1890)

INTRODUCTION

WHENEVER anyone in Britain is asked to name an animal trap they will usually reply a mouse, rat or gin trap. These answers are very vague to say the least. In this book I have tried to show different traps from a collector's point of view. Where possible, background information about them or their manufacturer, if any is known, has been given. I have tried to record the earliest known reference to the various trap makers and this also applies to the traps. However, it is almost impossible to say for how long a certain trap was in production.

This book is not intended as an A to Z reference guide to all the available types of traps found in Britain. It is a general reference book on British traps for the casual collector and hopefully a help to the serious student. I realise that my research is very much incomplete and I am in no doubt that I will have omitted many a type of trap and trap maker.

Information on traps and their manufacturers is hard to obtain in Britain due mainly to the absence of documents from the old trapmaking firms. The author would be most grateful to hear from any reader who has information e.g. catalogues, letterheads, bills, photographs etc. relating to the traps or the manufacturers mentioned in this book or about any others unknown to him.

Some people are confused and query the legality of possessing banned traps. They should not be because the law is quite simple with regard to traps in Britain. It is not an offence to possess any type of trap including the banned gin and pole traps. However, it is an offence to use any type of banned trap. Just because traps are illegal to use does not restrict anyone from collecting them or just hanging some on the lounge wall above the fire. All types of traps can be legally purchased, sold or even given away as gifts without any infringement of the law.

A New Era of Traps

With the imminent banning of the gin trap in 1958, other types of traps had to be designed and produced prior to this date for stringent testing. They obviously had to be as efficient as the old gin traps that they were to replace and yet meet the standards of humaneness as required by the Spring Trap Approval Order 1957. Some made it, but most failed for various reasons. A report in the September 1957 issue of the *Gamekeeper* magazine stated:

> The Humane Traps Advisory Committee has now submitted its third report to the Minister of Agriculture, Fisheries and Food, and to the Secretary of State for Scotland. In all, 174 traps have been examined since the Committee was established in 1954, and three are now recommended for approval for use against rabbits; and three for approval for use against small ground vermin.
>
> No trap suitable for open trapping (which the Minister may authorize in special circumstances) has yet come to light.
>
> Of traps which may be approved the Committee remark, quite truly, 'the crucial test is whether they are acceptable to the users,' and they go on to suggest some form of financial support to the marketing of approved traps so that users can decide which they fancy – the support might be given by the Government buying a supply of traps which would be available to users 'on loan' (loan being qualified, rather quaintly, by the words 'at a nominal charge' – which surely means hiring?). It is, at any rate, good news that the Committee is anxious about the actual marketing of approved traps, for the date of abolition of the gin trap rolls on apace (July 31st, 1958) and it is still difficult to believe that a sufficient number of substitutes will be available by then.

Further comments regarding these new humane traps is to be found in *The Shooting Times & Country Magazine* of 20th April 1962 and appears under the sub heading Humane Killers, where the reporter 'Auceps' says:

> I went last week to see Mr. W. M. F. Vane, MP, Parliamentary Secretary to the Ministry of Agriculture, present cheques to five inventors whose work has contributed towards the development of humane traps. It will be remembered that the Committee on Cruelty to Wild Animals, under the chairmanship of Mr. J. Scott Henderson, who was also chairman of the independent Awards Panel, and present on this occasion, unamimously condemned the gin as barbaric, although an efficient trap. Since the banning of the gin at the end of July 1958, a great deal of work has been put into the development of humane traps and no less than 174 designs were examined, of which only seven measured up to the panel's requirements. Mr. Vane commented that although it had been a long time coming, this day was well worth waiting for, and it proved that governments were not altogether soulless, as after the Scott Henderson report, no time had

been lost in setting up the awards scheme with a fund of £5,000 provided by the Government, so as to encourage the speedy invention of humane traps. He then presented cheques as follows: to Mr. F.E. Sawyer, Netheravon, Salisbury, £1,000 for work in connection with the development of the Imbra humane rabbit and vermin traps; Mr. R.W. Juby, Aylestone Hill, Hereford, received £750 for work in connection with the development of the Juby humane rabbit and vermin trap; to Mr. J.V. Legg, Buriton, Petersfield, Hants, £200 for work on the development of humane squirrel traps; and to Mr. R.C. Fuller, of Horsham, £100 for work on the development of humane squirrel traps.

It was a pity that Mr. Fenn of Astwood Bank, Redditch was not well enough to collect his £850 award in person. His small vermin trap is one of the most ingenious designs, and one that has proved a boon to game preservers.

Two thousand pounds remain in the kitty. Anyone who can design an effective humane fox trap stands a chance of winning a prize.

The law in Britain for approved spring traps requires that all these traps, and snares, are checked at least once in 24 hours, but out of humaneness it is better to voluntarily check them twice during the day, e.g. dawn and dusk.

Any unauthorised person interfering with any trap or snare is guilty of criminal damage and can be prosecuted under Section 1(1) of the 1971 Criminal Damage Act which states, 'A person who without lawful excuse destroys or damages any property belonging to another, intending to destroy or damage such property, or being reckless as to whether such property would be destroyed or damaged, shall be guilty of an offence.'

For six years discussions have taken place in various parts of the world by the International Standards Organisation 'to establish a voluntary inter-national standard for the testing of both killing and restraining traps.' Once this information is compiled and assessed, trap standards of performance, e.g. killing time taken by a trap or the amount of damage, if any, to an animal caught in a restraining trap, can then be used to upgrade certain types of traps, thereby improving the conditions for the trapped animal by treating it more humanely.

In July 1997, by a qualified majority, the General Affairs Council of the European Union, voted for the approval of the International Agreement on Humane Trapping Standards. Other countries agreeing to these humane trapping standards included Canada and Russia. According to Article 7 of the Agreement, all mechanical traps used for killing or restraining animals will have to undergo tests to ensure that they comply fully with the humane

Spring Traps Approval Orders Issued for England & Wales

SI 1957 No. 2216   The Spring Traps Approval Order 1957

SI 1966 No. 849   The Spring Traps Approval (Amendment) Order 1966

SI 1968 No. 645   The Spring Traps Approval (Amendment) Order 1968

SI 1970 No. 50   The Spring Traps Approval (Amendment) Order 1970

SI 1975 No. 1647   The Spring Traps Approval Order 1975

SI 1982 No. 53   The Spring Traps Approval (Variation) Order 1982

SI 1988 No. 2111   The Spring Traps Approval (Variation) Order 1988

SI 1993 No. 189   The Spring Traps Approval (Variation) Order 1993

SI 1995 No. 2427   The Spring Traps Approval Order 1995

Approved Spring Traps

Type of Trap	Target Species
Fenn vermin trap Mark I, II, III, IV Lloyd trap Payne Mark I Sawyer vermin trap Springer (multipurpose) No. 4	Small ground vermin, e.g. rat, weasel, stoat etc., but not those species listed in Schedules 5 and 6 of the Wildlife and Countryside Act 1981.
Fenn rabbit trap Mark I Fenn vermin trap Mark VI (dual purpose) Fuller Squirrel trap Imbra trap Mark I, II Juby trap Mark I, II Springer (multipurpose) No. 6	Larger ground vermin, e.g. rabbit, mink, grey squirrel etc., but not those species listed in Schedules 5 and 6 of the Wildlife and Countryside Act 1981.

All the above traps are, or were, British made.

Foreign Made Approved Spring Traps

Type of Trap	Target Species
Aldrich spring-activated animal snare	Large, non indigenous, mammalian carnivores
BMI Magnum 55	Small ground vermin (conditions as above).
BMI Magnum 110 Victor Conibear 110-2 BMI Magnum 116 Victor Conibear 120-2 Kania Trap 2000.	Larger ground vermin (conditions as above)

The Aldrich, BMI and Victor Conibear traps are all made in the United States of America, whilst the Kania trap is made in Canada.

standards agreed to. An exception to this agreement is made to allow indigenous hunters, who use traditional wooden-type traps, to carry on doing so without unnecessary restrictions being imposed upon their traditional way of life. Presently it has not been decided how each member country will enforce these humane standards or who will be responsible for testing existing and new traps. However, these new humane trapping standards will apply to every type, from a bear trap to a mouse trap.

All traps on the British Government Approved Trap List must now comply with European Union Regulation 3254/91. This Regulation prohibits the use of the so-called 'leg hold' traps and therefore reduces the risk of trapping a non target species. All traps must be set inside a natural or artificial tunnel, and the use of a spring trap, even an approved trap, in any other way is illegal.

With a population in Britain of nearly 60 million people this makes our tiny island one of the most densely populated countries in Europe. Due to most people now being born and brought up in cities or large towns, it is true to say that the British population has lost contact with the countryside and its wildlife. People generally see animals only in artificial surroundings such as city parks or man-made nature reserves.

Urban people see animals differently from the country person and these differences have contributed to the flourishing of the 'Animal Rights' organisations in Britain. What these well-meaning people often fail to see is that with proper control of the various wild animals through humane trapping methods, and more efficient traps, both mankind and surprisingly the animals can benefit from each other. With properly regulated humane trapping, wild fur-bearing species can be managed so that a known area of land can support a certain density of animals, thereby allowing mankind to harvest the surplus animals produced annually. Instead of animals reproducing to such an extent that they literally eat themselves out of 'house and home' and then either die of starvation, disease or territorial conflict, surely it is wiser to utilise this renewable natural surplus for either their fur or meat.

Many misconceptions occur about modern trapping. One is that traps with teeth are still used to catch animals and cause them suffering. But it is not in the wild fur harvester's interest to cause pain and distress to any wild caught animal as this would only encourage the animal to try and struggle free over a longer period of time, thereby rubbing and causing damage to the prime fur. This the trapper is anxious to avoid as he will receive a better price for the undamaged pelt. It is much better from the fur harvester's point of view to restrain the animal with minimum but sufficient force which allows the animal to quickly accept that it is being restrained for the moment and in its own best interest to remain calm and quiet so as not to attract attention to itself and so fall prey to some large predator out looking for an easy meal. For smaller fur bearers such as the stoat, which turns to ermine in the winter, a humane killer trap can be used, thus avoiding any unnecessary struggling.

Catching a large animal such as a fox or a coyote by the foot with modern modified so-called 'leg hold' traps is in the best interest of the animal as it causes minimum suffering. That may seem a strange claim to make, but when you consider what part of the animal is in contact with the scorching hot desert or the freezing cold and icy wastelands of the Arctic, or what part of the animal has to dig down through the soil to get at some unfortunate prey, the foot must be the toughest animal part.

I acknowledge that most of the old types of gin traps were cruel and barbaric in use due to their scalloped or riveted spiked teeth etc. Most makers didn't even bother to remove the sharp edges that were left on the jaws of the gin traps after manufacture. This resulted in the caught rabbit unintentially cutting off its own leg during its struggle to get free. Many times, a three legged rabbit lived to tell the tale of being caught in, and escaping from, a gin trap. Hugh Barrett gives an eye witness account of rabbit trapping when he recalled his early years helping a warrener during the 1930s. In his 1967 book *Early to Rise a Suffolk Morning* he remembers that all farms were so overrun with rabbits that the warrener was kept at his work the year round. He recounts:

> On a summer evening you might count a hundred all nibbling at the same time: with field glasses, you would see three times that number on any field bordered by woods or scrub. For a week or more in June I did duty with the warrener, and this opened a new door on the world, because he started work as soon as it was light, a little after three in the morning, and finished near dusk, which was after ten at night. The whole estate was riddled with rabbits (and) Vernon (the warrener) had laid traps in the entrances to burrows along three sides of the field: two hundred and fifty of them, and a hundred snares in runs out on the young barley. Nearing the trapping site the occasional clink of iron chain against stone was heard, as rabbits struggling to free themselves from the bite of the gin, told us we had a catch. The traps were laid every few yards and one in four had a rabbit in. After killing the trapped rabbit Vernon then threw the rabbit and trap to Hugh, to collect together, as he was moving on to a fresh trapping site. However, any traps which were empty he sprung and threw along with the others on to the field, too. Had he intended trapping in the same place the next night, he would merely have covered the pressure plates of the traps, so that no pheasant could be caught during the day, and then come round again in the evening, to remove the covers and sprinkle the plates with fresh earth, which attracts rabbits.

DON'T USE GINS!

IT HAS BEEN PROVED THAT RABBITS ACTUALLY INCREASE IN NUMBERS WHEN GINS ARE USED.

They are most unsuitable for rats, as they so often escape by twisting off a foot. Write for full illustrated particulars of latest efficient ways of trapping rabbits, rats, mice, moles, etc.; with full instructions for using long nets. Please help distribute Trapping and Fur Crusade Leaflets.

Major Van Der Byl, Wappenham, Towcester, Northants

FROM FEB. 1937 *GAME & GUN*

"VICTIMS OF THE STEEL - TOOTHED TRAP!"

Do You Realise that

Millions of rabbits are caught every year in the steel-toothed trap, and often linger for many hours with shattered or lacerated limbs ?

Surely this unnecessary torture should not be tolerated in a country which is known as a nation of animal lovers.

You Can Help to Prevent this Cruelty

BY URGING THE USE OF HUMANE METHODS RECOMMENDED BY THE R.S.P.C.A.

BY REFUSING TO BUY OR EAT TRAPPED RABBITS.

BY PASSING THIS INFORMATION ON TO YOUR FRIENDS.

Further details regarding humane substitutes for the steel-toothed trap will be gladly supplied by the

CHIEF SECRETARY, R.S.P.C.A.
105 Jermyn Street, London, S.W.1

(RIGHT) 1933 ADVERT

Obviously speaking from experience, Hugh Barrett considered gin traps 'horrible enough' and stated:

> . . . caught by one leg the rabbit struggles until the bone breaks, and then struggles the more, turning over and over, round and round, until the skin gives way and the poor brute is held by the tough tendons alone. Snares catch them round the neck – or well-set snares do – and often the animal is strangled pretty quickly; but sometimes as they twist and turn the wire breaks, or they pull up the peg that tethers it to the ground and go off with a tight wire round the neck to die a lingering death, down a hole, or get tangled up in a bush by the trailing wire and die there.

This widespread unnecessary suffering was mainly caused by lazy or slack trapping procedures due to the trapper trying to get as many traps set as possible in the shortest possible time. Another obvious cause was the inexperienced trapper. In Henry Lane's trap catalogue, *Traps and Trapping* (2nd edition 1926), the reason for these three legged rabbits is explained:

> **Reasons for Placing the Peg under the Trap.** – Very important reasons underlie the advice given with regard to the position of the peg. A peg driven outside the hole and away from the trap prevents the rabbit, when caught, from obeying its natural instinct to draw back into the hole. When the peg is placed in the hole the rabbit can retreat, dragging the trap with it the full distance allowed by the chain. In this

position the rabbit does not struggle to anything like the extent it would if gyrating around a peg set outside the hole. Safely hidden its fatalistic tendencies cause it to remain quiet, suffering a minimum of pain and not tempted to scream. I do not hesitate to say that ten per cent of the rabbits which are trapped outside the hole twist off their legs and so escape in a mutilated condition. A very important advantage incidental to placing both trap and peg in the position indicated is that foxes do not pull the rabbits out of the traps. They do not even attempt to scratch them out of the hole. The poaching dog has also to be considered. It will patrol the traps night after night, and drag the rabbits out wholesale. If a rabbit can draw well back into the hole there is little risk of wholesale losses from this cause, for even if the dog is doing its worst the time required to scratch out a single rabbit is considerable. Such dogs are usually chary of going any depth into a hole. Most of them have been caught in a trap at some time or another.

However, modern types of gin traps or long springs as they are known in the USA, are designed to be efficient as well as humane in the capture and restraint of any wild animal, such as a wolf for example. Indeed the following resolution was passed by the International Union for Conservation of Nature and Natural Resources/Survival Service Commission, Wolf Specialist Group, at its meeting in Leon, Spain on 22nd October 1993:

> Whereas it is often necessary to live-trap wolves for research that promotes conservation, and whereas every method of live-capturing animals presents a potential danger to the animal, now therefore be it resolved that the IUCN/SSC Wolf Specialist Group supports the use of modified steel foothold traps to live-trap wolves for conservation research as being the most efficient, effective, and practical method available of catching wolves while minimizing possible injuries. Steel foothold traps represent a method safe enough to be used in any context including wildlife refuges, protected areas or for endangered wolf populations.

Another unfortunate misconception is that because of the practice of trapping, animal populations will be brought to the edge of extinction just as the beaver was in America at the end of the fur trade years. Attitudes have changed and modern trappers are very concerned about the wildlife they hunt. After all, part of the fur harvesters' yearly income is derived from the quality of prime fur and the continued harvesting of surplus animals.

Modern trapping in North America is conducted humanely as no traps are allowed to be used which have teeth on them. Trapping is also regulated by the individual State Fish and Game or Natural Resources Department. The aims are still the same, fur harvesting, predator control in stock-rearing areas, and animal damage control, e.g. racoons in some city-dweller's chimney or beavers' dams flooding a farmer's grain crop. The individual trapper buys his or her State Trapping Licence each year and this permits the trapper to trap the various fur bearers during the stated trapping season on State-owned land, and also on private land if separate permission has been obtained. Most States now require a person who has never trapped before to complete a trapper education course. Again this is in the interests of a humane death for the intended animals and also shows the novice trapper how to skin the animal properly and prepare the pelts to obtain the best results. These courses are usually run in conjunction with the State Fish and Game Department and the Trappers Association of the individual State concerned. Upon completion of this course which includes both a written and a practical assessment, and having passed the exam, the novice trapper is allowed to purchase a trapping licence.

Each year in North America the trappers have to catch, to help keep the animal population level and healthy, approximately 70% of coyotes, 90% of muskrats, 25% of grey fox, 25% of bobcats and 75% of racoons. In fact in the United States of America, five million racoons are caught annually as well as nine million muskrats, 500,000 coyotes, 600,000 beaver, 400,000 red fox, 350,000 grey fox and 400,000 wild mink, and yet still no fur bearer is endangered by trapping. The States of Louisiana and Ohio are the top producing fur states in America, and yet they are both very heavily pop-ulated with people and animals. Both coexist in harmony, most of the time.

Only now in these enlightened times of scientific study of animal habits and populations and continuing humane trap research as carried out by such organisations as the Fur Institute of Canada, can traps be regarded as efficient humane tools of the conservationist, and not as cruel instruments of man as they were in the old days of the fur trade and the British Empire.

In Britain the old Victorian gamekeeper shot and trapped any creature that threatened his master's pheasants or other game. Even the beautiful kingfisher was on the gamekeeper's list of vermin. Why? Because its crime was to feed on the trout and salmon parr. Attitudes and values have changed and today's gamekeepers know that they are the guardians of the countryside and must work within the constraints of Government legislation. The gin trap has been banned from use in Britain since 1958 and relegated to the pages of a collector's book or hung menacingly from a sitting room wall. Government approved traps must now be used. Fines for doing otherwise are heavy.

Although the estimated total of 5,000 gamekeepers now employed throughout the British countryside still practise the art of vermin and predator control purely for the benefit of game, other forms of wildlife also benefit indirectly. Whilst he feeds his pheasants with grain in a quiet corner of what was probably a much larger estate before World War II, other creatures such as birds and voles also benefit from the spilt and scattered grain. Other creature benefits produced unintentionally by the gamekeeper include less pressure being exerted through predation by such species as mink and weasels.

Even though the gamekeeper keeps down the total number of predators such as stoats, foxes and magpies, he realises that each creature has a role to play in nature's eternal plan. There are now several colleges throughout Britain that have full-time courses on gamekeeping and emphasis is put on wildlife conservation. Other organisations which also hold special courses including trapping are the British Association for Shooting and Conservation, and the Game Conservancy Trust. These courses here, and in America, are proving that gamekeeping and fur harvesting can go hand in hand with the better known conservation ideas to produce an ecological balance in our ever changing countryside.

We must all remember the quote from King George VI, 'The wildlife of today is not ours to dispose of as we please. We have it in trust, we must account for it to those who come after.'

VERMIN CONTROL IN 1885

Chapter One

BACKGROUND

NO-ONE can say for sure when the first properly built trap was made in Britain. It was most likely just a deep hole dug in the ground on an established animal trail that hunter/gatherers had observed animals using on a regular basis. Having decided on the best site for the pit, and having excavated it to a suitable depth, they would then simply cover it over with light branches and grasses until it blended in with the surroundings. The animal or herd of animals would either stumble and fall into it of their own accord or could be chased in the direction of the waiting trap. A later modification to this simple hole would be the inclusion of one or more embedded upright pointed wooden stakes securely fixed into the bottom of the hole, and so thereby impaling the unfortunate animal when it fell into the pit. The wooden stakes would immobilise the animal quicker and lessen the chances of the animal just falling into the pit and remaining either unharmed or only slightly injured, and thereby posing a dangerous threat.

DEADFALL TRAP (c1870)

As time went by, primitive man would try to catch these animals more efficiently and also probably more selectively. It was obviously better to put time and effort into catching an animal that was of use to you than one that was not. Nets, snares and especially deadfall traps would have been used extensively on regularly used animal travel ways and also at their drinking places. In areas of peat bog a type of trap known as a treadle trap has been discovered in Ireland, Wales and Scotland. The dating of these traps, by pollen analysis, has shown that at least an Irish trap found at Drumacaladerry Bog, in North Donegal, can be dated back to around 1000BC, which is the late Bronze Age. Further evidence exists as to their use, as can be seen on the Clonmacnois Stone, again in Ireland, which dates back to around the 8th or 9th century AD. One scene on this sculptured cross slab shows a deer caught by the hoof in one of these traps. These traps were usually used in groups in marshy ground or at favourite watering places and they are mostly made of oak. One found in the moss of Auqharney, Aberdeenshire, Scotland, was made of the wood of the alder tree.

Treadle traps were of a heavy construction, rectangular in shape and varying in length from just over two feet to almost five feet in length. In the centre of the trap is cut out an opening of about nine inches by four inches. The underside of the trap was hollowed out and a flat wooden, crudely hinged flap or valve was held open by a wooden peg inserted between the valve and the side of the trap body. These were kept under tension by a willow bow-shaped spring, which was fixed in place at the furthest opposite ends of the trap. Willow wood is known for its springy qualities and suppleness. When the deer knocked out the peg with its hoof, the bowed willow spring's tension was released and as it straightened itself out quickly pushed the flap or valve against the body of the trap and in doing so captured the deer's hoof between them. Due to the awkward size and weight of the oak trap, the deer could not move too far from where it was caught. Using these traps in groups against a herd of deer or wild boar, would probably result in at least the capture of one individual. Once burdened by the trap attached to its hoof, it would soon be overtaken and killed by the pursuing hunter with spear or bow and arrow.

Little is known about traps during the Roman occupation of Britain, but bee-hive-shaped mole traps have been excavated at known Roman sites. It is most likely that pits and nets were again the most commonly used traps by the Romans in Britain. A mosaic showing submerged nets in shallow water, presumably for catching fish, is in the British Museum in London.

Another simple way to catch fish can be seen on the island of Lismore in Argyll, Scotland. Here stands the ruins of Castle Coeffin, which is thought to date from the 13th century and lies in close proximity to the diocesan cathedral which is known to have been established on the island some time during the late 12th or early 13th century. Situated in a gently shelving bay to the southeast of the castle is a tidal fish trap of unknown age. This is approximately U-shaped on plan and takes the form of a broad dry stone wall laid directly upon the sea bed a little below high water level. Obviously when the tide receded, any fish left behind this low retained wall had no means of escape and were easily caught.

There is a well-known connection between the church and fish, and certain monastic orders purposely built freshwater carp stew ponds to supplement their diets. The monks of Paisley in Scotland had been setting nets and constructing traps on the River Clyde to catch salmon and sea trout since they were first granted a charter to do so in 1165.

On the River Eden at Corby Castle, near Carlisle, and still remaining in working order, are salmon 'coops', which stretch across the water. These permanent salmon traps are reputed to be the first ones ever built in England and date from the early part of Henry I's reign (about 1115). It is recorded in a charter granted by Ranulf Mechin, the Earl of Chester, to the monks of Wetheral that 'the monks were to be allowed a fishery and sluice pool in the land of Chorkeby'. This charter was confirmed by Henry I in 1131. These salmon 'coops' or traps 'consist of heavy masonry piers in the river, like those of a bridge. Across the upstream ends of the piers are stout oak grilles; the downstream ends are closed by two grilles placed v-shaped, with a narrow entrance at the apex. A rather similar principle to a lobster pot in a horizontal position'. A similar system was also employed in the trapping of eels. A series of wicker traps, set in line on the river bottom, could be individually raised and emptied of its contents and then lowered back into the river to continue working. An obvious advantage to this system of semi permanent traps, is that during times of flooding all the traps could be raised above the raging river and therefore hopefully out of harm's way.

EEL BUCKS
CIRCA 1890

Another early fish trap, but this time of a portable type, was found during the 1990s excavation work which took place in what was the moat that surrounded the Tower of London. A wicker fish trap was discovered, which was still held in place by flint weights on each side of its open end. This trap although fragile was in relatively good condition and the digs director, Graham Keevill, said that it dated from about 1500.

The monks of Wetheral were not the only monks to be setting traps. Indeed the monks of Melrose, who were living in the Scottish border country of Eskdale, had been setting traps, although it is not known of what type, for wolves etc. since the reign of William the Lion (1165-1214) in order to protect their crops and livestock. However, in a dispute between the monks and the descendants of Robert de Avenel, who granted the pastoral rights to them originally, it was decided by a judgement of King Alexander II in 1235 that the monks had no right to hunt over the lands in dispute and were restricted from setting traps, excepting for wolves.

In England two hereditary chief foresters, known as foresters of fee, living in Derbyshire and called John le Wolfehunte and Thomas Foljambe, were both skilled wolf hunters in the latter part of the 13th century. They were commanded by the king 'to set traps each year in March and September in those places in the forest where hounds had scented wolves'. These two men were also allowed to 'employ a sworn servant to carry the traps'. In England the wolf was hunted for sport between 25th December and 25th March in the lesser populated areas by the nobleman with his mastiffs, 'highland greyhounds' and prized Irish wolfhounds. These dogs were also used seriously, outside of the hunting season, for the total eradication of wolves where these animals were a greater threat to the villagers and their livestock in the more densely inhabited districts.

The county of Yorkshire seems to have retained a remnant wolf population later than any other part of England. Even though, during the reign of Henry VII (1485-1509) due to the burning and cutting down of forests to create farmland and bounties paid for dead wolves, the wolf was fading into the mists of history and was being regarded as extinct in England. In Scotland the wolf evaded extinction, due mainly to the ideal combination of low human population with vast areas of wilderness and forests, for a few centuries more until MacQueen of Pall-a'-Chrocain killed the last one in 1743 near Inverness. The wolf survived even longer in Ireland even though in the 'book of information' compiled by Robert Legge in 1584 by order of Sir John Perrott, it stated that for the 'destruction of ravening and devouring wolves, some order might be had, as when any lease is granted, to put in some clause that the tenant endeavour himself to spoil and kill wolves with traps, snares, or such devices as he may devise'. Then around the dates of 1766-1770 'the woods yield no more, and all the rav'nous race extinct'.

Snares were probably still the most commonly used devices around this time for acquiring food silently and also for vermin destruction due to their cheapness in construction and being simple to make and operate. In Abraham Fleming's translation in 1576 of Caius Johannes book, published under the title *Englishe Dogges*, it states:

> Another sorte there is which hunteth the foxe and the badger. . . whom we call terrars, . . . drive them out of their hollow harbours, in . . . speedy flight, and being desirous of the next refuge, are otherwise taken and intrapped with snares and nettes layde ouer holes to the same purpose.

Colourful song birds were caught by various means out in the countryside, for selling to the 'bird fancy' in the larger cities. Here they were sold to become caged birds for the admiration and entertainment of the wealthier Victorian families. Other song birds though, met with a different fate. Birds, not now associated with being eaten in Britain, were also caught in large numbers. Wheatear snaring was an activity mainly confined to the very south of England and was indulged in by the shepherds while tending their flocks on the Sussex Downs. In the book *Nature in Downland* by W.H. Hudson, published in 1900, the author writes that the annual wheatear harvest was formerly a source of considerable profit to the shepherds of the South Downs. He claimed the most successful actually made more by wheatear-catching from July to September than the farmers paid them for the whole year's shepherding.

Describing the trapping he writes:

> In July the shepherds made their 'coops,' as their traps were called – a T-shaped trench about fourteen inches long, over which the two long narrow sods cut neatly out of the turf were adjusted, grass downwards. A small opening was left at the end for ingress, and there was room in the passage for the bird to pass through toward the chinks of light coming from the two ends of the cross passage. At the inner end of the passage a horse-hair springe was set, by which the bird was caught by the neck as it passed in, but the noose did not as a rule strangle the bird . . . the shepherds made so many coops, placed at small distances apart, that the downs in some places looked as if they had been ploughed. In September, when the season was over, the sods were carefully put back, roots down, in their places, and the smooth green surface was restored to the hills.

Wheatear snaring ceased around 1880-90 due to the sheep farmers stopping the shepherds from this practice as they were supposedly neglecting their shepherding duties. Other bird catchers though, still continued to supply the local poulterers and markets of London and Brighton with 'hundreds of dozens' of netted larks at a price of about a shilling a dozen. Larger nets were also employed on the sea shore to intercept known flight lines of wildfowl. These large nets were also used effectively when hung across woodland glades, again on known flight lines, of woodcock and other such game birds. Once the net was hung up in position, the birds would be quietly disturbed and taking wing would naturally follow their known escape route through the woodland glade and into the waiting net which would blend naturally into the background. There they would hang, entangled in the netting, struggling and waiting their ultimate fate.

Another use for nets, but on a much grander and permanent basis, came with the introduction of the duck decoy, which was also referred to as the decoy pipe. An early type of decoy was originally owned by Sir John Wooley at Pyrford in Surrey during the reign of Elizabeth I (1558–1603). However, it is thought that the first properly planned decoy in England was built about 1620 by Sir William Woodhouse at Waxham in Norfolk. The idea of using purposely built duck decoys was really imported from Holland where they were in common use. Charles II had taken sanctuary in Holland, after his father King Charles I had been executed in 1649. On his restoration to the throne in 1660, the idea of catching wildfowl more efficiently and on a much larger scale was brought to England with him. King Charles II now ordered his own duck decoy to be constructed in Saint James Park in London and this was completed in 1665. The supervision of the construction of this decoy was done by a dutchman called Sydrach Hilcus and records still exist as to the materials used, e.g. poles, reeds and nets etc, and the costs involved. From the dutch word *eendekooi*, which literally means a duck cage, the English word decoy is derived.

Basically, a duck decoy consists ideally of a shallow pool of water between one and three acres in size, secluded by trees and sheltered from the worst of the weather, where ducks can come and fly in and out unmolested and also rest in peace in total seclusion. From three to six pipes, or arms, are usually found on most decoys but eight have been known. These pipes curve away gently from the pond into the surrounding woodland leading their intended victims towards their doom. The mouth of each pipe should be no less than 21 feet wide, and the first hoop that carries the netting should be at a height of at least 12 feet above the surface of the water. Each pipe is approximately 50 to 70 yards in length, with each hoop carrying the netting getting progressively smaller in height, until at the end of the pipe they are only 2 feet high and the water only a few inches deep. Once the duck have been enticed quite a way down the netted tunnel and have reached a certain point, the decoyman and his dog, known as a piper, show themselves and start to chase the ducks further down into the netted, narrowing tunnel. The ducks

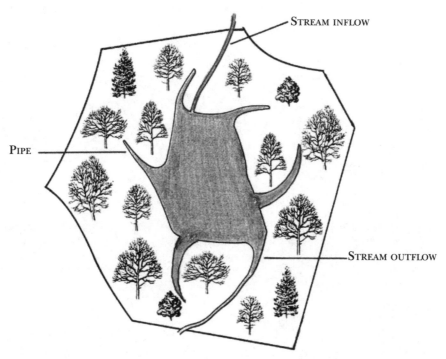

STREAM INFLOW

PIPE

STREAM OUTFLOW

AERIAL VIEW OF DUCK DECOY

rapidly take fright and flap away from them further down the netted tunnel, where they are unable to take to their wings and escape. At the end of the pipe, where they eventually all congregate crammed together, is the detachable catching net from which they are taken and killed. Obviously the call ducks, as the tame ducks were known, which acted as decoys to attract the wild ducks onto the 'safe pond' were easily identified by certain markings, e.g. notches cut into the webbed feet etc and so spared the fate of their associates.

In England 188 duck decoys were known, and mainly situated on the eastern side of England, whilst five are known to have existed in Wales. Strangely, no purposely built decoys are known in Scotland. In the north of Scotland between Nairn and Elgin, near Findhorn Bay on the Moray Firth, one was under construction but for some unknown reason was never completed. Duck decoying was obviously most successfully achieved during the winter, when natural food for the birds was hard to find. Keeping the water from freezing over and by artificial feeding and the use of the tame 'call birds', the wild ducks would be encouraged to visit and stay on the 'safe pond'. There is no doubt as to how effective these decoys were as records show. In its first five operating months during 1721 Steeple Decoy in Essex took 16,364 assorted duck, whilst 13,180 duck were taken at Dowsly Decoy in Lincolnshire between 1st October 1765 and 1st April 1766. From

LINCOLNSHIRE DUCK DECOY, CIRCA 1870

September 1833 to April 1868 the Ashby Decoy in Leicestershire took 95,836 assorted duck.

Due to the various drainage acts which were introduced to produce more viable agricultural farming land from what was regarded then as unproductive wetlands, the decline of the decoys started. Increased disturbance from the ever encroaching expanding railway network throughout the land took its toll and by the mid 1850s the working decoys were rapidly being abandoned and falling into neglect. Today only four working decoys exist and these are worked for conservation organisations. The assorted wildfowl that are caught are now leg-ringed or otherwise marked with large bright wing tags for identification purposes and released unharmed. This is all done in the pursuit of scientific knowledge with regard to bird migration etc.

Over the years both metal and wooden traps would gradually evolve and improve in design and efficiency until by 1590 the style of traps were well established as is shown in Leonard Mascall's book published in London in that year. In *A Booke of Engines and Traps to take Polecats. Buzardes, Rattes, Mice and all other Kindes of Vermine and Beasts Whatsover, most profitable for all Warriners, and such as delight in this kinde of sport and pastime*, he describes 35 mechanical devices and also gives many herbal and chemical recipes for destroying or driving off pests. Traps mentioned include single and double square box traps for catching mice and rats alive. The deadfall, in its same form continued to be used right into the early 1900s, as did a version of the universal 'piece of wood extending over the edge of a table top with a water container below'. This version though consisted of vanes, which were smeared with bait, attached to a spindle, which although attached to the table top rotated freely under the weight of a mouse thereby dropping the mouse into the awaiting container of water below.

Another type of mouse trap was the 'spring trappe' which operated a choker loop once the mouse had gnawed through a string which obstructed its way to the bait. Again similar versions were sold and advertised into the 1950s in Britain. All these traps were made of wood, but one trap he described as 'the gripping trappe made all of yrone, the lowest barre and the ring or hoope with two clickets'. We would recognise this trap today, from the illustration in the book, as a double flat-springed, round-jawed gin trap with spiked teeth and a treadle plate.

Then in the 1590s a law was passed by Parliament, due to the concerns of the nobility, that excessive hare poaching was taking place by 'men of vulgar sort', that after the 1st August 1604, 'any person destroying, tracing, or coursing hare in snow, or at any time taking or destroying any hares with hare pipes, cords or any such instruments or engines, should be committed to the common gaol for three months without bail, unless for the offender paid 20 shillings for the use of the poor of the parish'.

In a later book of 1686, also printed in England and titled *The Gentleman's Recreation* it states that 'Iron traps can readily be bought throughout England, and that most people know how to open or set them'. This book also shows an illustration of a single-springed, round-jawed, spike-toothed gin-type trap, taken from Francois Fortin's French trapping manual of 1660. Again in Fortin's trapping manual it is mentioned that such traps may be purchased from ironmongers and merchants everywhere.

With such traps being readily available throughout England and parts of Europe, it is not very surprising that they would find their way over to the North American continent. These traps would have arrived, as essentials, with the explorers and settlers in Canada, New England States and the Carolinas, in the early 1600s. It is estimated that by 1770, more than 400,000 immigrants had crossed the Atlantic from Europe in the hope of starting a new life there. Once ashore, inland from the Atlantic coast, lay a vast wilderness to be explored and settled. Woodland would be felled and cleared to form good farming land, over many backbreaking years, and further expansion into the surrounding areas would be a natural progression. However, danger and hardship was always a part of normal daily life for these people. With the constant uncertainties that existed, everybody learned to rely upon their own instincts for survival. Precious seed crops and livestock would need to be protected from vermin and predators and initially assorted types of traps would have been employed, with the smoothbore musket, and later on the 'long rifle', employed to protect themselves from large dangerous animals and especially the unfriendly native Indians, that they would encounter. These same traps would be used extensively in the expansion of the growing fur trade.

An early indication that gin traps were being used in the New World is shown in correspondence to employees of an English partnership called the Newfoundland Company in the early 1600s whereby they were instructed '. . . and by hunting shewtinge, trapps and gins you shall tacke and kill stackes beavers, oatters, foxes and have care to save and preserve their furres'. Around the mid 1600s felt hats manufactured from beaver pelts became a very popular fashion in Europe. This fashion for beaver hats and other fur started the fur trade boom that was to last for around two hundred years. Indeed the fur trappers routes would eventually open up the interior of North America and Canada to the settlers from the eastern coasts.

One company to realise and take advantage of this untapped fur resource in Canada was founded in 1670 by English Royal Charter and called the Hudson Bay Company. This company would dominate the Canadian fur trade within a very short period of time. Nearly a century later a rival company would challenge their position. Over many decades the Scottish Highlanders had been emigrating to the eastern maritime regions of Canada and eventually in the 1760s they were converging upon Montreal to set up various small businesses. Simon McTavish, a leading Scottish trader, brought about a series of mergers, with other mainly Scottish merchants, in 1775 to form a group known as the North West Company. Their employees becoming known as Nor'westers.

During the 1790s the Canadian fur trade was at its height and Simon McTavish was known by then as 'the Marquis of the Montreal fur trade'. Eventually after many years of fierce rivalry, which did neither business any good, the North West Company merged with the Hudson Bay Company in 1821. The Nor'westers name was swallowed up, with total control of both merged businesses going to the Hudson Bay Company.

Records show that between the years 1751 and 1783 the Hudson Bay Company imported from England to their trading posts, along with other more general goods, various sizes of traps with double springs. One entry states 'steel traps for foxes with double springs', but unfortunately no sizes are given. Another report, during the winter of 1785-1786, of double-springed traps supplied by the Hudson Bay Company were said to be five feet in length and weighing 70 pounds and used for trapping wolves and wolverines.

Other smaller traps were also being imported, as is shown in a 1760 advertisement offering steel rat traps from England, from a Benjamin Kendall who was a Philadelphia storekeeper. Unfortunately no mention is made of the maker's name or from where in England these traps were made.

There is reputed to exist an old ballad which mentions that during the reign of King Charles II (1660-1685), the small village of Wednesfield was already known for its trapmaking activities. It is known though that steel traps were being made in the late 1700s in the Birmingham area with one individual listed as a maker of fox and mantraps.

Regular problems were encountered with the imported traps to the New World. Such problems as traps being broken by wolves, springs coming off or broken by the extreme cold, weak springs and insufficient strength of the traps were all mentioned in journals.

The problem of poor quality metal had also been noticed back in England, but by a Quaker of Dutch extraction. Whilst practising his craft of clock maker in Doncaster, he had become so dissatisfied with the quality of the metal he was using for his clock springs that he started to experiment in producing a better quality of steel. About 1740 he moved to a village called Handsworth near Sheffield, thereby gaining access to specialised knowledge and containers, which were used to melt materials at very high temperatures, at a local glass works at Catcliffe. Steel at that time was called 'blister steel' which derived its name from its characteristic appearance. Blister steel was good for many uses, but its major drawback was that it had never reached its real melting point whilst being made, and so was never completely uniform within, and therefore not totally reliable.

In 1742 after years of extensive experimenting both at Doncaster and finally near Sheffield, Benjamin Huntsman who was born in 1704 at Barton on Humber in Lincolnshire, changed all that with his new process of crucible steel. He had managed to melt steel at such a high temperature that for the first time the steel melted completely, and therefore the chemical reactions became uniform throughout the steel. He died in 1776 but his discovery put Sheffield firmly on the steel-making map. People and businesses though were reluctant to change and iron still reigned supreme. Even in a report sent to the Hudson Bay Company Governor and Committee in London in 1821 it stated,

'The supplies of this department generally are of good quality, the ironmongery excepted, which is a real disgrace to the tradesmen who furnish it. The beaver traps (marked MS on the bait plate) are too weak and made of the worst British iron, whereas they should be made of the best Swedish. . . The cross plate is too slight and should be fastened by a screw and nut instead of a clenched nail. The traps are now packed up as required for use whereas the pieces should be packed up separately in order to be put together at pleasure, which would prevent breakage in the transport hither: the Indians complain that the traps are altogether too slight, so weak as not to hold a full grown beaver.'

In another report to London in 1822 again from George Simpson he states,

'Course iron works such as hatchets, beaver traps, ice chisels etc. we find can be manufactured at this place on much lower terms than imported from England, we have therefore indented for very few, our blacksmiths understand the temper required for this climate better than English tradesmen usually do, but it will always be necessary that strict attention is paid to the quality and description of iron applied for, as hitherto we have had great cause of complaint on that head.'

Another problem for the English trap makers around this time was that during the 1830s the fashion for felt beaver hats started to change. Silk hats became fashionable and the European demand for fur started to decline.

During the early days of pelt preparation, a solution containing mercury was brushed onto the pelt in preparation for the felting process. Unaware of the dangers of using mercury, many hatters suffered from Minimatas Disease, otherwise known as mercury poisoning. This condition was the cause of erratic or irrational behaviour as the hatter's mental health deteriorated and created the term Mad as a Hatter.

With the demand for fur lessening, so did the demand for traps. The Hudson Bay Company had leased from Russia all its North American holdings (namely Alaska) from 1840 to 1860 at a yearly cost of 2000 otter pelts. When Russia decided to sell off this vast wilderness, the Company tried to persuade Great Britain to purchase the land, and even offered to repay the purchase price with interest, if the Hudson Bay Company was granted exclusive rights to take fur in the territory. Great Britain declined the offer and when America purchased the Russian holdings in 1867 the Company's activities ceased in that area.

The trap makers then had to look to other countries to sell their products. With the expansion of the British Empire the Victorian trap makers soon took advantage.

Even though Benjamin Huntsman had produced a better product earlier, in the early 1850s wrought iron was still being used extensively throughout the metal trades. Steel was still only being used on a comparatively small scale and only then for special purposes, e.g. various springs, tools etc. Iron was in a period of boom as railways spread the length and breadth of Britain, but 1856 saw the metal that was to ultimately replace iron. Henry Bessemer, of French ancestry, but born in England in 1813, devised the idea of a high speed blast of cold air through the heated mass of pig iron, thereby quickly burning out any impurities in the metal. Regulating the length of the blast of air through the iron could now produce either malleable iron (without carbon) or steel. This method made really good steel provided that suitable iron, and a special added ingredient – manganese – were used. Mild steel could now be made by bulk production methods, and the turn of the century would see iron finally relegated to second place.

According to the book *Smith's Work*, which was published in 1899, wrought iron was made in four qualities, the grades being 'Ordinary' or common, 'Best', 'Best, Best', and 'Best, Best, Best'. The Lowmoor iron and the treble Best qualities of Staffordshire iron were considered to be comparatively close-grained and tough – wrought iron was never perfectly homogeneous, whilst mild steel was of the same character throughout. *Smith's Work* explains, 'in order to render this material (wrought iron) more homogeneous, the pasty mass is compressed under steam hammers or tilt hammers, and is passed beneath squeezers of different types, is cut up again and reheated, and the operations of hammering, squeezing and rolling are repeated, the homogeneous quality of the iron improving with each repetition.

On the subject of steel springs, the book explains:

'springs are hardened in the usual way by heating to a cherry red, and quenching in water then they are smeared with tallow or lard, and heated over the fire, moving them to and fro until the tallow catches fire, and blazes and burns off. The springs are then laid upon the forge, or in the ashes to cool down. If the work is of irregular thickness, the burning of the oil should be repeated 2 or 3 times. Small springs made in quantities and often put into a sheet iron pan and covered with oil, and held over the fire until the oil blazes and burns off. Moving and shaking the pan about causes the temper to be more uniform. In the case of heavy springs the operation may be repeated 2 or 3 times.'

Meanwhile during the early 1800s the small village of Wednesfield, which lies to the north east of Wolverhampton, became the trapmaking centre for Britain. This trade probably grew from the local blacksmiths who made such items as hinges, hasps and brackets for the local rural communities and nearby towns. The village lies in the north of an area in the Midlands called the 'Black Country', which received its name from the grimy conditions caused by the industrial activity in this area with coal mines and iron works. From this small rural village on the edge of the busy industrial heartland traps were to be produced first by hand, then later by machinery which would win trade medals at various exhibitions around the world including Brussels and also in the southern hemisphere. To quote Lane's catalogue of 1926, when they had just been awarded a gold medal in the New Zealand and South Seas International Exhibition, Dunedin, 1925-1926, regarding the two different types of manufacture,

> 'It is interesting to note that both hand and machine made traps were included in the exhibit and we think that, since the latter type formed a large percentage of all the types exhibited and were actually taken from stock, merely being polished in certain places to define the outlines, and varnished to prevent rust, we have every reason to be proud of our achievements.'

These same trap makers were to produce traps of all sizes and designs for the considerable export trade which was being slowly built up during the mid 1800s. As well as producing traps for beaver, muskrat and other North American animals, traps were also made to catch the lion in Africa, tiger in India, and even down to the common rabbit gin for export to Australia.

After the American War of Independence in 1776, British convicts could no longer be transported to the American colonies (as had been authorised by Parliament since 1717) and so the Government then decided that the offenders should be sent to the 'Australian wilderness' instead to serve out their sentences. The first fleet had arrived in Sydney Cove in 1788 and comprised around 1,000 convicts and their jailers. It is possible that some of the earliest rabbits in Australia arrived by this route, purely as a renewable food source. In 1827 it was reported that Tasmania had by then a large number of rabbits. Ten years later in 1837, 14 rabbits were listed among the Everard family livestock at Glenelg. In 1842, John Daw listed a warren amongst his capital assets on his property in what is now suburban Adelaide. All these rabbits are thought to be domestic stock, but in 1859 Thomas Austin of 'Barwon Park' Geelong, introduced 24 wild rabbits off the clipper *Lightning*. Within six years, 1865 approximately, it is said that 20,000 rabbits were killed on the estate. By the time the last convict ship *The Hougoumont* sailed to Western Australia in 1868, Eastern Australia was being quickly overrun by the rabbits, a process which still continues today. The extent to which rabbits were multiplying in a country with suitable habitat and few predators can be seen when the senior research officer of the South Australia State Government's Animal and Plant Control Commission visited one ranch during a period of drought in 1988. Dr. Brian Cooke visited the 7,252 square kilometre Quinyambie Cattle Station which lies several hundred kilometres north of Adelaide on the border between the State of South Australia and New South Wales, and estimated 24 million rabbits were on the land. According to the Bureau of Agricultural and Resource Economics, the wild rabbit population is estimated to exceed 200 million or approximately thirteen rabbits for every Australian.

One company to take advantage of this massive buildup in the rabbit population was W.&G. Sidebotham, who started to build up a large export trade to Australia. In the early 1900s thousands of rabbit gin traps made by this company would be packed into large metal tanks which were made by Davis's of Cannock Road, Wolverhampton, and shipped out for destinations on the other side of the world. These large tanks would ultimately be used as water containers in the Australian outback. These far-travelled traps made by Sidebotham's and various other manufacturers were basically 4 inch jawed gin traps, but also larger jawed double-springed traps were exported to catch dingoes (wild dogs) and the introduced red fox from Britain.

Other important export markets included the British colonies in Africa. Unexpectedly and 'without any previous notification', due to humanitarian concerns, the Governor of Nigeria, Sir Walter Egerton imposed a prohibitory tariff of one shilling on each trap being imported into the country. According to the local newspaper, the *Express and Star* of 7th December 1908, this action caused 'considerable anxiety in the locality, where so many look to this class of work for their sustenance'. This unexpected 'prohibition has resulted in leaving large stocks of traps on the hands of manufacturers and merchants . . . involving much loss and privation to men, women and children there, and in injuriously affecting businesses which have been carried on there for generations.' The Wednesfield Steel Vermin Trap Manufacturers Association according to the newspaper, have been in correspondence with the Colonial Office. They also enlisted the help of their local member of Parliament for East Wolverhampton, the Honourable Member, Alderman George R. Thorne by getting him to ask a question in Parliament.

The reason the Governor had imposed the tariff was due to 'the extensive use for trapping birds and small animals, and even deer (with) the cruel iron toothed spring trap. Round Ibadan probably 40 to 50 per cent of the bush fowl shot have only one leg, the other having been torn off in a trap.'

Mr William Sidebotham commenting on the shilling duty payable on each trap said, 'The duty is six times the value of some of the traps, of which they buy all sizes. The trade as a whole is affected. The loss would equal one third of the whole trade of the district, which is a serious item.' A newspaper report goes on to say that 'a great difficulty is, in fact, experienced in finding the men work in consequence of the loss of this trade, which as an individual market is probably the biggest for this kind of thing in the world, with the exception of Australia and New Zealand, and has been largely developed within the last seven years.'

Mr Sidebotham continued, 'We could formerly rely on two days' work a week for this one market.' The newspaper reported, 'Many of the goods made and rejected are stamped with the makers' names and trade marks, and are useless for other buyers; and shipments are even lying at Liverpool.'

The Colonial Office was quoted as saying that the trap trade 'must recognise a strong and increasing feeling in this country based against the use of traps of this nature.'

James Roberts, who had taken a prominent part in the protest, defended the trap as the most humane and effective instrument for the extermination of vermin, and it was pointed out that although a special prize has been offered to the inventor of a trap which shall pass the test of the humanitarians, the money is still unclaimed.

Colonel Seely had been informed that approximately 2,000,000 traps were made each year at Wednesfield, and that quite one third of that output would be for South Nigerian markets, the balance being distributed amongst Australia, New Zealand, South Africa, Canada, South America, India, China, the Straits Settlements, and the United Kingdom. The Wednesfield Trap Manufacturers' Association were informed that the Governor of the colony was expected to reach England shortly 'when he will be consulted'.

The *Wolverhampton Chronicle* of 31st March 1909 recorded the outcome of this dispute under the heading of Trapmakers' Victory. It read:

> It is satisfactory to find that as a result of the representations
> which have been made at the Colonial Office, and the thorough-
> ness with which the Hon. member for East Wolverhampton, Mr.
> George R. Thorne, has carried forward his important share in the
> negotiations, the trapmakers of Wednesfield have gained a victory
> with respect to the Nigerian impost. On Thursday a deputation
> waited upon Colonel Seely at the Colonial Office, there being also
> present the Governor of Nigeria (Sir Walter Egerton), Mr. George
> R. Thorne MP. (plus) The Master Trapmakers' Association was
> represented by Mr James Roberts (chairman), Mr W. Sidebotham
> (secretary), and Mr Joseph Tonks; the workmens' representatives
> being Messrs. E. Dudley, W. Hadley and Councillor Taylor JP. All
> the points on behalf of the industry were set forth, Mr Thorne
> introducing the deputation, and emphasising the importance of
> the issues to the district from the wages aspect. As an illustration
> of this Mr Roberts mentioned that large stocks of traps had been
> left on hand in consequence of the impost; in 1907 there were
> 126,239 traps sent into the port; in 1908 206,000; and that
> whereas he paid in wages for the month of February,1908, £225,
> he only paid for the corresponding month of this year £73. Three
> hundred persons are enganged in the trap trade generally and if
> the duty were insisted upon, misery and want would be increased
> in the locality.

It was reported that while the Governor had no wish to cause any hardship, he was still concerned about the humanitarian aspect of the gin trap. With this in mind he suggested the importation of traps without teeth, a suggestion that was accepted by the deputation. Samples of toothless traps were to be sent to the Colonial Office.

Trap designs varied as is shown in documents held by the National Union of Lock and Metal Workers at Willenhall, England. In these documents mention is made of the Trap Makers being 'specialists in the complexities of hawk, flat bird traps, single or double spring vermin traps, four qualities of rabbit traps, and twenty-four grades of rat trap, mole traps and 'real Dorset traps'.' In fact according to a 1953 advertisement, before World War II there were upwards of 150 different traps manufactured by the (Henry) Lane firm. Some of the better-known trap makers of the time, apart from the above two, were Griffiths, Roberts and the large Marshall family. Various members of this family had been involved in the trap making trade since the early 1800s at Wednesfield. George Marshall who lived at March End in 1813, seems to have had an established business at this time and may even have been one of the first trap makers in the Wednesfield area. Descendants of the Marshall family continued in the trap making trade until its virtual extinction.

An early effect on trap production occurred in 1827 when lethal booby traps, e.g. spring guns, and mantraps were banned from use in Britain. A spring gun is a small cannon-like device which usually swivelled in the poacher's direction upon the trip wire being snagged by a leg or foot. This action resulted in the discharge of a load of shot immediately in the person's direction and caused horrific injuries to the legs and the lower torso. The next legislation to follow came in 1904 with the banning from use of pole traps for catching such birds as crows, hawks and even kingfishers. This Act abolished the pole trap, or any trap put on or in an elevated position . . .

> 'from and after the passing of this Act every person who on any pole, tree, or cairn of earth, or stones, shall affix, place, or set, any spring trap, gin, or other similar instrument calculated to inflict bodily injury to any wild bird coming in contact therewith, and every person who shall knowingly permit or suffer, or cause any such trap to be so affixed, placed or set, shall be guilty of an offence, and shall be liable on summary conviction to a penalty not exceeding 40 shillings, and for a second or subsequent offence to a penalty not exceeding £5.'

After World War I, due to the enormous loss of manpower during the conflict, the rabbit and grey squirrel population flourished, mainly unchecked. Attention now turned to the growing menace of the introduced American Grey Squirrel which was inflicting damage to commercial forestry and fruit bearing trees. During 1931 the National Anti-Grey Squirrel campaign was founded 'under the auspices of *The Field*.' In May 1931, the Ministry of Agriculture called a conference of representatives of all the organisations connected with the cultivation and ownership of agricultural and forest lands,

THE NATIONAL
ANTI-GREY SQUIRREL CAMPAIGN

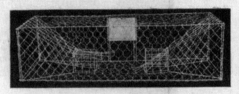

30 inches Long, 10 inches Wide, 8 inches High.

The "Campaign" Trap and Side-Cage
Approved by the Campaign.

THIS TRAP has been specially designed and will catch Grey Squirrels without hurting them. It is always "set" and only requires to be properly camouflaged and baited. It will hold several squirrels at a time.

PRICE :   Traps   Side Cages

Nothing is ever likely to go wrong with it, but care should be taken to see that the entrance gates work freely, and that the wires at the foot of them lie flat on the bottom of the cage.

Its maximum efficiency can be secured if rough boards are fixed along each side to produce a "tunnel" effect, after which a few branches or some bracken should be placed over it, leaving the ends clear. *This is important.*

The best bait is maize, nuts, banana skins, coco-nut, etc., which should be scattered liberally inside the trap.

It should be placed near the foot of a tree which the squirrels are known to frequent, or in one of their known "runs."

The best time to trap is, of course, when food is scarce. It is naturally more difficult to induce squirrels into traps when fresh food is abundant.

Captured squirrels can be either shot or drowned, preferably the latter. To do this the whole trap need not be immersed in the water, as a small door is provided in the side of the trap through which the squirrels can be driven into a small receptacle of wire netting, which can easily be made by any handy man, or specially designed side-cages can be obtained from the same source as the traps.

Grey Squirrel skins can be made into excellent fur gloves or fur coats, or the skins can be sold at prices varying from 3d. to 6d. each, according to size.

1931 SINGLE-SIDED LEAFLET

when it was unanimously agreed that the grey squirrel was a serious pest and that all possible steps should be taken to exterminate it. According to A.D.Middleton in his book *The Grey Squirrel*:

> The most successful trap is undoubtedly a large wire cage
> with a sleeve entrance, allowing easy entry of the squirrels but
> making it very difficult for them to find the right way out
> again. This form of trap, constructed in various ways by
> different people, has been found to catch large numbers of
> squirrels and has the advantage that any other animals or
> birds caught accidentally can be either released or dealt with
> according to the discretion of the trapper; maize and wheat
> have been found to be most effective baits. Such traps can be
> left in likely places where squirrels are active, and require
> very little attention beyond removing the catch daily and
> sprinkling a handful of corn in the bottom of the cage. Mr
> Laurence Swainson, the organiser of the National Anti-Grey
> Squirrel Campaign, has recently devised an improved form of
> this type of trap, which will soon be on the market.

His address was given as 'Moorlands, Boxmoor, Hertfordshire' where full particulars could be obtained. In December 1931 Gilbertson & Page were offering for sale the 'Campaign' trap at a cost of 10/- each and the separate side cage, if required, at 4/6d each.

In 1933 it had been reliably estimated that as many as 50 million rabbits were being controlled by trapping and other methods throughout Britain. Four years later in 1937, a report of the Select Committee of the House of Lords on Agriculture (damage by rabbits) reported:

> 'The Committee was appointed to consider what measures
> could be taken to lessen damage by rabbits and whether the
> prohibition of the use of gin traps would assist the object
> aimed at. The principal recommendations are:-
> (1) Legislation should be introduced to empower county
> councils, after fair enquiry, to order the destruction of rabbits on
> any land where damage is being caused to adjoining property.
> Failure to comply with the Order would lead to legal
> proceedings.
> (2) County councils to provide trained men with the
> necessary tackle for killing rabbits; these men could be
> employed for hire by the owners of the land, at the discretion
> of the council.
> (3) That any injured owner should be entitled to claim
> compensation for damage caused by a neighbour's rabbits.
> (4) That abolishing the gin trap would not assist in reducing
> rabbits, but that a gin trap with rubber jaws would be more
> humane than the present type.'

In their April 1937 issue, the *Game and Gun* magazine commented:

'All those recommendations appear reasonable, but it is doubtful
whether alone that they would effect a great reduction in rabbits.
The real position is that it is impossible to kill down rabbits very
closely without the expenditure of a good deal of time and money;
having regard to the enormous damage done by rabbits to crops
and also seedling trees, both trouble and expense should be faced
to reduce their numbers. Rabbits are best attacked when stocks are
low, and it is then that the time and money expended on their
destruction will have most lasting result. The best time to kill
rabbits is in November and December, just when gamekeepers are
busy with shooting; it would be a great help if landowners and
shooting tenants would employ extra men in those months to assist
their keepers in destroying rabbits.'

Then came the introduction to Britain in October 1953 of the contagious
viral disease myxomatosis, which is carried and spread by the rabbit flea. It is
reported in the December 1953 issue of *The Gamekeeper and Countryside*
magazine:

Myxomatosis was first noticed in Britain this autumn on an
estate near Edenbridge, Kent. The affected area was
immediately wired in, and vigorous attempts made to isolate
the outbreak by destroying the entire colony of rabbits. Some
weeks later a further outbreak was reported near
Robertsbridge, Sussex – twenty five miles from the primary
source, and today (November 6th) it is reported that some
600 acres of the South Downs near Lewes have infected
rabbits. It is obviously not practical to isolate an area of this
size, and there may well be other outbreaks that have not
been noticed or reported. Gamekeepers and others are urged
to report all cases of doubtful rabbit disease to their local pest
officers, and to await instructions.

Unfortunately, the genie was out of the bottle by now, as this disease very
quickly spread throughout the countryside resulting in many millions of rabbits
dying an agonising death. In fact, within two years of its introduction, it was
estimated that 95% of the whole rabbit population had been eliminated.
Therefore the need for a large amount of rabbit traps to control what had
been an enormous rabbit problem for farmers also disappeared with the
rabbits.

A more subtle blow to the vulnerable trapmaking industry was the
introduction and widespread use of gassing powders for the killing of remnant
rabbit populations and other infestations of vermin such as rat colonies.
(Incidently, the commonly used gas sodium cyanide, known commercially as
cymag, was withdrawn from sale by its manufacturer Sorex at the end of

THE BURRUN GAS PUMP

The Burrun Gas Pump is recommended for use with "Cymag" and other "gassing" powder. It is a strongly-made piece of equipment giving great pressure which forces the dust into places not otherwise readily accessible. It also has a special dust cut-off valve. By this device the dust is blown in first, and then forced to every part of the warren or burrow by pumping air only. In this way less gas is used with greater effect. There is little to go wrong with the Burrun Pump. All working parts are strongly made, non-corroding, and easy to get at for cleaning. It is constructed to be held in place with the feet, both hands being free to operate the pump.

THE MURPHY CHEMICAL COMPANY LTD
MURPHEX HANDBOOK 2ND EDITION, 1953

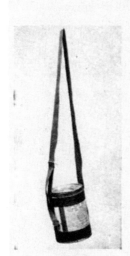

MURPHEX "CYMAG" TIN SLING

This carrier sling has been produced at the suggestion of a County Pest Officer. It is constructed of robust army-type webbing. A tin of "Cymag" slips easily into the holder, where it is firmly held without danger of being dislodged. The carrying strap can be supported on the shoulder during transportation, or shortened to handle-length when the spoon method of baiting is used.

This is an invaluable piece of equipment when gassing. It leaves the operator's hands free and minimizes risk of spillage. There is less danger of the fingers being injured by jagged edges resulting from the removal of the hermetic seal of the tin.

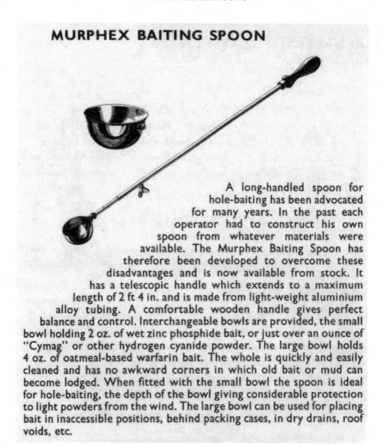

MURPHEX BAITING SPOON

A long-handled spoon for hole-baiting has been advocated for many years. In the past each operator had to construct his own spoon from whatever materials were available. The Murphex Baiting Spoon has therefore been developed to overcome these disadvantages and is now available from stock. It has a telescopic handle which extends to a maximum length of 2 ft 4 in. and is made from light-weight aluminium alloy tubing. A comfortable wooden handle gives perfect balance and control. Interchangeable bowls are provided, the small bowl holding 2 oz. of wet zinc phosphide bait, or just over an ounce of "Cymag" or other hydrogen cyanide powder. The large bowl holds 4 oz. of oatmeal-based warfarin bait. The whole is quickly and easily cleaned and has no awkward corners in which old bait or mud can become lodged. When fitted with the small bowl the spoon is ideal for hole-baiting, the depth of the bowl giving considerable protection to light powders from the wind. The large bowl can be used for placing bait in inaccessible positions, behind packing cases, in dry drains, roof voids, etc.

2003. Thereafter, its use or disposal was only permitted until 31st December 2004. To be in possession of cymag after that date is illegal.)

Two Acts of Parliament introduced in 1954 neant that the gin trap's days were numbered. In the 1954 Bird Protection Act (Section 5) it became illegal for anyone to set in position any spring trap or gin which by its nature and being so placed could cause bodily injury to any wild bird coming into contact with it. In the 1954 Pests Act (Section 8) it became an offence in England and Wales after 31st July 1958 to use any spring trap other than one which was approved by the Government. This same Act also made use of the gin trap illegal. The gin trap was later banned from use in Northern Ireland in 1969.

The banning of the gin trap in 1958 was also endorsed in Scotland for the taking of small ground vermin such as rats, rabbits, stoats, weasels etc. but delayed until 1st April 1973 for the taking of otters and foxes. This delay was due to the difficulty of finding an alternatively effective trap, to the universally efficient and simply operated gin trap, by the hill farmers and game fishing interests.

THIS IS A LEGAL LARSEN TRAP
UNDER THE WILDLIFE & COUNTRYSIDE ACT 1981

THESE TRAPS ARE LAWFUL UNDER A GENERAL LICENCE ISSUED BY THE STATUTORY AUTHORITIES IN ENGLAND, WALES AND SCOTLAND PROVIDED CONDITIONS OF THE LICENCE ARE MET. THE CONDITIONS ARE THAT:

• THE DECOY BIRD MUST BE PROVIDED WITH ADEQUATE FOOD, WATER, SHELTER AND A PERCH FOR THE ENTIRE PERIOD WHICH IT IS USED.

• ONLY CROW, MAGPIE, JACKDAW, JAY AND ROOK MAY BE KEPT OR CONFINED IN A LARSEN TRAP AS A DECOY. THESE ARE THE TARGET PEST SPECIES.

• WHEN NOT IN USE, THE TRAP MUST BE RENDERED INCAPABLE OF HOLDING OR CATCHING BIRDS.

• EACH LARSEN TRAP, WHICH CONTAINS A LIVE DECOY BIRD, MUST BE INSPECTED ON AT LEAST ONE OCCASION IN ANY 24-HOUR PERIOD.

THE PEST SPECIES MENTIONED ABOVE TAKE A CONSIDERABLE AMOUNT OF EGGS AND CHICKS OF BOTH GAMEBIRDS AND SONGBIRDS EACH YEAR.

THE USE OF THESE TRAPS AND THE CONTROL OF PESTS IS WELL RECOGNISED AS AN IMPORTANT CONSERVATION MEASURE.

POLICE WILDLIFE LIAISON OFFICERS WILL INVESTIGATE THE ILLEGAL USE OF TRAPS. THEY WILL ALSO INVESTIGATE INTERFERENCE OR THE VANDALISM OF LEGALLY SET TRAPS WHICH IS A CRIMINAL OFFENCE. FOR FURTHER ADVICE CONTACT YOUR NEAREST POLICE STATION.

PLEASE RESPECT LEGAL PEST CONTROL

PRODUCED BY THE BRITISH ASSOCIATION FOR SHOOTING AND CONSERVATION IN CONSULTATION WITH THE PARTNERSHIP FOR ACTION AGAINST WILDLIFE CRIME.

MODERN PLASTIC SIGN FOR ATTACHING TO A LIVE CATCH TRAP

Even now, at the time of writing, there is no effective British-made trap suitable for the control of foxes and so most fox control is carried out by shooting, where safe to do so, and the use of snares on large farms and estates. The less effective large fox wire cage traps can be useful in urban situations where foxes have become a nuisance animal, due to people habitually leaving food out for them. Being tamer and less suspicious they are more likely to enter this type of trap set for them by the suburban householder or allotment keeper. The use of all types of snares for the control of foxes etc. is now under constant threat of being banned, due to the activities of animal rights groups.

With the implementation of the gin trap ban in Scotland in 1973, the final nail was hammered into the old British trap makers' coffin. A few new trap makers had emerged to produce the approved traps that replaced the gins. However, only one, A.A. Fenn's approved trap, arose like the proverbial phoenix from the ashes of long dead trap makers' forges to take the place of the popular gin.

With the exception of the Fenn/Springer traps, trap making in Britain is now mainly confined to the production of wire cage traps, mole traps and commonly seen 'breakback' types of mouse and rat traps. Regarding modern traps, if approval is sought to enable a new spring trap to be marketed a specimen first has to be submitted to the Ministry of Agriculture, Fisheries and Food, now called D.E.F.R.A, The Department for Environment, Food and Rural Affairs. If the trap satisfies standards of humaneness and efficiency an amendment order has to be made through Parliament to the Spring Traps Approval Order 1957. The legislation governing mole, mouse and rat traps comes under the Small Ground Vermin Traps Order 1958.

Lastly, it is illegal under the terms of the Deer Act 1963 to use any trap, snare or poisoned or stupefying bait, net or arrow, spear or similar missile to catch or kill a deer. An exception to this Deer Act is possible for some scientific or educational purpose. A permit must be obtained from the appropriate Government department for the use of nets, traps and certain drugs in order to catch deer. The Wildlife and Countryside Act 1981 again sanctioned the legality of using traps as long as certain conditions were met. The Criminal Justice Act 1991 now deals with offences for breaking the game laws.

LARSEN TRAP
(PHOTO PERMISSION
MICHAEL ROBERTS)

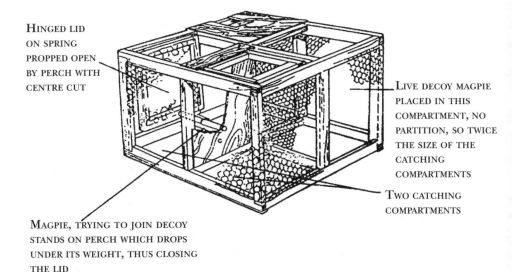

HINGED LID
ON SPRING
PROPPED OPEN
BY PERCH WITH
CENTRE CUT

LIVE DECOY MAGPIE
PLACED IN THIS
COMPARTMENT, NO
PARTITION, SO TWICE
THE SIZE OF THE
CATCHING
COMPARTMENTS

TWO CATCHING
COMPARTMENTS

MAGPIE, TRYING TO JOIN DECOY
STANDS ON PERCH WHICH DROPS
UNDER ITS WEIGHT, THUS CLOSING
THE LID

Larsen Trap

Larsen traps were designed by a Danish gamekeeper in the 1950s. In Denmark, it has been suggested that this trap alone was responsible for the significant reduction in the national magpie population from 1965.

Larsen traps will catch all corvid pest species (ie crows, magpies, jackdaws, jays, rooks) at all times of the year, but their particular value is in catching crows and magpies when these birds set up their breeding territories. The trap mechanism involves a spring door to each catching compartment, which when set is held open by a split perch. The perch gives way, and the bird's momentum takes it past the bottom of the door, which flips up – *et voila!* Because Larsen traps are small they can be easily moved around. Traps can be moved to deal with specific pairs of crows or magpies, and a few traps can thus be made to cover quite a large area.

Larsens are live-catch traps. Why catch alive? Because of the risk of catching birds other than corvids. Virtually all such non-target birds are protected by law, and must be released alive and unharmed. Having said this, we have experienced very few captures of non-target species in Larsen traps, another point in their favour. Finches and tits often visit them, but are too small to trigger the mechanism, and can in any case escape through the mesh sides. Of course, many legally protected bird species suffer from corvid predation on their eggs or young, and the Larsen trap is potentially an effective tool in the conservation of these birds too. There is no 'natural balance' between corvids and the birds they prey on, because they also feed to a great extent on other foods provided – directly or indirectly – by man.

(PHOTO AND TEXT PERMISSION MICHAEL ROBERTS *MODERN VERMIN CONTROL*)

WOMEN CHAIN MAKERS AT CRADLEY HEATH C. 1912
(reproduced from the original held at
Dudley Archives & Local History Service)

193, WOLVERHAMPTON ROAD, HEATH TOWN,

Wolverhampton, *Aug 18*th 190*3*

Mr Hodson

Bought of J. G. FORREST,

Manufacturer of all kinds of Chain for the Trap Trade.

LETTER HEAD OF J.G.FORREST, CHAIN MAKER

Chapter Two

TRAP MAKING

TRAP MAKING in the early years of the nineteenth century involved working in very poor conditions. In common with most industrial workers, long hours and low pay would be encountered as well as the noisy dirty environment surrounding the trap trade. In these conditions the old trap makers' health would have suffered.

In the beginning each trap would be made entirely by hand and by the same person from start to finish. Wrought iron would be heated in a forge, then hammered repeatedly on an anvil until it formed the desired shape. Springs would be tempered and retempered until the elasticity and quality was achieved. Bait plates would be formed out of flattened iron hammered thin and then cut out by chisel. Tongues and tills would be filed out and shaped, teeth being riveted onto the jaws or painstakingly cut by hand into them. Finally when all the individual parts had been made, the pieces would be assembled together.

Next would be the testing of the trap to see if the jaws snapped shut quickly enough and to make sure that nothing stuck or needed some other minor adjustment, which impeded its efficiency. Once satisfied with the quality of the trap the trap maker would either stamp his name or other recognisable mark into the spring, usually just behind the eye, and/or the plate. If he was working for another trap maker or firm he would stamp on their name or mark.

Even 'the best in the world', according to a Henry Lane Ltd. advert in 1930, sold 'cheaper unbranded lines'. Stamped or not stamped, the trap maker would then start to repeat the whole slow process once more, all the time with a background noise of hammers beating metal into shape on non yielding anvils, and with sweat and dirt everywhere. This small backyard producer of traps would also make his own chain for attaching to his traps. During the mid 1800s, Wednesfield and Wednesfield Heath were still rather isolated and very rural in outlook, but because of general improvements in

CHAINS

5

BEST JAPANNED WELDED COIL CHAIN, Twisted or Straight Link.

No. 410.   No. 411.

Links per Foot	...	9	10	12	14	16	18	20	22	24		per Dozen Yards.
Strength 2 Gauge	...											
,, 3 ,,	...											,, ,, ,,
,, 4 ,,	...											,, ,, ,,
,, 6 ,,	...											,, ,, ,,
,, 8 ,,	...											,, ,, ,,
,, 10 ,,	...											,, ,, ,,
,, 12 ,,	...											,, ,, ,,

Supplied SELF-COLOUR or GALVANIZED if required.
PACKED IN PARCELS CONTAINING ONE DOZEN YARDS.
SPECIAL QUOTATIONS FOR LARGE QUANTITIES. 20% DISCOUNT FROM NETT PRICES FOR 1 GROSS YARDS.

STRAIGHT LINK COIL CHAIN (By Weight).

8 ozs.   10 ozs.   12 ozs.   16 ozs.   1¼ lbs. per Yard.
per Cwt.

1½ lbs.   2 lbs.   2½ lbs.   3 lbs. per Yard.
per Cwt.

Cwt. extra for Japanned.   Self-Colour.

MANGER CHAINS (1½ yards)
Barrel Swivel and Spring Hook.

16 Link × 6 Gauge.   18 Link × 7 Gauge.

		Japanned
With Common	Open Hook	Galvanized
With Spring	Hook	Japanned
		Galvanized

Price Per Dozen.

MACHINE MADE WELDLESS CHAIN.
SINGLE LINK SCALE OR JACK CHAIN.   DOUBLE LINK SCALE OR JACK CHAIN.

No. 200.   No. 201.

Single.	...	6	8	10	12	14	16	18 Wire Gauge.
Bright Iron	...							
Tinned or Galvanized	...							

Double.	...	6	8	10	12	14	16	18 Wire Gauge.
Bright Iron	...							
Tinned or Galvanized	...							

Single.   Above prices per DOZEN YARDS. For One Gross Yards of one size 25% Discount from Nett Prices.   Double.

TWISTED LINK WELDLESS CHAIN.

No. 202
Gauge.

Strength No.	2	3	4	6	8	10	12	16	18
Japanned ..									
Galvanized .									

Dozen Yards.

10% Discount from Nett Prices for One Gross Yards.

BEST QUALITY SPRING HOOKS.

Sizes up to   3   3¼   3½   3¾   4 in.
Japanned
Tinned or
Galvanized

SPRING HOOK with EYE to SWIVEL.
per dozen extra up to 3½ inch.
per dozen extra above 3½ inch.
For quantities not less than One Gross of
a size 10% Discount off Nett Prices.

No. 32.

SPECIAL PRICES QUOTED FOR QUANTITIES.

JAPANNED "S" HOOKS.

Sizes   1   1½   1¾   2   2¼   3 inch.
per Cwt.
per Gross

Assorted Gross Lots   per Gross.
Assorted by weight   per Cwt.

No. 167.

CHAIN SWIVELS.

No. 165. Japanned.

Size Overall 1¾ 2   2¼ 2½ 2¾ 3   3½ 4 inch.
Price   ...

Per Dozen.

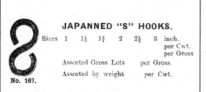

CHAINS FOR THE TRAP TRADE FROM THE SEPTEMBER 1947
CATALOGUE OF SWINNERTON & CO, STOURBRIDGE,
WORCESTERSHIRE

the quality and production of iron in nearby areas of the Black Country, people started moving from the countryside into the more industrial areas of Wolverhampton seeking better wages and conditions. This migration would create a large number of unskilled and semiskilled people eager to find any type of work. Some of these people would find work in the trap trade as this area of metal working expanded, whilst others would find employment making keys and locks.

Adult wages in the key, lock and trap making trades in the district in 1863 amounted to 15 shillings to 25 shillings weekly in Wednesfield, 18 shillings to 30 shillings weekly in Willenhall and 25 shillings to 40 shillings weekly in Wolverhampton and Walsall.

Wolverhampton didn't always get the most skilled men, but usually keysmiths tended to get less wages than locksmiths, so the latter were mostly to be found in the larger towns making the more sophisticated products. This situation didn't apply though to the trap makers due to their trade being less skilled than either key or lock makers and also because the trap makers had a virtual monopoly in Wednesfield and so could keep wages lower. A young boy under the age of 15 would get three shillings a week by 1910, with an extra shilling a week if he had been in the trap making trade for a year and was over the age of 15. If some men decided to work on a 'piece work' rate rather than a daily rate of pay some of the more skilled and quicker workers could earn better wages for themselves by producing more traps per day of the smaller and medium sizes. Slowly the changes would come with the introduction of jigs and hand presses, which would make for easier repetition of standard made parts and also slightly speed up production.

The trade of trap making by hand would slowly be superseded by the new and more efficient machinery such as the Crossley gas engine introduced into the John Marshall Works around 1910 to drive the shafting for his power presses. The larger and more efficient trap manufacturers would also be starting to buy in quantities of ready-made chain for attaching to their traps from specialist chain manufacturers. Two such local chain manufacturers were Wood Brothers and J.G. Forrest, both of Wednesfield Heath.

In an undated Lane catalogue, but *circa* 1908/1913, mention is made that 'H. Lane tests the springs of his best traps at least fourteen days before putting them in stock, and also warrants them for twelve months. He cannot, therefore, risk sending traps away without being set some days, as springs cannot be depended upon unless they are so tested.' To get a more accurate idea of the complex trap making process, I make no apology for reproducing totally from Henry Lane's catalogue of 1928, the sections called 'Past and Present Methods' and 'The Intricacies of Spring Making'. After all who is better qualified than a trap maker to explain how to make a trap?

THE INTRICACIES OF SPRING MAKING

One of the most difficult, if not the most difficult part of the trap to make is the spring. To begin with, the grain of the steel is closer, and therefore tougher than the metal used for the other parts of the trap. Then, owing to the fact that the design of the trap renders the attachment of the spring semi-floating, every detail of shape must be deadly accurate, as also must be the hardening and tempering, to ensure satisfactory results. Should any point be wrong in the finished spring, the result may be that it either catches the plate when depressed, or tends to draw the jaws out of the trap when sprung. These faults can only be rectified in handmade traps, where each base-piece or 'stock' is pierced separately to suit one spring. No such opportunity offers in the case of machine-made traps, and it is therefore necessary to ensure uniformity. The respective methods of the hand and machine-made springs are depicted opposite, and only a very short explanation is required.

It will be observed that the old style entails nine operations, requiring the material to be heated six times, and a great number of blows with the hammer. The new style is completed in five operations – two heats, and five blows of a power press, and no hammer work whatever.

In the finished article, the old style produced irregularity, where the new style produces uniformity. The hardening and tempering of the springs is described on another page, under the heading of 'Methods, Past and Present, Employed in the Manufacture of Steel Vermin Traps.'

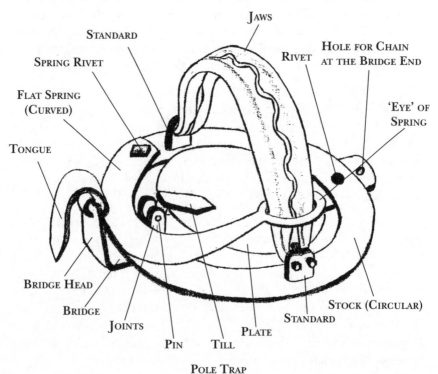

POLE TRAP

HAND MADE

A.	Piece of iron cut off bar.	
B.	Piece of spring steel cut off bar.	
a.	One end of the iron tapered for welding.	one heat
b.	One end of the steel tapered for welding.	one heat
C.	The two welded and shouldered	one heat
D.	The iron end split open with chisel.	one heat
E.	The iron end opened and arms rounded.	one heat
F.	The two ends bent round and crossed over for welding.	
G.	The two ends welded and the eye forged to correct shape.	one heat

MACHINE MADE

H.	The steel cut off from bar with end rounded.		one blow
I.	The steel pierced and trimmed.		one blow
J	Eye formed to shape	one heat	
K.	Eye embossed	one heat	one heat
L	Eye shaped and tapered	one heat	one heat

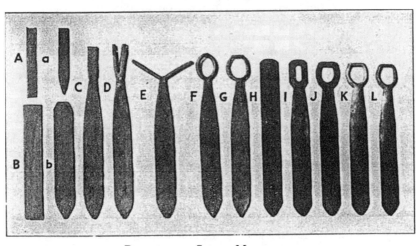

PROCESSES IN SPRING MANUFACTURE

DORSET

ORDINARY AND ORDINARY RABBIT

AMERICAN

DIFFERENT TONGUE STYLES

METHODS, PAST AND PRESENT, EMPLOYED IN THE MANUFACTURE OF STEEL VERMIN TRAPS.

In the early part of the Nineteenth Century, the manufacture of Steel Traps was centred in Wednesfield, and formed the staple trade of the place. No machinery was used, and the only appliances required were a smith's forge, a vice, a few hammers, files and chisels. Later on, the use of hand-presses for cutting out material into the various shapes required, was adopted. These were followed in the course of time by presses driven first by steam engines, later by gas engines, and finally by electric motors.

The present type of Power and Hand-presses, illustrated on page 17, are capable of doing a great variety of work – various 'Press Tools' are fitted into the presses, and the material can be cut into the shape required, pierced, or bent at various angles. If sufficient ingenuity be displayed in the design of the 'Press Tools,' a number of operations can be performed at one blow. It is imperative, however, that these 'Press Tools' are made to a fine limit of accuracy, an error of one thousandth part of an inch being sufficient to render the set useless in many cases. It follows, however, that when these tools are properly made, the greatest accuracy and uniformity are obtained and ensured in the finished parts and traps.

We have for many years designed and made our own 'Press Tools,' and have thus been able to produce certain types of traps entirely by machinery, an achievement that has never yet been attained by any other firm. The cost of producing a trap by machinery is, nevertheless, a very expensive business, and the outlay would not be warranted unless a reasonable demand were assured. A glance at the illustration on the opposite page will give a rough idea of the amount of highly accurate work entailed in making the machinery necessary for the production of one trap of one size and quality. The result is, however, that the traps thus produced are absolutely uniform in quality, the quality is of the highest, and all parts are easily replaceable.

ELECTRIC FURNACE USED FOR HARDENING SPRINGS
AND TOOLS FOR TRAPS.

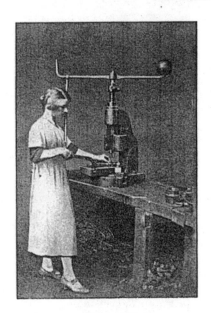

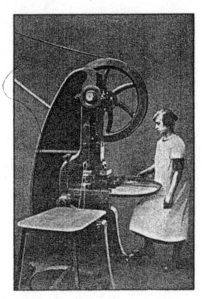

HAND PRESS   POWER PRESS.

METHODS PAST & PRESENT FROM THE 1928 CATALOGUE
OF HENRY LANE LTD. (ABOVE & OVER)

OLD AND NEW METHODS.

Since the formation of the Company, most of the 1919 plant has been discarded and been replaced by new and more up-to-date appliances, which enable us to turn out more reliable goods, thereby benefiting our customers. Coal gas is used extensively for heating furnaces of various kinds, and the electric furnace illustrated on opposite page, which is of the very latest design, has recently been installed for the accurate and uniform heat treatment of the springs for the traps, and the tools wherewith the traps are made. Without this furnace it is impossible to guarantee continually the correct results in hardening, and as the life of the trap mainly depends on the life of the spring, it is an invaluable addition to our plant.

The illustrations on page 18 show the chief changes from the old method to the new. Fig. 1 depicts a smith forging the eye of a spring, while in Fig. 2 is shown the method employed in forming the eye of the spring belonging to the trap illustrated on page 54, and which is entirely machine made. Fig. 3 shows a skilled workman filing up the brass catches used in the old hand made traps, while Fig. 4 shows the new pattern being milled automatically to the correct size. Fig. 5 shows the smith drawing the temper on the spring after hardening, to give them the necessary elasticity (one of the most highly-skilled operations on the trap) and in Fig. 6 our modern method is depicted – the hardened springs are placed in a lead or salt bath that maintains the required temperature, and, after remaining therein for a specified time, the springs are removed from the bath, correctly 'tempered'.

Though we do not claim to have reached perfection, we do claim that our products and methods of production are superior to those of other manufacturers in this country or any other. We have a great number of visitors from time to time, and are always pleased to show anyone over our works who is interested in our manufactures, whether they are purchasers or not.

FROM HENRY LANE LTD. CATALOGUE FEB 1928

DIAGRAM OF NAMED PARTS FROM
H. LANE'S 1ST FEBRUARY 1928 CATALOGUE

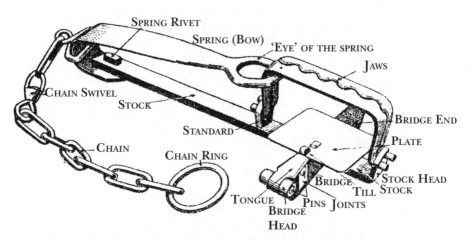

A BOW SPRING GIN TRAP. NOTE THAT THE SPRING GOES OVER THE
END OF THE STOCK AND FIXES UNDERNEATH. SEE LANE'S IMPROVED
DORSET RABBIT TRAP ON PAGE 128

UNUSUAL HOOK FIXING FOR THE S HOOK AND CHAIN

Gin Traps

The terms gin and trap are derived from the words 'engine' and 'treppe'. Engine was used historically for any mechanical device which did not require human effort to make it work. Once the gin trap was set it remained operational until an unsuspecting animal or human trod on the trap plate thereby releasing the jaws to either kill or capture the victim. The word trap comes from the old English 'treppe' or 'traeppe', properly a step, which is very apt as the animal steps onto the trap plate and in so doing sets it off.

On British gin traps there are three main types of springs used: flat, bow and wire. The first type was the simple form known as the flat spring. The second spring to be employed was the bow, which is the spring most people associate with gin traps. The last type is obviously the wire spring, and was in use before 1895. All of these spring types were still produced until the closing years of the trap trade.

The flat springs lost their strength and holding power after continuous use and because of this gradually gave way to the more efficient bow springs. Latterly these springs were mainly used for such small traps as bird and some rat traps, although in an illustrated price list of W.&G. Sidebotham *circa* 1955 double flat spring traps with jaw sizes ranging from 8 inches up to 16 inches were being offered to the African market. In Britain though, gin traps used were mainly of the single spring variety due to the large dangerous predatory animals being hunted, by various means, to extinction centuries earlier.

The absence of large and powerful predators in Britain might help to explain the difficulties experienced by the early trap makers, as well as the poor quality of metal that they were using here. Some manufacturers were incapable of producing traps which could be totally relied on for catching and holding such types of animals during the start of the fur trade in the New World. Obviously the trap makers would not realise the power exerted by a large trapped animal desperate to free itself and the combined effects that extreme minus temperatures could create on metal springs thereby causing breakages or bent parts which would allow the animal to escape eventually. Such conditions would not be normally encountered with our milder climate and smaller wildlife.

Later in the 1880s trap making doesn't seem to have improved much, regardless of weather conditions, as W. Carnegie, writing in his book *Practical Trapping of Vermin and Birds*, complained that 'Gins are generally loosely and clumsily put together'. Even in Robert's patent of 1895 mention is made of frequent breakages to the springs. To quote from his patent:

> 'My improvements consist in the spring part of the ordinary spring trap, . . . with stock, spring, jaws and bridge for

TRAP SPRINGS

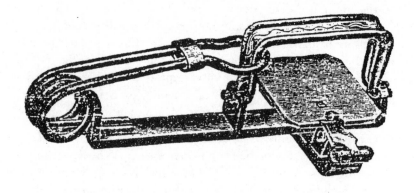

A TRAP FOR THE TRAPPER – WIRE SPRING RABBIT TRAPS 4" JAWS REAL DORSET, GALVANISED PLATES, BRASS CATCHES AND COMPLETE WITH CHAINS

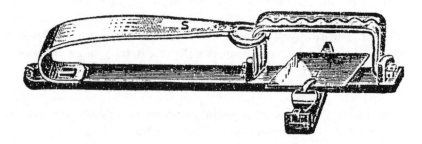

BOW SPRING RABBIT TRAPS 4" JAWS, REAL DORSET, GALVANISED PLATES, BRASS CATCHES COMPLETE WITH CHAINS

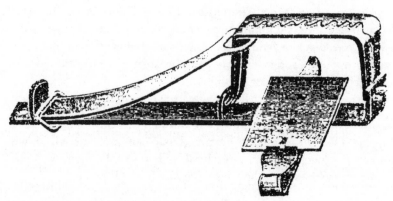

RUN OR RAT TRAPS FLAT SPRING AS ILLUSTRATION AND COMPLETE WITH CHAINS

catching rabbits, vermin and other animals and has for its
object the prevention of breakages which frequently occur in
the flat, bow, or loop spring now used . . . also to give greater
elasticity and more uniform pressure and following up power
than those now in use'.

In Britain the trap makers home market for larger traps was limited to
mantraps and traps for such animals as the fox, otter and badger with the
largest jaw sizes for these animals not usually exceeding 8 inches in length.
Although limited at home, in the sizes of traps used, the traps for the export
trade were not. Originally these double spring traps would have had their
springs solidly attached to a straight stock on either side of the jaws. The very
large traps such as used for lions and bears would also have been heavy (140
lb.) and awkward (96 inches long) to transport around the country.

An improvement in design to these traps, and a solution to the
transportation problem, came with the idea of folding one or both springs.
With this modification it became a lot easier to pack the traps into a much
smaller space and more convenient and easier to handle whilst travelling
over rough and inhospitable terrain. Another benefit was that when setting
the trap, the springs could now be adjusted to suit the different site conditions
encountered. Folding springs were called swivel springs in Bellamy's patent of
1860.

Normally bow springs were fixed, by a rivet, to the top side of the stock
just in front of the hole drilled into the end from which the trap chain was
attached. However, in a patent of 1878, the single bow spring of an ordinary
rabbit trap was designed to bend over the end of the stock and be fastened in
the normal way to the underside. This arrangement included a separate
eyed attachment for the trap chain which was also held in place by the same
rivet holding the spring to the stock. The reason for the spring being attached
under the stock was to very slightly lower the height of the spring and so help
in its concealment when set. Thomas Beech and Henry Lane, as well as Joseph
Yeo just mentioned, are known to have produced traps with this under stock
spring fixing feature on them, as well as other manufacturers.

'VEE' Spring

V-shaped springs can either be formed from one piece of metal to form the
stock and then continue on to form the spring or else just comprise the V-
shaped spring which would then be attached to the separate U-shaped base
or stock. This fourth type of spring appears in the Lane's of Wednesfield
adverts called the 'Vee flat spring'. The earliest advert that I know of showing
Lane's 'Vee flat spring' appears in a *Shooting Times* magazine during World
War II. Prior to this, in a 1931 advert by Spratt's of London, Lane's new flat
spring trap was illustrated with an accompanying patent number (No 288,894/

27). This patent 'relates to a new method of fixing the lower arms of V-shaped springs to U-shaped bases of metal spring traps for animals.'

However, in 1925, H. Lane (Australia) had made a trade mark application to register the name, flat spring. A Lane's flat spring trap (1929 pattern) advert states 'improved pattern, with spring and base in one piece.' These single V-shaped springs were made non-folding, but other single spring V-shaped spring traps including the Gilpa double grip, which was advertised in 1933 and Lane's American Muskrat trap, made *circa* 1907, both had a folding spring. Another maker with a 'V' shaped spring rabbit trap was Sidebotham's. They produced their 'light folding spring' rabbit traps with chains in 'DZIN REGD' quality with both brass fittings at 25/6d per dozen and with iron fittings at 21/- per dozen. The Dinkum is the wire spring version and sold at the same time for 21/9d per dozen with iron fittings around 1933. Both types were for 4 inch jawed traps.

It should be noted though, when considering V-shaped springs, that earlier made double springs on some traps were of this design and that it was intended for the springs to fold away to enable easier carrying and packaging. Roberts made double folding springs on their fox/dog traps with 9 inch/10 inch jaws, as did Lane's on their 'Leppan' lion and tiger traps. Lastly, not forgetting in Joseph Bellamy's patent of 1860, he mentions 'swivel shaped' springs, which would undoubtedly be V-shaped.

Forged Springs

This type of spring, either flat or bow shaped, is hand made and so usually, but not always, predates machine made or pressed springs. Obviously, when machines were being introduced to speed up trap production, hand-forged traps would still be made during the transition period. Some trap makers though would not be able to afford to invest money in new machinery and would continue to produce handmade traps, but due to their competitors being more efficient and therefore probably cheaper, they would eventually cease business altogether.

However, a September 1947 catalogue of Swinnerton & Co of Stourbridge in Worcestershire, who are 'Manufacturers of wrought and pressed ironwork', states that 'Wrought welded chains, and hand-forged springs can be supplied with traps at extra cost.' In an earlier catalogue of theirs, September 1927, they are stated to be 'Manufacturers & Merchants', so maybe the trap springs and 'spare parts for all traps supplied' were bought from established Trap Makers and resold by Swinnerton & Co. with their own trade mark stamped on them. Their trade mark being the letter S inside a diamond shape.

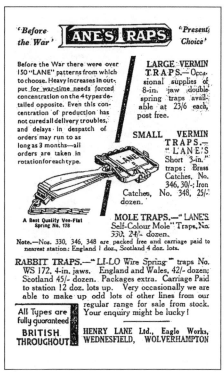

HENRY LANE LTD. 1949 'V SPRING' ADVERT

Left-handed Gin Traps

An unknown company listed in their undated catalogue, export trade section No 59 Griffin: Left handed Scotch vermin traps in sizes 4inch–7inch (jaw sizes) graded in half inch increases and ranging in price from 8 shillings to 14 shillings each. The price increasing by one shilling per size increase. The catalogue also states 'All traps marked with the 'Griffin' brand are tested and warranted.' Left handed curved spring pole traps are also known.

Interesting variations of the use of small flat springs can be seen in Henry Lane's catalogue (date unknown) where they are incorporated in single and double spring traps for American muskrats and in a single spring square-jawed British kingfisher trap. In all these variations the springs operate from inside the jaws, from under the plate. This type of trap has most likely been copied from the American style of trap known as the under spring, also referred to as jump traps, due to their action of jumping up when the plate is stepped on. However, according to James A. Bateman in his book *Animal Traps and Trapping*, published in 1971, this 'jump trap' style originally goes back to seventeenth century Austria, but instead of the flat spring being used as now, a form of bow spring was utilised.

Another interesting variation to be found in the same catalogue is the

POLE TRAP WITH LEFT HAND
SPRING AND PLAIN JAWS

heron or hawk trap which has two bow springs back to back with the jaws and bait spikes plate assembly above them. Some traps, such as the large bear trap that is displayed on the wall of the sporting gallery in the White Tower at the Tower of London also have secondary springs included in their design. These secondary springs are aligned in the opposite direction to, and immediately beneath, the larger main springs. The size of the secondary springs on the above mentioned trap are approximately half the size of the main springs, being around 15 inches in length. Presumably these secondary springs were added to help produce more holding power in the trap, as it would be known by the trap makers, that over a long period of use the main flat springs would eventually become weaker and so lose their effectiveness.

Another trap with the secondary springs feature, but instead having round jaws and plate, is in the collection of the National Museum of Antiquities of Scotland in Edinburgh. This trap was gifted to the Museum in 1872 by G.T. Cranstoun. The smaller 4 inch jawed rabbit traps in both bow and wire spring variations were also made with a secondary spring, but in the form of a compression coil spring. This type of coil spring has both ends tapered so that the coil spring 'sits' better between the stock and spring.

Other spring variations included W. Sidebotham's 'Eclipse' model, rabbit gin trap of *circa* 1890, which had a removable spring. Another type of removable spring was patented in 1907 by Henry Lane. Lastly, a dog or otter trap with an improved adjustable spring was exhibited at the Midland Counties Trade and Industrial Exhibition at Birmingham in 1892 by James Roberts.

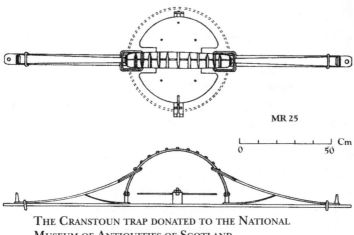

MR 25

THE CRANSTOUN TRAP DONATED TO THE NATIONAL
MUSEUM OF ANTIQUITIES OF SCOTLAND

The greatest overall size differences regarding straight stocked gin traps seems to range from the largest at approximately 96 inches in length, down to around seven inches in length. The first size of trap is a double flat spring bear/lion trap, whilst the latter size, the small single bow or flat spring bird trap. Jaw length of the two traps would be 36 inches approximately for the double spring and two inches approximately for the single spring bird trap. Obviously, although there would be roughly standardised sizes for certain types of traps, hand made traps would vary slightly due to human error or just because of utilising any quantity of spare metal found in the workshop. To quote from the book *Smiths' Work* of 1899, 'Good metal being rather costly, a careful smith will preserve odds and ends of iron and steel for small work, and for welding to other portions, so saving the cutting off of small pieces from long bars.'

A SECONDARY SPRING IN THE
FORM OF A COMPRESSION
COIL SPRING

Bridges

The earliest type of bridge seems to be what is known as an axle bridge. The 'seesaw' type of treadle plate was fixed across the bridge of the trap into opposite lugs, one made from the end of the bridge and the other from a separately made joint opposite the bridge head and tongue. The 'axle' that carried the plate was pivoted on these two opposite points of the bridge. The most common bridges are usually made of flat metal and either cross over or under the stock, being fixed at the point of overlay by a rivet. In some hand-forged gin traps, both the stock and bridge are formed into the same piece of metal. In this case the bridge is level with the stock and neither goes under nor over the stock, as in the more normal types. Bridges also have attached to them separately the joints by which the trap plate is fixed, via the till. One exception to this is a patent of W.H. Tildesley's in 1895 whereby the bridge is formed with a 'hump' in it to which the plate is directly attached by two projecting 'ears' or lugs from either side of the 'hump'. This 'hump' eliminates the need for separate joints for attaching the plate to and therefore the construction is simplified and manufacturing costs reduced.

In 1907, in the United States of America, a very similar style of 'humped cross' (bridge) was patented, and this is now a common feature on many styles of American trap, e.g. the Victor Long Spring and Oneida Jump Traps. Sidebotham's produced a 5 inch jawed wire spring gin trap with brass fittings, galvanised plate, and with the bridge galvanised. It is not known if galvanised bridges were also used on other sized traps produced by them. However, stamped on the galvanised plate is the name Sidebotham and also Gray Inverness, who was probably the retailer. The galvanised bridge may be an exclusive feature and produced especially for Gray's of Inverness. Another trap which has a galvanised plate and bridge is the 4 inch jaw wire spring trap made by Collins. The brass tongue has Collins No 0 stamped on the top. Collins became part of Sidebotham's, so it is not known whether this trap was produced by Collins before they became part of Sidebotham's, or whether Sidebotham's produced these traps using the Collins name and numbers.

Lastly, what Robert Smith describes in his book published in 1768 as a fox trap, and now more commonly known as an otter trap, has the strange feature of not having a bridge on the trap. What would have been the bridge head containing the tongue, is fixed to the outside of the square frame so that the tongue is above the top of the frame edge, and continues down just below the bottom edge of the frame. Here the flat piece of metal, which has been cut in the middle, has the two ends turned towards each other so that the plate's till may be pivoted between them by the pin which goes through them all. The till curves upwards from its pivoting point and ends in a horizontal 'diamond' shape secured underneath the trap plate.

A later design improvement to the 'square framed' trap made it easier to produce. This involved the simplification of the design between the tongue and drop plate. What was produced resulted in the now common bridge arrangement found on ordinary gin traps. The earlier difference was that the 'square framed' trap had the bridge assembly going under the plate and being fixed to the two opposite outer sides of the square frame. Due to this new arrangement the plate pivoted on joints which were attached to the bridge. This new feature now made the horizontal bar with the two 'plate stops' obsolete, and so was discontinued. This new bridge design became a standard feature in gin traps, resulting in the unnecessary 'square frame' also quickly becoming redundant.

The square framed otter gin trap, as illustrated in an unnamed and undated catalogue, is referred to as the Ringwood Frame Otter Trap. As this square frame style of trap is of early manufacture, it is possible that the early Dorset county trap makers first produced this type of trap, or sold a variation of it, in the area near the village of Ringwood. Although Ringwood is in Hampshire, it is in fact situated on the county boundaries of both Hampshire and Dorset. The famous Dorset trap making family of Shave didn't live too far away at Sturminster Marshall. The undated trap illustration states: 'Ringwood Frame Otter Traps, Spiked, with long chain attached'. Idstone writing in 1872 about an otter trap made by William Shave's great grandfather says that the jaws were, 'bristling with thickly set spike teeth, not only along the surface, but at the angle of the jaws'. Continuing he states: 'Give him (the otter) plenty of chain, six feet, and he will drown himself; and this, old Shave well knew, for he has attached a strong six feet chain to his old trap'.

It is just possible that the early Dorset trap makers sold locally, a lot of these square framed fox traps, as illustrated in Robert Smith's 1768 book, but with extra spiked teeth especially for catching otters. The River Avon is a famous trout stream at Ringwood, and otters would be viewed as predatory vermin which had to be permanently eradicated from the river to protect the stock of trout and other game fish. If these square framed fox traps with the extra spiked teeth and extra long chains were sold in large numbers in the Ringwood area, and along the course of the River Avon for especially catching otters, it is possible that the trap makers would receive orders from distant landowners for Ringwood Style Otter Traps for use on their own rivers. Eventually, the trap makers would start to distinguish this type of trap from the more common square framed fox trap by calling it the Ringwood Frame Otter Trap.

Idstone, whilst studying one of his old traps stated that he didn't think that the frame under the trap jaws served any purpose at all and commented: 'As you always find in old traps, the maker. . . surrounded the jaws with a substantial iron frame. There are abundant reasons for doing away with this unnecessary addition. . . This useless frame of substantial wrought iron.'

Although the square framed gin traps are mostly found with a flat spring, examples are known of having a bow spring instead.

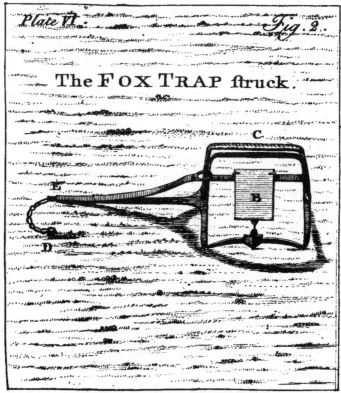

ROBERT SMITH'S FOX TRAP IN 'STRUCK' MODE

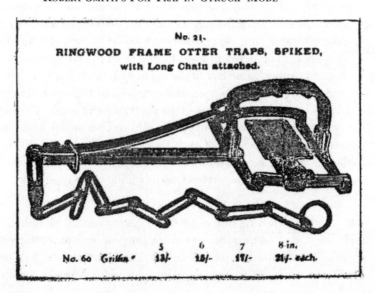

Trap Plates

These can be divided into three basic types. The first type is the **treadle plate** which was attached to two opposite points (lugs) on the bridge, known as an axle bridge, and thus created a seesaw effect. Although these were the earliest type of plates made, they were certainly still being made up to the beginning of World War I in 1914, and it is possible that they continued to be produced long after this date.

Old pattern tiger and bear traps with the flat springs were offered for sale in a T.E. Thomson & Co. Ltd. of Calcutta, India catalogue dated 1938. The wide tongue though in the illustration does suggest that it is a conventional drop plate in an old style trap, but it is possible that if a treadle plate was preferred and ordered, the trap makers would oblige. However, in W.&G. Sidebotham's illustrated price list of *circa* 1955, mentioned earlier, the illustrations show clearly that both types of plates were being offered for sale to at least the African market.

Whilst double flat springed traps with jaw sizes of 8, 9, 10 and 12 inches were being offered with conventional drop plates, the larger double flat springed lion or tiger traps with spiked jaw sizes of 12, 14, 15 and 16 inches were offered with the treadle plate fixture. Some traps with these treadle plates can also be found with five or six straight or wavy spikes fixed to them for attaching a meat bait. These spiked bait plates were made for both the larger single and double flat springed traps. Treadle plates were also made with two or four holes in them to facilitate tying a bait to them. Another version seen on the large bear trap previously mentioned in the White Tower has, instead of four holes, four large diamond shapes in it, which may originally have been round but have eroded.

The second and most common type is usually just called the plate or **drop plate**. This type of plate either has no holes in it or else two or four depending on size or type of trap. When a plate has holes through it, it is often referred to as a bait plate. The normal way a plate 'falls', when an animal steps onto it is in the same direction as the bridge, e.g. across the stock. A variation to this normal operation of the plate was patented by Joseph Bellamy in December 1860, whereby the bridge was discontinued, and the plate is attached to the joints in the normal way except that it faces away from the spring along the stock. The tongue was also discontinued, instead the end of the spring (eye) engages the heel of the catch or set (till), to which the plate is fixed. Once the trap plate is depressed it 'falls' in the direction of the stock thereby releasing the end of the spring which immediately travels upwards closing the jaws in the normal manner.

In October 1878, J. Yeo patented an opposite version to Joseph Bellamy's, whereby the plate 'falls' towards the spring and not away from it as in Joseph

Bellamy's patent. Once the spring is depressed and the jaws fully opened, a triangular tongue hinged on the stock head (which is formed from the stock) crossed the jaws and engages the till (catch) which is part of the plate assembly. Once an animal treads upon the plate, the trap operates in the normal way.

British trap plates are usually found made in a square form or in the shape of a letter H on some of the larger sized traps. The H shape was formed due to pieces being cut out of the plate on opposite sides to allow the springs to rise up without hindrance from the large plate. Exceptions to the usual square plate occur in pole traps which by their design are circular due to being placed upon high posts for the capture of hawks, owls etc. and so obviously have round plates. Another exception noted earlier is the double-springed trap which was donated in 1872 by G.T. Cranstoun to the National Museum of Antiquities of Scotland which also has a round plate and the unusual secondary springs. Two further exceptions are the 'Shave' rubber-jawed gin trap and some of W.H. Tildesley's round jaw rat traps.

Otter traps are flat-springed with the stock and spring only going as far as the square frame upon which the jaws are mounted. The square frame has two opposite sides turned up at right angles and from one is attached the tongue, which holds the jaw down when in the set position. On the opposite side of the square frame from the tongue is a flat metal bar going in the same direction as the stock but approximately half way between the stock and the edge of the upturned side of the square frame. From this flat bar are mounted two 7-shaped plate stops (as I call them as I can see no other purpose for them) pointing in towards each other and located either side of the plate. When the trap is set and the plate raised, the plate is held in a level position by the 'stops'. Although only now found on otter traps previously they were found on certain mantraps.

The third category of trap plates is really a mixture of what does not 'fit in' with the previous types. This section consists of a mantrap sold by Christie's which had two 'C' scrolls back to back although working on the drop principle. Another mantrap with an unusual trap plate is the square humane type made by the various iron founders of West Bromwich. This consists of a cross-shaped 'plate' which was held in place, when the jaws were opened, by the tension of the jaws wanting to close together. Once this device was triggered off, by the person stepping on it, the cross-shaped plate fell out of the square formed by the open jaws, allowing the capture of the unfortunate person's leg.

Other forms of **bait plates**, mainly in use with traps for birds, but still working on the drop plate idea, have prongs for attaching the meat or fish bait. Yet another bird trap, a pole trap, employed a circular ring for placing upon it an egg to entice members of the crow family to their doom. A further bird trap exhibited by James Roberts in 1892 at Birmingham, had a 'cup attachment instead of a plate for holding the bait'. He also exhibited a 'Cat trap, the spring is made to go off by pulling the plate up instead of pressing down as ordinarily' and a 'Rabbit trap with improved plate protector'. This plate protector was presumably for use in sandy soil conditions, and would stop the loose soil from accumulating underneath the plate which would stop the plate from 'dropping'. Roberts also exhibited a 'Dorset rabbit trap, extra best, with brass plate attachment size 4 inches'.

In 1895, W.&G. Sidebotham applied for a patent whereby their trap could also be set in motion by the dual action of either depressing the trap plate in the normal manner or by raising the same plate. Most early plates were made of iron but, as the understanding of metals grew, brass and galvanised plates also appeared. Gin traps with brass tongues and galvanised plates became known as 'Dorset' type traps. William Shave of Dorset County in England advertised himself as 'The original Dorset trap maker' in 1868. Traps with brass plates were produced by Roberts, Sidebotham and S. Griffiths. The traps which included this type of brass plate seem to have been known as 'wet set' traps, and may indicate that they were specifically made for trapping in river or salt water conditions. Again, the brass plate idea was to prevent the plate from rusting through too quickly and so extending the life of the trap.

Standards

The usual type of standard to which the jaws are attached is basically a single piece of metal through which two holes have been made to allow the jaw ends to fit through and therefore pivot on. The standard is then attached to the stock by passing through it and being welded underneath. Alternately, the standard can have a threaded end whereby it goes through the hole in the stock and is held in place by a threaded nut. Another earlier type of standard that is secured by a nut under the stock consists of two wide flat pieces of metal being joined together, leaving a space between them in the top half. Into this space, in the top of the standard, goes the ends of the jaws. The whole jaw is constructed out of thin wide metal tapering in width where it enters the space in the standard. Two holes are made through both sides of the standard and a single hold made in each end of the jaws. These are then all aligned up with a rivet which secures them in place and also allows them to turn. Yet a third variation can be found on Henry Lane's 'Leppan' lion and tiger traps. Having only seen an illustration and not an actual trap I can only make an assumption. However, the illustration clearly shows that both jaw ends, which would normally be bent at a right angle and just push into the two receiving holes of the standard, are in fact kept in line with the jaw and which must end in a hole. The single jaw hole on each jaw is aligned with the corresponding holes in the standards and a rivet then passed through these aligned holes. Again, once the rivet is fixed into place the jaws can then easily pivot on them. From above, when in the set position, it looks like a row of knuckles. How the two standards are attached to the stock is uncertain. However, the standard is possibly a wide U-shaped fitting and held in place by a threaded nut underneath.

Jaws

From catalogue information, it seems that three styles of jaws were produced by the various trap makers. These jaw styles consisted of the plain or flat jaw, bevelled jaw (which means cut to an oblique angle or sloped off) and the grooved jaw, which was also sometimes referred to as being ridged. An illustrated Tonks catalogue shows traps with jaws stated to be made in both the bevelled and the grooved styles. This same catalogue also refers to 'strong Dorset or grooved jaw rabbit traps.'

There are also three shapes of trap jaws common to gin traps, with the square jaw being the last type to evolve. In Robert Smith's book of 1768, he says,

'. . . I would advise that your steel traps for the fox should be square in the jaw, and not round as the common traps are usually made, and strike but five inches high and seven inches long in the jaw with saw teeth. . .'

Plate VI, Fig 2 in his book shows the type of fox trap referred to in the struck position (closed). This style of trap is now more commonly called an otter trap, but presumably both species of animals would have been caught with this type of trap in previous years. Approximately one hundred years later, square and early round jawed traps are mentioned in the Bellamy patent of 1860,

'The jaws (d,d,) which are here shewn square, may be oval or round as in the old traps if required, and they need not be toothed, as they may be formed of flat iron instead of bevelled iron, in which they would resemble the ordinary beaver trap. I can also make the jaws of my small traps similar to those of an ordinary beaver trap, out of plain flat iron instead of bevelled iron, as I shall for some uses require no teeth or serrated edge to such jaws'.

From the above comments it can be seen that the early styles of traps were commonly fitted with teeth rather than being left as plain jaws. In the early days the teeth would be merely spikes attached to either the upper or lower portion of the jaws. Some types include both a serrated toothed edge to the jaws as well as the larger spiked teeth. Serrated teeth appear commonly on the smaller types of traps for such creatures as rats. Early attempts at producing more humane gin traps include the 'off set' jaws featured in the large double flat-springed mantrap with the two 'C' scrolls 'plate' previously mentioned.

This attempt was followed in December 1891 by J. Johnstone who patented the idea that instead of the trap jaws being formed with teeth, they should be fitted with a strip of India rubber to hold the animal when caught. In a 1907 Army & Navy Stores catalogue the 'Shave' humane rubber-jawed traps for rabbits were being offered for sale at two shillings and six pence each or 28 shillings per dozen. In the same catalogue, Burgess's (improved) humane traps for rabbits or vermin were also offered for sale, but to order only. Described as 'similar in construction to an ordinary run trap, but the jaws being covered with India rubber, hold the animal caught firmly without breaking its legs. 4 inch jaws. Each 3/3, doz 36/0.' Obviously this was an idea ahead of its time, as only now in the United States of America are rubber-jawed traps being taken seriously by the trapping industry. This has been partly due to public opinion, but also to the trappers' own desire to cause the least discomfort possible to a caught animal, whilst still retaining a firm hold.

The first rubber-jawed traps commercially produced in North America were the 'Cush-in-grip' in 1936. These were produced by a company called Charles D. Briddell Inc, of Crisfield, Somerset County, Maryland. This company no longer exists, but two modern day manufacturers of rubber-jawed traps (also known as padded jaws) in North America are Woodstream Corporation and Butera Manufacturing. Woodstream manufacture padded traps called 'soft catch' in sizes No 1, No $1^1/_2$ and No 3. Butera produce padded traps in only two sizes, the No $1^1/_2$ and the No 2, and call their traps 'cushion catch'.

After the rubber-jawed traps produced around the early 1900s, came the 'Gilpa' double grip trap. This trap was made as an ordinary gin trap, but with the exception of inner jaws and had no teeth. Another feature of this trap was its single folding spring. This style of trap, which was produced around the very early 1930s seems to have had its origins in the double-jawed traps produced in North America for catching fur-bearing species without damaging the prime fur. To quote from the *Game and Gun & The Anglers Monthly* magazine of July 1933,

> 'Our tests in the field have shown that it certainly seems to fulfil all the claims which have been advanced in its favour, while it is undoubtedly extremely effective. The double jaws soften the closing blow, which does not break the bone or lacerate the flesh, and so it is extremely unlikely that any animal could escape by wringing off its foot. The price is 36 shillings a dozen, while a sample trap can be obtained for three shillings and six pence post free on application to Messrs. Gilbertson & Page Ltd.'

Indeed these small gin traps with a jaw spread of $4^1/_2$ inches were ideal to grip weasels by the body and kill them instantly.

Stocks

The most common type of stock found on British single spring gin traps consists of the stock head being bent upright and formed from the main stock. This type can be found on most of the various gin traps right up to the last ones made. In Joseph Bellamy's patent of 1860, the drawing included with this patent shows a variation to the normal pattern. In this patent the stock head is not formed in the usual way by being bent upwards from the stock. Instead, two standards are made separately and then attached to the stock. Due to the 'front' standard being attached separately rather than being formed from the stock, it therefore had to be positioned slightly further in to allow for a better fitting, and so making it more secure. This produced a slightly extended stock in front of the front standard. In Bellamy's patent of 1860, his drawing of a flat-springed gin trap has an extended stock but no mention was made regarding this unusual feature. In a slightly later trapping illustration dated 1890, a bow spring trap is shown which also has an extended stock. Other trap makers who also produced extended stocked gin traps included Griffiths, Sidebotham, Williams and Roberts.

In an undated poster (which may date from the early 1900s) Roberts advertised a new branded trap called the 3 star, ***, brand which showed a trap with special features including (a) projecting end of stock and (b) the jaws not having the close grip of the older patterns. Most of the extended stocked gins had bow springs as can be seen in catalogues dated 1920 and 1922. In the 1922 catalogue they are priced at 10/- (ten shillings) per dozen with chains. Sidebotham's also produced extended stocked traps with wire springs. In James Roberts' patent of 1895 his wire spring is secured to the stock by means of a rivet through an eye formed by the wire. When later wire springs were employed to operate a trap, the rear end of the stock was formed to make a bracket by being bent upwards in the same manner as the stock head. A hole was then made at the curve for the ends of the wire spring to fit through and thereby rest secured upon the stock.

Strangely, in W.H. Tildesley's patent of 1895 which deals with improvements to the bridge and plate attachments, his drawings show a separate stock attachment by a rivet to just inside the jaw standard, but again as in Bellamy's patent, no special mention is made of it.

In 1902 Alexander Allan Cruickshank patented a design which shortened the stock to just behind the jaw standard, and fixed to it either a single or double wire spring. The wire spring then formed most of the stock and in doing so lightened the weight of these traps considerably. This patent also allowed for the easy removal and replacement of a spring if the need arose. Although correct to say wire spring, and not wire stock, to help distinguish between this type of trap from the normal wire spring trap with a solid stock, it is easier to refer to this trap as having a wire spring and wire stock, as at first glance this type of trap looks to have a wire stock. Various manufacturers took up this general idea, and later patents show many methods of attaching and securing both bow and wire springs to a shortened stock.

Then in another Tildesley patent, dated 1927, the stock and spring are formed out of one continuous single length of spring steel with part of the stock, and part of the spring (immediately behind the eye) being bent into channel form for added strength whilst reducing the overall trap weight.

Although most stocks for gin traps were made from strips of flat metal, some, notably the square framed 'otter traps', have the stock made from square bar. The square bar can also be found attached to the frame turned to make a diamond shaped stock.

Joints

The joints are the two smaller 'standards' that are attached to the bridge and sit underneath the tongue on a normal trap. To these joints is attached, by a pin or rivet upon which it pivots, the till and plate. On some of the smaller 2 inch, $2^1/_2$ inch and 3 inch jawed traps it can be found that one of the joints has been omitted. The till is therefore riveted to a single joint with just enough 'slack' to allow it to move up and down freely.

In Lane's 1928 catalogue, with regard to the machine-made ordinary Dorset trap, mention is made that the trap has the 'plate hinged on brass pin, between brass standards. Brass pin for tongue'. Presumably the brass 'standards' are the joints as shown elsewhere in the diagrams of parts in the same catalogue and that the brass 'standards' were made separately rather than in one piece as SIDEBOTHAM'S, Williams' and Lane's brass pillars for the bridge head are. Again in an even earlier undated catalogue, *circa* 1908-13, of Lane's, mention is made that 'these traps (registered Dorset rabbit trap A1 brand) are practically the same as No 6, excepting that they are fitted with brass joints in addition to brass catches, and with a chain of extra strength'.

Tongues

These were first formed out of iron but later on were made from brass, copper and steel, with some being galvanised. Most tongues are attached to the bridge head end of the bridge and are fixed to it by means of a square hole. Part of the tongue goes through this hole and is folded back onto itself. Being a loose fitting, this allows the tongue to 'wag' back and forth without coming off. A simple but effective arrangement.

The other most commonly seen type of fitting comprises the bridge head end of the bridge being cut out in the middle at the top, forming a U shape. The two separate ends are then rolled over to form a clear tubular passageway for the pin to go through. The middle space is for the brass tongue to fit into, which also has a hole for the pin to pass through. The pin goes through all of the three sections with the brass tongue freely pivoting on the pin. In Joseph Yeo's patent of 28 October 1878, patent no 4326, there is no bridge arrangement on this trap, so the tongue is fixed to the trap's stockhead and can only engage the plate's till when the jaws are in the horizontal or set position.

In 1858 Henry Lane's introduced 'the brass catches and hinges' which were to help overcome the problem of rust forming on the iron tongues and joints and so reducing the efficiency of any trap. Copper was also used for trap tongues, but is not as common as the other metals. Mention is made in W. Carnegie's book *Practical Trapping* first published in the 1880s, of H. Lane of Wednesfield who made gin traps where

> 'the spring, the most important part of the trap, is always
> thoroughly well tempered, is strong, but nevertheless easily
> pressed down when the trap is being set; the flap (tongue)
> and catch (till) and other important parts, in which most
> makers fail, are of copper, and do not wear away like iron, or
> rust, which would clog the trap and prevent its acting. The
> plate is square, with the four corners taken off, and is of zinc,
> being so fitted as to be level with the jaws when set. . .'

In the *Keeper's Book* by Walker & Mackie, published in 1904, the same comments are quoted as above to Carnegie but this time refer to Burgess's spring trap. The probable explanation is that Lane's made the traps, but Burgess sold the ones that he bought from Lane's, stamped with his own name or mark.

Some types of gin traps are designed to be used without a normal tongue and are known as either tongueless or dogless. The term dogless comes from America where the tongue is known as the dog. In Britain this design was patented in 1933 by Samuel and Sidney Patten, who were by then trading under the name of James Roberts. The tongueless style of trap discontinued with the use of the upright portion of the bridge that the tongue was normally attached to. In place of the usual joints was a pivoted, one piece tongue and till. The till now engaged directly the jaw of the gin trap when in the set position. This style of trap was produced in both bow and wire spring versions. Another different version of the tongueless trap was also produced by Collins, and Tildesley's even produced a self-setting tongueless trap as early as 1887.

Brass Pillars

Advertised in a 1931 *Game and Gun & The Anglers Monthly* magazine and also several Midland gun company catalogues (1936-39) are Sidebotham's gamekeeper rabbit and vermin traps complete with chains, in jaw sizes 3", $3^1/_2$", 4", $4^1/_2$" and 5". The gamekeeper star (*) quality are fitted with brass pillars in addition to brass fittings (tongue and till), the brass pillars taking the place of the normal bridge head. Sidebotham's are not the only manufacturer that I have found to produce traps with the brass pillar feature as J. Williams and H. Lane did also. The brass pillar feature is also to be found illustrated earlier. Advertised in a 1913 catalogue of Gilbertson & Page Ltd. is Lane's D-shaped 'Egg' pole trap, 'specially suitable for catching jays, magpies and other egg stealing vermin', whilst a September 1950 advert of theirs simply states, 'GILPA rabbit and vermin traps. Specials with brass catches and pillars.'

Pole Traps

These traps were produced with or without teeth and also with India rubber-covered jaws. Sizes ranged from the two inch-jawed kingfisher trap up to the eight inch-jawed traps for use against all kinds of large birds of prey. Most pole traps were fitted with a single spring, but the seven and eight inch-jawed traps were usually fitted with double springs and setters.

Another design of pole trap used an egg placed upon a metal ring for bait, but worked in exactly the same manner as other pole traps except that it caught the bird, usually a crow or magpie, by the head or neck. These traps were made to look like a nest and could be used either on the ground, to represent a partridge nest or placed high in a hedgerow or other suitable tree. In 1872 'Idstone' describes an earlier improved hawk trap thus:

> 'The old hawk trap has a narrow trigger plate. This new one has simply a notch at the end of this perch or narrow plate, which holds down one of the toothless jaws, and acts beautifully; for if one jaw is held flat, of course both are. The largest is a circle of 6in. in diameter, the jaws (closed) $3^1/_2$in. deep. This is a very serviceable trap, and would take any hawk (even the largest peregrine) by the leg; whilst the usual trap, 4in. in the jaws, although seldom failing to secure the bird, almost always catches them by the toe. This little trap is used by keepers to place in the nests, for which the larger one is too cumbrous. I need hardly add that these traps are used without bait, and placed on the top of a post in some bleak and barren spot.'

A more humane type of pole trap was invented by Mr. C.M. Pelham-Burn, just prior to these traps being banned from use in 1904, for use on his own moors in Morayshire, Scotland. His design simply consisted of high striking jaws which by catching the bird by the middle of the body, instantly killed it, as opposed to the more normal way of being caught by the legs, which resulted with the bird hanging alive and upside down, awaiting death to come from exhaustion caused by its frantic efforts to escape. Whilst these high striking 'humane' jaws on pole traps also became illegal for catching birds, references are made to their use for catching feral cats and dogs in 1906 and 1909. Carnegie writes in his book *Practical Game Preserving* (1906, 3rd edition), 'The form of trap known as the hugger trap . . . is very useful for poaching cats and dogs. The taking of the bait releases the jaws which seize or hug the victim round the neck and kill it'. Carnegie writing about Round (pole) traps in his book *How to trap and snare* in 1908, says:

> The jaws may be plain or toothed, according to the quarry to be taken, and most manufacturers can supply these traps with the trigger action reversed, i.e. so that the treadle has to be raised in order to discharge the trap. It is frequently necessary when trapping to employ a bait fixed to the treadle in order to take the bird or animal by the neck. In such instances the creature is very prone to seize the bait, and, without in any way depressing the treadle, take it away by pulling. In such instances a trap with the ordinary catch would fail to act, whereas with the working arrangement reversed, it would do so. Traps fitted this way are usually termed 'hugger' traps, and the principle is applied to the larger sizes for taking poaching dogs and cats.

George Abbey, whilst referring to cats in his book *The Balance of Nature* in 1909 states,

> 'The trap employed may be that known as the patent hugger, 10in. jaws, which being furnished with sharp spikes, kills the animal at once, and tells no tale.'

POLE TRAP WITH OFFSET JAWS

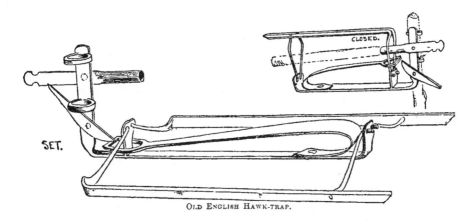

OLD ENGLISH HAWK-TRAP.

OLD ENGLISH HAWK TRAP FROM *HISTORY OF FOWLING*
(1897) BY REV. H.A. MACPHERSON – the diagram shows
this trap both set and closed. In the set trap the rings
by which the trap could be secured to a pole or
branch of a tree are well shown. There is also an iron
socket, apparently intended to receive a piece of
wood, upon which a hawk might alight. It was sprung
of course by the weight of the bird. The trap measures
8" in length; breadth when expanded is 5"

HUGGER TRAP FOR POACHING CATS AND DOGS FROM
PRACTICAL GAME PRESERVING (1906) BY WILLIAM CARNEGIE

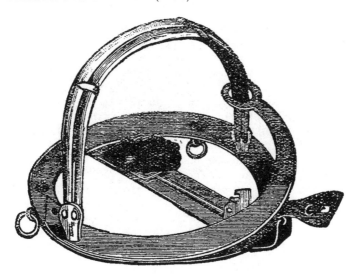

A TRAP FOR WINGED VERMIN ON THE MOOR
[FROM *THE GAMEKEEPER* JANUARY 1932]

The designer of the trap illustrated below is an Argyllshire gamekeeper and he considers his design offers certain advantages to trappers, particularly on grouse moors.

He has spent a lifetime trapping winged vermin on grouse moors with rabbit traps, but has always considered the rabbit trap unsuitable for the purpose. In the ordinary trap a 'hoodie' is apt to twist its foot off and escape, the new trap revolves with the movement of the bird. The trap is a round one and the chain is fixed to a swivel-bolt placed in the centre of the trap through a hole in the under cross-bar. He considers that the new trap is far less likely to be sprung without a kill. In fact, he has never known his new trap sprung without a capture, neither has he ever had a foot or claw left in it.

The size of the trap being only $5\frac{1}{2}$ inches, it can be set with the least disturbance to the ground; also it can be set on a small round island in a water hole. The jaws of the trap are thick and blunt and do not smash a bird's leg, neither would they sink into a sheep's leg if one should get caught, but they would give a chance for the leg to be pulled out. In place of the usual pan for springing the trap there is a small ring which offers one or two advantages which the expert trapper may readily realise.

The inventor would very much like to receive criticism of his trap from readers of *The Gamekeeper*.

Although pole traps were banned in 1904, from use in elevated positions, Carnegie again writing in his book *How to trap and snare* in 1908 states:

> Round traps can still, however, be employed in a number of positions, both for ground and winged vermin, where the ordinary Dorset trap is inconvenient, if not unsuitable, and they must accordingly be included in the armoury of the trapper.

Maybe the game preservers were just trying to get around the pole trap legislation by using smaller traps against winged vermin on the ground, whilst the larger types also on the ground, against feral cats and dogs. Certainly Sidebotham's were advertising for sale in the *Game & Gun*, 1933, round traps in 4", 4¹/₂" and 5" diameter sizes. Even S.Young & Sons (Misterton) Ltd in their 1957/8 catalogue advertise for sale Traps (Round) with the caption 'Round Steel Traps, with 4" smooth jaws 12/- each (as illustrated), 5", Traps 15/6 each post paid.' The illustration in their catalogue clearly shows a pole trap with a round plate.

Dorset Traps

Seemingly the term 'Dorset trap' comes from the excellent tempering qualities of the trap springs produced by the small number of Dorset-based trap makers or blacksmiths. A later improvement seems to have been the introduction of jaws with teeth formed out of the jaws rather than being attached separately either under or above the jaws. Idstone states in his book published in 1872:

> 'I am very much inclined to think that the original 'gin' had no teeth at all. Decidedly the first application of teeth was in the form of spikes, which folded over each other underneath the jaws. All the old frame traps are thus formed – at any rate, all that I have seen – whilst the spring instead of being bent over in a loop, is simply bolted with one large stud and eye. I am inclined to think this the best manner of attaching the spring after all, though not so pleasing to the eye. . .
> Dorset traps have been celebrated for something like one hundred and thirty years, for their lightness, their durability, the equal elasticity of the spring – I mean its being as firm at the top when the trap is sprung as when it is set – and for the flatness of the trap when open rendering it adapted for shallow or stony ground and requiring very little earth to cover spring and jaws.'

He also states that Dorset traps have found their way into every county of England and that pseudo-Dorset traps are not made in this county. He wrote:

> 'The secret of tempering was bought by the present maker's (Shave?) great grandfather of a travelling tinker, and the 'gin' thus made rapidly became a favourite. I am not sure that the pattern itself was not furnished by this itinerant tinman, but I

do know that the same cute hand instructed his pupil in the
art of tempering.'

Couldn't the above statement refer to the introduction of the now
commonly accepted 'bow spring' design of gin traps? I certainly think so. He
then goes on to describe a Dorset trap thus:

'With a chain and swivel 12in. long it weighs 1lb. 11oz. The
genuine article which I recommend, but which, to speak more
correctly, commends itself, is exactly 12in. long; the jaws are 4in.
from hinge to hinge, and when closed they are $2^1/_2$in. high. At
the same time the extreme height of the spring is $2^1/_4$in. and 1in.
less at its narrowest part. There are eleven teeth in each jaw, and
the trigger plate is about $2^3/_4$in. by $2^1/_2$in. The jaws and trigger
plate can be covered with 1in. of earth, and no part of the
spring exceeds $1^1/_2$in. in depth when set.'

Comparing another make of spring with a Dorset spring he says that
'the springs of both these traps are as nearly as possible 60lb, but, whilst in
the Dorsetshire trap I get this power by a depression of 1 inch, in the inferior
article I have to go $1^1/_2$ inches or nearly 2 inches, rendering the setting of a
Dorset made one far superior and much more easy.'

Unfortunately Idstone's book does not have an illustration of the Dorset
trap that he refers to. However, much later illustrated catalogues, such as
Tonks, refer to 'strong Dorset or grooved jaw rabbit traps.' This statement
implies that only Dorset traps had the grooved style of jaws. Another illustrated
catalogue, this time of Eliza Tinsley & Co, also states 'Pattern Nos 204 Dorset
jaw run or rat traps with chains.' The 204 illustration again shows a trap with
the grooved jaws. Lastly a Lewis Anglo catalogue states 'Item No 2276 real
Dorset rabbit trap. Grooved jaws. With galv. plates and brass fittings. 4 inch
jaws.' Again unfortunately none of these catalogues are dated.

In Mark Hovell's book *Rats and How To Destroy Them*, first published in
1924, whilst referring to Dorset traps he states, 'It is therefore unnecessary,
in the writer's opinion, to get a 'Dorset' trap, which has a brass catch and
galvanised treadle and is consequently more expensive.' Over the years it
seems that real Dorset traps had come to be thought of as superior made
traps having grooved jaws, a galvanised plate and brass fittings, e.g. tongue
and till. Whereas the sham 'Dorset' type has the same grooved jaws but only
iron fittings and a self coloured plate, i.e. not galvanised. These 'modern'
Dorset traps were made with either a bow spring, as in the original models,
or later on with a wire spring. However, in Idstone's detailed description of a
Dorset trap in 1872, he never once mentions a galvanised plate or brass
fittings being on the trap. This would be correct, obviously, as the brass fittings
were only introduced by H. Lane's in 1858 and in Idstone's own words, 'Dorset
traps have been celebrated for something like one hundred and thirty years. . .'

so this would mean that the original Dorset trap was first produced around the mid-1700s.

Quality Marks

These usually appear on the spring just behind the 'eye', if of the asterisk (* a star-shaped mark) type, the best quality being denoted by a single 'star', two stars for second quality, three for third quality. Fourth quality traps were also sometimes made, but usually makers tended only to produce traps down to third quality. In place of the asterisks can be found another simple way of denoting quality. This was done by replacing the asterisks with a letter and number, e.g. A1 quality or third quality A3. Both the asterisk and A1 type of systems were used by Sidebotham's. Lane's like Sidebotham's also sometimes produced a fourth quality trap. Lane's marked some of their traps, by putting a quality number e.g. 2, 3, 4 on to the brass tongue, but they still had their maker's name on the spring as well.

A very similar trap to these just mentioned is to be found with the spring stamped H. Lane A1 maker. These traps differ by having the joints made of brass as well as the tongue. They also have a chain of extra strength.

Quality marks should not be confused with size or type marks, that some trap makers put on their traps, e.g. Tildesley round jaw rat traps 0, 4, 5 (sizes) etc. These types of marks/numbers are usually found on the plate, but can also be found occasionally on the tongue, especially if made of brass, such as the 4 inch jaw bow spring trap stamped Collins behind the 'eye' of the spring, and with the number 8 stamped on the top of the brass tongue.

Another example of a type mark is Lane's 4 inch jawed Li-Lo wire spring trap that has stamped on its brass tongue the numbers 172. These numbers refer to its identification at the factory as can be seen in a Lane's advert of 1954 which states 'No WS 172', (Number Wire Spring 172). Another Li-Lo brand of trap also listed in the same advert is the 4 inch jawed Vee flat spring, being No. NF 184. Presumably NF refers to the factory identification as the new flat (spring) with 184 being its reference number and which would be stamped onto its brass tongue, but having not seen this type of trap personally, it's only a guess. However in a previously illustrated advert of 1949, from the *Shooting Times*, the illustration is of 'A best quality Vee-flat spring No. 178' which shows this type of trap with Lane on the plate. This type of trap definitely has the 178 number stamped on its brass tongue. The same type of trap, but sold by The Country Gentlemen's Association, has stamped in small capital letters under the embossed word LANE on the plate C.G.A.179 SPECIAL. The brass tongue also has stamped on it 179. This numbering seems to confirm that it refers to its identification at the factory. The 5 inch jaw version of the Vee-flat spring trap has stamped on its brass tongue 10FS. This trap also has Lane on the plate and an unusual feature for a gin trap, a wire safety catch. This wire safety catch is fixed through a hole on the end of the bridge to hold the 'free' jaw whilst setting the trap.

LANE'S 10FS TRAP WITH
THE WIRE SAFETY CATCH

LANE'S LI-LO
WIRE SPRING TRAP

Two slightly different 4 inch jawed bow spring Li-Lo versions have the number 000 stamped on to their brass tongues. The slight differences are that one trap has the normal Li-Lo embossed plate whilst the other version has Li-Lo stamped on the plate in small capital letters. Li-Lo is also stamped on the bow spring behind the eye of this trap. Yet another version exists of the LI-LO stamped on the plate in small capital letters. On this trap the number 20 is stamped on the brass tongue, while stamped on the plate under LI-LO are the words in larger capital letters, FAIRBURN & TULETT. There is nothing stamped on the pressed bow spring. This is another example of a business selling a bought-in product that has been stamped with their own business name. Their name can also be found on Alarm Guns, which they are also known to have sold. Incidentally, Thomas Tullet was from Horsham in Sussex, but was head gamekeeper on the Wentworth estate from 1901 until he retired in 1945 and died in 1954. His son, Thomas Henry Tullet, was also a gamekeeper, initially at Wentworth and then later at the Chatsworth estate and at Knepp Castle in Sussex. In 1933 he formed a partnership with Norman Fairburn producing dog food at the mill in Mill Lane, Greasbrough, which is on the Wentworth estate. In 1951 he formed Pointer Products (Pet Food Manufacturers) with his son Thomas. They had premises on the Eastwood Trading Estate in Rotherham, near Sheffield. Thomas Henry Tullet died in 1983.

Lastly, a double folding spring trap with Li-Lo embossed on the plate, and having 8 inch jaws, only has an ordinary metal tongue and not a brass one as the other Li-Lo traps have. This trap has no reference number on it, but it may be Trap No. 282 which is referred to as 'large vermin traps' in the already mentioned 1954 advert. The advert stated that 'Occasional supplies of 8 inch jaw traps with powerful double springs are available.'

It should be remembered that other manufacturers may have had a

"Gamekeeper" Brand.

These Traps are made in "High-Grade" Qualities only, and Every Trap is Thoroughly Tested and Warranted Sound.

"Gamekeeper" Real Dorset Rabbit Traps.

Brass Catch.   Galvanized Plate.

		8 in.	3½ or 4 in.	4½ in.	5 in. Jaws.	
✳	Best, extra strong	28/-	28/-	32/-	36/-	per doz
✳ ✳	quality ...	—	17/-	20/-	26/-	,,
✳ ✳ ✳	,,	—	14/6	17/6	20/6	,,
✳ ✳ ✳ ✳	,,	—	12/-	15/-	18/-	,,

"Gamekeeper" Plain Rabbit Traps.

Iron Catch.

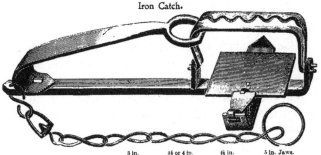

		3 in.	3½ or 4 in.	4½ in.	5 in. Jaws.	
✳	Best, extra strong	19/-	19/-	23/-	27/-	per doz.
✳ ✳	quality ...	—	13/-	16/-	19/-	,,
✳ ✳ ✳	,,	—	11/-	14/-	17/-	,,
✳ ✳ ✳ ✳	9/-	—	9/-	12/-	15/-	,,

Carriage Paid *on all Orders above* 40/- *value to the principal Railway Stations in England and Wales.*

Ordinary Rabbit Traps.

PLAIN OR GROOVED JAWS.

	Jaws ...	4	4½	5 inch.
" A 1 "	Quality ...	16/-	18/6	21/- per doz.
" A 2 "	,, ...	13/-	15/-	17/- ,,
" A 3 "	,, ...	10/-	12/-	14/- ,,

Complete with Best Chains.

SIDEBOTHAM'S TRAPS QUALITY MARKS

different system for identifying the quality of their individual traps or types, so the above comments are only a generalisation.

The more motivated and enterprising of the trapmakers were always trying to find a better design of trap or 'triggering mechanism' to sell to their potential customers. This endless search resulted in many patents, registered designs and trade marks being filed and these are known collectively as industrial property rights. The Oxford English Dictionary gives the following definitions of the words patent and trade mark. PATENT, is the privilege granted to a person or persons, the sole right to make, use or sell some invention. TRADEMARK is a mark, now secured by legal registration used by a manufacturer or trader to distinguish goods from similar wares or other firms.

After the Copyright of Designs Act 1839, designs could be officially registered, although from 1839 until 1842 no official mark or insignia were used. However, from 1842 until 1883 a complicated system of coded 'diamond marks' were used. Then in 1884, the much more sensible idea of consecutive numbers was introduced. These numbers are nearly always prefixed by Rd or Redg No.

Star & Crescent Mark
Confusion abounds among trap collectors as to why so many different trap makers stamped their traps with the 'Star & Crescent' when a trade mark is used to distinguish goods from similar wares or other firms. The answer to this question I believe, lies with the outbreak of the Crimea War (1854-1856). In 1854, when Russia invaded the Balkans and sank the Turkish fleet at Sinope, Britain and France declared war on Russia. This was because of their mistrust of Russian ambitions in the region. In the widely read *Punch* Magazine during 1854 there appeared a political cartoon showing the Imperial Eagle of Russia caught in a 'mantrap', with, upon its chest, a shield with Saint George of England slaying the 'evil dragon'. On the trap plate is a crescent representing Turkey which was being trodden underfoot by the Russians. With the Russian Eagle caught in the trap, this cartoon was basically implying to the general public that Russia was now in a situation that it would find hard to get out of. This cartoon I believe, the trap makers of the day, took to their hearts and embraced as a sign of patriotism. Rather than originally being a registered trade mark, the 'star & crescent' (of Turkey) just became a general motif used by the trap makers. Later established trapmakers such as Sidebotham's (est 1865) simply carried on the tradition of this well established patriotic motif. However the business of James Roberts which was established in 1867, seems to have 'hijacked' the star and crescent from general usage and registered it as his own trade mark. According to the *Trade Mark Journal* his date of application to register this mark was 4th January 1883, although he states that it had been in use by him since 'about one year before 13th

August 1875'. How this 'sharp business practice' was looked upon by the older established trap making families we can only guess. Joseph Tonks' (est 1825) catalogue of *circa* 1925, shows that they were still producing and offering for sale a 'star and crescent' brand of rabbit trap regardless of Roberts registered trade mark.

TRAPPED.

PUNCH'S CRIMEA CARTOON OF 1854

Swastika Trade Mark

A similar situation to the above, probably occurred regarding the Swastika Trade Mark as registered and used by the business of Eliza Tinsley in 1921. Another business to use the swastika motif was W.H. Tildesley, where the swastika is to be found made into a surrounding border on the leaflet for their Dorset Jaw Rabbit Trap No 0509. Germany was re-emerging, after the devastation of World War I, with the Nazi Party and its Swastika sign, becoming a strong symbol of nationhood with plenty of buying power, and so therefore just right for selling all types of British goods. Trap making was only a small part of both businesses mentioned above, so the management would be looking at the 'bigger picture' regarding trade with Germany.

Some Interesting Trade Marks Found on Traps

The CARRINGTON trade mark was registered on 3rd February 1887 by John Connell & Company, Dunster House, Mark Lane, London who described themselves as merchants.

Advert found in a Sheffield Directory of 1887 showing the Kangaroo Brand. This registered trade mark (date of registration unknown) showing a pictorial kangaroo belonged to Robert Sorby & Sons, Carver Street, Sheffield, who advertised themselves as sole manufacturers of a large variety of edged tools etc. This pictorial Kangaroo trade mark can be found with the letters R.S.B. next to it, which may denote the Robert Sorby Brand, thereby differentiating this brand of gin trap from the very similar pictorial kangaroo brand of gin trap registered by John Butler in 1907.

LYNG. The business of William Cross and Son Ltd, Lyng Foundry, West Bromwich, Staffordshire registered this name on 25th October 1894. However they stated that the 'Mark (had been) used by applicants and predecessors in business at least thirty nine years before 13th August 1875, i.e. *circa* 1836. They stated that they were manufacturers of all types of metal goods and list a wide range of products, but the only type of trap they now listed seems to have been mole traps.

SPART (Traps spelled backwards) This trade mark name was registered on 21st January 1902 by William Henry Pritchard, Caledonian Works, Hickman Street, Wednesfield, near Wolverhampton, Staffordshire. He described himself as a 'Manufacturer and Factor – of all kinds of metal vermin traps and gins'.

Another Sheffield business advertising in a Sheffield Directory of 1905 are Ibbotson Brothers & Company Limited, Globe Steel Works, Alma Street, Sheffield who were merchants & manufacturers of 'steel of every description' and seem to have made 'files, saws, steel forgings, axles, spiral springs of all kinds'. Their trade mark was the word GLOBE and a pictorial Globe. Date of registration unknown, but established in 1809.

Interestingly, the business of John E. Butler Ltd, 5 Birmingham Road, Walsall, Staffordshire, described as Merchants, registered a pictorial Kangaroo on 29th May 1907. This kangaroo is almost identical to Sheffield company, Robert Sorby & Sons' Kangaroo Brand. Gin traps with a pictorial kangaroo and BB stamped next to it may be from this merchant's business. The extra BB would be to differenciate between the trade marks and may simply imply 'Butler Brand'.

BLUE DIAMOND. This trade mark was registered by the New Zealand Hardware Co, Ltd 3, Cumberland Street South, Dunedin, New Zealand 22nd September 1908. By Consent. Address for Service in the United Kingdom was, c/o Marks & Clerk, 18, Southampton Buildings, London.

MOA. Another earlier trade mark registered 18th November 1890 by this company who were described as Hardware Merchants is a pictorial bird

with N.Z. to the right of its head, whilst under its feet is MOA. Address for service in the United Kingdom, c/o Keep Brothers, 11, Broad Street, Birmingham.

RATCATCHERS (1860)

Chapter Three

THE TRAP MAKERS
OF WEDNESFIELD

IN THIS CHAPTER I have arranged the known trap makers of Wednesfield in alphabetical order for ease of reference. I have also included separately other known trap makers or manufacturers from other areas in the following chapter. It must also be pointed out that even if a certain trap has a name on it that name may not be of a manufacturer. Then as now, items were produced by well-known makers for a wholesaler or retailer using that company or individual's name or brand name.

GILPA is one such example and is merely the abbreviation of the two names that form the company, i.e. Gilbertson and Page. This company was established in 1873, although the 'GILPA' trademark was only registered on 17th February 1930, and sold various game foods and equipment to farms and estates throughout Britain. A similar business, Spratt's of London, also had their name stamped on traps. Also Craig can be found stamped on the spring of some gin traps, but stamped under the brass tongue can be found the name of J. Williams and Son, Maker.

This list of trap makers does not imply that they all had their own business either. It is merely a list of people whose trade at that time was trap making. Some obviously had their own businesses whilst others were employed by large trap making companies such as Lane's, or a relative may have employed them. Certain individuals also carried on other occupations at the same time as their trap making, the most common being beer retailers, in premises with names such as 'Albion', 'Angel Inn', or 'Bull's Head'. This situation must have been a convenient arrangement for some trap makers who, after a long day making traps in dirty and sweaty conditions in some backyard building, would be ready to quench his well-earned thirst. It would also be handy to have another income to rely on when trap sales were poor.

Although trap making was heavy and hot work, and thought of as a man's job, just as chain making was, women were employed in both trades. In chain making the women normally made the smaller gauge chain which would be less than half an inch in diameter. Her job would include making twisted chains which were used for cart traces, harness work, cow ties and small dog chains. It was also probably a woman who made the trap chains for the normal sized gin traps. As in the chain making trade, the women employed making traps would be engaged in making the smaller and lighter traps for rats and such vermin, although one woman in 1838 is listed as 'rat trap maker and man'!

Premises would be shared by the tradesmen to cut down costs, especially by related tradesmen. Due to family relationships of some of these tradesmen, I have only recorded their names and not tried to unravel their kinship. Another reason is because of incorrect spellings by parish clerks some surnames have changed over the years. One example will illustrate. John Tonk's ancestors' surname was originally spelled Tomkys – over the years the generations have spelled their surname through written mistakes, firstly as Tonkys and then as Tonks.

Over time, family-run businesses such as Lane's and Marshall's invested more money into their trap works and started to expand by employing more workers and building up their home and export trade. Obviously some disputes would arise between employer and employee with the outcome that eventually the workers formed themselves into the Wednesfield Spring Trap Makers Society in 1890. By 1900 it had 126 members, but eight years later the numbers had started to fall, resulting in only 68 members in 1910.

Around 1905 the Trap Makers Association was formed and one of its founder members, William Sidebotham, became the employers' secretary. In a decision to avoid unfair competition between the various trap makers, a set price for their products was agreed between them. This arrangement between rival trap makers in an effort to set certain prices to each other's mutual benefit had previously been tried privately between W.H. Tildesley of Willenhall and Bellamy & Son of Wednesfield in 1903. The Trap Makers Association also agreed with the Trade Union representatives to wage increases and conditions through negotiations.

About 1911 the Wednesfield Spring Trap Makers Society was then merged with the National Amalgamated Lockmakers and Metal Workers Male and Female Trade Society, finally dropping the name Wednesfield in 1916. The Midlands Counties Trade Federation was formed out of a joint body of many small Trade Unions, which were trying to help each other by having one influential organisation speaking and acting on their behalf for the benefit of all members. The only paid official was John Taylor J.P. who was paid expenses only.

World War I between 1914 to 1918 drew heavily on metal reserves and manpower in Britain, but relations between employer and employee at that time were good. Mentioned in the National Amalgamated Lock Makers Male and Female Trade Society Report of 1917 is, 'Your Executive Council are pleased to report that the best of feeling exists between the employers and your society. This has proved a most useful factor in obtaining past advances in wages, and we appeal to the workers to do all in their power to retain the present good relationship'. The report also stated 'that every man is a member of the Union and with few exceptions the females also.'

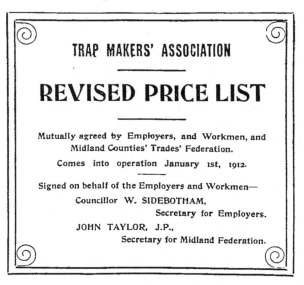

TRAP MAKERS' ASSOCIATION

REVISED PRICE LIST

Mutually agreed by Employers, and Workmen, and Midland Counties' Trades' Federation.

Comes into operation January 1st, 1912.

Signed on behalf of the Employers and Workmen—

Councillor W. SIDEBOTHAM,
Secretary for Employers.

JOHN TAYLOR, J.P.,
Secretary for Midland Federation.

A few years later, in the Union's report of 1921, things were different. It states: 'An application received in June, from the Trap Manufacturers, for a reduction of a 35% off piece workers and 20% off day workers resulted, after negotiations had taken place, in the application being withdrawn.' The employers had not given up though, and in the Union's report of 1922, 'the Manufacturers in the trap industry applied for a reduction in wages, and after repeated meetings with the men and employers, the Executive decided that a reduction was in the best interests of both parties.' However, some men did not agree with this decision, and upon a ballot being taken persuaded 75% of the workers to vote against any reduction at all. Eventually 'The Executive being of the opinion that a strike would only lead to disaster, again met the men, and eventually the matter was left in the hands of the Society, when the 20% (reduction) was accepted on their behalf'. The following year, 1923, the trade had been good for the trap manufacturers and some overtime was being worked in a few of the factories. Due to the overtime situation the Union had managed to obtain employment for certain members who had been out (unemployed) for some considerable time.

Unfortunately the trap makers still only received 'the rates of pay which were in operation last year.'

The report then says: 'To the Trap Makers we appeal for a better spirit of brotherhood than exists at the present time. . . certain men and women do not carry out their obligations which are not only due but should be their first thoughts on pay day.'

Clearly some men and women were not in agreement with some Union policies and were not bothering to pay their Union subscriptions. A few years later, the 1927 report goes on to say: 'While the majority of trap makers still remain loyal to the Union, it is regretted that others have ceased to do so. If there is one body of workers above another who have benefited through the activities of this Union it is the trap makers.'

In the years after World War II large estates were broken up and sold off. Never again would there be employed the vast number of gamekeepers or other workers associated with the estates or large farms. Modern machinery was also replacing the agricultural workers on the land. According to a report in the *Wolverhampton Chronicle*, dated 26th August 1955, 'The spread of myxomatosis has caused a considerable fall in sale of traps used for catching rabbits in England. This together with the Pests Act would appear to spell doom for the Wednesfield trapmakers.' However, when the reporter contacted Mr A.V. Sidebotham, a partner in the firm of W & G Sidebotham he found 'a thriving factory, working almost to capacity'. Explaining the situation, Mr Sidebotham commented that, 'although sales for the home market had dropped very considerably due to the spread of myxomatosis, the export trade was not affected. The firm exports traps to South, East and West Africa, Australia, and other countries. Traps are being made for catching leopards, lions, wild dogs, foxes, and small vermin, such as rats. The Pests Act will not affect the sale of traps for the export market and will only restrict the sale of rabbit traps in this country. It does not mean the end of manufacture, nor does the Act intend this.' The article ends: 'of the 45 people employed at the factory in Rookery Street, 14 of them are women press operators.'

The imminent banning of the gin trap in 1958, of course, also affected the few remaining trap makers. Many had closed their doors for good earlier, but Sidebotham's bravely struggled on dependent on mole traps and the production of several approved traps, which would replace the gin. Although they tried for many years to carry on, even with subcontracted work for Land and Range Rover cars, even they had to cease business in the very early 1980s. Finally the Spring Trap Makers Society which had been formed in 1890 and had become affiliated to the Trade Union Congress, ceased to exist in March 1988, thus severing the link with the old trap makers.

To quote White's Directory of 1834,

> 'Wednesfield is a township and chapelry in the south division of
> Offlow Hundred, two miles north east of Wolverhampton, and on
> the Wyrley and Essington Canal. It contains upwards of 3000
> acres of land, and 1,879 inhabitants residing in the large village
> of Wednesfield, and the neighbouring hamlets of Wednesfield
> Heath, March End, Nechell, Wood End, and Wood Hayes.
> Immense quantities of locks, keys and traps of every description,
> are manufactured here for the Birmingham and Wolverhampton
> merchants'.

Listed below are some of the men and women who lived, and worked in the
trap making trade – even briefly, in this area, but please remember that when
using this chapter as a guide to the trap makers' dates of working that all the
dates are only approximate. Any trap maker could have been producing
traps for many years before or after these known dates without the need to
advertise his address or products. Indeed, some trap makers may not have
been able to afford to spend hard-earned money on listing his address or
advertising his products, and purely relied upon local trade by 'way of mouth'.
According to *Benn's Encyclopaedia* of 1930,

> 'For over 150 years Wednesfield has supplied animal and
> vermin traps for all markets of the world. A dozen
> Wednesfield firms, employing about 200 people, have an
> annual output of over two million traps, and their products
> range from bird and rabbit to lion and tiger traps.'

Of the dozen businesses mentioned, only seven placed an advert, which helps
to illustrate my point. Another anomaly occurs with the 1841 Census records
which were 'rounded down' by five years, so this Census year only gives
approximate ages of people. A further anomaly to occur involves some patents.
The patent drawing and the trap that finally appears can differ widely,
although maintaining the basis of the Patentee's original idea. The reason
for this is simply that when the Patentee approached a trap maker about
producing his patent, the trap maker may have suggested an easier way of
operating the trap or altering the patent slightly to allow ease of production
and therefore reducing costs and making the trap a more viable product to
sell. Some traps only varied slightly from the original drawing but others can
differ greatly. A good example of this is the Davis humane rabbit trap which
was made in very limited numbers, with a flat spring, instead of the 'spring
being of full bow form' as it is described in John Davis's patent. W.&G.
Sidebotham's obviously either looked at the drawings or prototype trap and
instantly decided that an ordinary flat spring would work as efficiently, or
better, and also be easier to produce.

Wednesfield Trap Makers

Year refers to the known dates of operation; the earliest known date of a trapmaker's trade/identification mark is shown in brackets e.g. BRAVO (1910).

ADEY, Abraham. Wednesfield. Year 1876 – 1940
Steel Trapmaker and shopkeeper 1876
Steel Trapmaker and shopkeeper, High Street, 1880, 1884, 1888, 1892, 1896, 1904.
Greengrocer, 40 High Street, 1916.
Steel Trapmaker, 40 High Street, 1921, 1924.
Adey, Abraham & Sons, steel Trap Makers, 17 High Street, 1928, 1932, 1936, 1940.

APPLEBY, James. Wednesfield. Year 1865
Hinge and Trapmaker and beer retailer, Wood End, 1865.

APPLEBY, Henry. Wednesfield. Year 1851
Hasp and Trapmaker 1851.

BAGGOT, James. Wednesfield. Year 1835 – 1841
Trapmaker, steel 1835.
In the 1841 Census, James Baggot of Church Street was aged 60 approx., and had an apprentice called Henry Lane who was aged 18 approximately.

BECKETT, Joseph. Wednesfield. Year 1838 – 1839
In both years described as a rat trap maker.

BECKETT, James. Wednesfield. Year 1834 – 1849
Trapmaker (rats, vermin etc.). 1834.
Steel Trapmaker, 1835, 1841, 1842, 1849.

THOMAS BEECH, GLOBE WORKS, WEDNESFIELD
ESTABLISHED 1852.
Registered Trade Mark: "BRAVO"
Other Trade Marks:
T BEECH,   T. BEECH,
   x   xx
        T. BEECH,
          xxx
Manufacturers of all kinds of
VERMIN, GAME
AND
WILD ANIMAL TRAPS
Suitable for Home and Export.

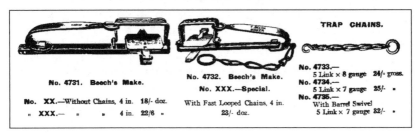

TRAP CHAINS.

No. 4731. Beech's Make.
No. XX.—Without Chains, 4 in. 18/- doz.
„ XXX.— „ „ 4 in. 22/6 „

No. 4732. Beech's Make.
No. XXX.—Special.
With Fast Looped Chains, 4 in. 23/- doz.

No. 4733.—
5 Link × 8 gauge 24/- gross.
No. 4734.—
5 Link × 7 gauge 25/- „
No. 4735.—
With Barrel Swivel
5 Link × 7 gauge 32/- „

BEECH'S UNUSUAL TRAP WITH BOTH BOW AND FLAT SPRING

BEECH, Thomas. Wednesfield. Year 1841 – 1955.

In the 1841 Census records, Thomas Beech of New Street, was a Trapmaker and aged about 23.

Trapmaker, 1849

Bird, Rat & Rabbit Trapmaker, New Street. 1865.

Steel Trapmaker, 1872.

Steel Trapmaker, Cross Street, 1876, 1880, 1884, 1888, 1896, 1904.

Steel Trapmaker, 2 Cross Street, 1916, 1921, 1924, 1928, 1931, 1932, 1936, 1940.

Beech, Thomas Ltd. Globe Works, Cross Street, 1948, 1951.

Trade/identification marks: BRAVO (1910),

T. BEECH

X

T. BEECH   T. BEECH

XX   XXX

nB (An upside-down horseshoe followed by the letter B).

Miscellaneous Information: Became incorporated as a limited company on 5th September 1940 and was dissolved on 10 March 1955. The company number was 363128. An unusual trap made by this business has a 6" jaw, drop plate and non-folding double springs. The unusual thing about this trap is that one spring is a bow spring and the other is a flat spring. The overall length of this trap is 26 inches.

BEECH, William. Wednesfield. Year 1892

Steel Trapmaker. Cross Street. 1892.

BELLAMY, George. Wednesfield. Year 1810 – 1924

According to an illustrated list of W.&G. Sidebotham, *circa* 1933, which claims they are the proprietors of this business, it states that George Bellamy & Sons, Atlas Works, Wednesfield, were established in 1810.

Grocer, Church Street, 1880

Grocer and steel Trapmaker, High Street, 1888, 1892.

Bellamy, George & Son. Steel trap & cabinet lock makers. High Street, 1896.

Steel Trap Makers, 6 High Street, 1904, 1916, 1921, 1924.

Trade/identification mark: CB (a horseshoe on its side followed by the letter B).

BELLAMY, Joseph, Wednesfield. Year 1845 – 1884

Steel Trapmaker 1845, 1849, 1850, 1851, 1854, 1855, 1860.

Directory advertisement, High Street, 1861, which states 'Manufacturer of steel traps for rats and birds, mice and vermin, rabbits, hawks, and beavers, foxes and wolves, otters, tigers, bears &c. Wrought traps for moles, musk, and muskrats. For home and export markets.

Steel Trapmaker 1864.
Vermin & game trap manufacturers, High Street, 1865.
Steel Trapmaker 1872, 1876, 1880, 1884.
Miscellaneous information: Provisional patent specification, number 2994, dated 6th December 1860, was sealed on 28th May 1861. Plate falls along stock away from the spring.

BELLAMY, Richard. Wednesfield. Year 1827 – 1841
Rat trap maker, 1827
Trapmaker of Graisley Lane and aged about 40 years in 1841 census.

BELLINGHAM, Richard. Wednesfield. Year 1839
Rat trap maker (& man) 1839.
This directory entry may be a spelling mistake for Bellimore.

BELLIMORE, Richard. Wednesfield. Year 1833 – 1842
Vermin & Mantrap maker 1833.
Trapmaker (rats, vermin etc.) 1834.
Trapmaker, steel 1835.
Rat trap maker (& man) 1838, 1839.
Trapmaker, steel 1841, 1842.

BOWEN, Alfred. Wednesfield. Year 1892 – 1896
Steel trap maker, High Street, 1892, 1896.

BUTLER, Mrs. Ann. Wednesfield Heath. Year 1880 – 1884
Steel trap maker, New Cross, 1880, 1884.

BUTLER, Charles. Wednesfield Heath. Year 1860 – 1876
Steel trap maker 1860
Steel trap manufacturer, New Cross, 1861, 1864, 1865.
Vermin trap maker, New Cross 1868, 1872, 1876.

CHAPMAN, Michael. Wednesfield. Year 1833 – 1855
Vermin trap maker 1833.
Trapmaker, steel 1835.
Rat Trapmaker 1838, 1839.
Steel Trapmaker 1841, 1842, 1845, 1849, 1850, 1851.
Trapmaker, steel 1854.
Trapmaker 1855.

CHESTER, John. Wednesfield Heath. Year 1884 – 1892
Co-Patentee with Arthur Lane, Patent Number 13,378, dated 9th October 1884, which was for improved springs in a mole trap.
Steel trap maker, New Cross, 1892.

COLLINS, Joseph. Wednesfield. Year 1880 – 1940
In a 1930 advertisement Collins claim that they have been 'established over a century' e.g. *circa* 1830.
Vermin trap maker, Hickman Street, 1880.
Vermin trap maker & Rose and Crown, Hickman Street, 1884.
Vermin trap maker, Graisley Lane 1888.
Steel trap maker, Graisley Lane, 1892, 1896, 1904, 1916, 1921.
Steel Trap Makers 72 Graisley Lane, 1924.
Steel Trap Makers Vulcan Works, 1928.
Steel Trap Makers Vulcan Works, Graisley Lane. 'Phone No Wolverhampton 2079 in 1931.
Steel Trap Makers Vulcan Works, Telegram Address 'Collins' Wednesfield. Telephone Number Wolverhampton 2079 in 1932.

COLLINS, Joseph & Sons. Steel Trap Makers, Vulcan Works, T. A. 'Collins' Wednesfield.

Telephone Number Fallings Park 31279 in 1936, 1940.

Trade/identification marks:

J.C (1885)
BUNYIP (1907)
BAIL-UP (1913)
MULGA (1913)
PLATYPUS (1913)
EMPIRE (1913)
BUZZARD (1914)
KIWIRE (1922)
Collins' Tested
Collins' No. 0
Collins' No. 00
Collins' No. 000

Miscellaneous information: Between 1913 and 1922, Sarah Collins was trading as Joseph Collins & Sons, 72 Graisley Lane, Wednesfield. Arthur Collins, Albert Collins and Bert Amos Collins applied for a patent, dated 19th November 1927, Number 31,097/27, which when accepted on 7th February 1929 became Patent No. 305,305. This patent was for 'fixing wire spring to trap base'. The three Collins were at that date 'trading together in copartnership as Joseph Collins and Sons'. Patent No 305,305 is to be found on a four inch jaw wire spring gin trap. This trap has a small section of a normal stock, coming from the standard, the end of which slopes upwards slightly. This upward slope allows the ends of the wire spring to pass through a hole in it and thus the wire spring forms the rest of the stock. The ends of the wire spring are then secured by the projections which are part of the standard. The brass tongue on this trap is stamped with Collins No 000. Collins also produced an unusual tongueless four inch jaw bow spring gin trap which has stamped on its galvanised plate the wording, Regd Setter No 388278 J. Collins. Eventually the business became part of W.&G. Sidebotham's.

CORBETT, James. Wednesfield Heath. Year 1833 – 1876

Rat trap maker and cabinet locksmith, 1833.

Trap maker for rats, vermin etc., 1834.

Trap maker (steel) 1835, 1841, 1842, 1845.

Iron dealer & steel trap maker 1849.

Iron & file dealer, steel trap & cabinet lock maker 1850.

Steel trap maker 1851, 1854, 1855, 1860, 1861, 1864.

Cabinet lock, steel trap & bracket maker 1865.

Steel trap maker 1872, 1876.

Miscellaneous information: In the 1841 Census record, Henry Rabold aged about 16, is listed as James Corbet's apprentice.

ECCLESTON, Joseph. Wednesfield Heath. Year 1827 – 1872

Rat trap maker 1827, 1833.

Trap maker for rats, vermin etc. 1834.

Trap maker, steel 1835.

ECCLESTONE (spelt with an E) Rat trap maker 1838, 1839.

Steel trap maker. 1841, 1842, 18345, 1849, 1850, 1851, 1854, 1855, 1860, 1864, 1872.

Miscellaneous information: In the 1841 Census record he is listed, with his sons William and Isaiah, whom are both aged about 20, as steel trap makers.

ECCLESTON, Joseph (Junior). Wednesfield Heath. Year 1876

Steel trap maker 1876.

ECCLESTON, William. Wednesfield Heath. Year 1865 – 1884

Steel trapmaker, Church Street 1865, Steel trapmaker 1880, 1884.

EVANS, James. Year 1833 – 1860

Steel trap maker 1860, 1854, 1850, 1849, 1845, 1842, 1841.

Rat trap maker 1839

Rat trap maker, Wood End 1838

Trap maker steel 1835

Trap maker rats, vermin etc. 1834

Rat trap maker 1833.

FORD, William. Wednesfield. Year 1854 – 1876
Steel trap maker, Chapel Street, 1876
Steel trap maker 1872
Steel vermin trap manufacturer, Chapel Street, 1865
Steel trap maker 1864, 1861
Beer retailer & steel trap maker 1860
Trap maker 1855
Trap maker, steel 1854.

GEE, Thomas. Wednesfield. Year 1841 – 1849
Rat trap maker, 1849.
In the 1841 Census record he was listed as an Apprentice to James Hope of Graisley Lane, and aged about 15.

GLOVER, Samuel (Senior). Wednesfield. Year 1888
Steel trap maker, North Road, 1888.

GLOVER, Henry. Wednesfield. Year 1904
Steel trap maker, North Street, 1904

GLOVER, John. Wednesfield. Year 1880 – 1884
Steel trap maker, North Road, 1880, 1884

W. R. & F. GLOVER
North Street, WEDNESFIELD
Manufacturers of all kinds of
STEEL GAME AND VERMIN TRAPS, ETC.,
FOR HOME AND EXPORT

GLOVER, William. Wednesfield. Year 1896 – 1961
Steel trap maker, North Street, 1896
Glover, Wm., Rowland & Frank. Steel Trap Makers, 18 North Street, 1928
Steel Trap Makers, Northern Works, North Street, 1931
Steel Trap Makers, 18 North Street, 1932, 1936
Steel Trap Makers, 18 North Street. Phone number Fallings Park 31121 in 1940.
Glover, W. R. & F. North Street, Tel. No. Fallings Park 31121 in 1948, 1951, 1955, 1957, 1959, 1961.
Miscellaneous information: Glover's 4 inch jawed wire spring gin trap,

known as the 'Clipfastner' has the Registered Design Number 693967. Some Glover traps have an embossed letter G on the plate. The brass tongue is stamped: Glovers No 6R

GOUGH, George. Wednesfield. Year 1841 – 1884
In the 1841 Census, George Gough was listed as an apprentice to Thomas Tomkys, Senior, and was aged about 20 years. He is next listed in the trade directories as a steel trap maker of New Street in 1876, 1880 and 1884.

GREEN, Henry William. Wednesfield Heath. Year 1888
Steel trap maker, New Cross 1888.

GREEN, Amos. Wednesfield. Year 1876
Steel trap maker, Graisley Lane 1876.

GREEN, James. Wednesfield. Year 1851 – 1892
Trap maker 1851
Trap maker, Wood End 1855
Steel trap maker 1861
Vermin trap maker, Wood End 1865
Steel trap maker, Wood End 1876, 1880, 1884, 1888, 1892.

GREEN, James Mrs. Wednesfield. Year 1896
Steel trap maker, Wood End 1896.

GREEN, Amos James. Wednesfield Heath. Year 1876 – 1884
Steel trap maker, New Cross 1876, 1880, 1884.

GRIFFITHS, Enoch & Co. Wednesfield. Year 1880 – 1904
Steel traps manufacturers, Victoria Works, Graisley Works, Wednesfield 1904
Steel Trap Makers, Paul Street (Wednes. Heath) 1896
GRIFFITHS, E & Co. St. Ann's Street, Willenhall listed as iron founders 1880.
E GRIFFITHS & Co, became part of W.&G. Sidebotham, and was the first trap maker to be taken over by Sidebotham's.

**GRIFFITHS, James. Wednesfield.
Year 1833 – 1841**
Rat trap maker 1833
Vermin trap maker 1841.

RABBIT & ANIMAL TRAPS
Registered Trade Marks:
"S. GRIFFITHS IXL."
ESTABLISHED 1840.
S. GRIFFITHS & SONS, CLYDE WORKS, WEDNESFIELD.

**GRIFFITHS, Samuel. Wednesfield.
Year 1840 – 1940.**
An advert states Established 1840.
Trap maker, steel 1841, 1842, 1845, 1849, 1850, 1851, 1854
Manufacturer of all kinds of steel vermin traps 1855
Trap maker 1860, 1861, 1864
Manufacturer of steel traps 1865
Beer retailer & steel trap maker 1872.
GRIFFITHS, S & Sons. Steel Trap Makers 1876
Manufacturers of steel traps, iron washers & bicycles 1880
Steel trap manufacturers 1884
Clyde Works, Steel trap, bicycle & safe manufacturer 1888, 1892.
Fire & burglar proof safe manufacturers; also makers of fireproof rooms, doors & frames, 1896.
Clyde Works, Wednesfield. Steel Trap Makers 1904
Fire & burglar proof safe manufacturers 1921
Fire & burglar proof safe manufacturers, Woden Road 1924
Steel Trap Makers, Bloxwich Road Wednesfield 1928, 1932, 1936.
Steel Trap Makers, 115 Lichfield Road, Wednesfield 1940.
Miscellaneous Information:
In 1841, Benjamin Wells, aged 15 approximately, was a trap maker's apprentice to Samuel Griffiths who was aged about 25.
In the Trade Marks Journal, application dated 7th April 1876, it was stated that fourteen years before the date of application I.X.L. had been used. The Name, Address and Calling of Applicant was stated as being Enoch Griffiths of and on behalf of the firm of Samuel Griffiths and Sons, Victoria Works, Wednesfield Heath, Manufacturers of Steel Traps and Iron Washers.
William Woodward, in 1887, traded as S. Griffiths & Sons, Clyde Works.
In July 1894 John Marshall was stated to be trading as S. Griffiths & Sons, Clyde Works, and seems to have been operating it as a separate business from his own.
In the 1920s trap making and safe making were listed under separate headings and addresses and seem to have become separate businesses. It is also thought that around the 1930s, the Samuel Griffiths trap making side of the business merged with John Marshall's of Lichfield Road.
Trade mark/Identification mark:

S. GRIFFITHS
XXX IXL (1865)
BONUM (1887)
IXL SPECIAL
IXL WONDER
IXL EMPRESS
IXL GEM
IXL ***
IXL **
IXL*
IXL (1862)

Patents:
On 26th March 1881, Thomas Douglas, a Gamekeeper, of Wire Bridge in the County of Peebles, Scotland provisionally patented his version of a rabbit trap. This was registered as Patent No 1349. Two versions of this trap are known.
(1) The first version as shown in the patent drawings has the small arched metal hoop attached to the straight cross bar, which goes under the trap plate. The ends of this cross bar turn upwards and over and enclose the ends of the metal hoop. At the front of the 'eye' of the spring is a transverse bar which when released rides upwards against the metal hoop.

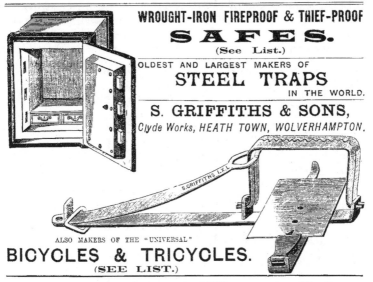

An 1888 advert from *The Ironmonger*

(2) In the second version, the straight cross bar has now both ends curved towards the spring. The metal hoop is now fixed through these ends. The transverse bar is now made slightly wider and also has a metal rod fixed alongside it, leaving a gap for the metal hoop to pass through when the spring is released. The second version is known to be stamped just behind the 'eye' of the spring with Douglas's Patent No 1349 1881, and on the stock just behind the brass tongue, S. Griffith's & Sons Makers.

Another trap known to be made by Griffiths was the Gem, which was patented on 3rd May 1911, being No 10,694. This trap with the unusual spring arrangement was patented by Arthur Anthony of 70 Villiers Street, Wolverhampton and Albert Nightingale of Park House, Park Road, Rug-

An 1882 advert from *The Ironmonger*

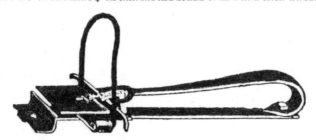

by. Both men being described as Engineers. The trap plate has the words, S. Griffiths IXL GEM.

A trap which might be a second version or a competitor's 'improved version' consists of the normal bow spring, having the compression spring, between it and the stock. This type of trap was also made in the extended stock version. A wire spring trap with the compression spring inserted is also known. All versions have no identification marks.

S.Griffiths also made a copy of Henry Lane's Heron trap.

GRUNDY, Harold. Wednesfield. Year 1835 – 1854

In 1835 and 1841 he is listed as a steel trap maker. In the 1841 Census he was living at Wood End, and was aged about 35 years.

Steel trap maker, 1842, 1845, 1850
Trap maker, Wood Hayes, 1851
Trap maker, steel, 1854.

GRUNDY, Henry. Wednesfield. Year 1833 – 1839

Rat trap maker, First Wood Hayes, 1833
Trap maker, rats, vermin etc. 1834
Rat trap maker, Wood End, 1838
Rat trap maker, 1839.

GRUNDY, Samuel. Wednesfield. Year 1833 – 1854

Rat trap maker, First Wood Hayes, 1833
Trap maker for rats, vermin etc., 1834
Trap maker, steel, 1835
Rat trap maker, Wood End, 1838
Steel trap maker, 1841, 1842, 1845, 1850, 1854.

HADEN, John. Wednesfield. Year 1888 – 1904

Trap manufacturer, Hickman Street, 1888
Steel trap maker, Hickman Street, 1892
Steel trap maker, New Cross (Wednesfield Heath) 1896

Steel trap maker, New Cross, 1904
Vermin trap maker, Cross Street, 1904.
Note two separate directory entries for 1904.

HAMES, Matthew. Wednesfield. Year 1841 – 1851

In the 1841 Census, Matthew Hames had two apprentices working with him at Church Street. They were Richard Ward, aged about 14 and John Chesterton who was aged about 11. He is listed in the trade directories as a steel trap maker in 1841, 1842, 1845, 1850, 1851.

HAMES, Ann Mrs. Wednesfield. Year 1854 – 1861

Steel trap maker, 1854, 1855, 1861.

HAMES, Henry. Wednesfield. Year 1818 – 1835

Trap maker, steel, 1835
Trap maker for rat, vermin etc., 1834

*HAINES, Henry.

Rat and mantrap maker, 1833

*HAINES, Henry.

Rat trap maker and huckster, 1833.

HAMES, Henry.

Rat, beaver, fox & man and humane mantrap maker, 1827.
manufacturer of rat, fox, beaver, and mantraps, 1818.
* Probably a misspelling for Hames. Two separate entries for 1833.
(Huckster: a retailer of small wares)

HAMES, Richard. Wednesfield. Year 1833 – 1849

Steel trap maker, 1849, 1842, 1841
Rat trap maker (and man), 1839, 1838
Trap maker, steel, 1835
Trap maker for rats, vermin etc. 1834

*HAINES, Richard.

Rat trap maker, 1833.
* Probably a misspelling for Hames.

HAMES, Mary. Wednesfield. Year 1838

Rat trap maker (and man), 1838.

HARRIS, Richard. Wednesfield. Year 1841– 1842
Trap maker, steel, High Street 1841,1842

HARRISON, Thomas. Wednesfield. Year 1834
Trap maker for rats, vermin etc. 1834.

HOPE, Michael. Wednesfield. Year 1827
Rat trap maker and huckster, 1827 (Huckster: a retailer of small wares)

HOPE, Edward. Wednesfield. Year 1827 – 1842
Hope, Edward & Sons. Rat Trap Makers, 1827
Rat trap maker, 1833
Trap maker for rats, vermin etc. 1834
Trap maker, steel 1835
Rat trap maker 1838, 1839
Trap maker, steel, 1841 (Church Street) & 1842.

HOPE, Sarah. Wednesfield. Year 1838 – 1842
Rat trap maker, 1838, 1839
Trap maker, steel, 1841, 1842.

HOPE, James. Wednesfield. Year 1833 – 1855
Rat trap maker, 1833
Trap maker for rats, vermin etc. 1834
Trap maker, steel, 1835
Rat trap maker, 1838, 1839.
In the 1841 Census records, James Hope is listed at Graisley Lane and is aged about 41 years. He also has an apprentice called Thomas Gee who was aged about 15.
Trap maker, steel, 1845, 1849, 1851, 1855.

HOPE, Joseph. Wednesfield. Year 1827 – 1835
Rat trap maker, 1827, 1833
Trap maker for rats, vermin etc. 1834
Trap maker, steel. 1835.

HOPE, John. Wednesfield. Year 1818 – 1827
Rat trap maker, 1818 & 1827.

JEFFERSON, Edward. Wednesfield. Year 1834
Trap maker for rats, vermin etc. 1834.

JEFFRIES, Edmund. Wednesfield. Year 1833
Rat trap maker, 1833.

KEMPSON, Luke. Wednesfield. Year 1841 – 1849
In the 1841 Census, at Graisley Lane, both Luke, aged 20 and William Kempson (brother?) aged 15 years approximately are both listed as trap makers. They are in the household of Thomas and Sarah Kempson.
Trap maker, steel, 1841, 1842, 1845, 1849.

KEMPSON, William. Wednesfield. Year 1841
Noted in the 1841 Census records with Luke Kempson (see above).

LANE, Henry. Wednesfield. Year 1841 – 1954
In the 1841 Census, James Baggott of Church Street, who was aged about 60, had an apprentice trap maker, Henry Lane who was about 18 years old. According to various adverts, H. Lane was established in 1844.
Trap maker, 1851
Manufacturer of all kinds of steel vermin traps, 1855
Steel trap maker, 1860, 1861, 1864
Manufacturer of game & vermin traps, Graseley Lane, 1865
Steel Trapmaker, 1872.
Advert in the *Iron* magazine states Manufacturer of every description of

TRAP MAKERS AT WEDNESFIELD C. 1912 OUTSIDE THE WORKS OF
HENRY LANE AT HICKMAN STREET, WEDNESFIELD, ENGLAND
(L TO R) BILL BRADLEY OF HICKMAN STREET; THOMAS WHITE
OF GRAISLEY LANE, DESCENDANT OF TRAP MAKING FAMILY OF
1818; FRANK MASON OF ROOKERY STREET; ALBERT JONES OF
THE RICKYARD. DIED IN FLANDERS 1915
(REPRODUCED FROM THE ORIGINAL HELD BY JOHN SMALLSHIRE)

TRADEMARKS OF HENRY LANE

steel trap, Eagle Works, 1874.

Steel trap maker, Graisley Lane, All kinds of steel traps, home & export. 1876 & 1880.

Steel trap maker, Graisley Lane. 1884, 1888, 1892.

Steel trap maker, Hickman Street, 1896. A second listing states (Estab. 1848) Manufacturer of every description of steel vermin traps. 1896, 1904, 1916, 1921.

(Estab. 1844) Manufacturer of every description of steel vermin traps. Eagle Works. 1924

Note: The change of establishment date from 1848 to 1844. This change was probably due to deciding to include the years since Henry Lane had learned his trade, and completed his apprenticeship.

In 1928 and 1932, H. Lane is listed as Eagle Works, Wednesfield, Wolverhampton, phone number 590.

In the directory listings of 1936, 1940, 1948, 1951, the address is the same but the telephone number is changed to Fallings Park 31190.

In the year 1954 the plant and premises were sold. Henry Lane's business had become a private limited liability company on 27th August 1920, but was finally dissolved on 3rd May 1974. The company's number being 169916.

Awards/Medals gained at Trade Exhibitions:

Hon. mention London 1862

First prize medals awarded at Belgium 1863. Melbourne 1888. Brussels 1897. Ghent 1913. New Zealand & South Seas Exhibition (Dunedin, N.Z.) 1926. The 1863 and 1888 trade medals were kindly given to the author by Ann, daughter of H.C. Lane, to add to my own trap collection. The (Dunedin N.Z.) 1926 medal remains with the Lane family, but the whereabouts of the 1897 and 1913 Belgian medals remains unknown.

Patents and improvements:

1858 7th May. Introduction of brass catches and hinges.

1884 Mole trap (improved flat springs version) Patent No 13,378. 9th October 1884. Arthur Lane and John Chester of New Cross, Heath Town, both trap makers, were the co-patentees.

1898 The 'Simplex' mole trap. Patent application dated 22nd November 1898 and accepted 14th January 1899. Henry Lane patentee. Patent No 24,581.

1902 Wire spring rabbit trap registered.

1907 Detachable spring. Patent application dated 30th January 1907 and accepted on 8th August 1907. Patent No. 2388. Henry Lane patentee.

1907 Improved method of attaching/detaching the cross piece to the base plate. Patent application dated 25th October 1907 and accepted on 27th August 1908. Patent No. 23,560. Henry Lane patentee.

1912 Wire spring rabbit trap. Patent application dated 16th July 1912 and accepted on 21st November 1912. Patent No 16,567. Henry Lane patentee.

1918 Wire spring rabbit trap. Patent application dated 9th October 1918. No 16,419/18, and accepted 16th January 1919 becoming Patent No 122,158. Henry Lane patentee.

1919 Wire spring rabbit trap. Patent application dated 7th November 1919. No 27,513/19. Accepted on 17th June 1920 becoming Patent No 144,553. Henry Lane patentee.

1921 Locked cross piece registered.

1924 Wire spring rabbit trap. Patent application dated 12th March 1924. No 6339/24, and accepted on 15th January 1925 becoming Patent No 227,310. Henry Chamberlain Lane patentee.

1926 Method of fixing a swivelling wire spring onto traps. Patent application dated 11th November 1926. No 28,417/26. Patent accepted on 9th June 1927 becoming Patent No.

HIGHEST AWARDS AT THE
FOLLOWING EXHIBITIONS

LONDON 1862
BELGIUM 1863
MELBOURNE 1888
BRUSSELS 1897
GHENT 1913
NEW ZEALAND &
SOUTH SEAS 1925/6

ESTABLISHED 1844.

HENRY LANE LIMITED.,

STEEL TRAP MANUFACTURERS.

EAGLE WORKS,
WEDNESFIELD,
WOLVERHAMPTON.

TELEPHONE:-
590 WOLVERHAMPTO

TELEGRAMS:-
'LANE L?. WEDNESFIEL

CODE:-
A. B. C. 5?? EDITION.

STATIONS:
L.M.S. WOLVERHAMPTO
" WEDNESFIEL
G.W.R. WOLVERHAMPTO

YOUR REF

OUR REF

1929 LETTERHEAD

272,098. Henry Chamberlain Lane patentee.

1926 Improved large trap plate. Patent application dated 21st August 1926, No 20,646/26 and accepted on 27th October 1927 becoming Patent No 279,200. Henry Lane patentee.

1927 Fixing of 'V' shaped springs. Patent application dated 5th September 1927 No. 23,222/27. Patent accepted on 19th April 1928 becoming Patent No 288,894. Henry Chamberlain Lane patentee.

1930 Swivel attachment. Patent application dated 19th May 1930. No 15,271/30, and accepted on 19th August 1931 becoming Patent No 355,262. Henry Chamberlain Lane patentee.

The Solicitors for the applicant, H.C. Lane, regarding Patent Numbers 272,098 (1926) No 279,200 (1926) No 288,894 (1927) were Watson & Everitt of 32 Prince of Wales Road, Norwich.

Overseas patents consist of:

Australia: No. 9546/13 (1913), No 9698/18 (1918), and Patent Application Serial No 14,251 (1920).

U.S.A.: No 1441,985 (1923).

New Zealand: No 52,222 (1924).

Lane's February 1928 catalogue states 'It may be noted that practically all the improvements in the design of the present day vermin traps have been due to the initiative of members of the firm'.

Regarding the quality of spring steel and explaining why Lane's were having to increase prices, a letter dated July 1929 states: 'ALTERATION OF PRICES. As a result of our inability to obtain regularly satisfactory results from our old quality of spring steel, we have been forced to experiment with steels at much higher prices. Tests were completed and a new steel has been incorporated during the past six months with absolutely satisfactory results. In some sizes the new steel costs just twice as much as our previous supplies, and in all cases there are heavy increases in the prices with the result that we have to advise that on August 1st 1929 Retail List prices will be advanced by 15% until further notice. We are taking this opportunity of increasing the margin of profit to wholesale buyers and are therefore reducing the trade discounts by only 10%.

Quotations from August 1st 1929 will be as follows:- RETAIL – Present List prices plus 15% net cash monthly. WHOLESALE – Present List prices less $7\frac{1}{2}$% and, where the gross value of the order exceeds £20 a further 5%. Cash discount of $2\frac{1}{2}$% for settlement during month following invoice.'

Identification/Trade Marks

(*See illustrations P. 102*)

H.Lane (before 1855)

H.Lane Wednesfield

H.Lane maker
H.Lane maker improved (1900)
H.Lane A1 maker (1908?-13)
running rabbit motif (1865)
heart shape with T M L inside (1889)
Chancery two boxers fighting motif (1907)
grip bird motif (1908)
defender single boxer (1920)
LI-LO (1929)
EAGLANE (1936)

'Henry Lane Limited and Messrs Dunlop jointly undertake that the mark shall be used only on goods which have been both manufactured or otherwise dealt with by Henry Lane Limited and offered for sale or otherwise dealt with by Messrs. Dunlop', Dunlop's address being George Dunlop & Son 95/97 Oxford Road, Reading.

The old established family name of Lane goes back in the Wednesfield area to around 1539. However, only two, Richard and Henry, are recorded in the early 1800s as being trap makers. Henry Lane started making traps in approximately 1844, and starting with the firm conviction that a sound business could only be built up by manufacturing goods of the highest quality, he met with such success that, in a few years, his products were known all over the world as the best obtainable. According to John Smallshire in his book *Wednesfield, the Field of Woden*, Lane's 'considerable works at High Street employed six men in 1848'. In the 1860s Henry Lane had become the overseer of the poor, and so by then must have been accepted as of some financial standing, and well respected within the community. When he moved from the High Street is unknown, but in 1865 he was working from premises on Graseley Lane. By the year 1874 his works were definitely known as 'Eagle Works' and he was advertising his products for 'home and export' in 1876.

His death occurred in the following year 1877. The management was then passed on to his eldest son, Arthur, who further increased the business and started to improve the methods of production, whilst still retaining the high standards. He died in 1891. Now the management passed on to Arthur's brother, Henry Lane, younger son of the founder. Between 1892 and 1896 Lane's had yet again moved premises. Again Smallshire's book mentions that 'There were ten men (employed *circa* 1898) when he moved to Hickman Street'. From now on Lane's would remain at these new premises.

With the increased demand for rabbit traps in Australia and New Zealand around this time, the skilled labour force could not produce sufficient traps to satisfy this increasing market by normal means. In 1915 the manufacturers' agent for Lane's traps sold in Australia was F. Walsh of George and Wynyard Streets in Sydney, but two years later another hardware manufacturers' agent, Frederick Carr, also of Sydney, had been appointed Lane's sole Australian agent.

The gradual upgrading of the existing plant and the devising of machinery to replace the need for skilled labour resulted in a totally new plant being installed in 1919. The factory was then 'the most up to date of its kind in the world.' The following year, the business was incorporated as a private limited liability company on 27th August 1920, with a similar company having been formed a month earlier in the same year in Australia. Henry Lane's eldest son, Arthur E Lane, became the manager of this overseas business, whilst his second son, Henry Chamberlain Lane, became a director and eventually a few years later, Works Manager of the Wednesfield company. Their father remained as the Managing Director at Wednesfield until his eventual

Reporting Progress.

"The new mode of fixing the
chain is a great improvement."

*R. Sharpe, Author of Board of Agriculture Booklet
on the Destruction of Vermin.*

HENRY LANE, LIMITED.
EAGLE WORKS,
WEDNESFIELD.
WOLVERHAMPTON.
STAFFS.

DECEMBER, 1930.   PUBLICATION No 811

*Extract from the "Shooting Times," Christmas
Number, 1930, reporting on Lane's No. 178
Trap and Chain.*

"This Trap has been tried out by our Kennel
Editor, who has found it a great success, in fact, he
assures us that he has never had a better trap in
his life."

History Repeats Itself!

FOR nearly ninety years the firm of Henry Lane, Limited, have been known all over the world for the excellence of their animal traps, and perhaps it is not surprising that they should have been the originators of practically every real improvement in traps that tend to lighten the trapper's labour. Among other improvements may be mentioned the following :—

Brass catches and hinges Design	Registered in 1858.
Present Mole Trap	Patented in 1884.
Wire Spring Trap Design	Registered in 1902.
Wire Spring Trap	Patented in 1912.
Wire Spring Trap	Patented in 1919.
Wire Spring Trap	Patented in 1920.
Locked Cross-piece Design	Registered in 1921.
Wire Spring Trap	Patented in 1924.
Improved Large Plate	Patented in 1926.
New Flat Spring Trap	Patented in 1927.

and now, at last, an absolutely satisfactory method of attaching the chain to the trap, for which a patent application numbered 15271 was made on May 19th, 1930.

All trappers know the extreme annoyance of finding a stake with a chain attached while the trap and victim are gone—a broken or bent S-hook, swivel hook, or wire connection being the immediately apparent cause. Of recent years all traps, high and low priced alike, have run the risk of being so lost. Prior to the disappearance of skilled labour in the hand-forged swivel trade it was possible to insure against such losses by the use of "Lane's" Improved Dorset, which was fitted with a sliding loop on the spring to which the chain (with a solid forged swivel) was welded. Malleable cast swivels, with their inevitable loss of freedom in working, did not satisfactorily replace the old forged swivel, and most makers employed an open hook for the swivel as being more regularly reliable. The S-hook connecting link was always liable to break or pull out, and so long as the swivel hook was made stronger than the S-hook, the danger of loss was not increased.

The improved attachment now introduced by Henry Lane, Limited, definitely eliminates any loss of traps on this old score, the whole connection being in every way as strong as the chain. Long use may rust it through, otherwise a file, saw or chisel are necessary to remove the chain from the trap.

Page Two

The small illustrations below comprise sketches to show the main principles on which the new attachment works. The shape of the parts is not strictly adhered to on account of the various types of traps to which they are fitted.

Fig. 1 shows a U-shaped swivel loop in which a double-headed eye-bolt turns freely, a round connecting bar passes through the two arms of the swivel loop, and after assembly to the trap is rivetted or bulged over at each end to prevent withdrawal. Figures 2 and 3 show the swivel loop and swivel eye-bolt in detail, so that the construction can be grasped at a glance from these illustrations.

Fig. 1.   Fig. 2.   Fig. 3.

In the Ordinary Dorset Trap, the swivel loop is somewhat different in shape from that shown above, as it is eventually attached to the trap as shown in the illustration on Page 4 (Fig. 4). In this case a short connecting bar is slipped through the existing chain hole in the stock of the trap.

In Fig. 5 below, the connecting bar is shown passing through the coil of the Wire Spring Trap, while in Fig. 6 the method of attaching to the new Patent Flat Spring Trap is shown. Special attention should be paid to the small prominences on the edges of the spring in this last illustration— they serve to prevent the attachment from sliding along the spring and keep the chain in correct position at the end of the trap. Each of these three illustrations show one link of a chain welded through the swivel eye-bolt.

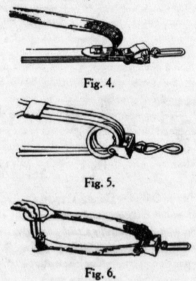

Fig. 4.

Fig. 5.

Fig. 6.

At the time of preparing this brochure for the press these new swivel attachments are standard at no extra cost on all our Best Quality Brass Catch Traps from 3-in. to 4½-in. sizes with the exception of the Improved Dorset Traps. Other lines will be gradually changed to incorporate the new attachment, and many of these lines can even now be so fitted if desired at a very slight extra cost.

It would not be out of place to mention here a few of the lesser known improvements incorporated in "Lane's" traps since January, 1929.

A new design of brass till has been adopted for all the better quality Machine Made lines, giving practically a flat surface to cover. The catch does not rise above the plate as in the old pattern, and where the old pattern required at least ¼-in. to cover the plate satisfactorily on this account, the new traps require no more than $\frac{1}{16}$-in. to cover. The advantage of this in wet weather or heavy soil is apparent.

All the best quality Machine Made traps are now fitted with jaws from which all the sharp edges have been removed. It is impossible for a rabbit to cut its leg off against the edges as in previous years, and the percentage of successful catches is correspondingly increased.

All springs other than those of the Wire Spring and New Patent Flat Spring Traps (of which more later) are made from a steel to our special analysis, rolled cold to prevent surface defects and incipient cracks, and scientifically hardened and tempered. Prior to the use of this new steel, and after the war, it became increasingly difficult to obtain reliable raw material, breakages being by no means uncommon both in and out of the factory. The new steel in many cases costs twice as much as the old, but we have the satisfaction of knowing that we have not had a single complaint over the new steel and can trace only two springs that have broken in or out of the works, out of tens of thousands of springs manufactured during the two years. Of these two springs one had not been tempered and could never have been made into a trap without breakage, the other had cracked in the hardening.

The Wire Spring Trap with its great strength and lightness needs no description as it is already widely known, but the New Patent Flat Spring Trap which embodies the same advantages may not be so well known, as it is a much more recent production, and we therefore give an illustration facing Page 8 of the Best Quality (No. 178 in our catalogue). The main features are the great reduction in weight made possible by the special spring, eliminating the need for a heavy stock as in the case of the Ordinary Dorset Traps. The chain, jaws and complete cross-piece are exactly the same as utilised in our Best Quality Machine Made Dorset Traps No. 160, and as such we guarantee all our No. 178 traps against faulty material or workmanship for all time.

Compared with the Machine Made Best Quality Dorset No. 160, at 53/9 per dozen, the No. 178 shows a distinct advantage, retailing at only 42/- per dozen.

The New Patent Flat Spring Trap is also made in cheaper qualities, our No. 180 and No. 182, details of which and all our other lines can be obtained, as also can all supplies be obtained, from one of the sources mentioned on Page 8.

SOURCES OF SUPPLY.

1. **Ironmongers in your district.**

2. **Large Associations and Stores,** e.g., Harrods, Army and Navy Society, Country Gentlemen's Association.

3. **Game and Dog Food Manufacturers, as below :—**
   James & Co., Hungerford.
   F. C. Lowe & Sons, Sittingbourne.
   Geo. Smith (Norwich) Ltd., Norwich.
   Spillers, Ltd., London.
   Spratt's Patent, Ltd., London.

```
SEE THE NAME "LANE" ON
EVERY TRAP.
```

Keep this Brochure with your Copy of the 2nd Edition of
" Traps and Trapping."

Page Eight

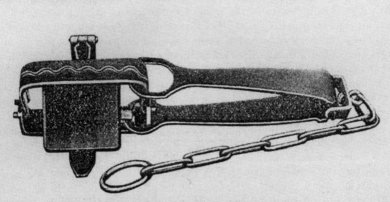

Lane's No. 178 Trap—An Aristocrat of Traps.

INVOICE

Inveraray Ironmongery Stores,
Inveraray,
Argyllshire,
Scotland.

Henry Lane Limited

TELEPHONE & TELEGRAMS:
WOLVERHAMPTON · FALLINGS · PARK · 31150
STATION: WOLVERHAMPTON L.M.S.

ESTABLISHED 1041
EAGLE WORKS · WEDNESFIELD
WOLVERHAMPTON
ENGLAND

ORDER No.	Letter.	DATE 2nd October, 1947.					
QUOTE INVOICE No.	ATM/I205/Y-3093.	DESPATCHED UNDER ADVICE NOTE(S) NO(S). 13873.					
	12 dozen "LI-LO" No. WS172 Traps & Chains S.P.	45/-	27	-	-		
	Less 25%		6	15	-		
			20	5	-		
	Returnable case No. 5	10/-	-	10	-		
						£ 20	15 -

death at the age of 83 on 19th January 1949.

Whilst H.C. Lane was the Works Manager, it is known that the small offices from which the work was directed were single storey and down at the end of the street, about a hundred yards away from the trap works in Hickman Street.

A condensed history of H.C. Lane's involvement with the family firm was kindly supplied by his daughter Ann, which follows in full:

He was born in 1904 and upon leaving school in 1919, he joined the family firm, dividing his time between basic office routine and the equivalent of a works apprenticeship till 1923, when he became Works Manager and converted all major production from skilled hand work to largely unskilled production by presswork and special purpose jig work. All tools and jigs were designed by him and made under his supervision on the premises. His part-time office work covered all such items as production planning, materials purchase, general correspondence, quotations and sales etc., but lacking full understanding of book keeping routine, he delayed filling a vacancy caused by the retirement of a book keeper in 1925, until by discovering and handling the routine work himself, he had fully mastered the procedure. The resultant interest in accounting developed over the years until he could produce full accounts for any period well before the audited accounts could be prepared. In 1927 for the first time he took over sole control of the business during the prolonged absence of his father on an African tour, and this control continued when his father largely retired from active participation in the business after 1928. From 1928 to 1939 he developed a sales plan concentrating on a trap design developed by him from his practical trapping experience of a trapper's needs. The main sales effort was in the home market where the particular design ultimately led the whole market in quality and popularity. This home trade was developed almost exclusively by mail advertising to and via the hardware and ironmongery retailers, with whom the most cordial relations were maintained. Export trade was also opened and developed in the 1930s in New Zealand, Belgium, France and various African markets, and the financing arrangements for each market were separately considered and adjusted to suit individual needs; thereafter, the individual requirements for commercial control and documentation procedures were personally devised and supervised before laying down an office organisation plan for the handling of future business from the particular markets.

While handling war subcontract work, he developed and established a system of photographic record of production processes; the system proved to be of extreme value in cases calling for later repeat production. Research into the technicalities of photography enabled him to reduce the system to almost foolproof levels. His record system interested other firms and thereafter he handled (as a sideline for his firm) the production of similar records for certain firms and he extended his photographic interest to the production of record and instructional motion picture films for his own and several external firms.

His daughter goes on to say that regarding 'press tool and jig work, as (the) designer of the wide variety of press tools and jig fixtures for trap production, he contributed articles describing the tools to *Engineer, Machinery, Machinist,* and *American Machinist,* and also a fifty column series to *Engineer* in 1931. His photographic contributions included 'A technical thesis on the optics of stereoscopic perception (which) secured the award of a fellowship of the Royal Photographic Society and was later published in the scientific section of the Society's official organ, the *Photographic Journal*. He also contributed various articles to *Camera Obscura*, *Amateur Photographer* and the *Photography Magazine*. On the subject of traps and trapping, 'Articles on this art or inexact science have been contributed to the farming and sporting press in this country and on the continent. The same practical knowledge of the subject lay behind the numerous instructional leaflets and pamphlets he had to prepare for his firm's use'.

Henry Chamberlain Lane was the sole family member operating the company when his father died in 1949, and as mentioned earlier, had been for many years previously. In the book *More Tales of the Old Gamekeepers* by Brian Martin, the retired gamekeeper George Cole mentions that he was having trouble with otters in the trout hatchery on the estate where he was working, 'so I had six Lane's double spring, 6in spiked jaw otter traps made. The ordinary gins wouldn't hold the otter. Trapping them was perfectly legal then.' He also recalled 'Old man Lane – he had a gold Albert (a short kind of watch chain, named after Prince Albert) across his chest and a little gold trap attached to it.' This small 'novelty' trap still exists and is now with family members living in New Zealand. However, it is not made of gold but of steel and nickel silver and is a perfect working model. The jaw size of this miniature working model is $1/2$ inch and so therefore one-eighth scale of a 4 inch jaw trap. The story behind its origin is that H.C. Lane occupied himself making the trap during the anxious hours prior to the birth of his son, Henry Robert Arthur Lane, on 29th September 1929.

World War II affected the company in two ways. Firstly rabbit trap production continued, albeit in a reduced capacity, to help with the national war effort for food production and crop protection, and secondly the company was required to produce pressings connected with the war effort. Much of the expertise in press tool design for rabbit traps enabled H.C. Lane to design and produce press tools to produce components which would normally have been regarded as impossible to produce on a power press. After the war, adverts of 1951-53 mention only the manufacture of six trap types due to the shortages of materials caused by the war but state, 'Before the war there were upwards of 150 different traps manufactured by the Lane firm in this country.'

Partly due to changing circumstances, such as the introduction of Myxomatosis in October 1953 and especially because of his wife's development of partial paralysis, H.C. Lane decided to sell the company and retire. From records held at Wolverhampton Archives & Local Studies Department it is clear that by 20th August 1954 H.C. Lane was already in negotiations to sell the trap making business and premises. In a letter dated 23rd August 1954, to Mr J.W.Stirk of Stirk & Co, Solicitors in Wolverhampton, he sent to them 'a plan (rather manhandled at various dates) showing the total premises in the block'. He also says that 'It is difficult to say what proportion of profit is attributable to the photographic section of the business. . . (however) in the year just closed expenses are shown as £34, depreciation £52, and analysis of sales for the period allocates £242 to photography.' He then goes on to say, 'I met the Chairman of the Humane Traps Advisory Committee over lunch last Wednesday, and I think I convinced him that an efficient humane trap will only be secured by expenditure on serious research. I was quite frank regarding my business plans, and he expressed a wish to retain the benefit of my specialist knowledge and development facilities. I indicated that I could not speak for any possible successors in my plant, but that to retain the services of a skilled key man with necessary overhead expenses for development and production of samples under my direction could not be expected at under £1,200 to £1,500 p.a., that my own fees would be additional, and that my experience in the search for a humane trap design for the past twenty five years would not permit me to give any guarantee of success. I have already told him that the Ministry have refused me any assistance beyond 'testing' and report on any samples we care to submit. He agreed with me that this was useless and I gathered that if his hands are tied in a similar fashion he would not be prepared to continue. I mention this because I think that Treasury support is likely to be more readily granted if I, as the consultant expert, have no financial interest in the results of experiments. Doubtless I could make alternative arrangements with some other firm in this district, or I could arrange for development work to be handled under my instructions at the Agricultral Engineering Research Establishment at Wrest Park, Silsoe, but I should obviously be happier if any successors to the plant here would be willing to accept the development contract which may be offered – needless to say I think such successors would be the better placed for a flying start in production of any finally approved designs which might be developed by the Ministry for general manufacture.'

In another letter to Mr J.W. Stirk, dated 30th August 1954, H.C. Lane confirms that his 'original intention was to treat the whole of the premises (owned or rented by the company) [N.B. this refers to his adjoining privately owned building which was rented to the company] as one block and my offer of sale would then include all premises, all manufacturing plant; all manufacturing stock-in-trade; such office equipment and records as would be necessary for the continuance of the manufacturing side of the business. I should exclude all photographic and optical equipment and stocks.' However, he goes on to explain that the situation had changed slightly and that he might retain the 'office block'. This 'office block' stretched from 81 Graisley Lane to 68 Hickman Street and contained all of his photographic darkrooms. In the letter of 30th August just quoted he says that 'I might add that in earlier conversations with you I had named an absolute minimum of £5,000 for plant, premises, stock-in-trade, and essential office equipment and records. I felt, and still feel, that even as a lock-up investment it should fetch £6,000 or more and in the event of the H.T. Committee working on the basis I have suggested to them which would provide up to £750 p.a. for my successor's overheads and a permanent free contract with me for advice on day-to-day trap business for a year or more, my minimum figure would be more in the region of £6,000 though in such a case the bulk could remain on suitable mortgage.' He finishes the letter by saying that the Humane Traps Advisory Committee 'Chairman is fully aware that I do not propose to delay sale negotiations on the offchance of my services being required by the Ministry. Discussions can therefore proceed on sale terms as 'with' and 'without' M. of A. research work.' In a further reply to Stirk & Co, dated 8th September 1954, this time regarding the implications of the Pests Act, H.C.Lane says,

'I suppose it might be possible to construe the present wording of the Bill so as to make it illegal to handle export trade (since it is proposed to make it an offence to be in possession of traps for sale which are not of an approved design) we were assured by the Ministry of Agriculture that the Bill would not affect export trade.' All these negotiations by the solicitors Stirk & Co of Wolverhampton on behalf of Cyril T. Squire of Messrs Thomas Squire & Co Ltd of Wednesfield seem to have been abandoned eventually.

Later, on 13th July 1955, a new company was registered as Lane's Li-Lo, Ltd. This private company was stated as having capital of £3,000. To acquire the trap manufacturing part of the business now carried on by Henry Lane Ltd., at Eagle Works, Wednesfield, and to carry on the business of manufacturers of and dealers in animal traps, etc. Permanent directors: Cyril F.J. Slater, 86 Sandringham Road, Penn, Wolverhampton; Joseph Ward, Broadlands, Nurton Hill Road, Pattingham, directors of Universal Engineering Co (Willenhall) Ltd; William G.Bassett, Harmere, Fibbersley, Willenhall. Secretary: Cyril F.J. Slater. Solicitors: J.H.Baxter and Co., Willenhall. Registered Office; Eagle Works, Hickman Street, Wednesfield.

Due to the activities and pressure from various anti trap organisations, H.C. Lane was co-opted by the Ministry of Agriculture to advise on the development of designs for humane rabbit traps. This resulted in major differences of opinion between H.C. Lane and the Ministry of Agriculture's 'humane trap' committee. Therefore he resigned in disgust and walked out. H.C. Lane died on 1st May 1979.

Other Traps

William George Everitt patented his safety tunnel trap on 21st May 1886,

being Patent No 6846. Two versions were thought to be known of this trap. The first has a normal bow spring and is for use against small ground vermin. The first version was still illustrated in a Lane's catalogue of 1928, but it is thought that this type of trap was still being produced up to around the beginning of World War II. Indeed in a Young's of Misterton catalogue dated 1940, Everitt's Safety Vermin Trap is illustrated and priced at 4/6 each post free, or 48/- per dozen, carriage paid.

In the second type the trap has a wire spring. It was always thought that this wire spring was Everitt's own version. However, my research has uncovered a patented copy of Everitt's Trap with a wire spring shown in the patent drawings. The Patent Application Date for this trap is 26th January 1940 (prov pat no. 1566/40) and the patentee was William Stewart Kidd MacLachlan of Keeper's Cottage, Balado, Kinross, Scotland. The complete specification was accepted on 25th March 1941, becoming patent number 534,996, by which time he had moved to Kirkhouse, Traquair, Innerleithen, Peeblesshire. This patent was for 'An improved trap for rabbits and like animals'. Part of his claim stated 'wherein the spring arms are formed at the ends of a coil spring or twin springs, and wherein the jaw or striker is in the form of a bifurcated or u-shaped member. . . wherein a removable locking pin is provided to lock the platform against movement after the jaw has been set in its operative position, and is withdrawn to free the platform after the trap is laid in position.'

A later mark II version of MacLachlan's rabbit trap was made which did away with the long wire spring usually associated with gin traps and instead used a compact coil spring as was being introduced in such traps as the

Sawyer Rabbit Trap. This made for a much neater arrangement as there was no awkward spring projecting out of one side of the trap's tunnel. This obviously made it easier to place in the entrance hole of the burrow. Presumably, Lane's made some traps for MacLachlan with the wire spring, but due to the start of World War II and steel rationing being introduced, this would soon discontinue. It is unknown who made the MacLachlan Mark II Rabbit Trap.

Alfred Clifford's (Patent trap) Hawley, Kent. In the book *The Balance of Nature* (published 1909) it states 'For capturing rats alive various galvanised wire cage traps are in vogue. Alfred Clifford's Patent Trap (Fig 88) has a trap door in the centre of floor and when set is perfectly level and cannot be noticed. The bait only requires to be laid on the floor of the trap. Immediately the animal puts its weight on the hinged floor the doors close. It has a clear run right through, thereby causing no suspicion whatever. Strongly made in galvanised iron and painted, it is very serviceable.' The illustration accompanying the text states that this trap is supplied by H. Lane, Eagle Works, Wednesfield, but it is not known if Lane's actually made this trap. In an unillustrated advert of 1907 this trap was offered in several sizes. Size No 1, 2ft 6in long (kept in stock) for catching rats, stoats, weasels etc. 5/3d. Size No 2, 3ft 6in long for rabbits (to order only) 15/0d. Wood packing 0/6d and 0/9d extra. Orders over two packed free. Special size traps for catching cats 34/0d, for foxes 62/0d (packing extra 4/0d.)

1844 **LANE'S TRAPS** **1953** **(T)** *" Stand the Test of Time "*

Before the War there were upwards of 150 different traps manufactured by the Lane Firm in this Country. During the War it became essential to secure maximum output by concentration on a minimum number of lines and this position has not yet materially improved. Of the lines now being made there are only six which are suited to trapping needs in this Country though it is hoped ultimately to increase the range when more normal conditions are reached.

LANE'S TRAPS MOLE TRAPS
"LANE'S" Mole Traps with deep curved jaws (Self Colour only). No. 330, 37/6 per doz.

LANE'S TRAPS SHORT FLAT SPRING TRAPS
For small vermin the "LANE'S ' SHORT 3-IN ' '" Traps, 3-in. Jaws only. **Brass Catch**, No. 346, 44/- per dozen; **Iron Catch**, No. 348, 39/- per dozen.

LANE'S TRAPS WIRE SPRING TRAPS
"LANE'S ' LI-LO ' —— BRAND " 4-in. Jaws No. WS172, 66/- per dozen.

LANE'S TRAPS VEE-FLAT SPRING ——
TRAPS. "LANE'S ' LI-LO ' BRAND " 4-in. Jaws No. NF184, 72/- per dozen. (Delivery delays on the No. NF184 may be greater than on other lines.)

LANE'S TRAPS LARGE VERMIN TRAPS
Occasional supplies of 8-in. Jaw traps with powerful double springs are available; No. 282, 26/- each. each, *post free.*

CARRIAGE AND PACKAGE TERMS

Where prices are quoted above " per dozen ", carriage to nearest station and packages are included on 6 dozen lots Scotland; 1 dozen lots England and Wales. For Scottish orders under 4 dozen but not under 1 dozen, add 5%. Orders of under 1 dozen to all destinations in Great Britain (except where quoted post free for single traps) are charged at the rate per dozen plus 10% to cover carriage and packing.

THIS ADVERT, *FROM HOW TO TRAP AND SNARE* 1908 EDITION, STATES THAT LANE'S WERE ALSO ONE OF THE MAKERS OF THE SARA TRAP. HOWEVER, THIS HUMANE TRAP WAS OBVIOUSLY NOT A SUCCESS AS IS SHOWN IN AN OPEN LETTER TO *THE SHOOTING TIMES & BRITISH SPORTSMAN* MAGAZINE OF 30TH APRIL 1949. IN IT HENRY C. LANE WRITES REGARDING HUMANE TRAPS AND SPRINGS: 'SIR, MR.MOSS, OF THE RSPCA TENDS TO CONFUSE THE ISSUES. SALES OF SO-CALLED HUMANE TRAPS ARE NO PROOF OF EFFICACY. THE USELESS 'SARA PATENT' SOLD IN THOUSANDS AT THE BEGINNING OF THIS CENTURY. SOME LANDOWNERS FORBID THEIR GAMEKEEPERS TO USE JAW TRAPS, AND THEN ALMOST ANYTHING IS BETTER THAN NOTHING. IF BY 'V' SPRING, MR MOSS MEANS THE USUAL FLAT SPRING HE MUST REFER TO WHAT WE CALL 'JUNK'. OUR AVERAGE FLAT SPRING LIFE IS CERTAINLY NOT LESS THAN TEN YEARS, WITH NUMEROUS CASES UP TO SIXTY YEARS. OUR CHEAPEST WIRE-SPRING RABBIT TRAP SPRINGS AVERAGE AT LEAST SIX YEARS' LIFE. ON THE OTHER HAND, THE CLOSE MULTI-COIL SPRING OF THE SAWYER TYPE IS MECHANICALLY INCAPABLE OF LASTING AS LONG AS THE OPEN-COIL UNDER NORMAL TRAPPING CONDITIONS. THE JAW TRAP CANNOT BE CLASSIFIED WITH THUMBSCREWS AND OTHER INSTRUMENTS OF UNNECESSARY TORTURE. WE ADMIT ITS USE ENTAILS SUFFERING, AS DOES A RING IN A BULL'S NOSE, OR AS DID A SURGEON'S KNIFE BEFORE THE INVENTION OF ANAESTHETICS – UNTIL A FULLY EFFICIENT SUBSTITUTE IS FOUND ITS CONTINUED USE IS NECESSARY, AND THE ONLY PROOF OF EFFICIENCY THAT COUNTS IS THAT OF SINGLE-HANDED TRAPPING RECORDS DURING A SEASON.'

HIGHEST AWARD
BRUSSELS, 1897.

STEEL TRAPS

HENRY LANE,

WEDNESFIELD,

STAFFS.

HIGHEST AWARD
MELBOURNE, 1888-9.

HON. MENTION
LONDON, 1862.

HIGHEST AWARD
BELGIUM, 1863.

ON THIS AND SUCCEEDING PAGES ARE EXTRACTS FROM THE
CATALOGUE (C. 1908 TO 1913) OF HENRY LANE, WEDNESFIELD

PRICE LIST.

Prices do not include Packages or Railway Carriage.

MOUSE OR SMALL BIRD TRAP.

No. 1.

With flat springs ... **4/6** per doz. ... **48/-** per gross subject.

With bow springs ... **6/-** „ „ ... **54/-** „ „ „

$2\frac{1}{4}$ inch jaws, unless otherwise ordered.

COMMON RAT TRAP.

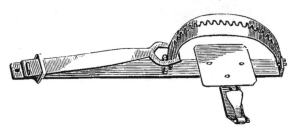

No. 2.

No. 1	2	3	4	5	6	
10/-	**11/-**	**12/-**	**13/-**	**14/-**	**16/-**	subject.

Supplied either with round or square jaws.

With bow springs, **2/-** per doz. extra.

RUN TRAP.

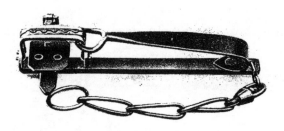

No. 3.

			2½	3 inch jaws.
Best	...	...	**12/-**	**16/-** per doz. subject.
Common	...	...	**10/-**	**12/-** " " "

An exceedingly handy trap for use in the runs of small Vermin.

SMALL DORSET VERMIN TRAP.

No. 4.

A most useful trap, though designed for the capture of Stoats, Weasels, &c., it is largely in demand for Rabbit catching. It is especially valuable in hunting districts, the smallness of the jaw insuring Foxes against serious injury should they spring the trap.

3 inch jaws, and fitted with brass catches, **30/-** per doz. subject.

Each trap is branded **H. LANE, MAKER.** on spring and catch.

SAFETY VERMIN TRAP

(EVERITT'S PATENT).

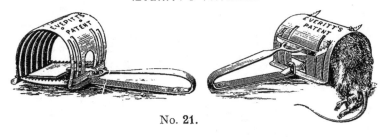

No. 21.

CLAIMS THE FOLLOWING ADVANTAGES:

Superior to all others for humanity and safety, as they can be set amongst Ground or Winged Game, Poultry, Dogs, Cats, &c., &c., without fear of their being caught or maimed.

They can be used with or without Bait, do not require fastening down, the victim being instantly killed, and for cheapness, simplicity and efficiency, are incomparable.

DIRECTIONS FOR USE.

For Rats, set the Traps where their runs enter buildings or enclosures. Securely block all superfluous holes, setting only against those most frequented. Cover the table with such material as sawdust or chaff, freely scattering it round, and when desirable, the entire Trap may be concealed, without fear of blocking; another method is to make tunnels of brick, tile, or tin, feeding inside with bruised Oats, Meal, &c., until freely used by the Vermin, when traps should be set to intercept.

For Stoats and Weasels, fix a bait a few inches from the ground, in the centre of an enclosure formed of a palisade or brushwood, leaving apertures for the Traps; thus one lure answers for three or more Traps, which can be left unattended for a considerable period with impunity, as the victim being killed outright, other Vermin are not suspicious of danger.

28/- per dozen, subject.

ORDINARY DORSET RABBIT TRAP.

N.B.—It is important that buyers should see that all Traps bear their proper brands.

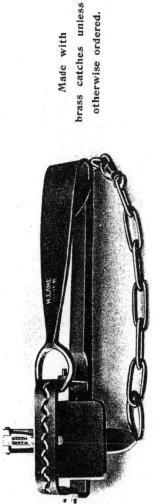

No. 6.

Made with brass catches unless otherwise ordered.

Excellence of material and workmanship are special points of this trap, thus producing an article which only requires a trial to prove its worth. With ordinary care it will last for years, and satisfy the most exacting demands. The second quality is a good reliable trap but in point of durability inferior to the above.

	3	3½	4	4½	5 inch jaws.	Brand on Spring.	Brand on Catch.
					48/- per doz. subject.	H. Lane, Maker.	H. Lane, Maker.
First Quality	30/-	35/-	35/-	40/-	48/-	H. Lane, Maker.	H. Lane, Maker.
Second Quality	26/-	27/-	27/-	33/-	40/- "	H. Lane	2
Third Quality	20/-	20/-	20/-	26/-	34/- "	H. Lane	3
Fourth Quality	17/-	17/-	17/-	21/-	25/- "	H. Lane	4

REGISTERED DORSET RABBIT TRAP.

No. 7.

AS USED ON THE ROYAL ESTATES AT WINDSOR and SANDRINGHAM.

These traps are practically the same as No. **6**, excepting that they are fitted with brass joints in addition to brass catches, and with a chain of extra strength.

3	3½	4	4½	5 inch jaws.
36/-	36/-	36/-	43/-	52/- per doz. subject.

Brand on Spring
H. LANE
A I
MAKER.

Brand on Catch
H. LANE,
MAKER.

IMPROVED DORSET RABBIT TRAP.

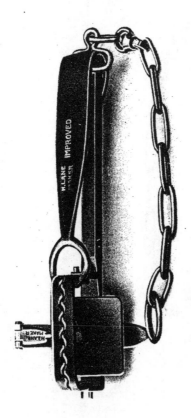

No. 14.

The advantages in this trap are as follows:—The spring comes round the end of the frame and is rivetted below instead of above it; it therefore lies lower when set, and requires a shallower hole in the ground to bury it. The chain cannot be detached from the trap, as a sliding link is substituted for the old-fashioned S hook, which latter frequently breaks and consequently the trap is often lost. The improved traps are fitted with brass catches, the springs are well tested, and the traps warranted to be both easy and certain in action.

3	3½	4	4½	5 inch jaws.
36/-	36/-	36/-	43/-	52/- per doz. subject.

Brand on Spring	Brand on Catch.
H. LANE, IMPROVED.	H. LANE
MAKER.	MAKER.

Mr. R. ROBERTS, of Taiman, Territorio del Chubut, Argentine Republic, writes in September, 1900, that he has found the No. 14 IMPROVED DORSET TRAP, with 5 inch jaws is quite capable of holding animals stronger than any wolf.

ORDINARY

RABBIT AND VERMIN TRAP.

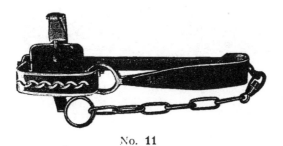

No. **11**

Large sizes from 6 to 8-inch jaws, suitable for jackals, dingoes, foxes, &c., are fitted with flat springs and setters unless otherwise ordered.

	3½	4	4½	5	6	7	8 inch. jaws.
Best quality	24/-	24/-	30/-	36/-	56/-	72/-	96/- doz. subject.
Cheaper quality	12/-	12/-	18/-	24/-	36/-	56/-	72/- ,, ,,

Above traps are fitted with iron catches only.

Special Quotations for Cheaper Qualities.

H. LANE'S WIRE SPRING RABBIT AND VERMIN TRAPS.

No. 6A.

The Trap, as above illustrated, will be found superior to any Wire Spring Trap that has yet been put upon the market.

It combines the maximum of strength with the minimum of weight; a 4-in. Trap complete with chain anly scaling 1½-lbs.

The springs are made of the finest cold drawn steel wire, and being detachable, may be renewed without difficulty.

The method of attaching the chain is much more secure than the old-fashioned **S** hook.

	3½	4	4½	5 in. jaws.	
1st quality, with brass catches	**31/3**	**31/3**	**35/-**	**40/-** per doz., subject.	
2nd quality, with brass catches	**25/-**	**25/-**	**27/6**	**31/3**	" "
1st quality, with iron catches	**18/-**	**18/-**	**21/-**	**25/-**	" "
2nd quality, with iron catches	**12/-**	**12/-**	**15/-**	**20/-**	" "

N.B.—In ordering please state whether Springs are required of full or medium strength, and whether plates are required of ordinary or large size.

OTTER TRAP.

No. 13.

Suitable also for Foxes, Badgers, Jackals, Dingoes, &c.

6-in. jaws	7-in. jaws.
10/-	**14/-** each, subject.

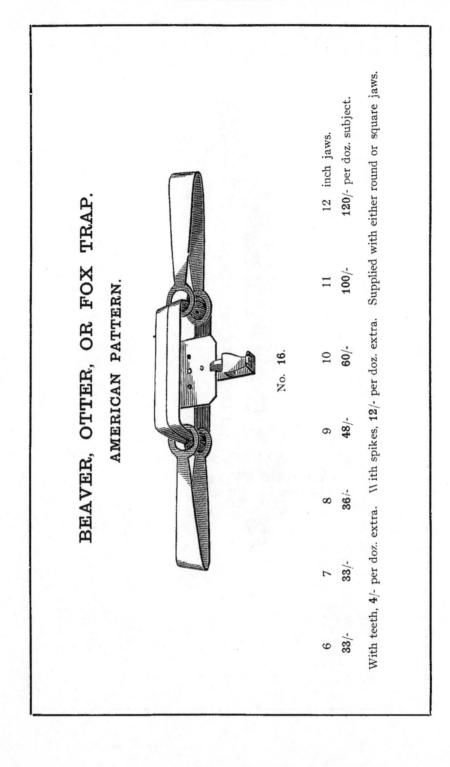

BEAVER, OTTER, OR FOX TRAP.

AMERICAN PATTERN.

No. 16.

6	7	8	9	10	11	12 inch jaws.
33/-	33/-	36/-	48/-	60/-	100/-	120/- per doz. subject.

With teeth, 4/- per doz. extra. With spikes, 12/- per doz. extra. Supplied with either round or square jaws.

OLD PATTERN MOLE TRAP.

PRICE—
Galvanized,
7/- per doz., subject.

PRICE—
Japanned,
5/- per doz., subject.

No. **10.**

MOLE TRAP, 1886 MODEL.

No. **5.**

PRICES—

Galvanized, **7/-** doz.

Japanned, **5/-** doz.

subject.

CLOSED.

OPEN.

MOLE TRAP, 1900 MODEL, or THE "SIMPLEX."

No. **5A.**

PRICES—

Galvanized, **7/-** doz.

Japanned, **5/-** doz.

subject.

OPEN.

CLOSED.

SMALL HAWK OR POLE TRAP.

No. **9.**

Made with or without teeth.

	4	4½	5	5½	6 inch jaws.
Best ...	**36/-**	**36/-**	**42/-**	**48/-**	**56/-** doz., subject.
Second quality	**30/-**	**30/-**	**36/-**	**42/-**	**48/-** " "

LARGE POLE TRAP.

No. **9**A.

Suitable for Eagles and all kinds of large birds of prey.

7	8 inch jaws.
11/-	**13/-** each, subject.

FITTED WITH DOUBLE SPRINGS AND SETTERS.

N.B.—It is perhaps superfluous to mention that the use of above Traps is now prohibited in the British Isles, but they are still largely used abroad, and for this reason are advertised in list.

KINGFISHER TRAP.

No. 20.

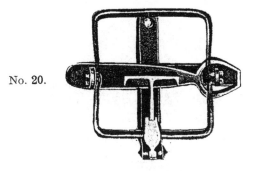

This trap was first made to special order, and is now largely used at Fish Hatcheries and by Fish Preservation Societies.

In setting, screw the trap to a stump in the water where the birds resort, place a piece of wood on the fork for them to alight on, or bait with a small fish. **21/-** per dozen, subject.

HERON OR HAWK TRAP.

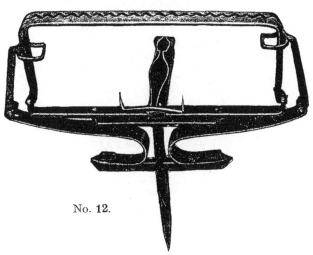

No. 12.

This trap is best known for catching herons. Bait with a fish, set in a suitable place, and a catch is insured. To capture hawks, place a short stick on the fork for them to alight on, or bait with a small bird on each spike. To set the trap get two wedge-shaped pieces of wood, press the spring down, and push the thin end of wedges between the top of the spring and bottom of the frame, lower the spring till the jaw opens wide enough to set the trap; then remove the two wedges from between the frame and springs.

12-inch jaws, **22/-** each, subject.

H. LANE'S
JAY OR MAGPIE TRAP.

No. 23.

The above trap is constructed so as to be used with an egg as a bait, which being placed on the ring as shown keeps the trap set. The moment the egg is removed the trap is sprung.

This trap is especially useful for the capture of Jays, Magpies, and other egg stealing vermin.

PRICE ... **60**/- per dozen subject.

ENGLISH PATTERN DOG TRAP.

No. 8.

Similar in pattern to the No. **6** Trap, but with spikes in jaws.

6	7	8 inch.
12/-	**14**/-	**16** ·- each, subject.

DOG OR WOLF TRAP,
IMPROVED AMERICAN PATTERN.

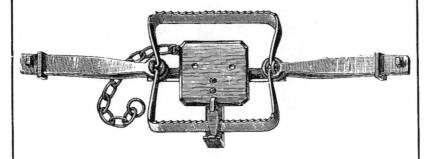

No. **16**A.

6	7	[8	9	10	11	12 inch.
42/-	**42**/-	**50**/-	**64**/-	**110**/-	**125**/-	**150**/- per doz., subject.

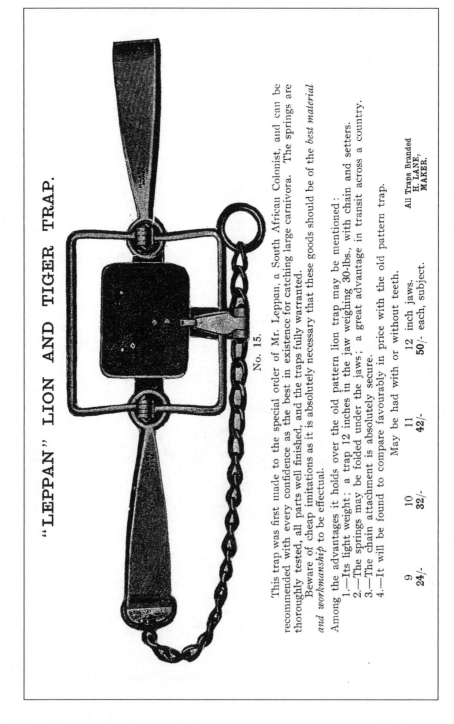

"LEPPAN" LION AND TIGER TRAP.

No. 15.

This trap was first made to the special order of Mr. Leppan, a South African Colonist, and can be recommended with every confidence as the best in existence for catching large carnivora. The springs are thoroughly tested, all parts well finished, and the traps fully warranted.

Beware of cheap imitations as it is absolutely necessary that these goods should be of the *best material and workmanship* to be effectual.

Among the advantages it holds over the old pattern lion trap may be mentioned :

1.—Its light weight; a trap 12 inches in the jaw weighing 30-lbs., with chain and setters.
2.—The springs may be folded under the jaws; a great advantage in transit across a country.
3.—The chain attachment is absolutely secure.
4.—It will be found to compare favourably in price with the old pattern trap.

May be had with or without teeth.

9	10	11	12 inch jaws.
24/-	32/-	42/-	50/- each, subject.

All Traps Branded
H. LANE,
MAKER.

LION, TIGER, OR BEAR TRAP.

OLD PATTERN.

No. 15A.

Weight 30	40	50	60	80	100	120 lbs. each.
9	10	11	12	14	16	18 inch jaws.

1/- per lb. subject.

H. Lane's Jay or Magpie Traps.

This Trap is made so as to be used with an egg bait, which being placed on the ring as shown, keeps the trap set. The moment the egg is removed the trap is sprung. Specially suitable for catching Jays, Magpies, and other egg-stealing vermin.

Price **45/-** per dozen.

(Sample Trap, **4/-** *postage paid.*)

GILBERTSON & PAGE LTD.
CATALOGUE OF **1913**

DOULBE SPRING
AMERICAN STEEL MUSK TRAP.

No. 32.

per dozen.

UNDATED CATALOGUE *CIRCA* **1906**

AMERICAN MUSK RAT TRAP.

No. 23.

4½	5	6-inch jaws.

per dozen.

UNDATED CATALOGUE *CIRCA* **1906**

AMERICAN STEEL MUSK TRAP.

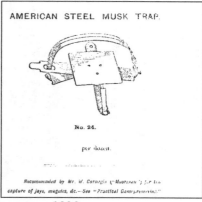

No. 24.

per dozen.

Recommended by Mr. W. Carnegie ("Moorman") for the capture of jays, magpies, &c.—See "Practical Gamepreserving."

UNDATED CATALOGUE *CIRCA* **1906**

BEST SPIKED DOG AND WOLF TRAP.

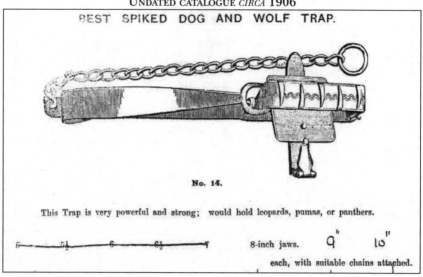

No. 14.

This Trap is very powerful and strong; would hold leopards, pumas, or panthers.

5	5½	6	6½	7	8-inch jaws.	9"	10"

each, with suitable chains attached.

THE HENRY LANE FACTORY AT NEWCASTLE, NSW IN 1929

Henry Lane (Australia) Limited

Douglas Edmund Hughes, born in 1899, was the son of Arthur Hughes and left school at 14 to be a tool room employee at a weekly wage of 6/3d per 52 hour week with Star Motors of Wolverhampton. A life long friendship started when Douglas met another toolmaker, John S. Hogg. During Douglas's early time involved with tool making he helped John Hogg and Joe Walsham from Dagenham. Later on John S. Hogg and a partner, Mr. Beller, acquired a business and John Hogg asked Douglas to work for him. It is thought that Mr. Beller was at some time a school teacher of Douglas's, and also a neighbour of Henry Lane when they were youngsters. At a later unknown date Douglas Hughes joined the Royal Navy as a Gunnery Artificer and was stationed to the North Sea and spent most of his shore leave on the east coast of Scotland. During Douglas's time in the Navy, John Hogg had become Works Manager at Henry Lane's Eagle Works in Hickman Street. After Douglas was demobbed from the Navy, he and Arthur Lane formed a strong friendship through their shared interest in motor bikes, which resulted in John Hogg persuading Douglas to work at Lane's.

Much later on, whilst working at Lane's John Hogg approached Douglas with a choice of two overseas ventures, Seattle, USA or Newcastle, Australia. Upon being interviewed regarding these positions by Henry Lane, the past stepped forward. During the conversation it was found out that previously Douglas's father, Arthur, had been a long time friend of H. Lane's. Their friendship had started at the gymnasium where they had been sports and sparring partners. Henry Lane also knew about the good solid friendship that had formed between Douglas and his son Arthur, who was to be the Works Manager in the new Australian venture, so the die was cast. On 19th July 1920 at the Wolverhampton Registry Office, Douglas, aged 21, married Lavinia Tonks who was two years younger. In a few short months they would be starting their married life together, far from friends and family, on the other side of the world in Australia. They left England on 17th September 1920, sailing on the S.S. *Berrima* and arrived in Sydney, Australia on 11th November 1920. The last sea leg of the journey was by the paddle ship *Namoi*, which sailed between Sydney and Newcastle. Douglas Hughes was later to describe his first sighting of the new plant as just 'three posts in a swamp.' Douglas's first job was to help erect the building and after, install the machinery. As his position in this new company was that of foreman toolmaker, he had then to get the business 'up and running' by training the local labour into becoming skilled when Australia's hardware industry was in its infancy years.

Originally Douglas was to be at this new plant for a period of two to five years, but it seems reasonable to assume that early on both Arthur Lane and Douglas Hughes received some inside information about the company from their fathers' connection back in England. Due to this, apparently they both negotiated the living income needed for the next three years to complete their five year optional engagement, with further options thereafter. Regardless of these early setbacks with the company Douglas stayed with Lane's for the rest of his working life. Douglas E. Hughes reluctantly retired from the company on 6th February 1964 due to ill health. His wife died in April 1964 and his own retirement was very short as he died a few months after his wife in July. He was cremated and interred with his parents in their grave back in the Borough Cemetery on Jeffcock Road, Wolverhampton, England.

The second employee sent from the Wednesfield business was Charles (Chaz) Jackson, who left his home at No 10 Graisley Lane, Wednesfield and arrived in Australia in very early 1921. Once in Australia Douglas, Lavinia and Chaz all stayed at a house not too far from Henry Lane's site. Charles Jackson was a trap tester by trade and had also to train the local labour. He remained with the company until his retirement in 1953 and also died about 1964.

John Edmund Hughes was born to Douglas and Lavinia on 20th July 1923 and as a small boy had played around the trap works and got to know some of the workers. When he left school at 14 he didn't immediately work at Lane's, but first did some nondescript jobs. However, when nearly aged fifteen, he was talked into working there on the production line. Coming up to sixteen and thinking of leaving and looking for a better paid job, John was then told that his next wage rise would bring his wage up to 18/9d per week. Soon he was approached about taking a job in the tool room. Once he had been shown around the tool room and told about the job he agreed to change his job within the company. However, he was told that he would have to sign an indenture for five years, with technical studies in his own time after work, if he wanted the tool room apprenticeship. John signed the five year agreement and being a youngster forgot to ask about the pay, presuming that it would be the same rate. Imagine his surprise on pay day when instead of his pay going up to 18/9d, it went down to 15/3d per week. Complaining about his new lower wages he was told that he could remove his name from the indenture papers if he paid the company £300. He declined their offer. His normal working week was 44 hours with an optional extra four hours overtime on Saturday morning. The tool room was operated in two groups A and B, and he was required to work his duty between the two groups every alternate week. Both groups were only together in emergencies on overtime. Just prior to the World War II period shift work was introduced and compulsory overtime was required. After the war normal hours returned and the introduction of a 40 hour week. John E. Hughes left Lane's in 1953.

Another family member who became an employee of Lane's was Jacob Tonks, father of Lavinia. Now, when living in England, Jake or Grump as he was known to his grandson John, was a foreman in a tool making and hardening section of a factory. He was born in 1875 and sold his house in Wolverhampton to his nephew Harold Tonks and he left England in 1934. Some time before the start of World War II he became employed as a security watchman, serving in this position during and after the war, eventually qualifying for his Australian pension whilst in his 70s. He died in 1967 aged 92.

My thanks go to John E. Hughes who kindly supplied me with his family's history regarding the establishment of Lane' in Australia.

In 1913 an Englishman, Frederick Carr began trading in central Sydney as a hardware manufacturers' agent. About this time, and certainly in 1915, the manufacturers' agent for Lane's Traps was F. Walsh of George and Wynyard Streets in Sydney. However in 1917 Henry Lane's appointed Mr. Carr as their sole Australian agent. A year later in 1918 the Australian Government introduced a 40% duty on imported products to help local industry. However, the duty on imported parts which would be assembled in Australia was at a much reduced rate. Due to this import tariff in Australia and the surplus of trap making equipment because of new machinery being installed at Wednesfield in England, Mr. Carr managed to persuade Lane's to set up an Australian company to manufacture their traps and therefore avoid the import tariff restrictions plus the added expense of shipping costs. It was decided that a private limited liability company would be formed to manufacture the English firm's patents in Australia. This company was to be known as Henry Lane (Australia) Limited, and an agreement was made between Henry Lane and the various shareholders of the newly formed company, namely that in exchange for the patent rights for Australia the new company agreed to allocate just over one third of its shares to the English concern.

Mr. Carr also decided in 1920, to reorganise his own business, by changing his business name of F.G. Carr Manufacturer's Agent (a hardware supply business) to Carr and Elliott. This change was done to reflect the partnership previously established between Mr. F. G. Carr and Mr. T.L. Elliott of Birmingham, England. Mr. Elliott had been locating new products, and companies in England on Mr. Carr's behalf.

The decision to acquire land in Newcastle for the new factory was quite simply based on the proximity to the Broken Hill Steel Plant which had been established there in 1912, and that shipping facilities were available for the easy importation of parts and for the distribution of finished traps etc. Shipping in those days was the main form of transportation around the coast, and there was a daily service between Sydney and Newcastle. Four acres of land were located and acquired at Clyde Street, Broadmeadow, a suburb of Newcastle, and although Douglas Hughes' first remarks about the site being a 'swamp', it was not a swamp in the proper sense of the word. The site, according to old local knowledge, was originally used by Chinese immigrants as vegetable gardens. Unfortunately for the Chinese their market gardens were in the way of development and so they were forcefully moved off the land. The market gardens would have needed good drainage, sweet soil, plenty of humus etc. and so it seems improbable that they would have attempted to grow vegetables in a swamp. Therefore the most logical answer to the 'swamp' is simply that with all of the various site preparations going on, such as the digging of foundations, drains, roadways etc. created the mess as seen by Douglas Hughes on his arrival at the site. If there had been any rain this would have turned the whole area into a 'sea of mud' and so hence the remarks of 'three posts in a swamp'. Eventually a galvanised iron shed of 2,500 square feet was erected on the site.

The establishment of the plant was assisted by Mr. Alfred Goninan, the owner of an engineering business, and a shareholder in the new company. It is thought that Mr. A. Goninan was a distant relative of the Lane family back in England or had some sort of family connections. Mr. Arthur E. Lane, grandson of the English founder Henry Lane, having joined the English business in 1917, became installed as the first Works Manager of this new Australian venture.

Due to the demand for rabbit traps being only seasonal, it was decided that other products which had a year round sales would also have to be made and put into production quickly. When the company finally began to assemble can openers and other products along with the traps, they were all branded with 'LA CARGO'. In 1923 the 'LA CARGO' trademark was registered. The trademark was formed by taking the first part of the three main directors' surnames, Lane, Carr, Goninan, the other directors being Walter Keep, Henry Magill, Albert Nettleton, James Taylor and William Small. Thus 'LA CARGO' stamped products became Henry Lane's entry into the main hardware market in Australia. When the 1927-32 depression occurred the Goninan participation ended and thereafter all products were branded Henry Lane or Lane.

The first trap produced at the New-castle factory, a wire spring rabbit trap, has been chrome plated and held pride of place in the manager's office. In 1927 the company decided to enter the builders' hardware field and in that year produced the first Australian made rim lock. From that decision has resulted Lane's becoming recognised as the major producer of a wide range of quality builders', domestic and general hardware in Australia. Due to this increase in products, the factory's building size was expanded to 20,000 square feet in 1928.

In the same year on 4th April, Arthur Edward Lane became the victim of a shark attack, in about three feet of water, and died due to his injuries. The attack was reported in the *Newcastle Herald* the following day under the title 'Shark Tragedy – South of Bar Beach – Merewether Victim'. For a number of years after Arthur Lane's untimely death, the members of the Wednesfield family received a small income from the Australian company but eventually this arrangement ceased with one capital payment for all their shares in this company.

Rabbit traps were originally a large part of the company's annual turnover and trap sales were the top sales item from March to November. However, trap production continued throughout the year so as to build up adequate stocks to allow immediate delivery with the main resumption of sales in March. Shift work trap production in 1934 was 240 dozen, which rose to 300 dozen in later years, the shifts being increased upon heavy demand for the traps as required.

During World War II it has been estimated that seven million traps were produced as rabbit skins were used to produce the Army 'Slouch' hats and the lining for Air Force flying suits etc. During the three years 1941-43, rabbit trap production peaked at over 1.25 million per annum.

From 1926 to 1968 there was a plant supervisor called James Hastie Harrower, who originally came from Dunfermline in Scotland. He was a major driving force in the plant, and because of his speed around the plant and his extremely forceful demands for more production, he became commonly known as 'The Flying Scotsman'. The plant workforce in 1934 consisted of 71 people, increasing during 1940-45 to 540. In 1981 the figure was down to 294 people employed and by 1995 this number had virtually halved to 142. This large reduction was mainly due to the competition from Taiwan/

Chinese imports.

The average yearly production of traps for the three years 1958-1960 was 20,000 dozen a year for Australian sales alone. Then in 1963 there had been a 50% increase in trap sales compared to the previous year. A year later in 1964, the total workforce of 350 comprised 40 toolmakers, 90 women on production work, 30 clerical staff and 190 males working in a supervisory and productive capacity. Also in 1964, Lane's had a flourishing export trade to Africa, Colombo, Singapore, New Guinea and New Zealand. These exports comprised mainly of rabbit traps, locks and latches. In 1964 it was estimated that approximately 110 tons of steel was used for manufacturing rabbit traps and that 30 tons was used in the production of dingo traps per year. The hot rolled spring steel used for making both types of traps being supplied by the Broken Hill Pty Co. Ltd.

In the Australian trade mark applications for 1930, H. Lane Ltd, applied to register the name Vampire, and in 1946 the trade mark LI-LO. Previously in 1915, the bird motif with the word GRIP under it had been registered.

Trap Types

1920:

Lane's production in Australia started with the wire spring (and 'wire stock') 1914 pattern rabbit trap, Australian Patent No 9698/18 and British Patent No 122,158 (1918). This trap was a variation of the earlier trap which was patented in Britain by Lane's in 1912 (Patent No 16,567) and patented in Australia in 1913 (Patent No 9546/13). Earlier wire spring traps 'kicked over' and a bracket was riveted to the rear end of the standard to cure this problem. This bracket gave more support to its 'wire stock' (which only clipped into the proper stock or base plate. The patent 9698/18 was another form of bracket fixing etc. used on this type

of trap. On the 1914 pattern trap, going through the spring 'loop' was an ordinary swivel and chain attachment with the chain ending in the usual chain ring through which was attached the metal peg. In an early 1930s advert for this trap, the illustration is shown with a different swivel arrangement, which has a patent application in Britain of May 1930 (No 15,271/30) becoming accepted in Britain in August 1931 as Patent No 355,262. This illustration also shows that the chain ring is now omitted and that the metal peg attaches directly through the end chain link.

1926:

Introduced in this year was the first 'flat' spring type trap. This consisted of a continuous combined flat metal stock and spring. This type of spring the English Lane's advertised in Britain as the 'Vee flat spring'. This type of trap also had the normal swivel, chain, chain ring and peg arrangement.

1929(?):

An improvement to the above trap appears in a variation known as Lane's No 29 flat spring pattern. The improvement was the introduction of a patent, No 16571/28, Spring Snubber and a solid head swivel peg. This new swivel peg was not a success and discontinued years later in favour of the peg with the 'D' shaped end and the chain attached by a ring to this.

Sometime unknown, Lane's produced a trap called the '41'. It is a 'flat spring' type but the difference is that it has a larger plate with turned down edges at an angle of 45 degrees. This trap was made for use in sandy conditions and also had a 15 inch long metal peg. It is thought that this trap also had the patent spring snubber (shock absorber) attached to its chain

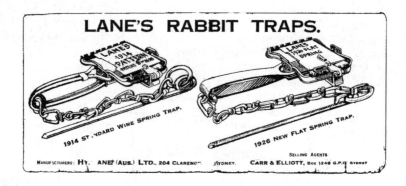

LANE'S RABBIT TRAPS.

1914 STANDARD WIRE SPRING TRAP.

1926 NEW FLAT SPRING TRAP.

SELLING AGENTS

MANUFACTURERS: HY. LANE (AUS.) LTD., 204 CLARENCE, SYDNEY. CARR & ELLIOTT, BOX 1248 G.P.O. SYDNEY

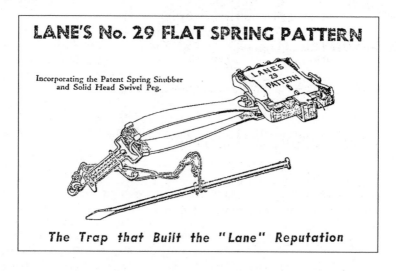

LANE'S No. 29 FLAT SPRING PATTERN

Incorporating the Patent Spring Snubber
and Solid Head Swivel Peg.

The Trap that Built the "Lane" Reputation

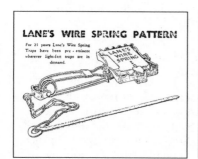

LANE'S WIRE SPRING PATTERN

For 21 years Lane's Wire Spring
Traps have been pre-eminent
wherever light-fast traps are in
demand.

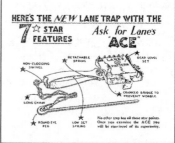

HERE'S THE *NEW* LANE TRAP WITH THE

7 ☆ STAR FEATURES   *Ask for Lane's* "ACE"

DETACHABLE SPRING

DEAD LEVEL SET

NON-CLOGGING SWIVEL

CRANKED BRIDGE TO PREVENT WOBBLE

LONG CHAIN

ROUND EYE PEG

LOW SET SPRING

No other trap has all these star points. Once you examine the ACE you will be convinced of its superiority.

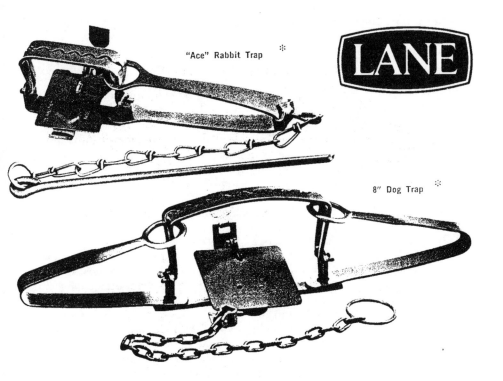

"Ace" Rabbit Trap ✳

LANE

8″ Dog Trap ✳

8″ Double-Spring Dog Traps

The 8″ Round Jaw Wild Dog or Dingo Trap is fitted with two folding, hardened and tempered springs, heat treated steel jaws and a large plate. The heavy anchoring chain has a large welded steel ring and every trap is unconditionally guaranteed.
Packing: In standard cases containing 6 traps.

"Ace" Rabbit Traps

Lane's "Ace" Rabbit Traps are light, fast and carry an unconditional guarantee against faulty workmanship or raw material. First introduced in 1933, over 10 million "Ace" Traps have been sold in Australia and overseas.
Supplied complete with chains and either the standard 12″ pegs or 15″ pegs for trapping in sandy country.
Packing: In standard cases containing 2 dozen.

LANE (AUSTRALIA) LTD 1969 CATALOGUE SHOWS THEIR
DOG TRAP AND THE 'ACE' RABBIT TRAP

when this feature became introduced. It seems that the '41' had been discontinued with the introduction of the 'Ace' trap.

1933:

The 'Ace' was originally made by Kenneth Royle as the 'KR' Trap. However, after Kenneth Royle had successfully fought an expensive law action against the American trap manufacturer Oneida Corporation, who contended his 'KR' trap contravened their 'loose spring' patent, he sold his tooling to Lane's who modified them to produce the 'Ace'. The trap has a raised ace (the playing card spade motif) on the plate. This was in the early 1930s. Comparisons between the No 29 and 'Ace' were conducted by Lane's who found that although the '29' was just as successful as a rabbit catcher as the 'Ace', its cost to manufacture was slightly higher, and so the decision was made in favour of the 'Ace'. The 'Ace' trap gradually took over from the No 29, which was a heavier and stronger trap, prior to 1940. The 'Ace' became the bulk of Lane's trap production and was still being made up to the end of 1996, when production finally ceased. Latterly only 4,800 rabbit traps were being made each year and the drop in sales was thought to be partly due to the actions of the Animal Protection Societies, but mainly due to a disease known as Rabbit Calicivirus Disease (RCD) 'escaping' from Wardang Island where a research programme was being conducted into controlling the rabbit population. This disease has been referred to in the media, incorrectly, as RHD, Rabbit Haemorrhagia Disease or VHD Viral Haemorrhagia Disease. The disease does not cause haemorrhaging, in fact just the opposite, as it clots the blood and usually causes death to occur within 48 hours. The disease is proving effective in dry areas and so may well eliminate the

need for traps on a large scale just as Myxomatosis did in Britain.

1938-39:

The exact date production of dingo traps started is unknown but it is around the 1938-39 period. Originally maximum production was 11,000 but it varied after initial production, probably due to the extra price compared to rabbit traps. Dingo trappers also seemed to be more careful with their traps and therefore didn't need to buy replacements as often as the rabbit trappers due to losses etc. The dog trap tooling was sold to a company in Perth, Western Australia, called Stockbrands, around the years 1974-5. However, Lane's still made the springs for these traps until finally in 1976 Stockbrands took the tools for spring manufacture. The reason why Lane's sold their tooling to Stockbrands was purely financial. Lane's local steel producer Broken Hill Pty required an order for steel far beyond a five year stock holding and the production was not a profitable item for Lane's, and so hence the decision to discontinue production. Stockbrands continued to make the Dingo/Wild dog traps identical to Lane's but added to the plate the words: Stockbrands made in W.A.

Special Items:

Chrome Plated Wire Spring (& wire stock) Rabbit Trap.

This trap has already been referred to as it was the first trap manufactured at Lane's Australian plant. It now resides in the Managers Office.

Gold Plated Wire Spring (& wire stock) Rabbit Trap 1924

This trap came from scrap disturbed during building work alterations. It was made workable, with all the parts original. Originally it was given to Mr. Robert Stewart Langfield by a farmer from Scone, which is approximately 100 miles north west of Newcastle. After a visit to another farmer, who is also a trap collector, Mr. Langfield arranged for the trap to be gold plated at Lane's. The main reason for this decision was its age, and also because it was in superb condition for plating. Mr. Langfield then presented this trap to Mr. Ian Ridgway of Cardinia, Victoria to add to his own collection where it now resides in a cedar cabinet.

Gold Plated 'Ace' Rabbit Trap
This trap, complete with gold plated chain and peg, was given to the author on 23rd July 1996 by Mrs. Susan Mangan, whilst on a visit to Scotland. It was presented by her, on behalf of her father, Mr. R.S. Langfield, who had greatly helped my research into the history of Lane's of Australia. He had started work at Lane's as a process worker in January 1934, later to become works manager in 1960, finally retiring in 1981 after more than 47 years of loyal service.

'Boom Times Just a Memory for Lane' Under the above heading according to the *Newcastle Herald* dated Thursday 16th September 1999, it was reported that Lane's would 'close its doors in Broadmeadow. . .' on Friday 24th September 1999. The article went on to state that 'The Lane Company had humble beginnings in the manufacture of rabbit traps. By the 1980s expansion had taken Lane to Victoria and around 22,000 different products were being manufactured in factories in Newcastle, Melbourne, Adelaide and Sydney. Among the products were door locks, hinges, brackets, deadlocks and castors. Over the years carpet sweepers and primus ovens were among items added to the list. The Newcastle factory also produced door locks for General Motors Holden for around three decades.' Lane's were 'Once recognised as Australia's largest hardware manufacturer . . . (with) the Newcastle factory employing 500 workers at its peak in the late 1950s'. However, 'early in 1997

Lane announced plans to halve its existing workforce of 135'. On the last day only 16 workers remained.

LANE, Richard. Wednesfield. Year 1833-1854
Trap maker, steel. 1854, 1850, 1845, 1835.
Trap maker for rats, vermin etc. 1834.
Rat trap maker. 1833.

LEWIS, George. Wednesfield. Year 1876-1904
Steel trap maker 1876
Steel trap maker & beer retailer, High Street, 1880, 1884, 1888, 1892, 1896.
Steel trap maker, Wood End, 1904.

LEWIS, Thomas Whittington. Wednesfield. Year 1921-1924
Steel trap maker. Wood End. 1921, 1924.

MARSHALL, Edward. Wednesfield. Year 1838 -1861
Steel trap maker 1861, 1860.
Steel trap maker, Porto Bello, Willenhall, 1854, 1845, 1838

MARSHALL, Enoch. Wednesfield. Year 1841-1864
In 1841 Census records he is listed as a trap maker at the High Street and aged 25 . From 1849 to 1864 he is just listed as a steel trap maker with no address given.

MARSHALL, George. Wednesfield. Year 1813-1855
In 1813 the Bishop transcripts describe him as a trap maker, of March End. In 1827 he is listed in the directories as a rat trap maker and as a trap maker for rats, vermin etc. in 1834. From 1835 he is described as a steel trap maker up to 1855. The 1841 Census records for March end show that George and his wife Mary were aged about 55. At the same address were two other people. John Edwards was aged about 15 and described as a Trap Makers' Apprentice, whilst the other John Watkins about 20 years old and described as a trap maker-jour-

neyman. The 1845 directory entry has a change of address to Neachill.

MARSHALL, John. Wednesfield. Year 1876-1968

The trade directories list him as a maker of all kinds of steel traps for home and export. High Street 1876. Then listed as of Lichfield Road in 1880, 1884, 1888, 1892, 1896. (Note that in John Marshall's patent of 1892 his address is given as of Albion Works, Bloxwich Road, Wednesfield). Bloxwich Road 1904, 1916, 1921, 1924, 1928.

Albion Works, Lichfield Road 1931. Bloxwich Road 1932, 1936.

115, Lichfield Road 1940.

It is interesting to note that on 30th July 1894 John Marshall, trading as S. Griffiths & Sons, Clyde Works, Wednesfield registered the S. Griffiths XXX IXL motif as a trade mark. From this information it seems that John Marshall already owned S. Griffiths & Sons but operated the firm as a separate business.

It is thought as mentioned previously under Samuel Griffiths, that Griffiths & Marshall's merged their trap making businesses together about the early 1930s. This may account for the Bloxwich Road address given in the 1932/36 trade directories. After the merger the joint business employed over twenty trap makers plus additional press workers who made standard blank parts for the traps. Due to this merger Marshall's Lichfield Road Works became the largest in Wednesfield. One of the last trap makers to work for Marshall's was George Jones who was employed from 1911 to 1968.

Trade/Identification Marks: Figure of a lion (1883). Scotchman (1890).

Patents etc.

In the book *The Balance of Nature* by George Abbey (Pub. 1909), Fig 87 shows the Exterminator Tunnel Rat Trap, which was supplied by Messrs. Wm. Burgess & Co. of Malvern Wells.

This trap looks remarkably similar to John Marshall's patent application dated 23rd May 1892 and which was accepted on 2nd July 1892 becoming Patent No 9715. The Exterminator Tunnel trap was made to catch small vermin such as rats, stoats, weasels etc and came in two models. The model illustrated killed the victim, while the second version had a door at each end of the tunnel which closed, capturing the victim alive. This model cost more, as it was a more elaborate design. Two mole trap versions of this patent were also made. The first was basically the same original trap design, but without the sides etc of the tunnel. The second version retained the tunnel but used coiled springs instead of the bow spring to operate it. The mole traps are thought to have been called The Climax.

Another trap made by Marshall's was the Sara Trap. This trap was patented by Frederic Sara of The Tors, Yelverton, Devonshire. He applied for his patent on 25th May 1907 and it was accepted on 17th October 1907 becoming Patent No 12,124. Marshall's were also thought to have stamped their miniature pole traps used against kingfishers with the word 'Dwarf'.

MARSHALL, Luke, Wednesfield. Year 1841-1931

Trap maker, steel, 1841, 1842.

The 'Angel Inn' and steel trap maker, 1849, 1850

Steel trap maker, 1851, 1854, 1855, 1860

Steel trap maker & beer retailer, 1861

Steel trap maker, 1864.

Marshall, Luke & Son. Steel Trap Makers. Neachell's Lane 1928, 1931. Shown on letter headed paper dated March 5th 1929 is the correct address of Nechell's Road, Wednesfield.

Luke Marshall was the son of George Marshall of March End and whilst working as a trap maker in the High Street took over his father's business

SCOTCHMAN

This billhead suggests that Luke Marshall either made padlocks or more likely, retailed them

Exterminator Tunnel Rat Trap made by John Marshall

about 1860 and employed two men and two boys. Luke's wife was Emma, and they had two sons, John and Samuel, both of whom followed into their father's trade. John established a successful business in his own right, whilst Samuel's small business eventually joined his father's, and may have operated separately for a while from the same premises.

MARSHALL, Emma Mrs. Wednesfield. Year 1864-1876
Steel trap maker, 1864, 1872
Steel trap maker, Marsh End, 1876 (misspelt for March End).
Emma was the wife of Luke Marshall and they had two sons who became trap makers, John of Lichfield Rd. and Samuel of Hadley's Fold and later Nechell's Road.

MARSHALL, Samuel. Wednesfield. Year 1880-1940
Steel trap maker, High Street, 1880, 1884, 1888, 1892, 1896.
Steel trap maker, Neachel Lane, 1904.
Steel trap maker, 139 Neachell Lane,

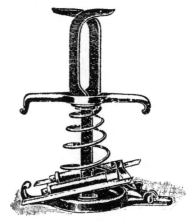

Trap sprung.

SARA TRAP

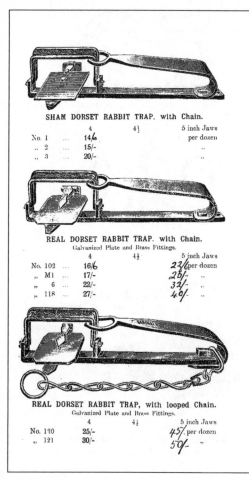

SHAM DORSET RABBIT TRAP. with Chain.

		4	4½	5 inch Jaws
No.	1	14/6		per dozen
,,	2	15/-		,,
,,	3	20/-		,,

REAL DORSET RABBIT TRAP. with Chain.
Galvanized Plate and Brass Fittings.

		4	4½	5 inch Jaws
No.	102	16/6	22/6	per dozen
,,	M1	17/-	26/-	,,
,,	6	22/-	32/-	,,
,,	118	27/-	40/-	,,

REAL DORSET RABBIT TRAP, with looped Chain.
Galvanized Plate and Brass Fittings.

		4	4½	5 inch Jaws
No.	120	25/-	45/-	per dozen
,,	121	30/-	50/-	,,

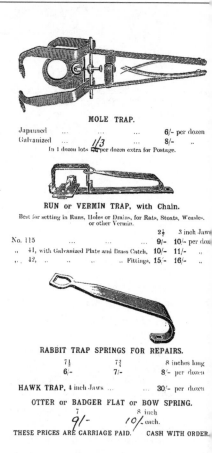

MOLE TRAP.

Japanned	...	...	...	6/- per dozen
Galvanized	...	1/3	...	8/- ,,

In 1 dozen lots 6d. per dozen extra for Postage.

RUN or VERMIN TRAP, with Chain.
Best for setting in Runs, Holes or Drains, for Rats, Stoats, Weasles, or other Vermin.

				2½	3 inch Jaws
No. 115	...	...	...	9/-	10/- per doz.
,, 41, with Galvanized Plate and Brass Catch,				10/-	11/- ,,
,, 42, ,, ,, ,, ,, ,, Fittings,				15/-	16/- ,,

RABBIT TRAP SPRINGS FOR REPAIRS.

7½	7¾	8 inches long
6/-	7/-	8/- per dozen

HAWK TRAP, 4 inch Jaws ... ... 30/- per dozen

OTTER or BADGER FLAT or BOW SPRING.

7	8 inch
9/-	10/- each.

THESE PRICES ARE CARRIAGE PAID.   CASH WITH ORDER.

THIS EXTRACT IS FROM AN UNDATED CATALOGUE OF SAMUEL MARSHALL

1916, 1921, 1924, 1928, 1932, 1936, 1940.
An undated catalogue shows the address as 139 Nechell's Road. Son of Luke and Emma Marshall, he eventually joined his business with his father's.

MARSHALL, William. Wednesfield. Year 1841-1872

In the 1841 Census records he is listed as a trap maker of Church Street.
Trap maker, steel, 1851, 1854, 1855, 1860, 1861, 1864.
Steel trap maker & Shopkeeper, Rookery Street, 1865
Steel trap maker, 1872.

MARSTON, Joseph. Wednesfield. Year 1827-1842

Rat trap maker, 1827, 1833
Trap maker for rats, vermin etc. 1834
Trap maker, steel, 1835, 1841, 1842.
In the 1841 Census record, he is listed at High Street, with his son William aged 38 years approximately, both as rat trap makers.

MARSTON, William. Wednesfield. Year 1841

Noted in the 1841 Census records with his father Joseph (see above).

MASON, Henry. Wednesfield. Year 1849-1884

Trap maker, 1849

Manufacturer of all kinds of steel traps, 1855
Rat trap manufacturer, High Street, 1865
Steel trap maker, 1872, 1876, 1880, 1884.

MORRIS, David. Wednesfield. Year 1851-1861
Steel trap maker, 1851, 1855, 1861.

NICHOLLS, Henry. Wednesfield, Year 1851
Trap maker, 1851.

NICHOLLS, Luke. Wednesfield. Year 1833-1839
Rat trap maker & retail brewer, 1833
Trap maker for rats, vermin etc. 1834
Trap maker, steel, 1835
Rat trap maker, 1838, 1839 (and beer retailer)
Note, that different surname spellings occur in the trade directories, Nicholls 1833, 1834, 1838. Nickols 1835. Nicholas and Nicholls in 1839.

NICHOLLS, Thomas, Wednesfield. Year 1833-1834
Rat trap maker, 1833
Trap maker for rats, vermin etc. 1834.

O'CONNER, William. Wednesfield. Year 1904
Steel trap maker, North Street, 1904

PHILLIPS, Nehemiah. Wednesfield. Year 1876-1904
Steel trap maker, North Road 1876
Manufacturer of all kinds of steel game, rat & vermin traps. North Road, 1880
Manufacturer of all kinds of steel game, rat & vermin traps for home and foreign markets. North Street, 1884
Manufacturer of all kinds of traps. North Street, 1888

PHILLIPS, Nehemiah
(Exor's of) Steel trap maker, North Street, 1892, 1896, 1904.

ROBERTS, James. Wednesfield. Year 1867-1932
Established in 1867 according to a known poster. In the trade directories he is listed as a
Steel trap maker, 1872
Steel trap maker, Hickman Street, 1876
North Road address in 1880, 1884, 1888 (1885/86 patents Reliance Works, North Street).
North Street, 1892, 1893, 1895, 1901, 1904
24 North Street 1916, 1921, 1924, 1928
24 North Street, Telephone No Wolverhampton 759 in 1931 and 1932.
Patents etc.:
Patents known to have been made by the James Roberts firm include:
Regd Design 25th June 1874 (Mole Trap)
Patent No 1817 10th February 1885 (Spring attachment for easier repairing of traps)
Patent No 5629 Application dated 24th April 1886, accepted 25th February 1887 (Box type plate protector)
Patent No 11,198 Application dated 15th June 1892, accepted 15th June 1893. This patent 'is designed to simplify the repairing of traps. In the improved trap (whether flat or bow spring) the usual, rivet, cotter or screw hole securing the spring to the stock is dispensed with. Substituted for it is a hole of oblong form – this allows the rivet, cotter or screw to be moved backward or forward so as to properly adjust the length of the spring to the trap.'
Another known variation of this trap consists of the bow spring going over the end of the stock but instead of fixing normally when in this underside position, the bow spring end curves upwards in a circular motion to be fixed underneath by the metal wedge which is now inside the curve of the spring. This trap is of the projecting

stock type and has the hole for the chain attachment going through this part of the extended stock.

Patent No 8985 Application dated 5th May 1893, accepted 7th April 1894 'affix the bridge of the trap to the stock in a firmer manner'.

Patent No 13,479 Application dated 13th July 1895, accepted 20th June 1896 Improvement in wire spring fixing to the trap.

Patent No 24,430 Application dated 2nd December 1901, accepted 2nd October 1902   Mole trap

All the above are James Roberts' own patents.

Patent application No 9239 dated 31st March 1932 and accepted in 1933, becoming Patent No 395,462 by Samuel & Sidney Patten trading as J. Roberts was for a tongueless gin trap. Stamped on the plates of this trap are Roberts Pat 395462 with either a number 53, for the pressed bow spring, or a number 51 for the wire spring version.

Patent No 12,418 Application dated 29th May 1907, and accepted 13th February 1908, by John Potter Junior of Sampford Courtenay, Devonshire who described himself as a Clerk. This trap is called the 'Ideal' and some traps have that name stamped on the trap tongue. Roberts can also be found stamped on the plate of some traps. An unusual variation of this 'Ideal' trap was advertised as 'The new 'Clyde' egg stealing trap'. Basically, all that was different from the normal trap was an oval cut out of the centre of the plate. The egg was then placed under the oval hole in the plate and rested on the coil spring below it. Obviously, because of the oval cut out of the plate most of the egg could still be seen. Due to the egg being under the plate, as opposed to being normally placed on top of a 'brass ring' as on most other types of 'egg traps', the advertising states that 'It is impossible for egg stealing vermin either to take the egg away or to suck the con-

tents without springing the trap.' However, to spring the trap, the trap plate had to be depressed in the normal way.

Patent No 209,999 An unusual dsign of trap is one that is called a 'Hare' trap, but why it should be known as this is not clear as the patent clearly states 'An improved humane rabbit or vermin trap. This is Harry Carne's, of Truro, Cornwall, patent which he applied for on 21st April 1923, No 10,836/23. The patent being accepted on 24th January 1924 being patent No 209,999.

In an S.Young & Sons of Misterton catalogue of *circa* 1931, there is an illustration of this trap which very much resembles the illustration in the original patent drawings. The patent specifications read 'The trap is set by pressing down the leaf spring, (in the drawing it is actually a bow spring) and the crank arms are then moved in such manner as to cause each to lie along the sides of the tread plate, the latter is then raised into a horizontal position, and the catch integral therewith engages with the lower bifurcated fork element, the pressure then being removed from the spring whereby the trap is set.' The text accompanying the illustration in the Young's catalogue says that the trap was 'Invented by a Trapper after 20 years' experimenting. This Trap will not catch or injure Dogs, Foxes, Birds, or Domestic animals, only Rabbits and Creeping Vermin. It does not require a chain. It kills the Rabbit quickly without injuring the flesh. There is no squeal, no rattle of chain, etc. Therefore other Rabbits are unaware Traps are set. Also Foxes, Dogs and Poachers are not attracted. Try and sample, Trap, 2/10, Post paid, 1 Dozen traps 25/6; 6 Traps 13/6. Carriage paid.' A Mark II version was also produced, which now had the normal bridge and tongue assembly which held the jaws open, that is found on the common

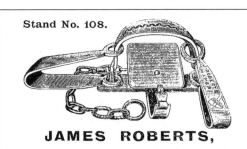

Stand No. 108.

JAMES ROBERTS,
RELIANCE WORKS, WEDNESFIELD, Staffs.

Patentee and Manufacturer of all kinds of Vermin, Rabbit, and Wild Animal Traps. For Home and Foreign Markets.

Illustrated Price Lists on Application.   Established 1867.

(TOP) A MOLE TRAP MARK II BY J. ROBERTS FIRST REGISTERED 25 JUNE 1874

(MIDDLE) HARRY CARNE'S MARK II HARE TRAP (PATENTED 1924) MADE BY J. ROBERTS

(BOTTOM) A 1902 ADVERT

gin trap. This trap is also found with Roberts stamped upon the spring.

Trade Marks/Identification Marks:
J Roberts (1868)
crescent over a star (1874)
A bent arm holding a flag (1888)
STREBOR (1896)
The Trio (1902)
'The essential particular of the trade mark is the combination of devices, and I disclaim any right to the exclusive use of the added matter'.
J Roberts (1867)
Maker
J. ROBERTS
***
RELIANCE
ELEPHANT (Motif)
SOVEREIGN
STREBOR SPECIAL.

Sometimes, along with the J. Roberts mark, can also be found on traps the marks A1, No 2, Patent 10.

Miscellaneous information:
At the Centennial International Exhibition held at Melbourne, 1888-1889, Class 38 (Portable Weapons, and Hunting and Shooting Equipment), J. Roberts gained a 2nd Order of Merit for the traps he exhibited whilst competing against another two British trap exhibitors there, H. Rogers, Sons & Co. of Wolverhampton and H. Lane of Wednesfield. Amongst the 1st Order of Merit group, 1st prize winners were H. Rogers, Sons & Co. Silver Medal and H. Lane Bronze Medal winner. Henry Rogers, Sons & Co. (*circa* 1830–late 1970s) were actually hardware merchants, which included a large exporting trade. They are not known to have manufactured their own traps.

Gold medals were awarded to James Roberts at Wolverhampton in 1891 and 1893. Another gold medal was awarded to him at the Midland Counties Trades & Industrial Exhibition held in the Bingley Hall, Birmingham between April 11th to May 14th 1892.

Of his stand, No 159a, the official catalogue states 'This exhibit of steel vermin, rabbit and animal traps contains a specimen of well-nigh every kind in that particular branch of manufacture, which are particularised below'. Listed below, as taken from that catalogue, is his extensive range of products.

No 1 is a large specimen of wild animal trap, weighing 140 lbs, length 6ft 6in, size of jaws 15in.

No 2 Dog or otter trap, with improved adjustable spring.

No 3 Sham Dorset trap, used for rabbits or foxes.

No 4 Rabbit or run trap, used for rabbits, also rats, stoats &c.

No 5 Lion trap, 7 in. jaw, with spikes and folding or swivel springs.

No 6 Beaver trap, double spring, fitted without teeth, so as not to injure the skin.

No 7 Kangaroo, dog, or otter trap, with double springs.

No 8 Kangaroo, dog or otter trap, with double folding springs.

No 9 Tiger trap, double springs, round jaw, fitted with spikes.

No 10 Fox or small dog trap, bow spring.

No 11 Hawk or owl trap, round, usually affixed on the top of poles for catching.

No 12 Wolf trap, strong, bow spring.

No 13 Heron trap, 12 in. jaw, for taking any kind of large birds, such as vultures &c.

No 14 Musk trap, for catching musk rats.

No 15 Bird trap, for any kind of small birds.

No 16 Bird trap, having a cup attachment instead of a plate for holding the bait.

No 17 Rabbit trap, size $4^{1}/_{2}$.

No 18 Cat trap, the spring is made to go off by pulling the plate up, instead of pressing down as ordinarily.

No 19 (Blank – no entry)

No 20 Rabbit trap, with improved plate protector. (Patent No 5629/1886 maybe?)

No 21 Vermin trap, round jaw for catching any kind of small vermin.

No 22 Dorset rabbit trap, 4 inch.

No 23 Bird trap, with round teeth.

No 24 Dorset rabbit trap, extra best, with brass plate attachment, size 4in.

No 25 Run or rat trap, Dorset jaw, size $2\frac{1}{2}$in.

No 26 American otter trap, made wholly of steel, double spring.

No 27 Tom tit trap, bow spring.

The largest trap weighs 140 lbs, and the smallest less than $\frac{1}{4}$ ounce.

In the Wolverhampton Art and Industrial Exhibition of 1902, James Roberts were advertised in the official catalogue as being on Stand No 108, with the illustration of a folding double springed 'Dog' trap.

In 1904 J.F.Good, a rabbit trap importer of Melbourne Australia, was advertising 'Rabbit traps fitted with Good's patent attachment Roberts 11/6.' The forged bow spring has stamped on it, J.Roberts No 2 (with the crescent and star motif). This is the same trap fitting as illustrated in Joseph Tonks catalogue of circa 1925.

J. Roberts was the third trap making business to be acquired by W.&G. Sidebotham. Obviously this was after the 1933 date of the Pattens' patent No 395,462 as they were still trading as J. Roberts then.

THE TRIO

J. ROBERTS, MAKER.

SIDEBOTHAM, William & George. Wednesfield. Year 1865-1984

According to headed notepaper William Sidebotham established his business in 1865. He is then listed in trade directories first as a steel trap maker only, in 1872. In 1874 William was advertising that he was the 'Manufacturer of all kinds of steel traps for game, vermin, and wild beasts, for home and export markets.' Then in 1876 and 1880 he is listed as a steel trap maker and shop keeper in Graisley Lane. In the 1884 and 1888 listings, he is still at Graisley Lane, but now with no mention of being a shop keeper. An advert in Hulley's Hardware of 1889/90 mentions that W. Sidebotham is the patentee and sole maker of the 'Eclipse' patent rabbit trap. It states that he is 'also maker of the 'Star and Crescent' brand of rabbit trap.'

SIDEBOTHAM, William & George.
Graisley Lane
Steel trap makers 1892-1904.
Steel trap makers, Graisley works, 1916-1921.
In 1924 their telephone number was Wolverhampton 768. In 1925 their address was found to be Graisley Works, Rookery Street, with the same 768 telephone number. This address and telephone number remains the same in the 1932 trade directory, but in the 1936-1948 listings the telephone number is Fallings Park 31368. Then in the 1951-1967 listings it alters from Fallings Park to Wolverhampton 31368. This same number is then prefixed by the number 7 in 1968 and Sidebotham's telephone number remained 731368 until the company ceased trading in 1984.
In the 1936 and 1940 directories, Sidebotham's are also listed separately as Wireless Engineers in Amos Lane.
Trade/Identification Marks:
Cockerel facing left with the word CHALLENGE underneath in a semi

Established 1865

W. & G. SIDEBOTHAM
Graisley Works, WEDNESFIELD

Manufacturers of all kinds of STEEL
Vermin, Game & Wild Animal Traps
FOR HOME AND EXPORT TRADE

Trade Brands :	Proprietors of
"GAMEKEEPER"	E. GRIFFITHS & CO.,
"BI-MO"	Victoria Works, Wednesfield
"DZIN"	GEO. BELLAMY & SONS,
"DINKUM"	Atlas Works, Wednesfield

circle (1890). Just the word CHALLENGE can be found also stamped on trap springs.
Gamekeeper facing left holding traps with the word GAMEKEEPER above (1898).
Interestingly this trade mark was originally registered on 18th August 1898, by Frank Hyde, Langdale Villa, Vicarage Road, Wednesfield, who described himself as a Factor. Previously in 1886 Josiah Hyde had registered the SHAVE trade mark, which also later became associated with Sidebotham's. Presumably there was a family connection between the two Hydes, which resulted in both the SHAVE & GAMEKEEPER trade marks being acquired by Sidebotham's.
BI-MO (1902).
DZIN (1922).
DINKUM (1925).
Star and crescent.
WANDGES.
Sidebotham's.
Sidebotham's Maker.

Patents:

Patent No 6016, Application date 22nd March 1895, accepted 7th March 1896.

The Patentees were William and George Sidebotham, who stated that 'according to this invention we so construct and arrange the parts by which the jaw is held open, that the jaw will be released by the lifting of the treadle or bait plate as well as by the depressing of the same, thus making it impossible for an animal to eat the bait without getting caught by the trap.'

Patent No 26,511 Application dated 13th November 1897, accepted 1st October 1898.

Again the Patentees were William and George Sidebotham who according to this improvement dispensed with the usual metal teeth found on gin traps and instead 'provide each of the jaws of the trap with an India rubber block secured to the jaws. . . (with) the surfaces of the said India rubber blocks being toothed, ribbed, or grooved so that when the jaws close upon the animal they will effectually hold the same without inflicting so much pain.' In this patent, W.&G. Sidebotham also mention that they are Cycle Saddle Spring Makers.

Patent No 19. Application dated 1st January 1900, accepted 3rd November 1900. 'Improvements in, and in the manufacture of springs for gin traps. . . and in tools for use in such manufacture.' The Patentees being William Sidebotham Junior and George James Sidebotham trading together in copartnership as W.&G. Sidebotham.

Patent No 251,732 Application dated 13th March 1925,

(No 6816/25) accepted 13th May 1926. An improvement for securing the wire spring (and wire stock) to the trap base or stock proper.

The Patentees were William Sidebotham, George James Sidebotham,

Harry Jabez Edward Sidebotham, Arthur Victor Sidebotham, and Harold William Sidebotham, all trading together in copartnership as W.&G. Sidebotham.

Patents relating to traps known to have been made by Sidebotham's include:

Application date 22nd February 1909. Patent accepted 21st October 1909, being Patent No 4349. The Patentee of this mole trap was a physician and surgeon called Charles Irvine Faulkner of Mount Temple, Clontarf, County Dublin, Eire.

Application date 7th September 1928 (No 25,775/28). Patent accepted 14th November 1929 becoming Patent No 321,493. John Davis of Southwood Lodge, Arundel Park, Sussex was the Patentee of this improved rabbit trap, which was designed 'to strike the rabbit or the like in the region of the heart and crush it against the top of the hole in which the trap is set'. It is thought that only a few trial traps were made, on an experimental basis, and which ultimately proved unsuccessful. The trap was known as the Davis Humane and was made with a flat spring, not as shown in the patent drawings.

Morgan Mole Trap:

On 11th February 1908, a Welsh farmer applied for a patent for a coiled spring operated mole trap. David Morgan of Bryncoch, Gwynfe, Llangadock was successful in getting his patent (No 3083) accepted on 8th October of the same year. However the patent and the actual trap made differed slightly. The patent drawing shows 'A frame consisting of a top bar, side bars and a supporting base. The trap and base are connected by four other vertical bars, there being thus three bars on each side of a central space. In the central space are pivoted two vertical catches, one turned to the left and the other to the right. . .' Around the middle vertical bar in each set of three bars, either side of the central space, is a coiled spring which when released operates a loop or noose which is 'free to pass up and down through a slot in the base.' To set, 'The trap is put in the likely run of the mole and set by pressing down the cross bar so that their inner ends engage with and are held down by the catches, the loops then hanging below the base.' Each spring was capable of working independently of the other. However in the trap produced by Sidebotham's they basically removed two vertical bars and coiled springs and also the complicated trigger mechanism in the central space. A single coiled spring was then put into this central space with one bar on either side of it joined together by the top bar.

Sidebotham's were also one of the six trapmakers to make the Sara trap.

Trap Query:

In a letter dated 14th June 1977 from Mr. A.H. Orchard, of Littleover, Derby, he offered to Sidebotham's the opportunity to manufacture cage traps with his improved 'mechanism of almost unbelievable sensitivity' which he had provisionally patented on 27th May 1977 (No 22419). Sidebotham's replied on 18th August 1977 requesting 'more information regarding the design and performance of this trap.' Unfortunately it is not known if this idea and prototype trap produced by Mr. Orchard (who incidentally was a retired designer engaged in the provision of intricate test apparatus whilst employed by Rolls Royce) was ever put into production on a trial basis.

Miscellaneous information:

In a completion order dated 12th March 1969, Messrs A.A. Fenn of Redditch received 120 doz 4 link x 10g JAPD chains with ring and small strong 'S' hook left open a little without swivel as before at 3/9d doz. The company of Eliza Tinsley in April 1971 also received 25 gross 4 link x 10g JAPD chains with ring and swivel but without 'S' hooks at 7/- doz, and 25 gross JAPD swivels with the turns closed at 3/- doz. A further order in December 1975 was for 1,000 black fox chains as before and 1,500 black standard swivels. Eliza Tinsley's also ordered for export to Ireland during 1975 and 1976 on several occasions 12 doz 3 inch jaw, 204, rat traps and chains and 12 doz 4 inch jaw No 202D Sham Dorset rabbit traps and chains. Other orders destined for Ireland (Eire) came from Messrs Joseph Murphy (Ballina) Ltd, Co., Mayo who ordered in February 1971 48 doz 3 inch square jaw run rat traps without chains at 40/6d doz, 18 doz 4 inch jaw '06' quality Sham Dorset rabbit traps with chains, iron fittings at 55/6d doz, 5 doz 5 inch jaw wire spring fox traps with chains, galvanised plates, brass fittings at 18/- each. William Carr & Sons Ltd. of County Cork ordered in November 1975 40 doz 4 inch jaw No 90 Real Dorset wire spring traps with galvanised plates, brass fittings with chains, 40 doz 4 inch jaw 'XX' Real Dorset traps, galvanised plates, brass fittings with chains, and 20 doz 4 inch jaw '06' Sham Dorset traps with iron fittings. Overseas orders included one in October 1975 from Messrs. Goode Durrant & Murray Ltd. of London and was for shipment per S.S. *Dalesman* to Belize and consisted of '2 ironhooped tea chests each containing 12 doz i.e., 12 doz 3 inch jaw '06' quality animal traps and chains at £6.75 per doz, 12 doz 4 inch jaw '06' quality ditto at £7.88 per doz.' Another order, this time from Messrs. Keep Brothers Ltd. of Birmingham and destined for Horsfords of St. Kitts in March 1976, consisted of '2 ironhooped tea chests at 60p each, each containing 3 dozen, i.e. 6 dozen 6 inch jaw 'S2' quality double folding spring large animal traps, with strong chains at £29.50 doz.' African orders in the latter quarter of 1975 included sev-

phone WOLVERHAMPTON **3.**   **ESTABLISHED 1865.**   Telegrams: Sidebotham, Wednesfield

W. & G. SIDEBOTHAM,

Steel Trap Manufacturers,

Graisley Works,

WEDNESFIELD,

STAFFS.

Trade Marks :

" BI-MO " Regd.

" DZIN " Regd.

" DINKUM " Regd.

We beg to call your attention to the various patterns of Steel Animal and Vermin Traps illustrated in this list; which are especially suited to the needs of the trappers and gamekeepers in this country.

All the "Gamekeeper" Brand Traps are Guaranteed first-class quality, and second to none as regards good value for money.

If we have not previously had the pleasure of doing business with you we are certain a trial order would convince you, and would lead to good repeat business.

The demand for the Wire Spring Traps, and the "DZIN" Folding Spring Traps; is increasing each season; as many of the modern trappers now prefer something lighter than the old pattern heavy type Rabbit Trap. Although these patterns are light in weight; and only weigh about 18-lbs. per dozen, yet they are strong in construction; and are fitted with strong, durable springs.

We have had more than 60 years experience in manufacturing and supplying Steel Traps; and our goods are the result of continually experimenting, and perfecting the various patterns.

PROPRIETORS OF   *Established 1810*

GRIFFITHS & CO.,

Victoria Works,

Wednesfield.

GEORGE BELLAMY & SONS

Atlas Works,

Wednesfield

CIRCA 1933 LEAFLET

TELEPHONE: WOLVERHAMPTON FALLINGS PARK 31368
TELEGRAMS: "SIDEBOTHAM, 31368 WOLVERHAMPTON."

ESTABLISHED 1865.

GAMEKEEPER

REGISTERED TRADE MARK

GRAISLEY WORKS, WEDNESFIELD, Staffordshire,........................194

M...

ORDER FROM

W. & G. SIDEBOTHAM,

MANUFACTURERS OF EVERY DESCRIPTION OF

STEEL VERMIN AND WILD ANIMAL TRAPS FOR HOME AND EXPORT TRADE.

Order No. 740

eral repeat orders from Messrs. Societe Commerciale L'Quest Africain for 200 doz 4 inch jaw 'S' quality single spring traps, but two years later in a letter dated 12th May 1977 to Messrs. William Rawlinson Ltd. of Liverpool in answer to their query regarding purchasing 4 inch jaw 'S' brand traps to export to Nigeria, Sidebotham's reply was that 'Unfortunately we are not in the position to export traps to Nigeria at the present time. There is confusion regarding size in their Customs Department and they will not allow traps of this size into their country. We have supplied plenty in the past, but until this query regarding size is cleared up, we can do nothing in this matter'. The situation was much better in South Africa as Sidebotham's obtained a further order from Greenstein & Rosen (Pty) Ltd. of Johannesburg in November 1979, which was ordered through Demick (Shipping) Ltd. of London, and totalled 20 doz 4 inch jaw traps at £12.90 per dozen, 40 doz 4 $^{1}/_{2}$ inch jaw traps at £16.18 per doz, 30 doz 6 inch jaw traps at £24.05 per doz, and 17 doz 7 inch jaw traps at £34.70 per doz. Again, in September 1981, these two same companies ordered 30 doz 6 inch jaw 'S' quality single spring steel animal traps complete with

chains at £28.14 doz and 20 doz 7 inch jaw, same as above, at a cost of £40.60 per doz.

British businesses supplied around the 1960s and 70s, with mainly scissor type mole traps included such companies as Messrs Swinnerton & Co. Ltd. of Stourbridge, Messrs Samuel Lewis & Co. Ltd. of Dudley, and of course Gilbertson & Page. An order in 1976 for Gilbertson & Page consisted of 500 strong chains, 2,500 standard chains, 1,250 strong swivels, 2,500 standard swivels and 200 mole traps. A later order for the company in March 1978 consisted of 250 Juby traps, but there seems to have been manufacturing problems around at that time, as a letter dated 18th August 1981 to Gilbertson & Page states, 'We would appreciate it if you would kindly let us know the position regarding the remainder of the 'Juby' traps outstanding on your order, and which are in the course of manufacture. We do of course, realise that your order for these traps was placed quite a while ago, and as we explained at the time, the firm who manufactured the castings for us went out of business and we experienced considerable difficulty in obtaining the patterns and finding another source of production. Now we have all the requisite parts in hand we are anxious to finalise this order'. Against this order of 250 Juby traps, which was placed in 1978, 100 traps at £3.87 each along with another order for 400 galvanised mole traps at 84p each were dispatched in March 1981 to Gilbertson & Page. In yet another letter to the company dated 8th September 1981 in reply to Gilbertson & Page's query regarding the remainder of the Juby traps, Sidebotham's stated 'Consequently we have a stock of these parts awaiting assembly, also completed Juby traps, which we (are) preparing against your above mentioned order, as we have received no cancellation of your instructions in the matter. We trust we may now continue to supply the balance of this order to you'. Another invoice for 150 Juby traps is dated 31/01/1982. Circumstantial evidence points to another trap called the 'Lloyd' as also being made by Sidebotham's. Unfortunately, no documentation has been located by me to verify this. The 'Lloyd' trap is basically a humane wire spring gin trap, but instead of having the normal jaws (complete with teeth) it has wire jaws, these jaws when in the set or open position form two 'L' shapes facing each other. Upon closing the two 'L' shaped jaws enclose the victim's body. In February 1962 Gilbertson & Page were advertising a new live catch crow trap called the 'Hoodie'. Like the Lloyd trap circumstantial evidence suggests that it also was made by Sidebotham's.

Gilbertson and Page were still selling the Hoodie crow trap in 1988 at a price of £19.75 each. When Quadtag purchased Gilbertson & Page's business, Quadtag's 1989 catalogue still advertised the Hoodie crow trap at £19.75, but in 1990 the price was £20.75 each. Presumably, all of these traps were old stock, which had been purchased when Sidebotham's ceased trading in 1984. Interestingly, in

Quadtag's 1991 catalogue a 'spring over net trap (magpie) £24.00' was advertised for sale. Did Quadtag find a new maker for the 'Hoodie' crow trap and decided as it was a new maker that the trap should also have a new name? In 1994 this trap was still priced at £24.00 plus £4.20 VAT. In 1995 the price had risen to £26.95 plus £4.72 VAT. Listed in their 1996 catalogue, are now two sizes of this trap. The magpie size (37cm diam) is still priced at £26.95 plus £4.72 VAT while a larger size (56 cm diam) for crows is priced at £36.90 plus £6.46 VAT. Quadtag still sold these two

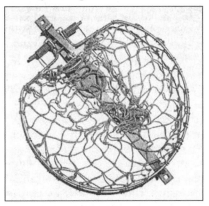

The "HOODIE" CROW TRAP

(Patent applied for)

The trap consists of an iron framework with a pan for egg or flesh bait and the usual type of spring catch which, when released, brings a net over the bird and captures it alive and unharmed. Suitable also for Jays and Magpies.

PRICE 47/6 EACH

Postage 2/9 extra.

GILBERTSON & PAGE LTD.
Tamworth Road · Hertford, Herts.

different sized traps at the same quoted prices up till they were purchased by Gamekeepa Feeds Limited in 2000. In a written reply (January 2005) to a letter enquiring about purchasing this type of trap, Gamekeepa Feeds Ltd state 'there are no leaflets available on the flip over crow trap nor do we have any illustrations of it. It is a spring-loaded trap (20 inches in diameter) with a net included in the price of £45.90 + VAT.' The maker of these later type 'Hoodie' crow traps remains unknown.

In a price list of steel traps, circa pre-1915, it states on the front cover that they are 'Makers to H.M. Commissioners of Works', and that their 'Annual output exceeds 150,000'. This same catalogue also states that customers initials would be 'stamped free on orders of 1 doz and upwards of rabbit or vermin traps'. Previously customers' initial and surname would be stamped onto the traps but this has been scored out on the catalogue and so presumably the stamping of surnames onto traps was discontinued. Sporting requisites such as leather cartridge belts, gun cases and bags etc. were also offered for sale. In an advert of 1931 Sidebotham's proclaimed, 'We are the largest trap manufacturer in the British Empire. We guarantee the quality of all our traps to be second to none'. Mentioned along with this boast were offered 'Gamekeeper' rabbit and vermin traps complete with chains in jaw sizes of 3, $3^1/_2$, 4, $4^1/_2$ and 5 inches. The 'Gamekeeper' quality * are fitted with brass pillars in addition to brass fittings. (Tongue & till). The 'Dinkum' with a wire stock and wire spring, is shown, at a price of 32/- per doz for 4 inch jawed first quality traps with brass fittings. Second quality 4 inch jawed traps with iron fittings are priced at 21/9 per doz.

In the last period of Sidebotham's years, as previously mentioned, work was subcontracted to them from the makers of Land and Range Rover vehicles, but in early 1984 the trap making building and contents were offered to the Black Country Museum Trust Ltd. at Dudley, just a short distance away. The building was re-erected on the open air site and the workshops reinstated internally as closely as to how they were left when business finally ceased. This trap making building now forms part of, with other preserved assorted buildings, a reconstructed village scene. The remaining buildings on the Rookery Street site, one of which was known commonly as the 'Monkey Muck Works' due to it previously being a manure works before being acquired by Sidebotham's, have since been demolished. The 'Monkey Muck Works' had been used as an engineering workshop by Sidebotham's, although the building is known to date from at least as early as 1886 and so may have been used as a trap making workshop prior to the reconstructed trap making single storey building, now in the museum, which was built *circa* 1912.

Below is a list of various punch marks found at Sidebotham's, and now in the reconstructed trap workshop. Note that some of these metal stamps may have been included in stock etc. when Sidebotham's acquired other trap-making businesses. Four trapmaking businesses known to have been part of Sidebotham's are noted on Sidebotham's headed notepaper. These are E. Griffiths & Co., Geo. Bellamy & Sons, James Roberts, and Joseph Collins & Sons.

In Mark Hovell's book *Rats, and How to Destroy Them*, published in 1924, he mentions that for the last forty years he has used traps manufactured by W.&G. Sidebotham's, 'And as he likes a strong trap, he has bought their 'Shave' Brand; but there is a lighter trap known as their No 6, which is less expensive, and does very well for rats, but probably is less durable.' He then mentions, 'The following prices taken from a recent list of Messrs. Sidebotham show the comparison between the sizes and qualities,' finally stating that, 'If a dozen or more traps are required they may be obtained with the purchasers initials stamped on them . . . without additional charge.'

Known Sidebotham punch marks are,

SIDEBOTHAM MAKER
SIDEBOTHAMS REGd 9
DZIN REGd
DZIN
Bi-MO REGd
SIDEBOTHAMS PAT 395462
GAMEKEEPER
APPROVED JUBY TRAP
HUMANE.

Other marks found on Sidebotham's traps include GRIPPA REGD, WANDGES, DINKUM, REGd 8, and for the Australian and New Zealand markets KOOKABURRA SPECIAL, ECHIDNA, MOA, NENE, KEA, KIWI, but at the moment the punches have not been located. The assorted list of various punches include, Roberts Pat 395462, Collins No 0, Collins No 00, Collins No 000, Collins No OX, Patent No 25348, REGd No 500389,

RdNo 780319, Gilpa, Gilpa Short, Gilpa Special, Gilpa Folder, Tonkins Special, Greens 500R L, Green's 500SL, Green's, Tinsley, Tinsley & Evers, Gray Inverness, Alex Martin Glasgow, P&R Fleming & Co., McKenzie, Cunningham, Bon-Accord, Stewart, Thistle, S Lewis & Co., C Homes, Stokes, Edward Owen & Co., W C Cavernil & Co. Ltd, James Hungerford, Eynon Fishguard, Rhydgal, P&R Phipps, Biscombes, W J Devote's, M Phillips, Hold Lac it, Worksop Manor, Styx, E G Price, Hiatt B-ham, Brand-on, Premier, Sharaff, Hero, Heap, Victor, Maywick, Amir, Hennessy, KWAC, County, Sweno, Woodrows, Shuker, Angove, Driscoe, M'dale.

Initials only:
K.B&A, N.C.D&M, A.E.C, D.C.L, G.B.O&Co LTD, W.W.A.F.C, J.G.&Co, F.H.&Co.
MADE IN ENGLAND, FABRIQUE EN ANGLETERRE, BEST, WARRANTED, TESTED, PATENT, XX.

Numbers only:
06, 29, 33, 44, 51, 52, 101, 101A, S120, 200, 200B, 201C, 402, 500, 500R, 500S, 912, 919, 2nd.

THE HUMANE TOOTHLESS VERMIN AND RABBIT TRAPS.

These toothless traps have been introduced to reduce suffering. They can also be fitted with rubber jaws which will further reduce pain.

The " Shave " toothless real Dorset vermin or rabbit traps, brass fittings, complete with chains.
Dozen .. 33/6

The " Shave " rubber jaw humane real Dorset rabbit traps, brass fittings, complete¹ with chains.
Dozen 38/6

Sent direct from makers. Carriage paid 2 dozen lots England and Wales.

ARMY & NAVY STORES LTD. CATALOGUE 1939-40

HARRY CRAVEN (LEFT) AND TED TONKS HOLDING
18 INCH JAWED LION TRAPS MADE AT W.&G. SIDEBOTHAM'S
OF WEDNESFIELD (*URALIA PRESS, WOLVERHAMPTON*)

Wednesfield Traps

Ted Tonks

I worked at Sidebotham's trap works in Wednesfield for thirty seven years. It was the last trap works to close, and they have now moved most of it to the Black Country Museum. Mind you, they can't rebuild it exactly as it was – it would be too dangerous! I can remember machines driven by belts that were so low that you had to stoop to get under them. It was quite a primitive place, and most of the workshops had earth floors. Occasionally a building was being demolished and the bosses obtained some second hand bricks with which to brick the floor, but I will always remember it as a hot dirty place with earth floors.

Trapmaking was very much a family business – if a father worked there, he would be followed by his sons, and daughters. This was also true for the bosses: The 'old man', William Sidebotham, had three sons, George, Harold and Arthur, who all went into the business. There was no snobbishness in those days, and we all lived together in the village of Wednesfield and were involved in the life of the community.

When I was a boy I worked for an electroplating firm in New Street, but through the Chapel, I got to know Harold Sidebotham. He was a Sunday School teacher, and we started a scout troop and a youth club. About 1924, when I was sixteen, I left the electroplating shop and went to work for Harold at Sidebotham's Trap Works. I began by doing 'odd jobs', and for forty eight hours I was paid ten shillings a week, but the idea was that I should learn all the jobs in the trap trade. When fully trained I would be able to become a foreman when one of the elderly men left.

There were two shops at Sidebotham's: one for making 'common traps', for export to countries like Africa, Australia and New Zealand, and one for making 'best traps', for catching otters and hawks etc., which were sold to the farmers. The 'best traps' had brass fittings, so that they could be set underwater if necessary, and they would not rust. Farmers and rat-catchers used to come to the works to buy these traps direct from us.

In the trap trade there are all sorts of jobs that have to be learned, such as forging, hardening and tempering, and we had to be able to work with the old hand bellows for doing intricate work. One rare example of 'modernisation' at Sidebotham's was that, if we wanted to do rush work, to forge the big springs that went in the big ovens, we had little blowers to add heat to the breeze on our hearths.

To temper the springs, after we had shaped them, and hardened them, we had to take them to a big oven where a dozen were heated at a time. As we put the springs into the oven we dipped a bit of fish oil on them. The art was not to make them red hot. We would see the flame, and suddenly it would burst – at that point we withdrew the springs and threw them on the floor to cool off.

After they had cooled, we had to test them, to see if they would be able to close the large jaws of the traps. Obviously, we had to be careful when testing traps. Even with the little hawk traps it was possible to trap your own thumbs, and someone would have to come and let you out! On the jaws of the large animal traps there were teeth, and some of the lion traps had spikes riveted to the jaws as well. We used to make these for Haile Selasie of Ethiopia, and I made the last six dozen exported from Sidebotham's. It took me four months to make them, as all the springs had to be hardened and tempered by hand.

In the big shop, the girls worked on the presses that bent the jaws to shape, and the men generally worked at the benches and forges assembling the traps. Every finished trap was inspected by the foreman. The trapmakers generally worked by their hearths, but one old chap worked an Oliver. There was a great deal of skill in making traps, and they had to be just right – even so, they were rough-finished, not all polished up and decorated to exhibition standard. Although it was hard work, I enjoyed it because there was a satisfaction in making something if you knew that it did its job well.

After about eight years I was considered good enough to do 'best work', and that's what I wanted to do. They offered me the foreman's job in the 'common work' shop, but I turned it down because I wanted to make 'best traps'. It was a good trade to be in. At twenty-one I was earning £3/2/6, and a year later I was earning an extra 5/-, which was a lot of money in those days. There weren't many folk earning £3 a week in those days, but we could earn that money by doing piecework, and people in the trap trade kept to themselves.

We earned every halfpence of our wages. We started at eight and finished at six, and never even stopped for lunch. I kept my lunch in my pocket and took a bite when the foreman wasn't looking. After the age of twenty-one you were allowed to smoke, but you weren't allowed to keep the cigarette in your mouth. After four and a half hours work on a Saturday I would go to Harold Sidebotham's home in Long Knowle to cut his lawn, after which I was given dinner in his house. Then I would run back to my house, change me, and rush to the football match. Some of the girls, after completing a day's work, went cleaning in 'The Smack' – the cinema in Rookery Street, that was looked after by Joe Purshouse, who, by day, was in charge of the Machine Shop.

But we also experienced hard times in the thirties. Sometimes we only worked two days a week, or were laid-off completely for a week. If a small order came in perhaps just three or four men would be called in to complete it. I was on the Means Test for five years. Sometimes work was more likely to pick up during the summer than the winter, especially when rabbits were more numerous. For some reason work picked up just before the War, and during the War itself we made traps for the Ministry of Supply. Traps were catching rabbits and rabbits were food, and if the rabbits were killed off, more food was saved!

I went in the Forces for five years, but after the War, I returned to Sidebotham's for eight or nine years, until I left after a row with one of the bosses. After I left, the trap trade declined, and myxomatosis finally killed off the trade in rabbit traps. Now we are not allowed to make traps, and the trade has vanished. Yet I can remember the time when we sent rabbit traps out to Australia in their hundreds. They were packed in tanks, supplied to us by the Globe Tank Factory, on Cannock Road, and these were used in Australia as water tanks.

Wednesfield was once dominated by the trap trade, and by the key-making trade. There was Roberts', of Victoria Road, who made common work, Marshall's in the town itself, and Beech's and Adey's in the High Street, and Henry Lane's, down by the canal bridge, that made exhibition standard traps. People may not like the idea of trapping animals, but rats, rabbits, and even moles, were a pest to the farmer, and our traps did a useful job.

TED TONKS WITH FINISHED AND UNFINISHED 18 INCH
JAWED LION TRAPS MADE AT W&G SIDEBOTHAM'S OF
WEDNESFIELD (*URALIA PRESS, WOLVERHAMPTON*)

ESTABLISHED 1865.

GRAISLEY WORKS,
WEDNESFIELD.

TRAP COMPLETE.

SPRING OF TRAP.

W. SIDEBOTHAM,
Patentee and Sole Maker of the "ECLIPSE" PATENT RABBIT TRAP.

For durability, facility in setting, and for cheapness unsurpassed in the market.

Spring can be removed, if broken, and re-fitted with new one in one minute—no Rivetting whatever. Lever is level with jaw, and can be more easily covered than the old-fashioned trap.

Manufacturer of all kinds of Steel Traps for Vermin, Game, and Wild Animals.

ALSO MAKER OF THE "STAR AND CRESCENT" BRAND OF RABBIT TRAP.

FOR HOME AND FOREIGN MARKETS.   LIST OF PRICES SUPPLIED ON APPLICATION.

HULLEY'S DIRECTORY 1889-90 ADVERT

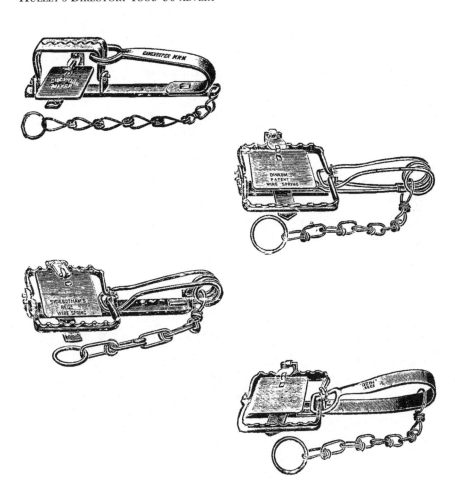

VARIOUS TYPES OF SIDEBOTHAM'S TRAPS – TOP LEFT, EXTENDED/PROJECTING STOCK; BOTTOM LEFT WIRE SPRING; TOP RIGHT, 'DINKUM' WIRE SPRING & WIRE STOCK; BOTTOM RIGHT, 'DZIN' LIGHT FOLDING SPRING TRAP.

Sidebotham's Patent Double=Action Trigger.

Two chances to one . . .

The Double-action trigger has the two chances, and the ordinary trigger has the one.

UP or down . . .

the Bait-plate may be moved, but in either case the Spring controlling the Jaws is released

Fitted to all traps in this List at same prices as ordinary traps.

THE ILLUSTRATIONS ON THIS PAGE AND THE FOLLOWING
PAGES ARE FROM A PRE-1915 SIDEBOTHAM'S CATALOGUE

LION, TIGER, or BEAR TRAPS.
DOUBLE SPRINGS (FLAT OR BOW).   SPIKED JAWS.   AXLE BRIDGE.

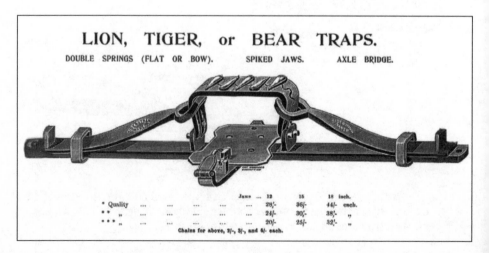

						Jaws ...	12	15	18 inch.
* Quality	...	...	...	...	...		28,-	36/-	44/- each.
* * „		...	...	...	...	...	24/-	30/-	38/- „
* * * „	...	...	...	...	...	...	20/-	25/-	32/- „
			Chains for above, 2/-, 3/-, and 4/- each.						

Pegs or Stakes.
FOR RABBIT TRAPS.

Iron, Plain 1/6 ; Twisted 2/6 per doz.
Hard Wood, 2/- per doz.

Rat Traps.

BEST QUALITY.   ROUND JAWS.   SHARP TEETH.

4½-in. Jaws...   ...   .   9/- per doz.

Complete with Chains.

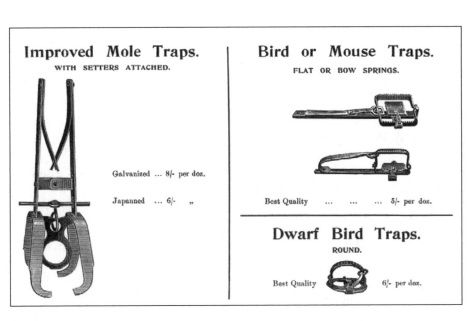

Improved Mole Traps.
WITH SETTERS ATTACHED.

Galvanized ... 8/- per doz.

Japanned ... 6/- „

Bird or Mouse Traps.
FLAT OR BOW SPRINGS.

Best Quality   ...   . 5/- per doz.

Dwarf Bird Traps.
ROUND.

Best Quality   6/- per doz.

Real Dorset Rabbit Traps.

BRASS MOUNTS AND GALVANIZED PLATES.

		Jaws 3"...	4	4½	5 inch.
*	Quality	12/-	21/-	24/-	29'- per doz.
* *	„	16/-	16/-	19/-	22/- „
* * *	„	...	12/-	15/-	18/- „

Complete with Best Chains.

Dorset Jaw Run Traps.

		Jaws ...	2½	3 inch.
*	Quality, Real Dorset, Brass Mounts	...	11/-	12/- per doz.
* *	„ Brass Catch	... ...	9/6	10/6 „
* * *	„	...	8/-	8/6 „

Complete with Best Chains.

Ordinary Rabbit Traps.

PLAIN OR GROOVED JAWS.

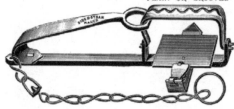

		Jaws ...	4	4½	5 inch.
"A 1"	Quality	...	16/-	18/6	21'- per doz.
"A 2"	„	...	13/-	15/-	17/- „
"A 3"	„	...	10/-	12/-	14/- „

Complete with Best Chains.

Hawk or Pole Traps.

WITH OR WITHOUT TEETH.

		Diameter ...	4½	5	6 inch.
*	Quality, Brass Mounts	... ...	21.-	25/-	35/- per doz.
* *	„	... ...	16/-	20/-	30/- „
* * *	„	... .	15.-	18/-	25/- „

Chains (if required) 1/6 or 2/6 per doz.

SMITH, Samuel. Wednesfield. Year 1841
Steel trap maker, 1841.

SMITH, Thomas. Wednesfield. Year 1841
Steel trap maker, High Street, 1841.

SPITTLE, Joseph. Wednesfield. Year 1827-1835
Vermin trap maker, 1827
Trap maker for rats, vermin etc. 1834.
In the same year also listed as a Hinge

Manufacturer.
Trap maker, Steel, 1835.

TAFFLEY, William. Wednesfield. Year 1876-1884
Steel trap maker and Shopkeeper, 1876, 1880, 1884.
It is interesting to note that a William Henry Taffley was a co-patentee with Boddis (Old Hill) Ltd, of an unusual trap that was patented in 1914. He is credited as being the inventor.

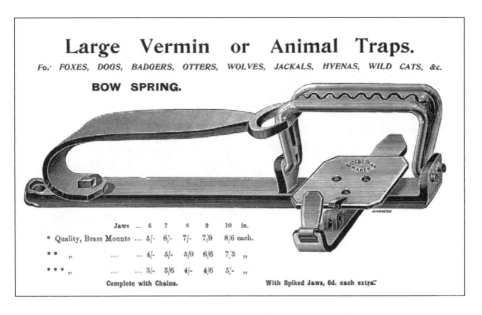

Large Vermin or Animal Traps.

FLAT SPRING.

Prices same as Bow Spring (see opposite page).

Large Vermin or Animal Traps.

Fo.· *FOXES, DOGS, BADGERS, OTTERS, WOLVES, JACKALS, HYENAS, WILD CATS, &c.*

BOW SPRING.

		Jaws	...	6	7	8	9	10	in.
*	Quality, Brass Mounts	...	5/-	6/-	7/-	7/9	8/6	each.
**	,,	...	..	4/-	5/-	5/9	6/6	7/3	,,
***	,,	...	...	3/-	3/6	4/-	4/6	5/-	,,

Complete with Chains.   With Spiked Jaws, 6d. each extra.

TOMKYS, Edward. Wednesfield. Year 1827
Steel trap maker, 1827.

TOMKYS, Charles. Wednesfield. Year 1833-1835
Rat trap maker, 1833 (Name spellt Tomkys)
Trap maker, Steel, 1835 (Name spellt Tonkys).

TOMKYS, George. Wednesfield. Year 1834-1849
Trap maker for rats, vermin etc. 1834
Rat trap maker, 1838, 1839
Steel trap maker 1841, 1842, 1845, 1849.

TOMKYS, John. Wednesfield. Year 1833-1842
Rat trap maker. & Victualler, The New Inn, 1833

DOUBLE SPRING (Flat, Bow, or Folding)

Large Vermin or Animal Traps.

OVAL JAWS.

Prices same as Square Jaws (see opposite page).

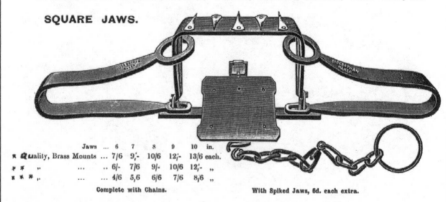

DOUBLE SPRING (Flat, Bow, or Folding)

Large Vermin or Animal Traps.

For FOXES, DOGS, BADGERS, OTTERS, WOLVES, JACKALS, HYENAS, WILD CATS, &c.

SQUARE JAWS.

Jaws	6	7	8	9	10 in.
⚹ Quality, Brass Mounts	7/6	9/-	10/6	12/-	13/6 each.
⚹ ⚹ „	.. 6/-	7/6	9/-	10/6	12/- „
⚹ ⚹ ⚹ „	... 4/6	5,6	6/6	7/6	8/6 „

Complete with Chains.

With Spiked Jaws, 6d. each extra.

Steel rat trap maker, 1838
Rat trap maker & Beer Retailer, 1839
Trap maker, Steel, 1841, 1842.

**TOMKYS, Samuel. Wednesfield.
Year 1827-1851**
Rat trap maker, 1827
Trap maker for rats, vermin etc. 1834
Rat trap maker 1838 1839
In the 1841 Census records, Luke
Hammersley who was aged about 15
years, was described as a trap maker's
apprentice to Samuel Tomkys.
Trap maker, 1845
Trap maker & Beer Retailer, 1849
Trap maker & Bull's Head, 1850
Trap maker, 1851.

**TOMKYS, Mrs M. Wednesfield. Year
1854**
Trap maker, 1854

TOMKYS, Thomas (Senior). Wednesfield. Year 1827-1855
Vermin trap maker, 1827
Trap maker for rats, vermin etc., 1834
Trap maker, Steel, 1835
Rat trap maker, 1838, 1839
Trap maker, Steel, 1841, 1842.
In the 1841 Census records for the High Street, it states that he had two apprentices, George Gough, aged 20 and Henry Light (?) aged about 13.
Trap maker, 1845, 1849, 1850, 1851, 1854, 1855.
Note: Different surname spelling. Tonkys 1835, 1841 * 1842.

TOMKYS, Thomas (Junior). Wednesfield. Year 1841-1855
Trap maker, Steel, 1841, 1842 (High Street)
Trap maker, 1851, 1855.
Note: Different surname spelling Tonks, also the Y is missing 1841, 1842.

TOMLINSON, Joseph. Wednesfield. Year 1849-1876
Trap maker, 1849
Steel trap maker, 1861
Vermin trap maker, High Street, 1865, 1868, 1872
Vermin trap manufacturer, High Street, 1874, 1876.
Note: See also, J Tomlinson, Birmingham.

TOMLINSON, William. Wednesfield. Year 1827-1835
Rat trap maker, 1827. 1833
Trap maker for rats, vermin etc. 1834
Trap maker, Steel, 1835

TOMLINSON, Samuel. Wednesfield Heath. Year 1874
Trap maker, Heath Street, Wednesfield Heath Town, 1874.

TOMLYNSON, Thomas, Wednesfield. Year 1838-1841
Rat trap maker, 1838
In the 1841 Census record, he was at Wood End and aged about 30 years.

TONKS, John (Senior). Wednesfield.
Year 1827-1865
Steel trap maker, 1827 *
Vermin trap maker, 1827 *
* Note: both of these entries were listed separately.
Trap maker for rats, vermin etc., 1834
Trap maker, Steel, 1835, 1841, 1842, 1845
'Albion' and Steel trap maker, 1849, 1850
Trap maker, 1851, 1855
Steel trap maker and 'Albion Inn' 1861
Beer Retailer and vermin trap maker, New Street, 1865.

TONKS, A. Wednesfield. Year 1931
Trap maker, Steel, 322, Wolverhampton Road, New Cross, 1931.

TONKS, Joseph. Wednesfield. Year 1825-1957
According to a trap catalogue this business was established in 1825.
Steel trap maker, 1872
Vermin trap manufacturer, New Street, 1876
Manufacturer of all kinds of steel traps, (established 1825) New Street, 1880-1896.
In a Trade Mark application, the address is stated as 9, New Street in 1897.
Steel trap maker, New Cross, 1904.
Between 1916-1924 the address is listed as 324, New Cross, Wednesfield Heath. Wednesfield Heath, otherwise Heath Town, became part of the town of Wolverhampton in 1927, so in 1928 the address is listed as 324 New Cross, Heath Town, Wolverhampton. Between 1948-1957 the address remains the same with the telephone number being Fallings Park 31069.
Identification/Trade Mark:
Eagle's talon (1897).
Registered Design:
Tonk's made a wire spring 4 inch jawed gin trap called The 'Triumph' which is the wire spring trap with the Registered Design Number 701,488.
Miscellaneous Information:
Tonks also made the 'Plate Protector'

patented by John Thomas Good, who was a farmer of 'Hudor' Glenthompson, shire of Ararat Victoria, Australia. His patent application is dated 15th May 1902, and was accepted on 17th July 1902, becoming Patent No 11,223. In April 1904, J.F. Good, Rabbit Trap Importer, of 396, Flinders Lane, Melbourne, Australia was advertising in the Farmer & Grazier 'Rabbit traps fitted with Good's patent attachment can be set in the driest sand without paper. They never get clogged. Catch every time. No spring traps. Prices, Griffiths 14/-, Roberts 11/6.' Tonks seemingly only started making these traps with this attachment around 1920-25 according to one of their catalogues. Traps are known to be stamped with KIWI on the bow spring, which have the 'secure welded or unbreakable connecting link' chain attachment fitted to them.

TONKS, George. Wednesfield. Year 1841

In the 1841 Census records for Rookery Street, George and Ann Tonks are aged about 51. He is recorded as a Trap Maker with three apprentices. They were Henry Townsend, aged about 18 years, William Walters, aged about 17, and Charles Cully, aged about 10.

TONKS, Samuel. Wednesfield. Year 1841-1842

Trap maker, Steel, 1841, 1842.

TOTTEY, John (Senior). Wednesfield. Year 1827-1860

Rat trap maker, 1827

Trap maker for rats, vermin etc. March End, 1834

Trap maker, Steel, 1835, 1841, 1842

Trap maker, Steel, March End, Neachill, 1845

Steel trap maker, 1849, 1850, 1854, 1860.

In 1841, at March End, in the household of John Tottey, was listed as a trap maker's apprentice, John Williams who was 20.

TONKS' TESTED TRAPS.

Manufacturers of Rabbit Traps, etc.,
with 100 years' experience.

"X J. TONKS" the oldest brand of Rabbit Trap sold in Australasia.

TERMS:

List Discount	%	Cash Discount	%
Delivery		Carriage	

Prices will be kept at present level as long as possible, but we reserve the right of alteration, if necessary, owing to exceptional fluctuations in Prices of Material, Labour or other expenses.

Best Weldless Embossed Spring Bird Traps.

Well made, serviceable, and good.   For catching small Birds or Vermin.

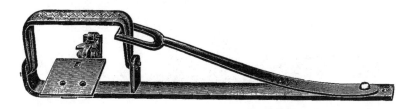

Size 2¼-inch jaw   ....   per doz.

Stakes for Rabbit Traps, Round or Square.

per doz.

TONKS' Real Dorset Rabbit Traps and Chains.

With Galvanized Plates and Brass Catches, these admit of much finer adjustment when setting, and are almost exclusively used by English Keepers and Trappers.

Made in three qualities.

Quality.	Size.			Price.	
"X J. TONKS"	4-inch Jaw	....	....		per doz.
"✳✳✳"	" "		....		"
"✳✳"	" "		....		"

"X J. TONKS" Celebrated Rabbit Traps.

The oldest brand of Rabbit Trap sold in Australia, and the Best hand forged Bar Steel Spring, with bevelled jaws, and manufactured of best wrought iron throughout. Patent unbreakable barrel swivel Chains. $2\frac{3}{4}$-inch or 3-inch plates with 4-inch jaws.

Price   per doz.

The strength of this brand has lately been increased with much stronger Spring, base and jaws, and is no doubt the best Trap of this well-known kind ever offered.

TONKS' Rabbit Traps.

✳ ✳ ✳

Well known second quality Rabbit Trap. Well made, with forged bar steel Spring and bevelled jaws, 2¾-inch plates and patent unbreakable swivel Chains.

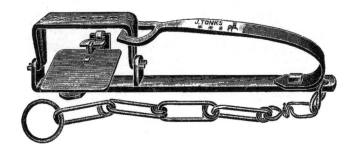

Quality.	Size.	Price.
" J. TONKS."	4-inch jaw.	per doz.
✳ ✳ ✳		

TONKS' "⟨✳ J. TONKS" Rabbit Traps.

The best brand of Star and Crescent Rabbit Traps sold in Australasia.

A thoroughly reliable light Trap, the strength of the Spring has recently been increased, and is the best Trap that can be offered of its kind.

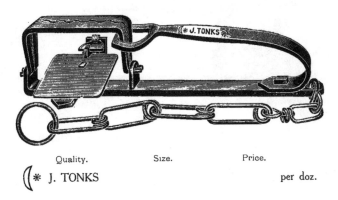

Quality.	Size.	Price.
⟨✳ J. TONKS		per doz.

Owing to special machining of Jaw ends, and the square end of Spring Bow, this Trap has a greater space inside Jaws, and the Rabbit is less likely to be thrown or knocked out, and consequently gives a very low percentage of sprung empty Traps.

TONKS' Reg'd. Wire Spring Rabbit Traps.

The Best on the Market.

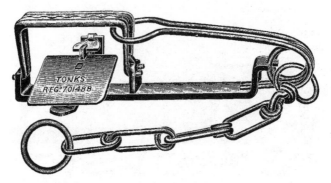

Quality.	Size.	Price.
TONKS' Reg'd. 701,488.	4-inch Jaw.	per doz.

The improved design for attaching the Spring to the base of the Trap, making it more secure, and striking straight without interfering with the resiliency of the Spring.

Springs are all manufactured by ourselves, and are of the very best tempered Steel Wire obtainable.

TONKS' Improved Embossed Weldless Spring Rabbit Traps.

Grooved Jaws.   Cheap.   Serviceable and good.

Quality.		Size.		Price.
No. 1.	....	4-inch Jaw	....	per doz.
No. 2.	....	" "	....	"
No. 3.	....	" "	....	"

With Patent unbreakable Chain and Swivel.   Spring of best bar Spring Steel.

TONKS' Rabbit Traps with Patent Cover.

This is a thoroughly serviceable and reliable improvement. I have manufactured these Traps now for several years in large quantities, and they are giving entire satisfaction.

They well repay the extra cost in time saved in covering in the ordinary way, and being sure Catchers save a lot of annoyance from the sprung empty Trap.

Made in one quality only—the Best.

Quality—X J. TONKS.   Size 4-inch Jaw.   Price   per doz.

Any of the **Rabbit Traps** shown in this list can be made without extra cost with **Projecting End on Base of Trap** which prevents jaws from being knocked or loosened, which sometimes happens when traps are accidently dropped in warehouse or store.

TONKS' Double Spring Dog Traps.

Strong Best Hand Forged Bar Steel Springs and Wrought Iron Bevelled Jaws.

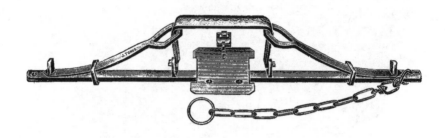

Quality.	Sizes	6	7	8	9	10-inch jaw.
" J. TONKS "						
✳ ✳						
	Price					per doz.

TONKS' Strong Dorset or Grooved Jaw Rabbit Traps.

Specially Manufactured for the New Zealand Markets.

With Secure Welded or Unbreakable Connecting Link.

Quality.	Size.	Price.
XXX	4-inch jaw.	per doz.
XX		

TOTTEY, John (Junior). Wednesfield. Year 1841
In the 1841 Census records John Tottey of High Street is aged about 25 and described as a rat trap maker. At the same address is also another rat trap maker Thomas Smith who was 20.

TOWNSEND, Henry. Wednesfield. Year 1841-1855
In 1841, Henry Townsend was an apprentice to George Tonks of Rookery Street.
Listed as a trap maker in 1849, 1851, 1855.

TOWNSEND, William. Wednesfield. Year 1874
Trap maker, Graisley Lane, 1874.

TURNER, John Bowen. Wednesfield. Year 1876
Steel trap maker, 1876.

WARIL (?) Bary. Wednesfield. Year 1841
In the 1841 Census records for Wood End, Bary Waril(?) was about 40 years old and described as a trap maker.

WARD, Benjamin. Wednesfield. Year 1834
Trap maker for rats, vermin etc. 1834.

WARD, Richard. Wednesfield. Year 1841-1904.
In 1841, when aged about 14, he was an apprentice to Matthew Hames at Church Street.
Steel trap maker, Church Street, 1865
Steel trap maker, 1872, 1876
Steel trap maker, High Street, 1880, 1884
Steel trap maker, Church Street, 1888, 1892, 1896
Ward, Richard & Sons, Steel trap makers, Church Street, 1904.

WATKINS, John. Wednesfield. Year 1841-1851
In the 1841 Census records, John Watkins is listed at the household of George and Mary Marshall, who was a trap maker at March End. John Watkins was listed as a trap maker journeyman, meaning one whose apprenticeship was completed and also one who worked by the day for pay. He is stated as being aged 20, but in the 1841 Census ages were rounded down to the nearest five years, therefore making his year of birth instead of 1821, between approximately 1816 and 1821, probably 1818. He is also recorded as being born in the county (Staffordshire) but unfortunately he has not been located. He is next found in the Wednesfield Trade Directories for the years 1845 and 1849 listed as a trap maker, but after these dates he disappears completely in Britain. However, in the American publication *The Steel Trap in North America* by Richard Gerstell, on Page 172 he mentions a John Watkins and says, 'The earliest written record I have found identifying Watkins as a trap maker is an entry in the 1850-51 Boston (Massachusetts) Directory: Watkins. John, Steel Trap and Hinge Maker, 75 West Dedham. The name John Watkins does not appear in the 1855 Directory. . .' Gerstell goes on to say, 'I have examined more than 100 traps bearing his name (and) all the Watkins traps I have seen are of intermediate size. Based on key design features the numerous traps produced in Watkin's shop fall into three broad groups. The traps in the first group are generally similar to devices commonly referred to as English Rabbit Gins.' The photograph accompanying the text shows a normal bow spring gin trap. He continues, 'Practically all Watkins traps bear the maker's name and a size number, but only a few show their place of manufacture. The lettered die stamps used in marking the devices read I. WATKINS, J. WATKINS, and BOSTON/MASS. Numbers 4, 5, 6, 7, 8, 9 are used.'
According to all this information he most likely sailed from Liverpool, Eng-

land, which was his nearest main port, sometime around 1849-50, arriving in Boston (?) Massachusetts where he took up residency and probably general blacksmith work before resuming his trap making occupation. Due to not being listed in the 1855 Trade Directory, maybe after a few years, once he had accumulated some money and a better knowledge of the country he had decided to travel further inland to be closer to a regular supply of steel, as at Wednesfield, plus his potential customers the fur trappers.

Obviously, there was more than one John Watkins in Boston, as Gerstell records: 'The name John Watkins first appears in the Boston city directory for 1843. In 1845, he is identified as a locksmith. . .' Note that John Watkins the trap maker is recorded as being found listed in the 1845 trade directory for Wednesfield, therefore he can't be on both sides of the Atlantic Ocean at the same time. The year 1850 is not the only year he made traps in America, because Gerstell thinks that he produced traps, 'perhaps for ten or twelve years afterwards'. There is also no proof that he only made the English-style of gin trap in 1850, while living in America. Gerstell states: 'Based on overall design and certain structural details, it seems likely that Watkins, with his English background, first made gin-type traps, then progressed to the double spring devices with plain riveted jaw posts, and finally turned out in largest numbers the bolted-post models preferred by most North American trappers. However, proof of this is lacking.' Indeed, a good trap maker skilled in his trade would be able to reproduce any trap, or part of it, that was brought to him to repair or even copy.

According to Gerstell on page 172 of his book, he states: 'An extraordinarily large number of surviving traps bearing his name seems to indicate that he was among the major producers of his time.' All that can be said is that any style of trap stamped with his name and Boston/Mass does not pre-date the year 1850, for obvious reasons. However, any trap that is only stamped J Watkins, may or may not, have been made at Boston, but unfortunately there is no way of knowing, as Gerstell points out: 'only a few (of Watkins traps) show their place of origin'. These traps may have been made in a totally different location, if he decided to move nearer to his potential customers, the fur trappers, or he may simply have decided to discontinue stamping his traps Boston/Mass, while still residing and making traps there. It is possible that the John Watkins who is recorded as a locksmith is a relative of John Watkins the trap maker. Due to their possible relationship, and already being established in Boston, this would give the trap maker a destination to emigrate to, and more importantly contacts there. Questions remain as to whether he stayed in the area, or moved on. However, the Boston directory of 1850-51 records him as a 'steel trap and hinge maker'. Did he only make traps for a certain period of time before concentrating on making hinges? A growing population in Boston would need hinges for doors and gates etc. His possible 'relative' was already established as a locksmith, and the two separate trades would fit nicely together as a joint family-type business. Indeed, Gerstell again records that: 'The name John Watkins does not appear in the 1855 directory, but a statistical summary of a Massachusetts industrial census taken that year includes the following entry –

'Establishments for manufacture of butts, or hinges, 1. Brass or composition butts or hinges, Made 1,000 dozen, value $5,000.00. Capital invested $3,000.00. Employees 7.' It is most likely that John Watkins had made some money out of his trap making, but perhaps decided to invest his capital in a more lucrative partnership with his already well-established locksmith 'relative' making hinges etc.

WHITE, William. Wednesfield. Year 1841-1864
In the 1841 Census he was at Lichfield Street and aged about 20.
Directory listings, Steel trap maker 1845, 1849, 1850, 1851, 1855, 1860, 1864.

WHITE, Thomas. Wednesfield. Year 1818
Listed as Rat trap maker, 1818.

WILLIAMS, John. Wednesfield. Year 1841-1966
In 1841 John Williams was an apprentice trap maker to John Tottey Senior of March End.
Trap maker, Wood End, 1851
Steel trap maker, 1854, 1855, 1860, 1861, 1864
Trap manufacturer, Taylor Street 1865
Steel trap maker, 1872
Steel trap maker, Taylor Street, 1876, 1880, 1884.

WILLIAMS, John & Son Steel Trap Makers, Taylor Street, 1888, 1892, 1896, 1904
Steel trap makers, 43 Taylor Street, 1916, 1921, 1924, 1928, 1931, 1932
Steel trap makers, 43 Taylor Street (Tel. Fallings Park 31240) 1936, 1940

WILLIAMS, John & Son, Crescent Works, Taylor Street, 1948, 1951, 1955, 1957, 1959, 1966.
Trade Marks/Miscellaneous Information:
Maker of the Terror and Ferret 'Snap Trap' rat traps. Williams famous '50

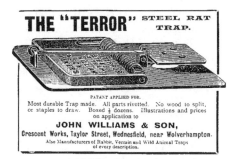

1905 ADVERT

1920 ADVERT

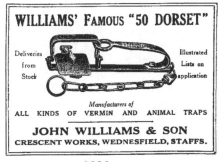

1929 ADVERT

1930 ADVERT FOR HERCULES TRAP
REGISTERED DESIGN NO. 714556

Dorset' bow spring gin trap. An improved wire spring gin trap known as the 'Hercules' (Rd 714556). In a Patent application dated 1st June 1905 and accepted on 15th March 1906 (Patent No 11,476 The Terror rat trap) Joseph Williams Senior and Junior were trading as John Williams & Son, Crescent Works, Taylor Street, Wednesfield. The Terror rat trap was being supplied by S. Young & Sons (Misterton) Ltd. in 1934 at a price of 12 shillings per dozen, which included carriage paid. Slightly later the prices were, for rats;12/9 dozen; 7/- half dozen; smaller quantities 1/6 each. For mice 5/- dozen; 3/- half dozen; smaller quantities 7d each. Post Paid. In a catalogue of theirs, dated 1st September 1940, the illustrated Terror humane steel rat trap was now being offered for sale at 16/- (sixteen shillings) a dozen; 8/6 half dozen; smaller quantities 1/9 each; three 4/6 post paid. They were also advertising for sale the Terror Mouse trap, but omitted to include a price, or an illustration! Luckily though, in another earlier catalogue of Young's *circa* 1937, Terror mouse traps were being offered for sale at 4/3d dozen; 2/4d half dozen, and small lots at $5^1/_2$d each all post paid .There was also an illustration with the prices. Unfortunately, this illustration shows a German-made (*circa* 1932 to 1937) metal mouse trap which is also called the Terror.

An improved version of the Terror rat trap, called the Ferret, appears in adverts in 1917 and 1920.

An unusual trap made by this business was patented by Harry Carne, Higher Town, Truro in 1925. His provisional application date for the patent was 10th February 1925, No.3688/25, with the complete specification being quickly accepted on 5th November 1925, and so becoming Patent No 242,133. This trap has stamped on it the initials

J.W.&S and also the patent number 242,133. Some traps also have the name Bantam stamped on it.

Another unusual design of trap made by this business was the Phelp's Patent Trap. This trap was provisionally patented on 27th May 1932 (No. 15,035/32) and again with a slight improvement one month later. (No.18,118/32) by Robert Melliar Phelps of 88, Sidwell Street, Exeter, in the county of Devon. The patent was accepted on 24th August 1933 and given the Patent No. 397,268.

This trap is basically a 'spring powered leg or foot snare'. The Mark I design had four projecting arms, one at each corner of the box which enclosed the trap plate. The Mark II version has what look like 'wire jaws' on top of the box, but are in fact guide bars for the chain noose. Both models have a detachable wire spring. This rabbit trap could 'be made ineffective during the day by leaving the safety catch in position over the arm of the spring, at dusk push catch to one side and trap is at once ready for its work through the hours of darkness. A fox or dog escape can easily be arranged, if desired, by cutting out a piece of chain where shown in Fig 4, and replacing by cord, gut or other suitable material. A fox will soon find this and bite free, but it is out of the reach of rabbits.' The setting instructions state: 'Dig out exactly as for the gin and place box in jump.' However, as it was designed to be used out in the open, rather than being placed in a hole in a rabbit burrow, the patent papers state: 'This construction does not allow of the trap being buried in the ground as the spring could not open sideways against the pressure of the surrounding earth.'

An interesting letter appeared in *Shooting Times & Country Magazine* during August 1978, from C.A. Swan, Ministry of Agriculture, Fisheries and Food, Worplesdon, Surrey, who was replying to a reader's letter and photograph, regarding an unknown trap. In his reply, he states: 'The 'unknown trap' depicted in your letters column is the treadle section of a Phelps fox trap. The hinged wires that appear at first to be jaws, hold a fine link chain noose which, when the treadle is hit by the foot of an animal, is thrown upwards and drawn tight around the animal's leg. The spring (not shown) that activates the noose is compressed and held under tension by the tiller in the way that the jaws of most spring traps, including the gin, are set. On release, the spring becomes detached from the treadle reducing the possibility of injury to the animal, by leaving the treadle section in the ground. The method of setting is to encircle a pegged-down bait with several traps, with the intention of catching a fox as it approaches the bait. I undertook trials of this trap on behalf of the Ministry of Agriculture in 1963. The trap is ingenious and well-made but not very selective. The bait almost always attracted much less cautious animals than the fox, including dogs, badgers, cats, and corvids, especially magpies.'

The 'unknown trap' in the photograph was a Phelps Mark II. In both the Mark I and Mark II versions, the wire spring, extended in line with the box section. The later Mark III version, has a round plate and enclosing round box section, and the wire spring is attached at a right angle to it. However, it is not known when the Mark III version was made.

WILLIAMS, Joseph. Wednesfield. Year 1904-1921
Beer retailer and Trap maker, High Street, 1904.
Steel trap maker, Taylor Street, 1916, 1921
Miscellaneous Information:
Refer to John Williams above.

WOOD, William. Wednesfield Heath. Year 1838
Listed as a Rat trap maker, 1838.

WOODWARD, Charles. Wednesfield. Year 1916-1924
Steel trap maker, Bloxwich Road, 1916, 1921, 1924.

WOODWARD, Victor. Wednesfield Heath. Year 1896-1904
Steel trap maker, Heath Street, 1896, 1904.

WOOTON, Jeremiah. Wednesfield. Year 1896
Steel trap maker, North Street, 1896.

THE VILLAGE BLACKSMITH (1906)

Chapter Four

TRAP MAKERS IN OTHER AREAS

R. ADCOCK & Co. London. Year 1937-1945

Reginald Adcock of 1 Victoria Street, Westminster, London SW1 applied for a patent for his deadfall trap on 23rd June 1937 (No 17457/37) and his complete specification was accepted on 7th September 1938 becoming Patent No. 491,681. He advertised his trap in the *Game & Gun* magazine in November 1937 by getting that magazine to test its efficiency. They 'found it to work perfectly.' Their article about this trap states, 'It would be difficult to imagine anything more simple or more deadly than the new Mortis rat trap. Made almost entirely of wood, there are no springs to rust or weaken, and instantaneous death of a

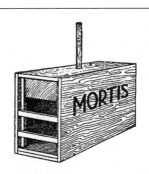

THE " MORTIS " TUNNEL RAT TRAP.

Destroys instantaneously and humanely. Constructed of wood —weather resisting, simple, safe and effective. Invaluable to keepers, farmers and sportsmen.
Price **12/6**

The " Mortis " Humane Rat Trap

DON'T let rats infest your building again this winter. Instal a "Mortis" Trap now.

The "Mortis" is the only trap that kills outright and completely conceals its victims. Rats do not become trap-shy with a "Mortis."

Refer to " Game & Gun," November, Page 745

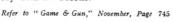

Price 17/6 delivered

Write for particulars of this new and deadly effective trap.

R. ADCOCK & CO., Westminster Chambers, 1, Victoria St. S.W.1

rat is ensured by the fall of a heavy rectangular block of wood which falls flat down into the tray which forms the base of the trap. This falling block is held up, when the trap is set, by a length of stout but pliable twisted wire, and is released immediately any rat touches the trigger plate, which occupies the whole width of the base of the trap and over one third the length. The accompanying illustration explains the system of working better than words and all that is necessary to do is to set the trap and bait the trigger plate with whatever bait is considered most suitable for the environment. We have tested this trap and found it to work perfectly and effectively, while we fancy that the older it got, the less suspicious would rats be. The only criticism which we raised was the obvious danger to cats and dogs, and to meet this criticism the makers fitted a wire guard. We have tested the trap with this guard but have found that although the guard prevents dogs and cats from actually entering the trap, it does not prevent them from inserting their paws to get hold of the bait, and a test carried out with a bit of fish as bait proved that two dogs and one cat immediately put their paws in to try to scrape the fish towards the edge of the trap. If the trap had been properly set this action would, of course, have sprung the trap and almost certainly resulted in a crushed paw. Provided this danger is realised and the trap is set only in such places which are not frequented by or open to dogs and cats, we can recommend this trap with every confidence. A battery of these traps in a warehouse, for example, would prove most efficacious, particularly as these traps merge in the floors and rafters, being made of wood, while usually the dead rat is completely hidden when the block falls and so there is no risk of alarming others. The 'Mortis' rat trap can be obtained from Messrs R.

Adcock & Co., 1 Victoria Street, Westminster, London, SW1, the price being 17s.6d. delivered.' A 1938 advert states that R Adcock & Co. are the manufacturers and patentees.

Another trap produced by Adcock & Co. was the Mortis tunnel rat trap which was advertised in the Army & Navy Stores Catalogue of 1939/40 at a price of 12/6d each. This trap was probably the result of the criticism of their previous trap to which they had added a wire guard.

ALBION Manufacturing, The Granary, Silfield Road, Wymondham, Norfolk NR18 9AU. Year 1885-present

This business was established in 1885,but didn't originally make traps. Only recently, *circa* the mid 1990s did this company start to manufacture live catch animal traps along with their other wire products. A few prototype live catch mole traps, with a galvanised body and vision panel along the whole top length of the trap were made. This trap is called The Mole Master and was illustrated in their 1998 brochure. While the brochure was being published it was decided that due to production problems and costs involved, it would be much simpler, cheaper and lighter to make the trap out of lengths of square plastic tubing. Therefore in early 1998, The Mole Master Mark 2 was introduced. This version is slightly different in design from the prototype, and is an oblong brown plastic trap with a clear plastic vision panel on its top side, which slides to open. As in the original prototype, the mole can enter through either end of the trap, through the non return flaps, but cannot push its way out again. The Mole Master Mark 2 version was in production for about two years when the design was again slightly changed. The Mark 3

MOLE MASTER MARK 2

MOLE MASTER MARK 3

version was now made with the clear plastic vision panel on the top of the trap being formed to overlap partly down both sides. It is also pivoted at one end , by the door 'hinge', so that it can be raised up to open instead of having to be slid open. Two types of the Mark 3 exist. The first type 'A' is the original shorter version, whilst the second type 'B' is slightly longer and is still in production. Throughout all of these changes the Mole Master name has remained unchanged as has the product code, No.ALBI-011. An experimental Mark 4, which has a 'soil box' fixed to the bottom of the Mark 3 trap has been developed, but at the moment there are no plans to commercially produce it. The idea behind this modification, is that sometimes a mole will push soil up to an obstacle that it comes across in its run, such as a trap, which then prevents it working successfully. However, if the mole pushed soil up to the door on this Mark 4 modification and keeps pushing, the soil will raise the clear plastic door, allowing the soil to be pushed further into the trap. Once clear of the doorway, the pushed soil will fall into the 'soil box', and so thereby create space for the raised door to drop down behind the entering mole and so catch the mole. This sequence of events would still happen without the 'soil box', by just lengthening the trap

considerably. From a mole trapper's point of view, the extra long trap would also be easier to place in the mole's run rather than trying to dig out a small oblong hole in the bottom of the run to allow the 'soil box' to fit in neatly.

ALLCOCK Manufacturing Company, Birkenhead. Year 1945-1960
Argyle Street, Birkenhead.
Identification / Trade Mark: KINDHART.
Allcock Manufacturing Co (a corporation organised and existing under the laws of the State of New York) 4 to 8, Argyle Street, Birkenhead, Cheshire; and Brandreth Works, Water Street, Ossining, New York; Manufacturers, registered this trade mark on 20th June 1944.
PRANG Registered by this company on 19th March 1945. Was this a spelling mistake for PRONG, which was registered a few months later on 25th June 1945?
This company produced a live catch, wire cage trap that was known as the Kindhart. This trap was intended for use against the rat and squirrel,

THE "KINDHART" RAT AND SQUIRREL TRAP.

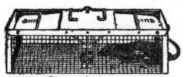

Open at both ends
Animal walks in unsuspectingly

Both ends shut
The animal is caught unhurt

The "Kindhart" Rat and Squirrel Trap will catch vermin such as Rats, Stoats, Weasels and Squirrels.

No danger to Animals, Poultry, Pigeons, Birds or Children.

Strongly made in close mesh and enamelled dark green.

Easiest trap to set,. Raise one of the doors and trap automatically sets itself. (No springs)

SIZE—20 inches long, 5½ inches wide, 5½ inches high.

Price   Post Paid.   Money back, if not satisfied.

according to the paper label attached to the top of the trap under the wire handle.

An all metal, coil spring operated, Breakback trap was also made by this company. This trap was made in both rat and mouse sized versions and had the trade mark name of Prong. The two different sized traps are both identical in colour and have a round bait plate with two bait spikes, side by side, protruding from it. The wording on the mouse trap label reads, 'The Easy Set, Prong Trade Mark, mouse trap, Model PR5, will not nip fingers, sensitive, easy setting, rustless – long lasting, made in England by Allcock M'F'G Birkenhead.' The rat trap version has slightly different wording to the mouse trap. Its label states 'The East Set, Prong Trade Mark, Rat Trap, Model PR ? (missing on label), can't nip fingers if instructions followed, easy setting – extra sensitive, can be washed to remove odours, camouflage colour scheme, all metal – rustless finish, made in England by Allcock M'F'G Co Birkenhead (inc.USA).'
Patent: Prong trap, provisional Patent No. 13108/45
Registered Design: Prong Trap, Design No. 843674
On an instruction leaflet that came

with the rat trap, the rat trap was priced at 1/11d each. On the reverse side of the same leaflet under the heading of 'Other Allcock Traps' the Prong mouse trap was priced at 10¹/₂d each whilst the Kindhart was priced at 12/6d each.

Messrs. ARLINGSTALL & Co. Warrington. Year 1896-1907.

The Keeper's Book, published in 1904, states, 'Brailsford Trap – this is a trap to catch rabbits alive, and is manufactured by Messrs Arlingstall and Co., Warrington.' It goes on to describe it as consisting of 'a wire cage, very strongly made and open at both ends, the door being kept up by a simple method of setting. There is a treadle made, and as soon as that is touched the doors close and the victim is imprisoned.' A 1907 advert shows that

1896 ADVERT

Brailsford's Wire Vermin Traps.

All Sizes, for Dogs, Cats, Rats, and all small vermin taken alive without torture.

Apply to **Mr. BRAILSFORD,**
Ightfield Kennels,
WHITCHURCH, SALOP.

Or to **Messrs. G. ARTINGSTALL & CO.,**
WARRINGTON.

these traps were also made for catching rats, cats, foxes, badgers, dogs, with prices according to size and quality ranging from 5/- (five shillings) up to 35/- packing extra. All the traps were sent direct from the manufacturers. In 1863 Richard Brailsford patented this trap being Patent No 3,008. Later, on 15th August 1903, W. Brailsford & Co, Poplar Cottage, Rossett, Wrexham, manufacturers of vermin traps in which metal predominates, registered the trade mark: W. Brailsford & Co.

BAKER, George Junior Ltd. Birmingham. Year 1923-1936

General wire workers. 192, 194 & 196 Great Hampton Row. 'Champion Wire Works'. An advert of 1923 shows a Champion folding rat trap. Patent No 11,894, and what looks to be a 'Wonder' type rat trap, both being wire cage traps.

BAKER, Joseph. Wolverhampton. Year 1849

Steel trap maker, Saint John Street, 1849. Also listed as an Iron and Steel Warehouse.

BARNES, Albert. Ulverston. Year 1909-1950s

According to a 1909 advert, Albert Barnes was the proprietor of a sporting goods shop in Market Place, Ulverston. On 29th November 1921 he applied for a patent (No 32,001/21) and this was accepted on 23rd November 1922, becoming Patent No 188,969. The patent was for a 'Wire twisting machine particularly adapted for the production of snares'. Adverts from 1923 and 1927 proclaim 'Rabbitwist' the world's best rabbit snare. Patentee Albert Barnes, 'Rabbitwist' Snare Works, Ulverston, England. Patent filed 32,001. Agents wanted'. Then in an application dated 25th October 1924 (No 25,395/24) he applied for a patent for a spring operated snare. The patent was accepted on 10th December 1925 becoming Patent No 243,872. Another patent application dated 26th September 1930 (No 28,877/30) and accepted on 28th December 1931 becoming Patent No 364,029, was basically minor improvements on his previous Patent No 243,872. The main difference is

BARNES' IMPROVED HUMANE RABBITJERK TRAP.
Regd. No. 28877.

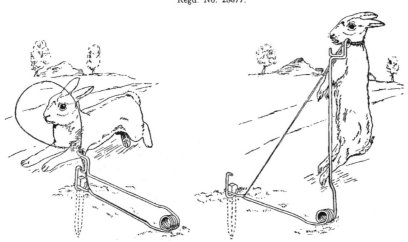

No squealing, no struggling, no pain. Instant death. The illustrations clearly show the method of use and the effect,
List No. B.T.3 Price 4/- Post 6d. Dozens, post free.

in Patent No 243,872 (1925). 'The extremity of the lower member is provided with a spike formed integrally thereon in a manner so as to be at right angles to the said member. . . The lower pointed end of the spike is adapted to enter the ground and thereby retain the device horizontally and firmly in its respective position,' whereas in Patent No 364,029 (1931) '. . . wherein the lower arm is formed with a loop through which a peg can be driven for securing the spring device to the ground.' In a Parker-Hale Ltd of Birmingham catalogue dated 1939, the price for one improved humane rabbitjerk trap is stated to be '2/6d, post 4d. Dozens, post free.' In a later 1941 catalogue of Parker-Hale's, it states 'Barnes Improved Humane Rabbitjerk Trap, Regd No 28,877' (which is the 1930 patent application number) was now being priced at 4/- each with postage costs increased to 6d. Dozens were still post free. In both the 1946 and 1947 Parker-Hale catalogues is an illustration of his 'Rabbitwist' snare, with Barnes Patent No 188,969 under it. In a 1947 Parker-Hale catalogue only the 'Rabbitwist' snare is advertised, and there is no mention of the Rabbitjerk trap. This is still the same situation in their 1950 and 1954 catalogues, so presumably production was discontinued with the outbreak of World War II. The Rabbitjerk 'powered snare' had an overall spring length of approximately 18 inches, whilst a smaller version the Ratjerk had an overall spring length of approximately 8 inches. It is not known if the Ratjerk was also made in the second version of this 'powered snare', whereby the loose peg was secured through the loop. Although the Ratjerk trap is known to exist, no reference source or illustration has been found for it at the moment.
The business was still trading under the Barnes name until the early 1950s but, with the introduction of myxomatosis around this time, there would obviously have ceased to be a demand for rabbit snares. However, in Parker-Hale's catalogue edition No 58 (1958) they are still listing 'Rabbitwist' snares, but these may just be old stock.

BETHEL RHODES & Sons. Keighley. Year 1930 – present.

Wire Works, North Street, 1936
Market Street, Keighley, 1953
Bethel Rhodes & Sons Ltd, Lawkholme Mills, Alice Street, 1988
Maker of the Monarch wire cage rat trap. They also make the 'Duffus' type of half barrel mole trap sold by Wilkinson of Burnley.

W. & J. BIRKENHEAD, Sale, Manchester Circa 1897

The full page advert for this insect trap, was found in the second edition (1897) of *Ferns and Fern Culture* by J. Birkenhead FRHS where they describe themselves as the 'inventors and manufacturers'. The first edition was published in 1892.

" Long rats, Lean rats, Skinny rats and Keen rats, Big rats, Brawny rats, Grey rats and Tawny rats."

They're all the same to the **MONARCH RAT TRAP**

½ inch mesh Galvanised after made. Beautiful silver finish, far ahead of the foreign article in durability, strength and appearance.

The MONARCH performs its functions with the thoroughness of which only a BRITISH Trap is capable—hence you can very confidently recommend it. Trade terms are generous and prices keen.

BETHEL RHODES & SONS
WIRE WORKS, NORTH STREET, KEIGHLEY

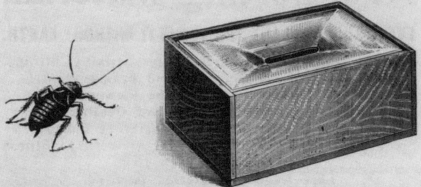
FROM FERNS AND FERN CULTURE BY J BIRKENHEAD FRHS, 2ND EDITION 1897

BLACK, George. Hatton, near Wragby. Lincolnshire. Year 1908-1926

According to the 1901 census returns for the village of Hatton, George Black states his age as 45 and his birthplace as Scopwick in Lincolnshire. He was living with his wife Rebecca and their children, Mary, John and Herbert, and his employment was a Gamekeeper. He is first mentioned in the Trade Directories in 1896 where he is listed as being Gamekeeper to the local landowner Coningsby Charles Sibthorp Esquire, of Canwick Hall, who is the sole landowner. He is next noted in the trade directories for the year 1900, as still being a

BLACK'S HAWK TRAP, 1933 ADVERT

gamekeeper for Coningsby Charles Sibthorp, but now of Sudbrooke Holme. This entry remains the same in the trade directories of 1905 and 1909. However, in 1913 he is to be found as gamekeeper to M.R. Waldo-Sibthorp. In 1919 he is still listed as being gamekeeper to M.R. Waldo-Sibthorp but now Montagu R. Waldo-Sibthorp Esq; is the sole landowner. This entry remains the same for the years of 1922 and 1926, his last listing.

Carnegie, writing in his second revised edition of his book *How to trap and Snare* circa 1910, says that this trap 'is being used on a large number of estates with great success.' Describing the trap he says, 'The trap consists of a wire cage, divided into two compartments, one above the other, the whole being about 2ft square. The lower and smaller compartment is for the confinement of a few live sparrows, which form the most attractive bait for a sparrow-hawk. Access to this compartment is gained through a small swing door at the bottom corner of the trap. The upper and larger compartment is for the hawk

to enter from the top. Nearly the whole of this includes a swing over door, which immediately closes behind the hawk, and the latter is thus securely trapped and practically uninjured. The capture is attended by no broken legs nor any suspension in mid air, as used to be the case with the pole trap.' He also points out that this trap is 'A great recommendation in the eyes of many (because) each hawk is captured alive and unharmed, and those who have doubts concerning the harmful nature of the kestrel or other predaceous bird can release it from the trap uninjured.' About its use, Carnegie says, 'From the outward appearance of this trap it might be supposed that no bird so cunning as the sparrow-hawk would allow itself to be caught so easily, but experience has proved the contary.' He continues, 'To ensure good results it should be situated where hawks are known to haunt, such as an open space between two coverts, or on a quiet stretch of waste land, where a few bare old trees may prove a good look-out position for the hawks. The trap should be placed upon four supporting sticks, one at each corner of the trap, to a height of about two feet. After it has been fixed, and the drop-lid set, a few privet branches should be stuck in the ground at the back of the trap, reaching up to the top of the door.'

It is not known for how long George Black actually made his own patented hawk trap, or if any of his family members made them. However, Gilbertson & Page Ltd were advertising 'Black's Hawk and Jay Trap, Price 34/9, Carriage paid' in their December 1938 issue of *The Gamekeeper.* Later, in their renamed *The Gamekeeper and Countryside Magazine* of September 1950, they were advertising 'The improved Hawk and Jay Trap. Very popular and efficient, price 55/- each, carriage paid.' In a later 1968 catalogue of S. Young & Sons (Misterton) Ltd, what seems to be an identical trap is being advertised as Young's Hawk Trap Cage. The text reads 'This Trap has been used with great success, also the Hawk is caught alive and unharmed. Very simple, yet effectual. The Trap should be fixed upon four supporting stakes, one at each corner, and about 2ft high. Also a few branches should be placed on ground at back of Trap, so as to reach to the top of the Trap door. The Trap is made of fine Galvanised Wire Netting, which is fitted to a strong wood framework. It has two compartments: the bottom compartment is used for putting a few live sparrows in, which forms an attractive bait. The Trap is about 2ft square and 2ft 3ins high. Price packed and carriage paid, £6.0.0. (The above Trap can be used for catching other kinds of birds.)'

In S.Young & Sons 1972 catalogue, their Hawk Trap Cage, is not offered for sale. They are still selling their Hawk Nets, as they did in their 1968 catalogue, but with the warning that 'Hawks are fully protected by law'. They also state, on the same page, The Protection of Birds Acts 1954 and 1967. It is illegal to use any form of spring trap, snare or net (including mist nets) to trap wild birds unless licensed to do so. Licences are normally only granted to those persons with permission to ring wild birds.'

BODDIS Lid. Cradley Heath. Year 1911-1956

That this business is obviously older than 1911 is due to E.J.&S. Boddis already registering the trade mark Advance in October 1911. However it is first noted as a limited company in a patent application dated 14th May 1914. This patent was accepted on 18th March 1915 and the patentees were the Company, Boddis (Old Hill) Ltd, Manufacturers and William Henry Taffley, Inventor, Boddis's address being given as Advance Works, Wrights Lane, Old Hill, Staffordshire. This patent was numbered No 11,888. Boddis is next found in an advert for various items, including traps in 1920, which states 'Boddis (Old Hill) Ltd, Advance Works, Old Hill, Staffs. Manufacturers of every description of vermin traps for home and export. Cradley Heath 111.' In 1924-28 they are listed as odd works makers, with the same telephone number. In 1932 their telephone number had changed to Cradley Heath 6311. Between 1936 and 1951 they are listed as steel pressings manufacturers of Wrights Lane, and still with the Cradley Heath 6311 telephone number. However, in 1954 the telephone number has altered to Cradley Heath 69276, but still with their same address. 1956 is the last listing I have found for this company.

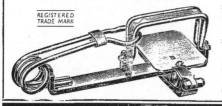
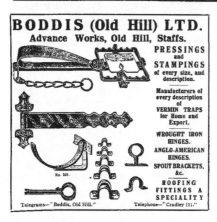
Trade/Identification Mark: Advance (1911), Defiance, Defiance Gem.
Patent: No 11,888. May 1914.
Presuming that at least one prototype trap was built the same as shown in the patent drawings, (Mark I), a similar version was known to have been put into production. This Mark II version known as the Terrier has a jaw length of $3^1/_2$ inches approximately and only differs slightly in construction. The three differences being
(a) No tongue assembly due to the 'eye' of the spring engaging the till;
(b) The spring having only one coil either side of the plate;
(c) The spring bridge moved to the centre of the trap.
Strangely, this modification results in a similar trap to what was previously patented in 1895. A provisional specification application dated 4th November was submitted by Alfred William Webster of Tufnell Park, Middlesex and also by two Australians, John Francis Ryan of Lancefield Junction, Victoria, a rabbit trapper and Thomas Joseph Whelan of Albert Park near Melbourne, a clerk. The Patent No 17872 was accepted on 12th September 1896. The trap is known as a Boss and the actual trap produced differs slightly from the patent drawings. In the drawings the plate falls towards the coil spring, along the stock, and away from the tongue which is behind the plate and which goes over both jaws where they pivot in the standard. However, in the actual trap the plate falls across the stock and has the normal tongue and bridge arrangement as found on gin traps. The tongue is next to the two coiled wire springs, which is fixed in line with the length of the jaws, at the bridge head, and goes over the single wire of the spring and one jaw to engage in the till on the plate as normal. Each of the two coils of the single wire spring being at opposite ends of the bridge to each other. The maker of this trap remains unknown.

Miscellaneous Information: Another business, Benjamin Priest & Sons, also used the Trade/Identification mark of Defiance, with a tiger's head and shoulders.

The first difference between the 4 inch jawed Defiance and the Defiance Gem is that in the last mentioned trap the overall length of the stock and spring is slightly shorter, and that the trap is made of a lighter thickness of metal, therefore reducing its weight slightly. The second difference is that the Defiance has the chain attached by a swivel, to a chain ring that goes through the wire spring 'loop' at the end of the stock. In the Defiance Gem the wire spring 'loop' at the end of the stock, is forced slightly apart in the middle, to allow the insertion of a double-sided flat piece of metal, which looks triangular shaped from above, and which has a hole in the end from which protrudes the 'question mark' shaped swivel. Both traps are usually stamped on their plates Defiance or Defiance Gem respectively. Smaller versions of the Gem, still with the same unusual 'triangular' swivel attachment, were made with jaw sizes of $2^{1}/_{2}$ and 3 inch jaws. However, these small traps only have Defiance stamped on their plates.

An interesting observation is that there was a William Taffley, trapmaker, in Wednesfield, who may have been the inventor mentioned in the 1914 Patent No 11,888.

BULLOCK, William & Co. West Bromwich. Year 1806 – present.

An advert of 1822/3 clearly shows that the Spon Lane Foundry at West Bromwich was well established by this date. Offered for sale amongst other items were humane man traps. In a later catalogue thought to date from the 1860s humane man traps were still being offered for sale as well as improved cast iron beetle traps and cast iron mole traps. The mole traps No 130 were priced at 7/- per dozen (two sets of jaws) whilst No 130A with three tangs were priced at 9/6d per dozen. With plates, one shilling per dozen extra.

In nearby Bullock Street, one of the houses in Twenty House Row was maintained by Bullocks as a school house for the education of the children of their employees. In 1885 George Salter (who make a variety of weighing scales etc.) acquired the business and site and still operate from it.

CLARK, E.&T. Wolverhampton. Year 1827

General Iron Founders, Horseley Fields, 1827, and maker of humane man traps.

CLARK, Thomas. Wolverhampton. Year 1833

(Late E.&T. Clark) General Iron Founders, 1833, and maker of humane mantraps.

CLARK, Thomas & Charles & Co. Wolverhampton. Year 1849 – 1921

General Iron Founders, and maker of humane mantraps, 1849 & 1850.

In their illustrated catalogue of general ironmongery for 1907, this company were advertising for sale only Japanned and galvanised mole traps plus the separate springs and setters. This same catalogue has handwritten alterations to the prices of the galvanised mole traps and is dated 7/1/10.

CIRCA 1860

This Trap will be found much superior to all others. The construction is such that Beetles are readily caught, and cannot possibly escape; but the principal advantage is, that they can be destroyed instantly, without ANY INJURY TO THE TRAP, which is of Cast Iron, ENAMELLED INSIDE, and may be cleaned with very little trouble.

DIRECTIONS FOR USE.

Bait the Trap with crumbs of bread, or beer is preferable, and place it where the Beetles resort; they will soon enter it in search of food, and will be unable to get out again; then pour boiling water into the Trap; which kills the Beetles; empty the Trap, and when wiped clean, bait it again for use.

696. BEETLE TRAP, painted white and enamelled inside, with Glass, 2s. 9d. each.

Extra Glass for ditto......... 4d. each.

1908 ADVERT

CLIFFORD, Alfred. Hawley near Dartmouth, Kent. Year 1891-1908 In the 1891 census records Alfred Clifford appears at Clermont House, Hawley Road Wilmington, where his profession is given as plumber. Living here also, are his parents James and Jane, and his brother Charles who is also described as a plumber.

On 17th November 1892 Alfred Clifford, Plumber and Sanitary Engineer, residing at the same address above, applied for a provisional patent (Number 20,846) for 'A New or Improved Eel Trap'. This invention 'consists of a half round, or any other suitable shape cylinder, made in any length composed of galvanised wire netting of small mesh on light galvanised iron frame or any other suitable material. One or both ends can be made cone-shaped of perforated zinc or other material (marked A on drawing) the small ends are furnished with flexible wire B, sharp pointed at ends next bait box which will prevent the exit of eels after they have passed into trap through small end of cones. One of the cone ends A is made separate from cylinder and attached to same by means of wire hinge C and stud slot D (or otherwise) so as to open and close to serve the purpose of a door and entrance combined thereby saving the cost of making a separate door, and being more easy to empty. In the centre of cylinder and attached to the movable end is placed a round or any other shape perforated zinc (or other suitable material) box E to hold suitable bait to entice the eels into trap.' This patent was accepted on 26th August 1893.

In 1893 he also exhibited at the Cornwall County Fisheries Exhibition at Truro, which was to be held between the 25th July and 16th August. At this exhibition he was situated in the Miscellaneous Trade Exhibits section, listed under Sporting implements; eel traps etc. Later, on 30th October 1893 he again applied for another provisional patent (number 20,455) this time for 'A New or Improved Rat or other Vermin or Animal Trap'. This trap was basically an oblong 'run through' type with a pivoted drop down door at each end. However, a clever idea was 'For the convenience of packing, the trap is made in sections and can be taken to pieces and put together again in a few minutes. So as to more particularly describe the different sections of trap and the convenience of packing same, I would state that there are six pieces in all of which the two sides are fastened by screws to the bottom and are easily removed. The two doors and top are fastened to sides by metal pins or pegs which can be adjusted or removed at pleasure. The whole of the parts can be packed in a small space on the bottom of trap or put

together for use without trouble.'

His next exhibition was The Fishery and Marine Exhibition at Scarborough, Yorkshire held between 31st May and 5th October 1895. According to a report in the *Scarborough Gazette*, dated 20th June 1895, 'Mr Alfred Clifford, Hawley, Kent, has a stall well filled with traps of many descriptions; eel traps, rat traps, and fox traps; also a selection of guns and English made fishing rods and fishing tackle.'

In Perry's Directory for Dartford of 1896, he is listed as 'Patent Sporting Works, Hawley Road'.

The 1901 census shows that Alfred Clifford was still living at Hawley Road with his parents, and that his age was 32 years. He was still being described as a plumber.

In an unillustrated advert from the Army & Navy Stores catalogue dated 1907, the prices and some sizes of Cliffords's Patent Vermin Traps are shown. The advert states, 'For catching animals alive. Specimen of the 2ft.6in. size on view in the department. No1. 2ft.6in. long (kept in stock), for catching rats, stoats, weasels, etc 5/3d. No2. 3ft.6in. long, for rabbits (to order only)15/0. Wood packing 0/6 and 0/9 extra. Orders over two packed free. Special size traps for catching cats, 34/0; for foxes, 62/0. (Packing extra, 4/0).'

Lastly, an advert appears, showing his two patented traps, in William Carnegie's book *How to Trap and Snare* in 1908.

COLBURN, Thomas. Wolverhampton. Year 1827-1833
Rat trap maker, Coles Croft, Stafford Street, Wolverhampton, 1827
Rat trap maker, 1833

CRUICKSHANK, Alexander Allan. Glasgow. Year 1901-1924

**CRUICKSHANK'S PATENT
RABBIT AND VERMIN TRAPS.**

(*Covered by Two Patents.*)

Stated by every keeper and trapper who has
tested them in practice to be the best ever produced.

TOOTHJAW TRAPS

(made with Medium or Full Plate as desired),
Dorset Type, complete with Chains, and fitted
with best Brass ·Mounts, 24/- per dozen. Free to
nearest railway station in 2½ dozen quantities. One
dozen sent carriage free, on rail, as a trial order.

A. A. CRUICKSHANK,
Craighall Warehouse,
MACKIE STREET, GLASGOW.

1904 ADVERT FROM
THE KEEPER'S BOOK

On 19th September 1902 Patent application number 20,460 was made, and accepted on 13th August 1903. This application was for a single detachable wire spring for gin traps, 'and has for its objects to enable such traps to be manufactured at considerably less cost than hitherto, whilst simultaneously giving greater power of spring, with facilities for detaching and renewing when worn or broken, ease in setting and durability in use, combined with extreme lightness as compared with the best known types in present use.' The person who applied for this patent was Alexander Allan Cruickshank of Atholl Cottage, Dumbarton and his occupation was that of Inland Revenue Officer. He had previously been granted another patent in 1901, No 1339, for an 'Elastic Medium' for use between trap and stake, which could also be used in conjunction with this second patent. By 1907-9, he was living in a house at 2, Albany Street, Kelvinside, Glasgow. According to a 1904 advert his busi-

ness address was Craighall Warehouse, Mackie Street, Glasgow. However, in the Post Office Directories of Glasgow for 1905-10, he is listed as Trap (Steel) Maker, Craighall Works, Masterton Street. Then in 1913-14, Allan Cruickshank Ltd. is at 67, McAlpine Street. Finally Allan Cruickshank Ltd. (Rabbit and Animal Traps), last address is at 14, Bishop Street, Anderston, Glasgow

Seemingly, two types of this trap were made. One type was with the normal steel jaws, as in the advert of 1904, whilst a humane version had rubber covered jaws, which 'any lady can put her hand on the plate and spring the trap without injury.' Cruickshank's traps only seem to have been made in 4 inch and 3 inch jaw sizes, and were advertised in Gilbertson & Page's Ltd. 1913 catalogue at 28/- doz. (4 inch) and 23/6d doz. (3 inch) carriage paid. In this catalogue no mention of the rubber jawed traps was made.

COLBOURN, Robert. Wolverhampton. Year 1838
Rat trap maker, Carribee Island, Wolverhampton, 1838

DAVIS, Joseph, Wednesbury. Year 1862/3
Directory of Wolverhampton Advertisement 1862/3 states Wednesbury Works, Short Lane Wednesbury. All kinds of steel traps or every description, and the latest new spring gun traps made of the best quality of steel and to any size.

DUFFUS, John and Son. Eassie, Forfarshire, Scotland. Year 1918 – present
The Duffus family were well known as mole catchers and travelled throughout the local area from farm to farm carrying out their trade. They would be paid a fee for clearing the farmer's land of the moles, but extra money would be earned in those far off days by selling the mole skins as they were a product much in demand by the fur

trade. In the early years they would be using the wooden full barrel mole traps which were in common use.

The exact date that the family of John Duffus of Eassie started making their own type of mole trap is unknown but it was definitely before 1918. The type that they originally made were constructed of a wooden cylindrical barrel body hollowed through the middle in the normal style of that period. However, their spring arrangement on this new trap was totally different. Instead of the more normal large loop wire spring arrangement which extended out to one side of the trap, they produced a much neater and more compact coil spring. This new design also had other benefits. Two of the new smaller coil springs could now be placed on top of the wooden body of the trap in line with either direction that the mole or moles were travelling, thereby enabling two moles to be caught at separate times. These traps were all hand made by members of the Duffus family and sold mainly locally.

A few years later, an improvement to these wooden traps was patented by John Duffus Senior and John Duffus Junior. This patent application of 27th September 1922 (no 21,309/22) was to become famous in Britain as the Duffus Half Barrel mole trap, with the patent being accepted on 13th September 1923 becoming Patent No 203,484. Although these improved traps were now made out of galvanised steel they were still hand made. This was a slow job as each body was individually cut out using only hand shears from the strips of sheet metal. All the holes and slots were either punched out or chiselled out, again by hand. Individual springs were cut to length and coiled etc. The business was carried on at this pace for many years by John Duffus Senior and his three sons, Henry, John and Larry. Eventually, over the years disaster

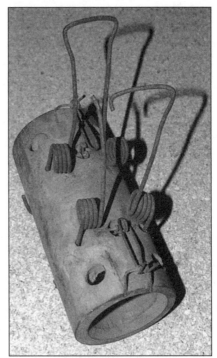

AN EARLY TYPE OF DUFFUS MOLE TRAP (FRONT SPRING BROKEN AND PARTS MISSING)

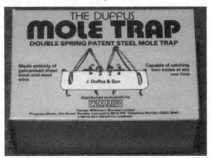

PACKAGING BOX FOR DUFFUS MOLE TRAP WHEN SOLD BY WILKINSON'S OF BURNLEY

struck the family. Henry's son, who was a pilot, was killed during World War II and John Junior's son died in 1953 of tuberculosis. Larry had emigrated to Canada. Due to there being no male heirs to carry on, it was decided to sell the business.

Meanwhile, John Junior had been helping out on a farm where Mr. David Jolly was working. One day Mr.

Duffus mentioned to David Jolly that he would not be at the farm tomorrow due to having to go and see a Solicitor about selling the mole trap making business. Mr. Jolly showed a serious interest in acquiring the business and they started discussing details. Eventually, the sum of £200 was agreed for the purchase of the business. Therefore in 1958 David Jolly became the proud owner of J. Duffus & Son and carried on the business still under its founder's name. The traps were still being produced totally by hand, until Mr. Jolly bought from the Singer Sewing Machine factory in Coatbridge one of their punching machines. This machine of course then had to be converted to punch the holes and slots needed in the sheet metal mole trap body, and this was done locally. This one improvement alone was a great saving in manual labour and time. Another help was the introduction of a guillotine machine which had been purchased from a book binding company in Dundee where it had been used to cut up silk. Now a morning's work cutting the sheet steel with the old hand shears could be done in fifteen minutes.

All the other hand operated 'machinery' was invented and made by David Jolly himself, to help speed up the process. However, everything is still finally assembled by hand. The galvanised sheets of steel are purchased from either Alexander's of Stirling or Brown & Tawse of Dundee, whilst the wire is supplied by Brunton's of Musselburgh. The original hand held punch is still used for stamping the name J. Duffus & Son on the traps and this accounts for the occasional 'light' stamping found on new traps. When David Jolly bought over the business in 1958 he continued to sell his traps through Spence & Gerrard of Edinburgh, as had John Duffus. When that business was taken over by Thomas Scott of Grassmarket, Edinburgh, he again continued to sell through the new owners. Then about 1970 Thomas Scott ceased trading and a little while later an agreement within Wilkinson's of Burnley England made them the sole distributors throughout Britain. The business was growing steadily through the years, with the result that about 1987 there were employed three full-time and three part-time people. The maximum number of traps that could be made per day was 100, but on average 1,000 were produced per month. Wilkinson's supplied the packaging boxes for the traps. Eventually, after many years, Wilkinson's stopped ordering Duffus traps and started producing their own copy. Due to the decline in orders over the years, and also because of the time-consuming hand assembly of the traps produced, it was decided that the business would only be operated by family members and on a very limited scale. Eventually David and his wife Frances decided to seek full-time employment outside of the business, but also to continue trap making as a low key operation, as they still receive orders. The mole traps are still made in the large shed at the rear of the Jolly's house and throughout the sale of Duffus traps there has never been a minimum number to order. Duffus mole traps have been exported to Sweden, Holland, Canada and South Africa. Unfortunately, none of David and Frances' children – Stephen, Vivienne or Cameron – are interested in continuing the mole trap making tradition. At this time production is still from Linnbank, Kilry, by Alyth, PH11 8HS.

DUKE, WARING, CRISP & CO., London, Year 1920-1932

1920-1925. Between these dates their address was 139 Wardour

(OPPOSITE) 1924 ADVERT FROM
RATS AND HOW TO DESTROY THEM
MARK HOVELL

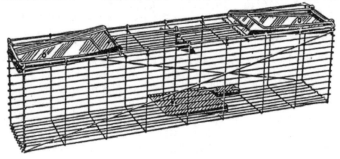
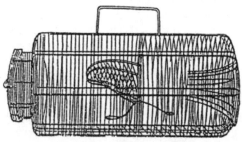

A 1917 ADVERT FOR DROWNING – *Benn's Encyclopaedia*

Street, London.
1932-1936. Their address is now Soho Works, Vauxhall Street, Kennington Oval.
In The Hardware Trade Journal for 1920, this company was advertising as 'Wire workers, Brass Finishers and Sieve Makers, Wire & Metal Merchants'. Next to an illustration of the 'Wonder' live catch rat trap, the advert continues 'Pattern Wire Rat Traps ex Stock'.

W. T. FRENCH & Son. Birmingham. Year 1916-1955

Mysto Works, Browning Street, Ladywood, Birmingham. 1917
In an advert of 1916 these 'Capito' type drowner mouse traps retailed at 2/- each, whilst in a later advert of 1925, they were being retailed at 2/9d each. The Trade Mark MYSTO was registered for metal mouse traps on 25th October 1916, whilst strangely for metal rat traps, the same word was registered on 13th February 1917. Alfred Edward French and Alfred William French trading as W.T.French & Son, 23 & 25 St.Mary Street, Ladywood, Birmingham, described themselves as manufacturers.

GREEN, Richard Limited. Cradley Heath. Year 1900-1939.

According to an advert this company

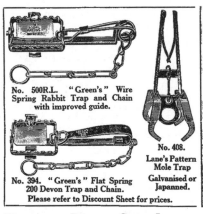

No. 500R.L. "Green's" Wire Spring Rabbit Trap and Chain with improved guide.

No. 408.
Lane's Pattern Mole Trap
Galvanised or Japanned.

No. 394. "Green's" Flat Spring 200 Devon Trap and Chain.
Please refer to Discount Sheet for prices.

TRAPS FROM RICHARD GREEN LTD. OF CRADLEY HEATH 1938/39

was established in 1900, and their premises were known as Cokeland Works.
1924. Green, Richard Ltd. Chain Makers, Cokeland Place.
1928. Their telegraph address was 'Ready, Cradley Heath' and their telephone numbers were 261 and 262.
1932. The telephone numbers were by then preceded by the number 6.
1938/39. Ironmongers catalogue showing among other items 'Green's Traps'.

Trade/Identification Marks: The initials RG intertwined on an upright oval (1919).

Miscellaneous Information: Steel punches found at W.&G. Sidebotham's Works included Green's, Green's 500SL, and Green's 500 RL. The 500RL trap is shown in the 1938/9 Ironmongers catalogue, and refers to Green's improved spring guide for wire spring gin traps. A 'rubber jawed' wire spring gin trap is also known to exist. This trap has stamped on its galvanised plate in three separate lines, one above each other, the words '500H Green's Humane'.

GRIPPER Manufacturing Co., Leicester, Year 1914-1969

The Gripper Manufacturing Co. seems to have had as its founder an Alexander Charles Harris. He is listed in the Trade Directories between 1898-1902 as Death and Harris, Engineers, Millwrights, and Ironfounders, Joseph Street and New Bridge Street. In 1904 he is listed as Proprietor of Death and Ellwood, Joseph Street and Clarendon Street. Thereafter in 1908-1912 as A.C. Harris, Engineer, 18 Portland Road. Around the same dates 'Gripper Patent rabbit traps – sure catchers' were being advertised in the magazine The Australian Farm & House (issues 1909 and 1911) by D.&W. Chandler (Ironmonger) of Fitzroy. However, the Gripper Manufacturing Co. first appears in the local Trade Directories in 1914 and

THE GRIPPER RAT TRAP

for Rats and other Vermin

(Registered No. 771051)

(Specially recommended by the R.S.P.C.A.)

Kills instantly in a humane way by hitting the animal a sharp blow on the head.

SPECIAL FEATURES.—It is lighter, simpler, more compact, more portable, and more efficient than the old steel-toothed gin. No chain or peg required, as the animal is killed on the spot.

The jaw forms a barrier when set, so that animals must approach bait from the right end. Two rats are often caught at the same time. It is undoubtedly the best rat trap made. Bait with a piece of fresh bloody meat for stoats ; or with a peanut for grey squirrels.

Size 5-in. jaw. Weight 10 oz. Price 27/- per doz. Carriage paid.

Sample trap 2/9 post free.

1941 ADVERT

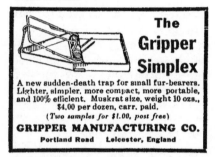

The Gripper Simplex

A new sudden-death trap for small fur-bearers. Lighter, simpler, more compact, more portable, and 100% efficient. Muskrat size, weight 10 ozs., $4.00 per dozen, carr. paid.

(Two samples for $1.00, post free)

GRIPPER MANUFACTURING CO.

Portland Road   Leicester, England

TWO AMERICAN ADVERTS

THE GRIPPER MOLE TRAP

Most efficient ever designed. Weight only 8¼ ozs. Galvanized. By Parcels post. 2 for $1.00; 5 for $2.00; 12 for $4.00.

GRIPPER MFG. CO.

Portland Rd., Leicester, England

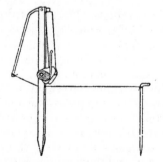

GRIPPER DEADFALL

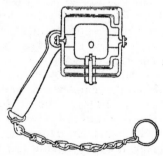

GILPA DOUBLE GRIP TRAP

were described as Mechanical Engineers of 18 Portland Road, Tel. 4360. After World War I, a round 1920, Mr. Harris asked the family-run business of R.C. Harrison, who operated a small foundry, making small brass castings, in Causeway Lane, Leicester, to make castings for him. These items consisted of all types of gripping devices mainly for domestic use, such as sugar tongs, coal tongs for the hearth etc. and were all of his own design. Production of these items was obviously the reason why the business took the name Gripper and presumably he had been making them for many years before. By the year 1925, the address had changed to 7 Portland Road, but it is not known exactly what year that this occurred. In 1927 Mr. Harris went to live at the Nether Hall in the village of Keyham, which is six miles from the centre of Leicester. His family consisted of a son named Tom and three daughters. It is very possible that around the 1930s A.C. Harris sold his business, as during the early 1930s they moved to Letchworth, Herts. It is said that the villagers were sorry to see them leave, as they were popular people.

In two separately published articles which appeared in the August 1932 and October 1933 issues of the American magazine *Fur-Fish-Game*, mention is made by Major C. Van Der Byl (see Notes) of three types of Gripper traps. The first in 1932 only mentions one type, the new humane steel trap, called the Gripper Simplex. Later adverts also showing this trap appeared in the same magazine in the December 1932 issue, along with the following months of January, February and March in 1933. The October 1933 article then mentions the Gripper Deadfall and the Gripper mole trap but no reference is made to the Gripper Simplex trap, and to quote from the article, he says, 'For the last two years I have been trying to design a humane and efficient rabbit trap. This trap called the Gripper Deadfall seems to answer the purpose.'

From the tone of the article it appears that Major C. Van Der Byl had some connection with this company. This is reinforced by the addition in the American article of a 'GILPA' double trap. In a small article sent to the magazine *Game and Gun & The Angler's Monthly* published in July 1933, the same illustration appears with the statements, 'Messrs. Gilbertson & Page recently sent for our trial one of their new 'GILPA' double grip traps. We understand that it has been developed by Major C. Van Der Byl from the double jawed traps which are now being used with success in America.' Presumably the 'GILPA' double grip trap was also manufactured by the Gripper Company but sold solely by Gilbertson & Page in Britain under their 'GILPA' brand name. Indeed the plate on the trap is stamped Gilpa Double Grip Rd No 780310. In 1932 the company are listed as Die Casters, which is probably why R.C. Harrison received no further orders from around this time, and then in 1954 as Specialist in Cast Iron Welding. Their last listing is in the Trade section of the local directory in 1969. In Britain the Simplex trap was advertised in 1934 as the Gripper Breakback rat trap and priced at 20/- per dozen, carriage paid from the company. The Gripper mole trap was also offered for sale at the same time,

priced at 12/- per dozen, but there was no mention of the Gripper deadfall trap. In a Gilbertson & Page unillustrated price list for September 1951 Gripper rat traps are advertised at 36/- per dozen.

GROSVENOR, Theodore L. Wolverhampton. Year 1928-1936

Animal trap makers, 12 & 13 King Street.

Galvanised hollow-ware manufacturer; 'Loud Speaker' and 'Grosvenor' brands; also animal traps, Japanned steel trunks, spades, shovels, packing tanks, safes etc. (12&13) King Street, T.A. 'Buckets', T.N. 1394 (1932).

Fireproof safes etc., 12&13 King Street, T.A. 'Buckets', T.N.21394 (1936).

H. STANLEY BLEYER Ltd. Birmingham. Year 1939-1953

In 1939 H. Stanley Bleyer of 107 Oxford Road, Moseley, Birmingham 13, was advertising imported traps as well as other general household items such as washboards, pegs etc. The traps he advertised were Lynx, Capito and Presto self setting mouse and rat traps. H. Stanley Bleyer Ltd. of 143-143a Conybere Street, Birmingham 12, registered the 'Impex' trade mark on 26th January 1949 and described the business as Merchants and Manufacturers. In 1951-1953 the address is noted as the Impex Works, Coneybere Street, suggesting this was the address where Impex mouse and rat traps were made.

However, evidence suggests that the all metal Impex mouse and rat traps were in fact made by W.H. Tildesley of Willenhall. (See illustration page 245) In the actual rat trap produced, the upright edges enclosing the trap plate have 'saw' type teeth cut into them, whereas in the smaller mouse trap version the same two long sides have no teeth serrations and there is no raised serrated front edge. Tildesley's trap

NOTES ON MAJOR CHARLES VAN DER BYL

In March 1936 the Major wrote a letter to the *Game & Gun* magazine which stated:

Another efficient and humane way of catching rabbits without the aid of gins is now being used on a Devon farm. A 6 volt motor cycle headlamp of the focusing type, which can be switched on and off, is used, and the battery is carried in a haversack. On entering a field, a long narrow beam is turned on a rabbit, which can then easily be caught by a dog, as long as the light is kept on the rabbit. Neighbouring rabbits crouch in the grass and can easily be detected by the light reflected from their eyes, and accounted for. A sheep dog was used which caught the rabbits and retrieved them. A bag of 27 rabbits was made thus in three quarters of an hour on one night, and 33 in one hour on the following night. This method is inexpensive, simple and humane; but a dark night without moon is essential for its success. This farmer has not set a trap or snare on his farm for seven years, and has kept his rabbits down entirely by this means. I am always ready to supply full particulars for the humane trapping of rabbits, rats, stoats, and especially moles, and can also send a white list of furs that can be worn with a clear conscience.

C. Van Der Byl, Major
The Fur Crusade & Humane Trapping Campaign
Wappenham,
Towcester

An advert, in the same magazine, of December 1936, for the Spade Twins, whilst not mentioning the Major or any of his organisations, but with the Wappenham Towcester address, states that they were 'Also specialists for humane traps recommended by R.S.P.C.A.'

Then in the September issue of 1937 he wrote 'May I inform readers of *Game and Gun* that I am surrendering my designs for the three well known Gripper traps, for rats, mice and moles, so that any manufacturer may now copy them? I do this because I believe them to be the best and most humane traps for these small animals; and I want to lessen the suffering caused by using other types. At present these Gripper traps are made only by the Gripper Mfg. Co., Portland Road, Leicester.'

In an October 1937 review of his book *My Fifty Years of Sport*, it was said that Major Charles Van Der Byl 'is probably best known to the present generation of younger sportsmen, and to the readers of *Game & Gun*, as an ardent and fearless critic of the cruelty of trapping. But to an older generation he is equally well known as a fearless rider to hounds, over fences or after the Indian boar; a great shot and gallant soldier. At the present time, when there is so much sickly sentimentality and ignorant abuse of field sports, there might easily have been a risk of the founder of the anti fur crusade being tarred with the same brush which has been used so lavishly on the ignorant but vociferous enthusiasts who attack hunting, shooting, fishing and all field sports so wantonly and recklessly. Major Van Der Byl could not have helped his cause more than by giving us this admirable book which is a delightful record of a soldier's life in England, Ireland, Africa and India. His chapter on the ethics of hunting is brim full of sound and practical common sense and humanity, and divorced completely from any prejudice, and thus makes quite one of the best expositions on this subject which we have ever read. A really admirable book, which is well worth reading.'

Concern was expressed in the *Shooting Times* of 9th March 1940 'about the ability of the men selected for anti aircraft duties on fishing vessels.' David Brotherstone wrote, 'I gather the class of men selected for this very important work are not sufficiently skilled for shooting at fast flying targets such as a Heinkel charging at a very high speed. We have a large number of crack clay target shots throughout the country who are slightly over the present military age, including the writer, who would be pleased to give their services.'

In the following issue the Major replied in typical style, 'I immediately cut out Mr. Brotherstone's letter from the *ST* last week and sent it to the Secretary of the Admiralty. To my mind, shooting at rocketing aeroplanes is about the ideal of sport, because there is a real fifty-fifty chance of being bombed or shot yourself whilst doing so. All sport is enhanced by a spice of the danger attached to it.' What more could be said about the man?

illustration has smooth raised edges to it, and so presumably, this is an illustrator's drawing of the Impex mouse trap.

The only markings on the trap, are to be found on the plate, and consist of a diamond shape, within it, the words Impex forming a plus sign with the P being in the centre of both crossing words. This is stamped on the left side of the bait spike, whilst on the right side is stamped Made in England. All the lettering is in capitals. Very similar German copies of the rat trap are being produced, but the easiest way to tell them apart is to turn them over so that the underside is showing. On the Impex rat trap you will see an embossed 'Y' shape with a separate 'dot' at the end of the right 'arm', between the two 'D' and two reversed 'D'-shaped pressed-out holes, whilst on the German made copy it is an embossed 'o' shape. Another difference is that the German copy has a wire safety catch fixed in the top left corner, whilst the Impex has no safety catch anywhere. Another similar copy, without a safety catch, has a much smaller plate on which is faintly stamped Simplex across the top, and below the bait spike along the bait

plate's bottom edge Made in France. All the words are in capital letters. Turning the trap over, there is an indented X shape with two continious lines, coming off the X, one either side of the cut-out base. The right hand side's straight line stops level with the top of the cut-out space, whilst the left hand side's straight line continues slightly. Unfortunately, other near identical copies exist, but their country of origin is unknown. The Impex Trap's Registered Design Number is 638438.

HODGETS, John. Birmingham. Year 1770-1780
Trap maker, rat, fitcher, fox, man & hinge. No 102 Digbeth, 1770
Trap & hinge maker, 102 Digbeth, 1780 (fitcher = polecat).

IZONS, WHITEHURST & IZON. West Bromwich. Year 1763-1924.
1763, Duke Street, Birmingham. Brass & general Ironfounders.
Reputedly, the goods manufactured at that time were man traps, rat traps, door knockers, kitchen stoves and other household goods.
Around the early 1780s. due to an increase of business the works were transferred from Birmingham to West Bromwich. In *Pigot's Directory* of 1822/3 Izons & Co. advertised humane man

HUMANE MAN TRAP.

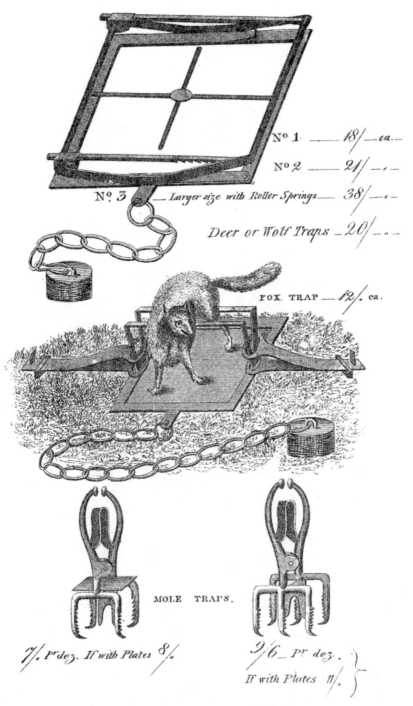

Nº 1 _____ 18/_ ca._

Nº 2 _____ 21/_ ,_

Nº 3 _____ Larger size with Roller Springs_____ 38/_ ,_

Deer or Wolf Traps _ 20/_ ,,_

FOX TRAP _ 12/_ ea.

MOLE TRAPS.

7/. Pr doz. If with Plates 8/.

9/6_ Pr doz.
If with Plates 11/.

IZONS UNDATED CATALOGUE OF *CIRCA* 1830-60

18/. 24/. 38/. ea.
Nº 1 2 3

Izons undated catalogue of *circa* 1830-60.
Note different spring from Bullock & Co's trap
illustrated on page 293

Sham and Real Dorset Rabbit Traps,
are made in the following Qualities. :—

LIGHT.	MEDIUM.	STRONG.	EXTRA STRONG.

X XX
ANGLO.

ANCHOR.

IN ORDERING STATE BRAND.

S LEWIS & CO MARKS

traps, fox traps, and mole traps. Unfortunately there is no illustration of them. However, in a later catalogue of theirs, which is thought to date from around 1830-60, the same type of traps are shown complete with prices. It is interesting to note that both the humane mantrap and the fox trap illustrated below it have the same basic square shape plus the same lug attachment for the trap chain. Strangely, the fox trap has no plate, and seems to have folding springs. The illustrator may have omitted the plate on purpose, so as not to clutter up his drawing, and the springs might just represent the normal straight stocked flat springs.

In an article that appeared in 'Piccadilly' January 1924 Izons & Co. Limited were quoted as 'The oldest makers of cast hollow-ware in the world.'

KENRICK, Archibald & Co. West Bromwich. Year 1780s – present.

Little is known about the traps made by Kenrick's, but it seems to have been the usual mole traps and humane man traps as mentioned in *Pigot's Directory* of 1822/3. An 1840 catalogue shows a humane man trap with an almost identical illustration of a poacher in the trap, as is also seen in Bullock's catalogue illustration. Kenrick's mole traps (two and three claws and plates) are also the same prices, with their two-claw cast iron mole traps still being offered for sale in a later 1914 catalogue.

Kendrick became involved in the manufacture of a wide range of ironmongery products and since World War II are widely known as a leading maker of castors.

LENCH, William. Birmingham. Year 1770-1780

Trap maker. No 8 Mill Lane, 1770 Trap & hinge maker, 9 Park Street, 1780.

LEWIS. Samuel & Co. Withymoor, near Dudley. Year 1750-present.

This very large business, according to an 1897 billhead, were 'Manufacturers of every description of Wrought Nails, Rivets, Chains, Cables, Anchors'. The list goes on, and they seem to have made just about everything. However, it is known that they did make mole hawk and gin traps, but this would only have been a small part of their business. One of their catalogues circa 1910/12 has illustrations showing that they made both flat and bow types of single spring gin traps with jaw lengths up to 8". Double folding spring traps with jaw lengths from 8" up to 14" were also illustrated and made 'for foxes, beavers and other wild animals'. Several known examples exist of forged single bow spring gin traps with a jaw length of $9^1/_2$". These traps have Anglo Lewis stamped on the spring near the eye. W & G Sidebotham had steel punches with S. Lewis & Co on them in their works when Sidebotham's ceased business in 1984. Therefore, it is most likely that later on S. Lewis & Co found it easier, and probably cheaper, to get Sidebotham's to make the traps on their behalf, stamping them with the Lewis name or trade marks. Sidebotham's are well known for putting various manufacturers' and especially retailers' names onto their traps.

Trade / Identification Marks: The Trade Mark LEWIS ANGLO was registered on 27th June 1910 by Samuel Lewis and Company Limited, Anglo Works, Northfield Road, Withymoor.

LONGMEADOW WILDLIFE MANAGEMENT Ltd. Dorset. Year 1989-2003

Lower Wincombe Lane, Donhead St. Mary, Shaftesbury, Dorset SP7 9DB
The firm of Longmeadow began trading in 1989 and was registered as a Limited Company in July 1994. This company design and manufacture all their own equipment, of which traps are only part of their production range. These traps consist of various types of wire mesh live catch models. Longmeadow decided to introduce a live catch mole trap onto the market to fill an existing need for such a trap for research purposes etc. Their idea for this type of trap was based on German wooden versions which was first thought to have been made in the early 1700s. The principle of the one way entry baffle door has been used since time immemorial and because of this the Longmeadow live catch mole trap is not patented. The mole trap was first released to the trade, in low profile, at Pest Tech 96 in November 1996 at the N.E.C. Birmingham. It went on sale to the general public in February 1997, at a cost of £10 per pair plus postage of £4.50. As with all traps it is not the mechanism, but the application that ensures its success, and whilst the tooling of the trap door profile was not a problem to an engineer the application of the trap took eighteen months to research. The live catch mole traps come as a pair, in two different lengths of 12" and 9" long.

They are both made of brown plastic tubing with a diameter of $2^3/_{16}$" and have a flap door at either end.
In the 1st June 2000 issue of *Shooting Times*, Longmeadow advertised their new mole trap, the Talpawl. The illustrated advert states 'It is a double-loop tunnel spring trap with stronger springing and more sensitive trip than

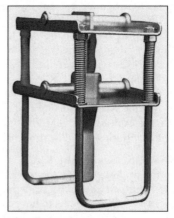

TALPAWL MOLE TRAP

standard traps. Its dual killing action promotes swift and effective dispatch. An optional stronger spring means the trap can be used in sticky clay soils.' The advertised price of £56.90 was a printing error, as the traps retail for about £10.00 each.
This trap was made for Longmeadow by a Midlands based manufacturer of car components. Only 1000 traps were ordered and produced, and no more are in production.

The owner of Longmeadow Wildlife

Management Ltd was Nigel Shearing, who sadly died in 2003 at the age of 56. Nigel Shearing was a regular contributor of pest control articles in the *Shooting Times & Country Magazine* and his obituary by Paul Quagliana, appeared in the 23rd October 2003 issue. Part of his obituary reads: 'A Colonel Morris came down the hill to his house with an original Larsen trap and asked Nigel if he could repair it. Nigel reckoned he could make a trap that was better, and that was the birth of his business Longmeadow Wildlife Management. As more people spoke to him with ideas, so his business grew, until one great day when he gave 12 police wildlife officers a talk on trapping and the law. Nigel was a highly efficient mole catcher and specialised in making live catching traps, including squirrel traps, mink traps and even a live catcher leopard trap to be sent to Africa. Once established, he approached the Game Conservancy Trust (GCT) with a prototype for a Larsen trap with an improved trip mechanism. Mike Swan, of the GCT, reckons it is still the best trip mechanism for side entry Larsens.' Quagliana continues saying, 'I will remember his traps for catching spider crabs' but also recalls, 'Like so many rural businesses, Nigel's was hit hard by foot and mouth, and never fully recovered.'

MALES. Warners Lane, Selsey, Chichester, West Sussex PO20 9EL. Year Mid 1990s to present
The firm of Males started making wire cage traps in the mid 1990s and their February 1997 catalogue states that they are 'designers and manufacturers of live catch animal traps.' They also produce two versions of a weatherproof poison hopper, 'The modified version (which) incorporates a clear PVC magnetic door which restricts access by non targeted rodents.'

MALES'S DOUBLE CATCH, SIDE ENTRY, 'LARSEN' TYPE CORVID TRAP

MARSHALL & Sons. Honiton, Devon. Year 1948
A 1948 advert indicates that they are snare makers.

NATIONAL PATENT COMPANY LIMITED. Johnstone, Near Glasgow. Year 1872-1956
Mouse, rat and mole trap manufacturers.
According to various adverts, this business was established in 1872. It was started by James Hunter and remained a family business. About 1905-6 a purpose-built factory was erected at South William Street, Johnstone, and this address is where the business remained until its demise in 1956. In early 1951, fire destroyed about half of the factory leaving only the outer walls standing as the roof of the building had collapsed inward. Although the company managed to rebuild and again start production of traps, they never recovered totally from this disaster and finally ceased trading in the middle of 1956.
The company produced two types of wooden mole traps. The full barrel type was known as the 'Perfection' whilst their half barrel version was simply known by that name. They also sold the various parts of the mole traps separately so that any mole catcher could just replace the part that was needed. In a Joseph Nichols & Son, Birmingham, catalogue of 1898-1900, Perfection full barrel mole traps were being advertised at 21/- doz.,

whilst in a later 1920 *Hardware Trade Journal* both full and half barrel mole traps were shown in a National Patent Company advert. In the P.&R. Fleming 1953 catalogue already mentioned, again both the full barrel Perfection and the half barrel mole traps were advertised.

The National Patent Company also made a wooden live catch mouse trap, for catching individual mice. Known as the 'Captor' it was made in two very similar versions, A and B, the only differences being that type 'A' has an extended base at the mouth of the trap and the two sides are angled to fit the door flush when closed. In the type 'B' both sides are oblong in shape and the door closes between them. There is also no extended base on this type. The first type of traps made by James Hunter were the ones known as 'choker loop' style, and as far as is known, were only made in sizes to catch mice. Choker loop traps that were produced included the Detective 2-4 holes, Never Fail (softwood version of the Detective), New Snapshot 2-6 holes. The three hole New Snapshot was still being advertised for sale by P.&R. Fleming & Co. of Glasgow in 1953 and also in *Benn's Encyclopaedia* in 1956, in one of the National Patents own adverts. Breakback types of traps, also known as snap traps, produced were the Ace, Allwire, Baitlock, Betta, Cheapa, Dart, Hero, Million, Nap, Unseen and Veto. There seems to be no rat size versions made of the Allwire and Nap traps, but mouse and rat versions were made for all the other models.

JOSEPH NICHOLS & SON Ltd, Cheapside, Birmingham B12-0PT Year 1841-present

This large business make and sell a vast range of general 'wirework & wire articles for every purpose' from wire waste paper litter bins found in recreation parks etc to large and complicated machinery guards.

Some of their wire products being sold under their AJAX brand. Previously, in their Victorian and other early catalogues were illustrated a large range of different

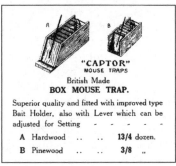

"CAPTOR"
MOUSE TRAPS
British Made
BOX MOUSE TRAP.
Superior quality and fitted with improved type Bait Holder, also with Lever which can be adjusted for Setting -   -   -   -   -
A   Hardwood ..   ..   **13/4** dozen.
B   Pinewood ..   ..   **3/8** ,,

FROM JOSEPH NICHOLS & SON
LTD CATALOGUE DATED 1935-38

types of traps. For example traps included, a wire cage rat trap that 'folded flat for packing', a similar type had a single, solid sheet metal, hinged drop down door. Another run-through type had a wire door at each end. This business also produced an 'imitation wonder rat trap', a 'galvanised round rat trap wire bottom'. This dome-shaped trap is the same shape as the rat trap shown in the Jack Black, rat catcher, illustration. Galvanised, single end opening, sloping wire eel traps were also produced as was a double, opposite ends opening, half barrel version.

Their catalogues also show that they sold, but may not have actually made, single and double, live catch bird traps, made of wood and wire. Other wood and wire traps, illustrated in their catalogues include, the Improved Cossack mouse and rat traps, which seem to be a slight variation of the 'Perfection' mouse and rat trap, whilst the 'improved rat trap' seems to be again a slight variation of the original Breakback mouse and rat trap. Other traps illustrated include

Rat Traps

No. 225

WELDED THROUGHOUT, RUST-RESISTANT FINISH

14″ × 8″ × 5″
360mm. × 203mm. × 127mm.

The strongest trap on the market and a proved success over many years

ANIMAL TRAP

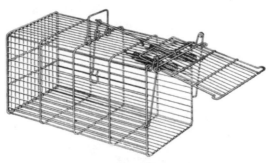

No. 226

Strong, Galvanized after made, Welded Mesh

16″ × 8½″ × 8″
406mm. × 216mm. × 203mm.

J. NICHOLS & SON, 1987 CATALOGUE

the Improved Plevna or London Perpetual, Acme, Premier Mouse trap plus the Little Nipper mouse and rat traps. The Nipper traps are still being made by Proctor Bros. A single entry and a double entry Free Kirk live catch mouse trap illustrated, seems to also have been made by Proctor's and known simply, in their catalogues as the 'Box' mouse trap.

Nichols also sold 2 different types of beetle trap. One was the Improved japanned circular zinc beetle trap which had a $7^1/_2$" diameter, whilst the second type was oblong in shape. The second type, just called Beetle Trap, was shaped like a triangle with the top cut off. It was made in 10, 11, 12, 13, and 14 inch lengths, and was probably made of wood. Lastly, illustrated in both of Nichols 1962 and 1987 catalogues is their $^3/_8$" diamond shaped wire mesh, circular Sparrow Trap, which was made with a door in its side. In 1987 the Sparrow Trap was priced individually at £13.40p plus VAT plus carriage. Earlier made sparrow traps, circa 1900, were made with $^1/_2$" diamond mesh, and could be purchased in either circular form at 18/- each or square 18" x 18" x 7" deep at 20/- each and were galvanised after being made.

The PERPETUAL Trap Co. Walsall. Year 1906-1910
65 Bridge Street, Walsall.
Maker of the self setting automatic mouse and rat exterminator called the Perpetual.

PRIEST, Benjamin & Sons. Old Hill, Staffordshire. Year 1900-1925
In an April 1900 advert, B. Priest & Sons, Bolt and Nut, Chain and Nail Works at Old Hill, Staffs were advertising the 'Perfect' patent reversible hinge, which they made and presumably had patented previously.

Trade/Identification Marks: The word Defiance in a curve above a tiger's head and shoulders facing to the right. The trade mark was registered in 1906 and their address was Providence Works, Old Hill. They stated that no claim was made to the exclusive use of the word 'Defiance'. In fact the word 'Defiance' was also used by Boddis (Old Hill) Ltd, Staffs, another trap making company.

Patents: George Frederick Mitchell of Cheriton Fitzpaine, Devon, whose occupation was stated as tailor, applied for a patent on 15th September 1905 (Patent No 18,632) with the complete specification being accepted on 12th July 1906. The complete specification states that his 'Invention relates to rabbit and other vermin traps more especially of the gin or steel spring type,

$^1/_2$" Mesh
10mm.

Door at side

SPARROW TRAPS
GALVANIZED AFTER MADE
18" diam. x 7" deep
457mm. x 180mm.

J. NICHOLS & SON, 1987 CATLAOGUE

the jaws of which are sometimes provided with rubber surfaces to avoid unnecessary injury to the entrapped rabbit or other vermin. Hitherto, in traps of this type provided with rubber, the latter has been riveted, cemented or screwed to the jaws and considerable difficulty has been involved in replacing the rubber when worn.'

His patent was designed to overcome this difficulty by clipping the rubber blocks on to the jaws of the trap, 'so that it can be readily removed when worn and replaced by new rubber.' In the book *How To Trap And Snare* by Carnegie (1908 edition) there is an advert which states that these adaptors can be obtained from Messrs. B. Priest & Sons, Old Hill, Staffs plus a separate illustration of a trap with the adaptors fitted, with the caption, 'Mitchell's Humane Trap'. The book also states, 'The adaptors containing the rubber can be applied to ordinary tooth jawed traps by filing the jaws to receive them or by taking them out and reversing them in their sockets. The makers, Messrs. Wilkins & Wright, Birmingham, claim that the rubber containers will outlast the traps. . .'

A patent application was lodged on 21st October 1919 (No 25762/19) by John Henry Priest, Works Manager, and accepted on 15th July 1920 becoming Patent No. 146,764. 'The invention comprises an improved spring for vermin traps and the like and the means for producing same. . . the object of this invention is to manufacture a spring of the aforesaid type which dispenses with the ordinary welded junction between the steel and iron parts of the spring, the improved spring being of enhanced strength in comparison with the springs of this character.' This is Patent No 15002/20 in Australia.

Another patent application dated 11th February 1925 (No 3800/25) by

Benjamin, James and John Priest together, and accepted on 9th April 1925, becoming Patent No 231,793 was for improving the attachment of a wire spring to its stock 'without interfering with the resilience of the wire and rendering it liable to fracture from fatigue.' Their solution consisted of 'securing the extremities of a wire spring to a trap body by welding the wire to projections of small surface area formed on the body. As the projections are of small area the welding operation can be carried out very rapidly and the metal of the spring does not become sufficiently heated to affect its resilience or to modify the effect of the previous heat treatment of the steel.'

PROCTER BROS. (Wire Works) Ltd. Newport, Gwent. Year 1740- present.

This business was established in 1740 (in Leeds, Yorkshire) according to various catalogue adverts, and originally made wire sieves and such like wire products for agricultural use. The business was then acquired by the Procter family in the 1870s. At this time the business was mainly making wire fencing and machine guarding products, which incidentally they still produce today. Then in 1898, a Leeds ironmonger called James Henry

MITCHELL'S HUMANE TRAP

Atkinson patented the Little Nipper mousetrap, the complete specification being granted on 30th December 1898, becoming Patent No 27,488. Procter's made and sold this trap, and in 1913 bought the patent, and have continued to make this very successful trap. In fact the annual production of Little Nipper mousetraps is about 100,000 per year and are sold worldwide. Since originally making the Little Nipper mousetrap, Procter's have made other types of mouse and rat traps, including the Nipper rat trap with both a wooden and a metal bait plate. Traps made in both mouse and rat sizes include the Sentry, Alert and the Felix. They also made a box live catch mouse trap. However, apart from the Sentry and Little Nipper mouse traps plus the Nipper rat trap, these other traps are no longer made. The business is now at Pantglas Industrial Estate, Bedwas, Newport, Gwent NP1 8XD.

QUEENSBURY Ltd. Chevington, Bury St. Edmunds, Suffolk IP29 5RG Year 1998-2005?

Tel: 01284 851004.

It is thought that when the patentee of this trap died, the company ceased to exist. Certainly, in early April 2005, a letter written to the company was returned to me unopened and marked 'addresse has gone away'. It is supposed that this trap was not a commercial success due to its excessive weight and price. It is not known if any traps were actually sold, but definitely two were made.The Queensbury trap is an unusual design of live catch fox trap and was offered for sale in 1998. The company's brochure states that 'The Queensbury trap is the result of extensive research and development into humane live-catch trap design. Although loosely based on the bent sapling and ground-net principle, it incorporates instead a number of high-tensile springs and cross-sectional tines which, when activated, interlock to form an impregnable steel wall. A pre-baited triggering mechanism ensures that the Queensbury trap operates quickly and securely, containing the target animal without serious injury and with minimal distress.' The company 'decided to market the Queensbury trap as a complete fox-control system, complete with baits, lures and trailing scents. . . (and) is currently priced at £329 plus £20 carriage and VAT at the current rate (Total £410).' This trap 'is made entirely in the United Kingdom from British steel coated with nontoxic corrosion-resistant polyester paint.'

RAT PAK. Moor Lane, Thorpe on the Hill, Lincoln LN6 9BW. Year 1986-present.

The 'Rat Pak' trap was designed by Brian J. White while working in the family poultry farming business for the specific control of rats. Poisons had been previously used but found to be ineffective due to the vast constant source of food available. The Rat Pak trap was initially designed to control the rats in the poultry house roof insulation cavities. Rats are known to use roof beams as travel ways and so the early Rat Pak traps were positioned on the beams so that the rats had to pass through them in order to gain access to the chicken feed below. After a little experimentation this proved to be very effective and so then the traps were placed at ground level in the farm feed mill. All the traps were unbaited, being on the 'run through' principle, so as to catch the rats as they tried to enter or leave the buildings in search of food. After a few prototypes had been made and used, one hundred traps were then made for his own use around the farm.

These traps proved to be efficient and so Brian White filed a patent for the trap on 17th March 1988, the patent being granted in 1989 (Patent No 2,216,764). However, because he continued to develop his design, the pat-

ent was discontinued. Later, 400 traps of a slightly different design were produced of the 'run through' type. However, all these traps were made with a 'foot trip' to operate the single killing bar, and it was being discovered that this mechanism was prone to clogging by excessive poultry feathers etc. He then decided to produce an 'overhead trip' which effectively eliminated the previous disadvantage and at the same time two killing bars were introduced. Now there was a killing bar either side of the tripping mechanism, which helped to stop quick rats running through successfully.

'Rat Pak' is wholly owned by Brian White and was initially a single handed spare time occupation, but since 1990 has become a full time job and now also employs another two men. Since his initial success with his original rat trap design, he has gone on to designing other traps which are also manufactured in the same farm workshop. He now supplies over 400 dealers and pest control companies throughout Britain with his products.

Trap development;

August 1986. Prototype rat trap made and trialed.

March 1988. Production model containing two triangular shaped 'stops' with square metal mesh. The rat has to run through the centre of the trap between the two diagonally opposite 'stops'. 'Foot trip' operated single killer bar.

April 1991. This current version of the rat trap was designed to be less vibration sensitive, easier to set, and also able to operate in dirtier conditions more efficiently. Two killer bars instead of the previous single one. It is also an 'open' run through type, but without the two 'triangular stops' or 'foot trip'. This trap is now operated by a metal square mesh V-shaped 'overhead trip' mechanism, which is situated from side to side in the middle of the trap.

January 1992. Rabbit trap launched

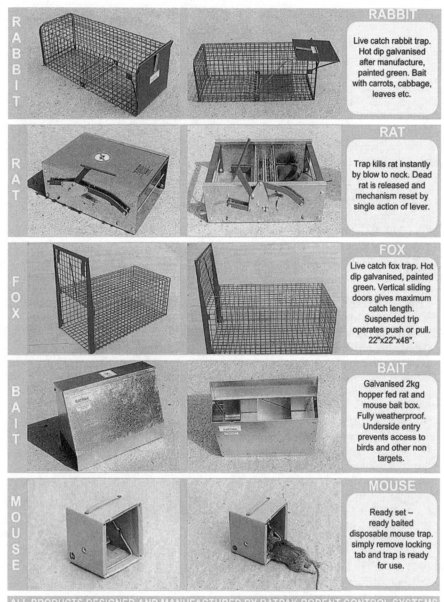

RABBIT

Live catch rabbit trap. Hot dip galvanised after manufacture, painted green. Bait with carrots, cabbage, leaves etc.

RAT

Trap kills rat instantly by blow to neck. Dead rat is released and mechanism reset by single action of lever.

FOX

Live catch fox trap. Hot dip galvanised, painted green. Vertical sliding doors gives maximum catch length. Suspended trip operates push or pull. 22"x22"x48".

BAIT

Galvanised 2kg hopper fed rat and mouse bait box. Fully weatherproof. Underside entry prevents access to birds and other non targets.

MOUSE

Ready set – ready baited disposable mouse trap. simply remove locking tab and trap is ready for use.

ALL PRODUCTS DESIGNED AND MANUFACTURED BY RATPAK RODENT CONTROL SYSTEMS

THE RANGES OF **RAT PAK** PEST CONTROL PRODUCTS

(live catch cage trap).

October 1992. Disposable self assembly cardboard mouse trap launched. This trap was never patented. The trap, when assembled, is formed into a cardboard cube and the metal killer bar is powered by an elastic band. There are no markings at all on the trap.

June 1993. Mouse trap modified to receive a steel chassis. The Mark II version consist of a metal chassis inside a thin cardboard outer casing. At the end of December 1994 production of the metal chassis mouse trap ceased. This was due totally to the rising demand for the company's poison bait boxes which were now a major seller.

MARK II MOUSE TRAP

REED, William Henry. Launceston. Year 1888-1957/8

On 28th May 1888 a patent application, No 7784, was made by William Henry Reed of Dunheved Iron Works, Launceston, Agricultural Implement Maker and James Walter Lawry of St. Dominick, St. Mellion, Farmer, both of the county of Cornwall, for a mole trap. The patent was accepted on 16th March 1889. This guillotine spear type mole trap was to become known as the Anglo-Impassable. In a 1907 Army and Navy Stores catalogue the illustration of 'The Slayer', with latest improvements and priced at 1/11d each, looks like this trap. However, the last known illustrated advert found by me was in a 1957/8 Young's of Misterton catalogue where the Anglo-Impassable was offered for sale at 18/6d each or three for 50/- carriage paid. There are three different models known. The Mark I has a complete circle welded to the top of the spring rod which drives down the spikes. The Mark II has the top of the spring rod formed into a circle, which is also of a heavier gauge metal than the Mark I model. A variation (A) of the Mark II trap consists of it being slightly

SINGLE KILLER BAR

ANGLO-IMPASSABLE MOLE TRAP

smaller than the normal Mark II trap in overall size, and with the spring rod 'eye' being of the same shape but again smaller. The trigger arm also has a shallower notch cut into it and only the very bottom of the trigger arm is tapered to allow for a flush fit.

SANKEY, Joseph & Sons Ltd. Bilston, Staffordshire

On the Demon Cockroach packaging box, is stated 'Made by Joseph Sankey & Sons Ltd'. The 'Demon' Cockroach/Beetle Trap was advertised from 1888 to 1940 regularly. However, I have only found one advert after 1940 in a Young's of Misterton catalogue of 1957/8. Maybe these traps were old forgotten stock. On 17th February 1887, 'William Frederick Lotz of the firm of Lotz, Abbott & Co. of 66 Queen Street, Cannon Street in the city of London, merchant, do hereby declare the nature of this invention, partly the result of a communication to me from abroad by Henry Abbott while temporarily residing in New York in the United States of America, and partly my own invention. . .' did apply for a provisional patent, No 2512, which was accepted on 15th July 1887. A very similar copy, in both shape and design to the 'Demon' trap, was called the 'Hedgehog' beetle trap. According to Crowden & Garrod's spring circular, of circa 1900, this trap was 'The latest pattern, 7,000 sold in Manchester in one week. Small 4/6d per doz. Large 9/- per doz'. This trap seems to differ from the 'Demon' by having oblong slots instead of the 'revolving butterfly wings' on the top, by which the beetles fall in.

SAUNDERS, Mark. Birmingham. Year 1770-1780

Trap maker, mouse. No 85 Digbeth, 1770 Mouse Trap Maker. 85 Digbeth, 1780.

SELFSET Ltd. Sunbury on Thames. Year 1947 – present.

Melbury Road, Woodthorpe, Nottingham. 1950-1958.
Falcon Works, Hanworth Road, Sunbury on Thames, Middlesex, England. 1959 – present.
In a letter dated 6th December 1984, the headed notepaper of which reads: 'Largest manufacturers of metal mouse and rat traps in the British Isles', it states that 'The Selfset one we have been manufacturing since 1947 and the Trapsit we have had on the market for the last ten years which we designed and patented but Rentokil have the selling rights of this. The Selfset one we find is very popular in England and overseas, and have been selling in the region of half a million every year over the past fifteen years and prior to that anything between 250,000 and 300,000. Very little variation has been made in the design but the manufacturing of this has been greatly improved and they are now made fully automatic which has enabled us to keep our price to a reasonable figure. The retail price of the mouse from the 1st Jan. 1985 will

be 45p and the rat 93p which includes VAT.' According to advertising brochures Selfset traps are made from Speltafast, a non rust steel. Three different variations of the rat trap are known. Type A has no spikes, type B has four spikes, type C has five spikes. The pointed spikes, on both types, are formed from out of the trap base, near its edge where the killer arm strikes.

SHAVE, William. Sturminster Marshall, Dorset. Year 1867-1871

1867 listed in directory as a shopkeeper.

1871 listed in directory as a grocer. However, in a provisional specification left at the office of the Commissioners of Patents on 3rd December 1867, William Shave declares himself as a trap manufacturer. In an advertisement in the *Ironmonger* dated 29th February 1868 an illustration shows a gin trap called the 'Idstone' trap which appears to be the trap referred to in the provisional specification. In a later catalogue of 1907, the Army & Navy Stores offered for sale 'The Shave' (humane) rubber jaw traps for rabbits at 2/6d each, or 28/0 per dozen.

An interesting reference in the above *Ironmonger* advert of 1868 states, 'Mr. Shave, the original Dorset trap maker, Patentee.' Could this advert be the answer to which family of trap makers produced the first 'Dorset' type trap way back in William Shave's great-grandfather's time?

The 'Idstone' trap was advertised, in 1868, as being made in 3", $3^{1}/_{2}$", 4", $4^{1}/_{2}$" 5" and 6" jaw sizes.

Idstone, writing in 1872, states that 'The usual Dorset trap made by Shave is 4 inches square, (meaning the jaws when in the open position) and when closed the jaws are $2^{1}/_{4}$ inches above the plate.' Then he goes on to describe 'an old otter trap, fished up from the (river) Stour after years of immersion, as good as the day it left the forge;

the S. – the monogram as we call it nowadays, of Shave's grandfather – being still distinguishable, and the springs as sharp as the day he tempered them. It will do the poor old smith little harm if I expatiate upon the barbarity of this instrument, $4^{1}/_{2}$ inches deep in the jaws when closed, and bristling with thickly set spike teeth, not only along the surface, but at the angle of the jaws. There is no occasion to use such severity, even to hold an otter, confessedly the most difficult of all British animals to catch and keep. Give him plenty of chain, six feet, and he will drown himself; and this, old Shave well knew, for he has attached a strong six feet chain to his old trap, with a well made and still acting swivel.'

The 'Shave' brand of trap was eventually made and sold by W.&G. Sidebotham of Wednesfield.

Miscellaneous Information:

The word 'Shave' was registered as a trademark on 20th May 1886 by Josiah Hyde, Dorset Works, 14 George Street, Parade, Birmingham. He described himself as a merchant and manufacturer.

Reviewing the information above, it is possible to logically speculate on the probable sequence of events regarding the 'Shave' brand of traps. The Shave family of trap makers, living in the county of Dorset, are thought to have made the original bow spring trap. Idstone writes: 'The secret of tempering was bought by the present maker's (Wm Shave) great-grandfather from a travelling tinker (gypsy) and the 'gin' thus made, rapidly became a favourite. I am not sure that the pattern itself was not furnished by this itinerant tinman.' Therefore presumably the original bow spring trap was first made by Wm Shave's great grandfather in the mid 1750s. Once the advantages of this type of spring were realised over the flat spring type, its fame would spread slowly outwards from Dorset, up through the Midlands and northwards. In 1871 William Shave, although regarding himself as a grocer, was still producing his 'shave' traps (but most likely on a small scale). This is verified by Idstone's writings in 1872. It would seem logical, therefore, that the original 'Shave' traps were only made by the Shave family, in small quantity, from about the mid 1700s until about 1885. The name 'Shave' was then registered as a trade mark by Josiah Hyde, Dorset Works, Birmingham in 1886. Prior to this 'Shave' registration, again according to Idstone, Wm Shave's grandfather made an otter trap which had the S monogram stamped on. Although this trap had been immersed in the River Stour for many years, it was recognisable as one of Shave's, without it having the full name stamped on. Remember, these early traps would not be mass produced in their hundreds, and would be relatively expensive, and would originally only have circulated in the local Dorset area where they would have become well known. Therefore, I suggest that any trap that has the stamp 'Shave' on it dates from after Josiah Hyde registered the trademark in 1886 and was never made by the Shave family. Josiah Hyde

described himself as a 'merchant & manufacturer' when he registered the 'Shave' trade mark. In all probability he would mainly be a merchant, e.g. retailer or wholesaler to other people or businesses. It is unknown what type of manufacturer he was, but he may not have been engaged in making traps.

Dorset Works, implies that the 'Shave' traps were made there, but businesses used to describe themselves as manufacturers even if they just put their own stamp on something that they had bought in and resold later. However, if J. Hyde had been retailing 'Shave' traps over many years, it is possible that Josiah Hyde did actually buy out William Shave's trap making business and transfer it to Birmingham. To safeguard his investment he registered the word 'Shave' as a trade mark, as 'Shave' traps would have been well known by then. Possibly, if J. Hyde didn't actually make his own 'Shave' traps, which was a very skilled job initially, and as he was most likely already dealing with established and well known trap makers, he would probably engage one trap maker to produce them for him. I say one trap maker, rather than several individuals, because he would want all of his traps to have a uniform shape or finish. If he ordered traps from several sources,

he would end up with different finishes as different trap makers would make them slightly different to each other. He would want them to look as though they were coming from the same factory (his). Now, if this sole trap maker, that he had a contract with happened to be W&G Sidebotham of Wednesfield, then this assumption would put the next piece into the jigsaw.

In 1924 Mark Hovell wrote in his book that for the last forty years he used traps manufactured by Sidebothams, and 'has bought their 'Shave' brand'.Note that he states *their* 'Shave' brand. Presumably therefore, the 'Shave' brand of traps had been purchased previously from J. Hyde by W&G Sidebotham at some time prior to 1924. The 'Shave' humane rubber jaw traps for rabbits are known to have been offered for sale from at least 1907 until 1939/40. A 4" inch jaw, round 'pole trap', stamped SHAVE, is known to exist which has a left handed spring, instead of the more usual right handed spring. On the end of the chain, the chain ring goes through a post pin by which

THE CELEBRATED "SHAVE" RABBIT AND VERMIN TRAPS.

The celebrated "Shave" Traps have a reputation of over 70 years' standing. The Registered Trade Mark "Shave" is stamped on each trap.

In ordering these, Members will please state if chains are required or not, chains being charged for extra, and only supplied when ordered.

5 in. traps and upwards are not kept in stock, but will be sent direct from the manufacturers. Samples may be seen in the Department.

"Real Dorset."			Each.	Per doz.
No. 21.	Brass mounted 4 in. jaw...		1/10	21/0
„ 21.	„	3 „	1/9	20/0
„ 9.	„	3 „ ...	1/5	16/0
„ 20.	„	4 „	1/4	15/0
„ 19.	„	4 „ ...	1/3	14/6

"Dorset."		Each.	Per doz.
3 in. jaw, 1st quality Run Traps ...		0/11	10/6
2½ „ ' „ „ „		0/10	9/6
3 „ 2nd „ „		0/10	9/6
2½ „ „ „		0/8	7/6

"Plain Rabbit."				Each.	Per doz.
No. 13.	4 in. jaw, not mounted ...			1/2	13/0
„ 12.	4 „	2nd quality		1/0	11/6
„ 11.	4 „	3rd „		0/10	9/6
„ 13.	5 „	not mounted ...		1/7	18/0
„ 12.	5 „	2nd quality		1/5	16/0
„ 11.	5 „	3rd „		1/2	13/6
Chains, light	....			0/2	1/9
„ heavy	....			0/4	3/6

"THE SHAVE." (Humane.)		Each.	Per doz.
Patent Rubber Jaw Traps for Rabbits......................		2/6	28/0
Chains, light	....	0/2	1/9
„ heavy	....	0/3½	3/0

ARMY & NAVY STORES
1907 CATALOGUE

MARK HOVELL'S
1924 COMMENTS

The price of steel traps varies somewhat with the price of iron, and for this reason they now cost more than formerly; but the following prices taken from a recent list of Messrs. Sidebotham show the comparison between the sizes and qualities.

ORDINARY RABBIT-TRAPS.
"Shave" brand without chains.

	5-inch	4-inch
1st quality	29s. per dozen	24s. per dozen
2nd „	25s. „	21s. „
3rd „	21s. „	18s. „

CHAINS.
Heavy ... 3s. per dozen   Medium ... 2s. per dozen

SIDEBOTHAM'S No. 6. SHAM DORSET.
Without chains.

5-inch	...	19s. per dozen
4-inch	...	16s. „

The same rate of prices applies to single traps and chains as per dozen.

If a dozen or more traps are required they may be obtained with the purchaser's initials stamped on them.

the trap is secured to the upright post.

J. SIMPSON & Sons, Otley. Year 1920-1930

Known from advert as the patentees and manufacturers of the Outwit rat trap.

SMITH, William. Birmingham. Year 1770-1780

Trap maker, mouse. No. 62 Coleshill Street, 1770

Mouse trap maker, 25 London Prentice Street, 1780.

J.J. THOMAS & Co. London. Year 1909-1921

In the book, *The Balance of Nature* published in 1909, it mentions that 'Traps for catching mice alive comprise numerous forms such as. . . the always set and baited Acme, Premier, Excelsior and Perpetual, in sizes catching up to twelve mice at a time, may be had of ironmongers or the manufacturers (Messrs J.J. Thomas & Co., 360 and 362 Edgware Road, London). The same book also mentions, with an illustration, that double cage traps for birds, especially bullfinches, can be obtained from the same address. In Young's of Misterton 1972 cata-

THOMAS & CO'S DOUBLE CAGE TRAP

logue this same design of trap '. . . the only trap that will successfully catch bullfinches' was being offered for sale at £2.12$\frac{1}{2}$ plus postage of 30p. In a 1921 advert, their address was 393 Edgware Road and they were offering Marvel rat traps (will catch from 10 to 15 rats at a time) plus mouse traps. Unfortunately there were no illustrations or prices.

1920 ADVERT

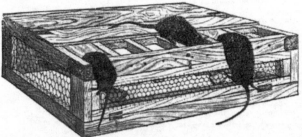

Patentees and Manufacturers: **J. SIMPSON & SONS,** OTLEY YORKS.

THE WORKFORCE OF W.H. TILDESLEY (DATE UNKNOWN) –
THE OWNER IS STANDING FAR RIGHT
(REPRODUCED FROM THE ORIGINAL HELD AT W.H. TILDESLEY LTD.)

WILLIAM HENRY TILDESLEY,
Willenhall. Year 1875-present.

This company was founded by William Henry Tildesley who was born in 1855, when he bought the small curry comb making business of the late Jesse Veal in 1875. The 'established 1800' date found on early headed notepaper probably refers to the Jesse Veal business. The business was located at 88 Walsall Street, Willenhall and W.H. Tildesley also lived there. From this address curry combs were supplied to Harrold Bros. of Birmingham for export to the United States of America. Other later destinations included Russia, Canada, Germany and such continental markets. However, other products were later made and sold including night latches, drop hammer forgings and of course steel traps.

On 25th October 1887 a patent application was filed and accepted on 31st August 1888 for a 'self setting' gin trap. This was Patent No 14,468 and consisted of one jaw being made complete with an 'ear' which opened the jaw when the spring was depressed. There was no tongue on the trap but the jaw engaged a 'C' type catch on the plate which had a slightly longer bottom curve. When the jaw pushed this catch down it had the effect of raising the plate up and the top of the 'C' shaped catch engaged the jaw. Releasing pressure on the spring, slowly, resulted in the jaw holding firm against this catch and stayed open. Traps with two 'ears' where also made. Another patent in 1889 (Patent No 8,648) was concerned with the forming of trap 'springs from a strip of steel in a quicker manner and without a weld or seam', whilst a patent applied for on 18th July 1895 and accepted on 23rd May 1896 (Patent No 13,769) concerned the cheaper construction of the bridge by being made 'humped' and therefore eliminating the need for the usual joints to hold the plate in place.

William Henry's fourth patent application was on 20th December 1904 and accepted on 2nd November 1905

(Patent No 27,922) was for yet another 'self setting' trap but this time a coil spring operated mole trap of the scissor type. In a letter dated 19th March 1902 Mr. Tildesley says about the packaging of traps, 'We pack usually in strong iron bound cases, as we find that the goods pack much more closely, and the cases are more dependable than cheap casks such as are generally used for these goods. We have sent thousands of dozens to the Bombay market and are doing a large Indian trade for repeat orders at the present time.' Overseas orders included in 1903 'Thousands of dozens of traps for the Australian markets' and again for the Indian market (Madras) '200 doz rat traps as follows. 100 doz No 4 at 13/- per doz, and 100 doz No 5 at 14/- per doz. 50 doz to be packed in a cask No 4 & 5 equally assorted and well oiled as usual.' With such good orders the last thing wanted in the trade would be a price war, therefore a meeting was arranged between Messrs Bellamy & Son of Wednesfield and W.H. Tildesley to agree fair terms of trade. What was agreed between the two trap makers is detailed in a letter dated 21st February 1903 from Tildesley to Bellamy, 'I beg to confirm arrangement with Mr. Bellamy made yesterday afternoon as follows

1st. That for the present we will not quote for common round jaw rat traps any better terms than 80% +10% casks charged, F.O.B. and as much more as possible.

2nd. That this quotation dates from March 1st next.

3rd. That should occasion occur for raising or lowering prices generally we will meet together and act together.

4th. That should either of us become suspicious of the other our respective books shall be open to some respectable person, say an accountant, so that independent testimony on the matter in dispute can be given.

Believing this to be a workable arrangement and having every confidence that it will be to our mutual advantage.'

However, in a letter dated 23rd October 1903, referring to the curry comb trade and import tariffs imposed by the USA, Russia and Germany, Tildesley complained to the Rt. Hon. Joseph Chamberlain of Highbury, Birmingham that 'I have the latest machinery and can only just compete on British soil.' An opportunity for Irish sales came about initially due to a verbal agreement on 27th November 1903 between Tildesley and Alabaster Bros. of Birmingham and later confirming them as sole agents for Ireland in a letter dated 15th February 1904 which stated, '. . . hereby appoint you my sole agents for Ireland to sell traps, curry combs and carriage treads on commission at 5% on nett returns, such returns being understood to mean the nett amount paid by customers for goods sent. This arrangement to be terminable by three months notice on either side.'

In 1904 the business was relocated to a greenfield site about 75 yards further along and across the road from 88 Walsall Street. The new address was on Bow Street, but still retained the Clifford Works name. This site is still the present location of W.H. Tildesley Ltd. albeit on a much expanded scale. On 2nd May 1904 a letter to Mr. Garratt of Edgbaston, Birmingham confirmed to him the lease of the premises of the old works at 88 Walsall Street, Willenhall at £40 per year to be paid quarterly commencing Midsummer 1904. Then in a letter sent to the Editor of the *Express and Star* Wolverhampton in July of that year about various concerns regarding the Willenhall surveyor's salary being doubled in three years, he complained, 'Rates going up. Trade going down. Value of house property reduced. Workmen existing on four days work per week. Manufacturers and tradesmen's profits reduced at least one third! Will one of the majority who voted for the increase in salary kindly give me his reason for so doing as there is a very wide spread feeling in the town against such a course.'

Although generally complaining in the July letter, in a reply to a letter from H.M. Admiralty, Engineer Overseer, Birmingham in December 1905, things had improved because mention was made of having a 'stamp shop 66' x 38'. This we are extending another 30' and putting down a stamp with 20 ton block. Have tea stamps with hammers ranging from 17cwt down to 1cwt and have a good annealing oven. Employ about 80 workpeople at present.'

Incidentally in 1906 the usual hours worked by a youth was 54 hours per week at 3d per hour.

Correspondence during August 1907 between W.H. Tildesley and Samuel Emery Junior of North Street, Wednesfield proves interesting. Emery, who was unemployed at the time, says 'that I have served you faithfully for more than a quarter of a century.' Tildesley's reply was that 'the state of the trade is such as to make it impossible to give you work without discharging others.' Emery then writes back saying that it was a 'miserable excuse when one considers that I introduced the trap trade... you know your real reason is far more contemptible than appears on the surface for is it not due to the fact that you are grinding down the wages of your poor slaves in the trap shop and that my dismissal from your service is the only way in which you can effect your purpose?'

In February 1918 Tildesley's were awarded two Army contracts for horse shoes. One contract was for light pattern No 3, 4 & 5, hind, whilst the other was for the weekly supply of 7,500

pairs. Five years later on 26th February 1923 the company was incorporated. Then on 30th July 1927 the last trap patent (Application No 20,237/27) was submitted, this time by Horace William Tildesley. The application was accepted on 15th March 1928 being Patent No 286,968. This patent was for the construction of the trap stock and spring out of one piece of continuous metal whilst being of a light weight. In order to keep its strength while also being lighter in weight, part of the stock had to be made with a channelled section. This idea also made production costs cheaper.

On 23rd November 1949, W.H. Tildesley died. A small drop forgings company was bought in 1972 and strangely this company was called G.A .Tildesley & Co. Ltd. The W.H. Tildesley Ltd. Company has certainly come a long way in diversifying its products since the first days of curry comb manufacturing as was shown in the 2nd September 1991 edition of the *Birmingham Evening Mail*. The company now supplies the world markets with specialist drop forgings etc. and their products can be found in some unusual places including windmills in Oregon, USA, and artificial limbs and Harrier Jump Jets. Yet for all these 'high tech' products the company still employs a workforce of 75 people and still makes curry combs and coil spring scissor mole traps.

Trade/Identification Marks: Acorn, Negro's head with a top hat on (1902).

Miscellaneous Information:

Experimental Traps:

Patentee: Harry Carne, Tregullas, Near Truro, Cornwall. (Farmer).

Date of Application: 14th July 1905.

Date Accepted: 1st March 1906.

Patent Number: 14,507

In an undated letter from Harry Carne regarding his conversation with W.H. Tildesley about rabbit traps for the June 1906 RSPCA competition he says 'whether my trap wins the prize

RAT TRAPS
No. 0510

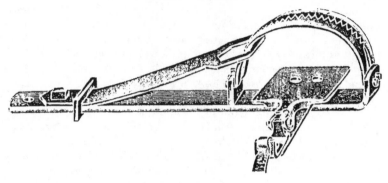

ROUND JAW

Size No.	...	3	4	5	6
Sizes of Jaws	...	4	$4\frac{1}{2}$	5	$5\frac{1}{2}$ ins.
Length overall	...	11	$11\frac{1}{2}$	$12\frac{1}{2}$	$13\frac{1}{2}$ ins.
Weight	...	...	12	$13\frac{1}{2}$	$14\frac{1}{2}$	16 ozs.

RAT TRAP SHIPPING SPECIFICATIONS

Size No.	1 Gross		2 Gross		5 Gross	
	Case Size	Gro. Wt.	Case Size	Gro. Wt.	Case Size	Gro. Wt.
		Cwt. qr. lbs		Cwt qr. lbs.		Cwt. qr. lbs.
3	20"x20"x20"	1 0 10	25"x25"x20"	2 1 0	33"x27"x31"	5 3 0
4	20"x20"x20"	1 0 14	25"x25"x20"	2 1 8	33"x27"x31"	5 3 14
5	22"x22"x20"	1 0 16	26"x26"x21"	2 2 4	33"x28"x32"	6 0 0
6	24"x24"x22"	1 0 20	26"x26"x23"	2 2 14	34"x30"x33"	6 2 0

W. H. TILDESLEY LTD.
CLIFFORD WORKS : WILLENHALL : STAFFS.

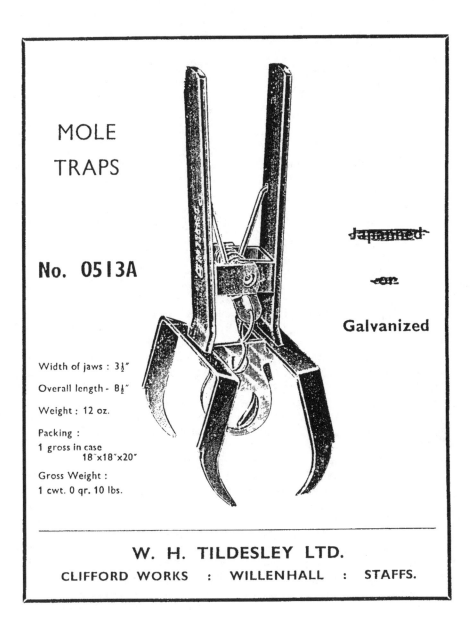

MOLE
TRAPS

No. 0513A

~~Japanned~~

~~or~~

Galvanized

Width of jaws : 3½"

Overall length - 8½"

Weight : 12 oz.

Packing :
1 gross in case
      18"x18"x20"

Gross Weight :
1 cwt. 0 qr. 10 lbs.

W. H. TILDESLEY LTD.

CLIFFORD WORKS : WILLENHALL : STAFFS.

or not does not lower it in my estimation. I am afraid 'the committee' are not 'experts' to give an opinion. However, they are going to try it and that's what I prefer. Let a gamekeeper give his opinion. What terms would you be prepared to offer, and I would sell them. I can give you bankers and other references, or I will sell the patent right 5/6'. In Tildesley's reply of 16th October 1905, he says, '. . . I think the better way would be for me to see the trap before I give an opinion as to the best thing to do. I am prepared to manufacture at a reasonable price and leave the sale of the goods to you. I might make some suggestions both as to the manufacture and the method of distribution of the goods when made but can not very well do either till I see the trap. . .'

Doubt was cast on the probability of the RSPCA prize being awarded as is shown in the letter dated 15th November 1905 from John S. Owens, AM. INST. C.E. of Westminster, London. 'I have not heard result yet of trap time, but have little doubt that none of those selected will do their work properly. Especially as to my knowledge the two killing traps are made on a principle which was patented and abandoned years ago. I think the prize will probably not be awarded which would be unfair, as it was offered for the best trap, not for a perfect one. Would you be inclined to cooperate with me in

producing a trap for the RSPCA competition in June?' Tildesley's reply was 'I shall be pleased to cooperate with you in producing a trap for the RSPCA competition in June.' Unfortunately, no further correspondence was found as to the outcome of this joint venture.

Patentee: George Louis Lavender, Druids Heath, Aldridge, Staffs (Managing Director) of Lime Works).

Date of Application: 17th November 1905.

Date Accepted: 29th March 1906.

Patent Number: 23,651

(Automatic mouse & vermin trap known as the Rotary Automatic Exterminator).

In G.L. Lavender's letter to Tildesley dated 3rd January 1906 he says 'I am pleased you have proved the effectiveness of the trap. What about the terms for working it, are you prepared to join me? If so I think the following would be fair. Value of patent £1,000. I will accept £300 and after paying a fair price for making will divide the profit with you. You being sole maker and provide tools etc. According to quotations you have already, it will not cost more than 10/- dozen. Say 1/- each and we sell at say 2/- giving us 6d each, a sale of 10,000 would give you the money back. I think this is fair, what do you think?' Tildesley's reply the next day was 'I am not prepared to take up a share in your patent, but do not object to making them and trying to put them on the market. To do this means two or three things. 1st, to make them and retail them at 2/- each. 2nd to make them and sell wholesale at 1/- each to the factors and merchants or 3rdly ignoring the merchants and factors, sell to ironmongers and retailers at a price for them to retail at 2/- each or 2/6d each. Either of these methods do not allow of anything life 2/- each for you to net. If you consider the expense and trouble of floating a new thing, I think you will come to my conclusion that as a sale, a patent is little worth, only as a protection against <u>competitors when you have made a trade</u> in a particular line of goods'.

Patentee: John Caleb Percy Webber, 96 Union Street, Plymouth. (Jeweller).

Date of Application: 16th November 1906.

Date Accepted: 30th May 1907.

Patent Number: 25,939 (Automatic vermin trap).

Writing to Mr. Webber on 8th October 1906 W.H. Tildesley stated 'I have examined carefully the sample of patent rabbit trap and also the specifications but do not think that either of them is likely to take with trappers or meet the requirements of the Society for the Suppression of Steel Traps. I beg to return sample and specifications and letters herewith by parcel post.'

An interesting series of letters concerning a member of the Society for the Suppression of Steel Traps Committee for Selecting a Humane Trap were found, and references to experimental Tildesley traps were included. The first dated 8th October 1906, was from Mr. Andrew Buxton of Hunson Bury, Ware, Herts. In it he says 'Mr. S. Trist has forwarded me your two letters which I would myself reply to by saying that I as a member of the Committee shall be very pleased to give any trap you care to send me a good trial. I did not attend the first meetings when the models were looked through but some made for striking the rabbit were too cumbersome and the impulse of the spring being released so great that the rabbit was thrown away from the traps and they were consequently useless. If you can make one such as you suggest in your letter it should be what we require so long as it can be set in the position required by law and is equal to the present steel trap in portability and efficiency.' Tildesley's reply of 9th

October 1906 was '. . . and shall be glad to send you a sample to try in a little time. I am addressing myself to the task of making a trap to set in the mouth of the hole occupying a space of not more than 6" in width and of striking high enough to kill a rabbit. I suppose that the Society will grant the prize to the person who can satisfy them. I understand no competitor has been awarded the prize as yet.' In a further letter to Mr. Buxton dated 16th October 1906 Tildesley writes, 'Under separate cover I am sending two patent applied for rabbit traps which may answer your purpose for a preliminary trial. I have several more, part made, of rather different construction which I will send you later on. In the meantime I shall be much obliged to have your opinion as to the effectiveness or otherwise of those I am sending you. Thanking you for your kindness in interesting yourself in this matter'. In an afterthought, he adds 'These samples will require a little care in setting as they are imperfect, the tongue being weak which holds the jaw down but I am sure you will not put them to a too severe trial at first'. Tildesley then wrote to Mr. Sidney Trist of London on 18th October 1906 enquiring about Mr. Buxton. He wrote, 'On the 16th inst. I forwarded to Mr. Buxton two rabbit traps which I have patented provisionally so that he may try them. I feel rather curious to know if you know what Mr. Buxton's position is i.e. whether he is well qualified to give an unbiased opinion. My reason for asking this is the ordinary business caution begotten of experience as that gentleman is an absolute stranger to me. Hoping I am not trespassing too much on your kindness'. Mr. Sidney Trist was the Honorary Secretary of the Society for the Suppression of Steel Traps, and replied on 19th October 1906 that 'You may quite rely upon Mr. Buxton. He is a relative of the famous Buxton's the Brewers, who are known for their philanthropy and interest in many movements. He is a country gentleman in Hertfordshire but he is also connected with the banking interest in the city, and you may rely absolutely upon his honour in every way; he is a practical man and quite understands the difficulties of the position from the standpoint of the trapper. I shall be glad to hear if anything results from the effort'. Obviously happy with the reply he received from Trist, he then, on 29th October 1906 wrote to Buxton 'I am sending under same cover herewith, two more patented traps for you to try. The double jawed trap is easy to set by me accustomed to handling these traps. When the spring is pressed down you can easily keep the jaws open and adjust the plate (treadle). The single jaw trap can easily be set by pulling open the jaws and allowing the square link or ring to run down the spring, being careful after setting to put the said ring at the chain end of the trap so as not to interfere with the working of same. I shall be glad of any suggested modifications you may choose to give me and if you think it necessary I shall be pleased to meet you and discuss any point you may have occur to you when trying these samples. These traps are the first crude attempts embodying the 'lazy scissor' principle.' Buxton's delayed reply was written to Tildesley on 9 November 1906 saying 'I regret having omitted to acknowledge your letter of 29th and 2 further traps with it owing to having been away. You have taken a deal of trouble designing the 4 traps and I have given them careful consideration. I find that the only one which is certain of catching is the double jawed one and that, that catches by the legs and is therefore the same as the ordinary steel trap and no more humane. The reason for this one and the others failing to kill the rabbit as you intended appears to be that the actual 'wings' of the traps are so short being only 3 or $3\frac{1}{2}$ inches in length, that when the rabbit comes from behind it simply grazes him underneath. When he comes from in front it is a just chance whether they catch his head or graze his nose and even if they struck the head or neck I think it would be some hours before the animal was killed if it was killed at all. We had sent us a very similar trap to the straight one of the first 2 you sent me only with longer 'wings' which were slightly curved at the ends for the intention of catching the rabbit alive round the neck. We found that this sometimes acted very successfully but it as often as not missed altogether. I am extremely sorry not to be able to give a more satisfactory report on your traps but considering the uncertainty of this action I can not consider this more humane than the gin and they are not more efficient and would be I should say more expensive. The prize has not yet been awarded and I fear if it ever will be as neither your traps nor others sent in are equal to the gin in cheapness and efficiency. I will return your traps tomorrow to Willenhall Station L.N.W.R. carriage paid'. Tildesley's last known letter sent to Buxton was dated 14th November 1906. In it he wrote 'Thanks for yours of the 9th inst. and my models which I have now received. I did not expect any of them to meet your requirements but feel that I can not yet give up my quest. Was the trap you speak of as being like one of mine submitted by a Mr. Carne of Truro? If so it opened above 14 inches and seemed to me too wide to set in a burrow. Will you kindly say how high a trap jaw should strike and how wide when opened it may be as I am not yet satisfied that the thing can not be made. The difficulty with me is that I am not a trapper only a mechanic and until this competition was brought to my notice had never troubled to enquire into the habits of the rabbits. I am learning still but the demands of business keep me from giving the time to a very interesting subject which I feel I should like'.

Prior to 1976 (exact date unknown) W.H. Tildesley Ltd donated to Walsall Museum a total of 42 assorted traps, not all being of their own manufacture as some are marked 'Oneida Community No 4 Jump, Sargent & Co No 1' etc, which are American manufacturers. Along with the traps, which included rabbit, mole and mouse trap, curry combs and step treads for carriages or cars were also donated.

Traps donated include:

Patentee: Frank Edmund Sawyer
Date of Application: 27th July 1936 (No 20702/36).
Date Accepted: 19th October 1937
Patent Number: 473,718 Prototype 'Imbra'.

Patentee: James Duncan, Easter Wairds, near Denny, Stirlingshire, Scotland.
Date of Application: 23rd August 1933 (No 23,558/32).
Date Accepted: 4th January 1934.
Patent Number: 403,767 Duncan Rabbit Trap.

Patentees: Samuel Collett & James Henry Collett of Otago, New Zealand.
Date of Application: 24th September 1895.
Date Accepted: 2nd November 1895.
Patent Number: 17,840.

Two versions of this patent were donated. The first is the one shown in the specifications, a small 'jump' type, whilst the second is a gin trap style of trap, but with the stock forming into a square box around the plate as a protection against soil accumulating under the plate. This trap is also similar to known traps found in Australia which are called 'Imperial Box Traps'. The maker of these 'Imperial Box Traps' remains

unknown but they have stamped on their plate Pat No 25,355/35 which may be an Australian patent number.

Tildesley's Patents:
No 286,968 (1928).
No 13,769 (1895). This trap has a round bait plate.
No 14,468 (1887). Two types donated. The first is a square jaw bow spring, tongueless. The second type is a round jaw with one 'ear or lug' for self setting and is tongueless. The spring is unusual in being neither bow or flat but a combination of both to look at. The end is riveted as is normal in flat springs, but then rises up at a slight angle and sits in the normal bow spring position. Another self setting gin trap (Patent No 12654, which was jointly patented by Cyril Walker and William Allsopp both of Wolverhampton in 1886), is set by the action of depressing the spring, which then acts upon a 'handle or lever' under the spring by pressing it down. When the 'lever' is depressed, the plate is raised at the same time which engages against the 'eye' of the spring. There is no bridge on this trap and the plate falls along the stock away from the 'eye'.

Cyril Walker's Patent self setting Rabbit and Vermin traps were advertised and illustrated in an undated catalogue of T.W.& J. Walker of Wolverhampton, who are stated to be Merchants in the trade directories for the years 1869-1874. The catalogue page states 'Rabbit Traps- Plain or Grooved Jaw' whilst the jaw sizes made were stated to be 4, $4^{1}/_{2}$ & 5 inch. The prices being respectively 8/6, 11/6, & 13/6 per doz, net cash, whilst chains for these traps could be obtained at 2/- per dozen extra. The Rat or Run Traps, again made in either Plain or Grooved Jaw, were made in jaw sizes of $2^{3}/_{4}$ and 3 inch. Their prices being 6/6 & 7/6 per doz net cash, with chains for them at 1/6 per dozen extra. The illustration shows both traps with an extended or projecting stock.

A trap which seems to be the one referred to in the above mentioned letters consists of a bow spring which operates jaws on the 'lazy scissors' principle. This trap, which has a Negro's head stamped on the spring also has Tildesley Patent Applied marked on the plate.

Another trap working on the 'lazy scissor' principle consists of only one set of jaws (a single pair of arms) and is operated by a flat spring. This trap is incomplete, and has no markings.

A trap with a conventional square gin type jaw and stock has a concealed coil spring which operates 'half' a normal trap spring (from the eye down) which is fixed to it by a rivet on top of the 'casing'. The plate also 'falls' along the line of the stock. This trap has a Negro's head trade mark on the spring.

An unusual type of 'jump' trap was also donated. This trap differs from the usual 'jump' type traps by having the plate directly attached to the flat spring, instead of being attached to one side as is normal. This jump trap is also a variation of the Walker and Allsopp's Patent No 12,654 of 1886, as two separate styles of traps were illustrated in the patent drawings.

Lastly, an unknown self setting double flat spring 'scissor type' mole trap was gifted to the museum.

Tildesley Stock 1927-1935:
1927. No 3 Jump traps
1928. Jump traps 1385 No 3. Plus jump trap chains.
1930. No 3 jump traps 1340
1931. Round jaw jump traps No 3. 1340
1935. No 3 square jaw jump traps.

According to the few remaining stock records at Tildesley's, jump traps were listed between 1927 and 1935. There seems to have been two jaw types made, but in how many sizes remains unknown. From the records it seems that round jaw jump traps size No 3 were listed as No 1340, whilst the same size of trap, but made with a square jaw seem to be listed as No 1385.

Working on the assumption that the previously mentioned unusual jump trap, the one with the plate attached to the flat spring, that was donated to the Walsall Museum by W H Tildesley's was also made by this company, it is possible that the stock listings refer to a more successful version which was produced. Two known types exist which only differ slightly from the museum item, but unfortunately none have any identifying marks etc. on them. They are a round jawed Kingfisher trap with serrated teeth, and a 4" square jawed trap with the normal scalloped teeth of most rabbit gin traps.

Traps in Stock at June 1927:
Round jaw rat (size) No 0-1-2-3-4-5-6-7-8 inclusive.
Square jaw rat trap (size) No 1-2-3-4-5 inclusive
Galvanised and japanned mole traps.
No 0503. Rabbit traps 4" & $4^1/_2$" (inch jaws).
No 0509a $3^1/_2$"-4"-5"
No 0502 Fox 6"-7"-8"
No 0511 Run $2^1/_2$"-3"
No 3 Jump traps.

June 1928:
Round jaw rat no 0-8 inclusive.
Square jaw rat No 1-2-3-4-5 plus also No 1 & No 3 with spiked jaws
Mole traps in both coil spring and old pattern (flat springs)
Bird trap $2^1/_4$"
Rabbit traps
0509a $3^1/_2$"-4"-$4^1/_2$"-5"
0509b $3^1/_2$"-4"-$4^1/_2$"-5"
0503 4"-$4^1/_2$"-5"
0514 4"
0515 4"

Jump traps
1385 No 3
Fox traps
0502 6"-7"-8"
Run
0511 2$\frac{1}{2}$"-3"
Chains
3 link, 6 link no swivel, jump trap chains

June 1929:
Round jaw traps No 0-7 inclusive, with also included, No 3 double jaws.
Square jaw No 1-5 inclusive, with also included No 3 & No 2 with spiked jaws
Galvanised and Japanned mole traps
Bird traps.
Rabbit traps
0509a 3$\frac{1}{2}$"-4"-5"
0509b 3$\frac{1}{2}$"-4"-5"
0503 3$\frac{1}{2}$"-4"-4$\frac{1}{2}$"-5"
0511 2$\frac{1}{2}$"-3" plus 3" special (run)
0515 4"
0502 6"-7"(fox)

June 1930:
Round jaw rat No 0-7 inclusive
Square jaw rat No 1-5 plus No 2 spiked (jaws). Also listed under this heading
No 3 jump traps
1340
Rabbit traps
0503 3$\frac{1}{2}$"-4"-4$\frac{1}{2}$"
Rabbit traps
0509a 3$\frac{1}{2}$"-4"-5"
0509b 3$\frac{1}{2}$"-4"-4$\frac{1}{2}$"-5"
0515 4"-4$\frac{1}{2}$"
0514 4$\frac{1}{2}$"
0502 6"-7"-8" (fox)
0511 2$\frac{1}{2}$"-3$\frac{1}{2}$" (run)
Mole traps. Japanned and galvanised.

June 1931:
Round jaw rat No 0-8 inclusive plus No 8 double jaw
Square jaw rat No 1-5 inclusive plus No 1 & No 3 with spiked jaws
Round jaw jump traps No 3. 1340
Rabbit traps
0509a 3$\frac{1}{2}$"-4"-5"
0509b 3$\frac{1}{2}$"-4"-4$\frac{1}{2}$"-5"
0503 3$\frac{1}{2}$"-4"-4$\frac{1}{2}$"
0514 4"
0515 4"

SAMUEL COLLETT
PATENT NO. 17,840 (1895)

JAMES DUNCAN. PATENT NO.
403,767 (1934)

FRANK SAWYER. PATENT NO.
473,718 (1936)

HORACE TILDESLEY. PATENT
No.286,968 (1928)

0502 6"-7"-8" (fox)
0511 2$\frac{1}{2}$"-3 " (run)
Mole traps. Japanned and galvanised.
Bird traps.
June 1935:
Round jaw rat No 0-8 inclusive
Bird traps
No 3 square jaw jump traps
0518 traps
Rabbit traps
0509a 4" plus 0509a chains
0509b 4" & 5"
0503 3$\frac{1}{2}$"-4"-4$\frac{1}{2}$"-5"
0502 6"-7"-8" (fox)
Run traps
0511 2$\frac{1}{2}$"-3" plus No 3 with brass
tongue & till & galvanised plate
Mole traps
Japanned and galvanised coil springs
Japanned and galvanised bent springs
(? U-shaped spring maybe ?)
Square jaw rat No 1-5 inclusive plus
No 2 & 3 with spiked jaws.
June 1938:
0509a and 0509b
Round jaw rat No 0-6 inclusive
Square jaw rat No 1-4 inclusive
Run traps 2$\frac{1}{2}$" & 3"
Mole traps
Bird traps.

TWO LATER, SIMILAR VARIATIONS
OF WALKER & ALLSOPP'S
PATENT NO 12654 (1886)

June 1948:
0510 Round jaw rat traps No 3-6
inclusive.
June 1950:
Rat traps No 3-5 inclusive

**TINSLEY, Eliza & Co Ltd. Cradley
Heath. Year 1851 – present.**
In 1813 at Wolverhampton was born
the daughter of Benjamin Butler. This
daughter Eliza, was at the age of 25
to marry Thomas Tinsley of Sedgley,
an established nailmonger. He was

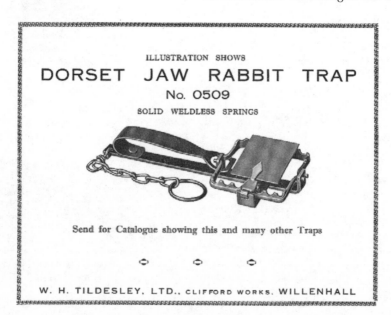

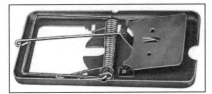

TILDESLEY'S ILLUSTRATION OF
IMPEX TRAP

A TILDESLEY MOLE TRAP,
NOW OBSOLETE

five years older than her when they married on 1st January 1839. During her twelve years of marriage to Thomas, she gave birth to six children. Her husband died in June 1851, and against all odds for a woman in that day and age, she decided to carry on her husband's business. Very quickly she established herself as a shrewd businesswoman and was respected for her honest business ability. She also had a reputation for being a fair and kind employer to her many workers, as well as a generous local benefactor. Although mainly involved in the wrought iron nail trade, her business expanded to include such products as rivets, chains and anchors as can be seen in an 1860 advertisement. In 1870 she decided to send to Melbourne, Australia her representative to set up a business in that country, trading on her established name and reputation. It is thought that her intention was to establish a similar business in this newly developing country. However, in 1872, she sold the English business to a partnership whilst the Australian business seems to have been an independent company with no links to Cradley Heath in England. Ten years later, on 18th April 1882, Eliza Tinsley died at her home in Sedgley.

The early history of when Tinsley's first started to produce animal traps is unknown, but it is known from an undated catalogue (which is later than 1932) of theirs that they produced the usual common types of gins for rats, rabbits, fox etc. This same undated catalogue also shows a 'scissor type' mole trap, and 'Griffin's Patent' mole, rabbiting and general trapping spades being offered for sale. It is not known if these 'Griffin's Patent' spades were made by Tinsley's or just retailed by them. When it became obvious to the company management that gin traps were to be banned, a decision to discontinue manufacture of them was taken well before the ban was implemented. However, after the introduction of the gin trap ban in 1958, Tinsley's still managed to sell and export to Ireland gin traps which they had purchased from W&G Sidebotham, as late as 1975-6. During the 1970s they were also purchasing quantities of fox chains, swivels etc. from Sidebotham's. W.&G. Sidebotham's probably stamped 'Tinsley' on the traps, for them to sell as their own products, as the metal punches bearing the Tinsley name were found amongst Sidebotham's machinery when the building and contents were sold to the Black Country Museum at Dudley.

Although only now producing their No 208 mole trap, which is an established seller, they did introduce for a short while an all metal break back rat trap. This trap was never particularly successful and after a prolonged period of poor sales was finally discontinued. In a Young's of Misterton catalogue dated 1972 there is an illustration of this trap and they were priced at 40p each. Along with this catalogue is a separate leaflet with price alterations from July 1st 1972. Mention is made for page 48 'Breakback traps, cannot supply.' The earliest reference to this trap that I have found is in Young's 1962 catalogue where the illustration is exactly the same, but priced at 4/- each plus 1/- postage. This trap doesn't appear in their 1957/8 catalogue. Two slightly different types of this trap were made, one with and one without a 'half moon' shaped support, where the trigger arm or tongue is attached.

Trade/Identification Marks:
E.T. (1856). T in a circle (1870). Eliza Tinsley & Co. (1874). Swastika (1921).

A BREAK BACK TRAP, MADE BY
TINSLEY FOR RATS

TOMKYS, Samuel. Wolverhampton. Year 1833-1838
Steel trap maker, 1833
Steel rat trap maker, Canal Street, Wolverhampton. 1838
Note different surname spelling: Tomkiss 1838.
See also S Tomkys, Wednesfield.

TOMLINSON, Joseph. Birmingham. Year 1854-1858
Steel trap maker. 16$\frac{1}{2}$ Loveday Street, 1858

Rat trap maker. 16$\frac{1}{2}$ Loveday Street, 1856
Steel trap maker, 16 Aston Street, 1854
Steel trap maker, 20 Court, Coleshill Street, 1854.

The TRAPPO Co. London. Year 1906-1920
7, Castle Street, Finsbury, London.
Maker of the 'New automatic mouse trap with mirrors.' Trade Mark: The business of Bielenberg & Co., 7, Castle Street, Finsbury, London E.C. who were importers of Foreign Goods, registered the name TRAPPO on 31st January 1906.

JOHN TURNER & Sons (Wire Works) Ltd. Sheffield. Year 1789-1983
Turner John. Wire worker & birdcage manufacturer. 98 Norfolk Street. 1876, 1879.
Advert showing 'Perfection Mouse Trap' dated 1st October 1877.
Turner John. Wireworker. Channing Hall Buildings, New Surrey Street and Ironmonger, Ladys Bridge Buildings Wicker. 1883
Turner John. Plain & ornamental wireworker. The Sheffield Wire Works, Channing Hall Buildings, New Surrey Street and 6 Wicker. 1884
In 1887 listed as Blind Manufacturer in New Surrey Street.
Listed in 1888 at 47 Newsurrey Street & Ladys Bridge Buildings Blonk Street.
In 1889 'New' was omitted from the address.
1893 listed as of 44 Arundel Lane & Surrey Street.
Manufacturer of every description of wirework for gardens, fencing, Sheffield Wire Works Est 1789. 47/49 Surrey Street & Arundel Lane. 1895, 1896, 1898.
In 1902, 1903, 1905 Works address was 3 Arundel Lane.
1907 John Turner & Sons, 47 Surrey Street. Works Sidney Street.

PATENT RABBIT TRAPS

WITH IMPROVED CATCH AND EASY RELEASE

Regd. No. 395462

STEEL SPRING PATTERN

No. 400   per dozen

WIRESPRING PATTERN

No. 402   per dozen

ADVANTAGES OVER THE OLD PATTERN

1. It is strongly made.

2. It is easier to set when the jaws are opened and the plate is raised. The Trap sets automatically.

3. It is slightly narrower than the old pattern and easier to cover when set.

4. It is finely adjusted and light pressure on the plate will spring the trap.

TINSLEY'S COPY OF ROBERTS TONGUELESS TRAP, PATENT NO 395462 (1933)

1908-1926 Works address Sylvester Gardens.
1934 Turner John & Sons (Wireworks) Ltd. 26 Arundel Street. Works 12 Eyre Lane.
1938 41 Howard Street. Works 12 Eyre Lane.
1944 240 Abbeydale Road. Works 12 Eyre Lane.
1951 11/14 West Bar Green. Works Eyre Lane.
1957 Office Swinton Street, Bridgehouses.
1961-1983 Lambert Street, West Bar. Ceased business on 14/09/1983.

VAUGHAN, H&T. Willenhall. Year 1874-1929

Standard Works, Willenhall. 1874 Henry Vaughan, Lock Manufacturer, Wood Street. 1877-80 Henry & Thomas Vaughan, Rim, Mortice & Deadlock Manufacturers, Wood Street. In 1880 they are mentioned as being lock makers at 27, Wood Street, and also Pawn Brokers at 24, Market Place. Pawnbroking is not mentioned after this date. In 1916 their telephone number was 56 Willenhall. In 1929, H&T Vaughan were taken over by Yale Locks. Obviously, from the above information this business was mainly involved in lock making. This poses the question, did they actually make traps for a short while or was it more likely that they bought them in with their own initials stamped on them, and just resold them to customers who had ordered them from their catalogue, in which a gin trap was illustrated with various sizes and prices accordingly? They were supposedly makers of various items including traps. Identical entries appear in the 1895 and January 1902 catalogues which show the ordinary bow spring gin trap that they supposedly made in sizes $3^1/_2$", 4" $4^1/_2$", 5" and $5^1/_2$".

J. VEAL (thought to be a Dorset trap maker) date: Pre 1800?
Identification Mark: J.V.

Idstone, when describing some old traps in his possession, states that the first trap weighs 60lbs of iron and 'It measures 6ft.7in. from end to end, and each spring is 2 ft.7in. long. As you always find in old traps, the maker was not content with a trigger and trigger plate, he surrounded the jaws with a substantial iron frame. There are abundant reasons for doing away with this unnecessary addition. This useless frame of substantial wrought iron is nineteen inches square. The jaws work in two double studs, each of which would, as Shave the trap maker tells me, take a quarter of a day to make. The closed jaws reach ten inches above the trigger plate, which is nearly a foot square, and each jaw is armed with seven spike teeth, an inch and a half long, and so set as to tear the flesh of any unhappy struggler. The combined strength of the two springs – for there is one at each side of the jaws – pulls at least 560lbs, enough to almost sever an ordinary birch wood broom handle at a blow. I have two of these formidable engines, and both were marked J.V. The workmanship is first rate and each trap must have cost the first owner three or four pounds. A few days ago a very large, powerful 'frame trap' , made doubtless for wild and martin cats was brought to me, bearing the same monogram as this pair of mantraps. It might have served as the model for these barbarous toils, and on the spring I found the name J. VEAL. – a Dorset maker, I believe, who lived before Hall, and one or two Dorset trapmakers who were famous in their day before the 'Shave period' to use the language of the scientific world.'

WAINE, Joseph & Co. Willenhall. Year 1892-1912

According to their January 1905 catalogue this company made a 'Speciality of catering for the different colonial and foreign markets. . .' and their products included such items as 'locks, latches, curry combs, safes, hinges, grindstones, vermin traps & etc.' Their address was Imperial Works, Wood Street, Willenhall, England. This is probably another business that bought in various specialty products from the actual makers, and resold them to their customers as being made by themselves.

WALKER, John. Birmingham. Year 1770
Rat trap and bed screw maker. No 2 Bow Street, 1770

WARD, Joseph. Birmingham. Year 1770-1780
Trap maker, mouse. Floodgate Street, 1770
Mouse trap maker. 10 Floodgate Street, 1780.

WHITLOCK BROS LTD. Great Yeldham, Essex 1882 – circa 1974/5
According to Kelly's Directory for Essex, in 1882, Francis, Hy.Ed. and John Whitlock were described variously as farmers, coal, corn, brick and artificial manure merchants. The first entry for the business is found twenty years later in 1902 – Whitlock Brothers, agricultural engnrs. After 1937 the business is listed in Kelly's manufacturers and merchants directory. In the 1974/5 volume they were recorded as being 'contractors, plant and equipment manufacturers'. They were not found in the 1986 volume.

Patents. In 1932 Joseph Henry Fuller Carey of Redditch, Worcestershire patented (No 389,410) a wooden tunnel trap, which had its two spring mechanisms fixed on the outside and on top of the tunnel. This trap was to be known as the 'A.B.C.' Humane Vermin Trap and was recommended by the R.S.P.C.A. In 1934, Gilbertson & Page advertised

this trap in their *Gamekeeper* magazine as Carey's A.B.C. Humane Safety Vermin Trap for rats, stoats, weasels etc at 5/- each with postage being 1/- extra. It was also sold and illustrated in Young's of Misterton's catalogues of 1937 and 1940. This trap was also sometimes referred to, by trappers, as the 'Whitlock' trap, presumably because it may have been originally sold by them or even known that this business made it.

Later, Whitlock Bros also made two other wooden tunnel traps, and three sizes of wood and wire netting traps, according to their advert of November 1961, which appeared in *The Gamekeeper and Countryside* magazine. These 'wood and wire netting' traps were advertised as 'Balchin' Humane Trapping Cages and have the Provisional Patent No.021215. In the February 1964 issue of the above mentioned magazine, Whitlock's were advertising 'Game Farm Equipment' which also showed a live catch, bird cage trap. This same advert, again, appearing in March 1966.

WILMOT, S.M. and Co. Ltd. Bristol. Year 1896-1960
The first entry for this firm in the street directories appears in 1896 and states, 'S.M. Wilmot and Co., Galvanised Iron Works, Albert Road, St. Philip's Marsh, Bristol.' The firm remained at this address until they ceased trading after 1960. By 1909 they had acquired the telegraph address of 'Galvaniser' and the telephone number 851. Their first listing as a Limited Company was in 1911. The firm's telephone number by 1939 was 76051 and by 1950 had changed to 77491. Their last entry was in the 1960 Directory where they were described as 'Sheet Metal Workers'. This firm mainly produced a variety of general metal wares, but in Carnegie's book, *Practical Trapping*

Vermin Traps.

Run Traps.

		2½-in.	3-in.
G847	Common ...	6/6	7/6 per dozen.
G848	Best ...	7/6	8/6 "

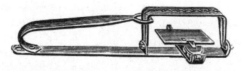

Rabbit Traps with Chains complete, Plain or Grooved Jaws.

			4-in.	4½-in	5-in. Jaws
G849	Quality,	Light	9/-	11/6	14/- per dozen.
G850	"	*	9/6	12/-	14/6 "
G851	"	A	10/6	13/-	15/6 "
G852	"	B	12/-	15/-	18/- "

Other Qualities on application.

Plain Bridge, Double Spring Wolf, Tiger and Kangaroo Traps.

			6-in.	7-in.	8-in.	9-in	10-in.	11-in.	12-in. Jaws.
*	**G853**	Quality	5/8	7/6	9/6	12/-	14/6	17/-	19/6 each.
**	**G854**	"	4/6	5/10	7/6	9/6	12/-	14/-	16/6 "
***	**G855**	"	3/8	4/10	6/4	8/2	10.-	12/-	14/6 "
		Chains.	4/6	6/-		9/6 per dozen.			

JOSEPH WAINE & CO, 1905 CATALOGUE

(5th edition, published in 1922) he states that Wilmot's 'also make a combined sparrow and rat trap (Wyatt's patent). This has proved most effectual.'

The Wyatt patent that Carnegie refers to was obtained by Charles Wyatt of Waterloo Farm, Frome in the County of Somerset, England, the date of application being 21st August 1903 (Patent No. 18,123) and being accepted on 23rd June 1904. The complete specification states 'In the annexed illustrative drawings forming part of this specification, Fig. 1 is a side sectional skeleton view of a trap made in accordance with my invention. Fig.2 being a plan view thereof, while Fig.3 is a sectional plan view of one end of the trap. Like letters of reference in-dicate corresponding parts wherever occurring throughout the several figures of the drawings. In carrying my invention into practice I construct the trap (a) of wire netting of suitable mesh, such as shown by Fig.3 and give such trap an approximate cylindrical form, the lower side or bottom (a') being flat to allow it to rest securely upon the ground. At one end, and at suitable intervals along the top and sides of the trap, I provide openings (b) for the birds to enter, such openings being in the form of conical or funnel shaped passages which extend some way into the interior of the trap. The entrance openings (b) in the outer walls of the trap a are given a considerably larger diameter than that of the exit openings (c) which communicate with the interior of the trap, the walls of the passages aforesaid tapering from the outer openings to the inner ones as indicated by (d). Within the trap, near one end thereof, I provide a conical or funnel shaped partition (e), all the entrance openings (b) aforesaid communicating with that part of the trap so partitioned off. The said conical partition (e) is provided with a small opening (e') in the apex, through which the trapped birds pass into the end (a2) of the trap, an opening being provided in the end wall of such trap, adjacent the opening (e') in the said partition (e), for the removal of the trapped birds, such opening being normally closed by means of a flexible mouth or bag provided with a slip noose or string threaded through such mouth or bag; or alternatively a hinged door (f) may be provided for closing the said opening. It will be understood from the foregoing that the birds find their way into the trap through the entrance passages aforesaid, from whence they pass through the opening (e') in the partition e into the end (a2) of the trap, the arrangement of the partition constituting a double trap, which, in conjunction with the peculiar form of the entrance openings, precludes any chance of the birds escaping when once they have entered the trap.'

The specification then ends '. . . sparrows and other birds, it may also be applied to the purpose of trapping rats and other vermin.'

YEO, Joseph. Edenhall. Year 1878-1884

According to the 1881 Census, Joseph Yeo and his family were residing at Helm View, in the village of Edenhall, which is near Penrith, Cumberland. Joseph was aged 41 and was married to Elizabeth. He was born in Freystrop, Pembrokeshire, but his wife was locally born at Kirkland. Their two children, Joseph Sewell, aged seven, and Mary Lily aged five, were both born at Culgaith which is not far from either Kirkland or Edenhall. Previously, on 28th October 1878, Joseph Yeo had applied for an improved animal trap patent which was sealed on 22nd April 1879. This patent, No 4326, was granted for a gin trap constructed without the normal bridge assembly. The plate dropped along the stock instead of the usual way across it. Another feature of this patent was that the end of the bow spring was attached to the underneath of the stock. Another trap presumably made by him is a 'spring powered noose or snare.' This trap has Regd, Maker, J.Yeo stamped into it. Nothing else is known about it. Although listed in the 1881 Census as a blacksmith, in the 1884 East Cumberland Directory for Edenhall Joe Yeo of Helm View is listed as a grocer.

YOUNG. Samuel & Sons, Misterton, Crewkerne, Somerset. Year 1895 – 1992

According to their letterhead, this business was established in 1895. In a small undated booklet of circa 1911, which is a 'Price list of Poultry eggs for sitting, and live chicks with mothers' the address is given as Samuel Young, The Misterton Poultry Yards & Appliance Works, Misterton, Crewkerne, Somerset. According to this booklet Samuel Young supplied a 'Large illustrated catalogue of coops, runs, foods, egg boxes, nets, traps. Every description for vermin. Lawn tennis, cricket and other nets.'

However, the first entry in various trade directories is to be found in 1914. This entry lists 'Samuel Young, poultry, pigeon , & cage bird appliances, rope & twine & net maker.' The name changes to Samuel Young & Son, and also the address Enterprise Works is added between 1919 and 1923. The telephone number Crewkerne 102 is

GEORGE YOUNG, AS FEATURED IN *THE SUNDAY TIMES MAGAZINE*
5TH OCTOBER 1980

added for the first time between 1923 and 1931.

The name changes again to S. Young & Sons (Misterton) Ltd with the telephone number changing to Crewkerne 161, between 1931 and 1935. The telephone number changes again to Crewkerne 3461 between 1965 and 1968. Once again the telephone number changes to Crewkerne 73461,between 1975 and 1978.

All directory entries stop between August 1992 and January 1994.

Through out this business's lifespan, they sold, 'Sporting appliances and Sundries' including 'Traps, fishing, poultry, & chicken appliances, and other products'. Although they made traps, they never made any gin traps, even though gin traps can be found with only their name stamped on them. Just like Gilbertson & Page, Spratt's and other such companies, gin traps were ordered from the actual gin trap makers and stamped with their own business name, and then sold on to Young's own customers. In an article that appeared in *The Sunday Times Magazine* dated 5th October 1980, Samuel Young's "five daughters and four sons all learnt the art of trap making. The girls specialised in hand-knotting nets – some fine enough to catch small birds and insects, others strong enough to hold deer. The boys did the wirework and carpentry. Even now everything is made by hand.' The article also quotes George as saying, 'I don't like suffering, cruelty or poison. We have never made a trap to kill or maim. We are very proud of that.' The article continues, 'At 74,George is the youngster of the family. With Sidney,77, and a part time staff of energetic pensioners, they deal with

an unending flow of customers. Winnie, Eva, and Lily, the surviving sisters, still come in to help.' This business was operated from converted farm buildings and 'Apart from their own products, Young's catalogue offers a formidable arsenal. Stacked around are eel-traps and spears, traps for fox, weasel, mole, mouse, pike, coypu, mink, squirrel, jackdaw, moorhen, rook, cat and rat. There are alarms to catch poachers, decoy birds, shellfish nets, gas pumps, bird scarers, owls to frighten little birds, whistles to call roe deer, ducks foxes, rabbits, and rooks.' They also sold 'baskets to carry poultry and racing pigeons, incubators for eggs, 'electric hen' chick nurseries, pheasant feeders and their exclusive ferret and pigeon tonics (from secret recipes).'

1972 was the last year that an illustrated catalogue was produced. After that date, a price list only, was introduced, in a very small booklet form. Later on, this price list changed to a double sided A4 single sheet of paper.

Young's also produced other booklets such as *The Art of Netting*, and *Rabbit Catching with long nets*. Unfortunately, most of these booklets do not have a publication date printed on them. One copy of The Art of Netting, that I know of, does though. The cover of this issue states in the top left hand corner, 'copyright 1/1/20 second edition price 1/-'. Through the middle of the cover at an angle is the title The Art of Netting, whilst underneath at the bottom right of the cover are the words 'published by S Young & Son, Misterton .s .o. Somerset'. Presumably, what is the first edition, has printed on its cover in the same place as the second edition, 'Copyright. Price 7d. Post Free. The

FOUR IN ONE PEST TRAP
PATENT NUMBER 526444
FOR MICE, COCKROACHES, WASPS, FLIES, MOLES, SLUGS, WOODLICE

Small mice, large mice, lean mice : grave old plodders, gay young friskers ; fathers, mothers, uncles, cousins ; cocking tails and pricking whiskers ; families by tens and dozens ; brothers, sisters, husbands, wives ; pop in the 4 in 1 and lose their lives.

Thousands of pounds are lost yearly, so all possible steps must be made to destroy these pests. The common house mouse is familiar to most housewives. Like the cockroach it will foul most human foods in the most unpleasant manner. Mice are prolific breeders, and it is most important to take all possible steps for their destruction.

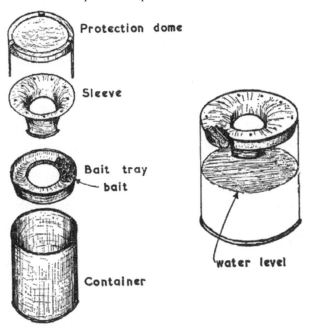

The most effective means of destroying these pests is by trapping them in the 4 in 1 Trap, which will trap up to 15 or 20 mice in one night, apart from cockroaches, slugs, woodlice and all ground pests, around infested stores, outhouses, frames, greenhouses, etc. A recent Act of Parliament clearly defines the duties of all owners and occupiers, and local authorities in the matter of rat and mice destruction. **Price 75p.**

Mr. Bill Sowerbutts of Penny Meadow, Ashton-under-Lyme – 21st January, 1959 – writes : We had the pleasure last Spring and Summer and since of testing your Vermin trap on our nurseries and market gardens and found it very successful indeed. Particularly in Spring when new sowings are being made we found it very valuable in preventing damage by mice and other small rodents. Best wishes. Yours sincerely Bill Sowerbutts. B.B.C. and T.V. fame.

YOUNG'S 1972 CATALOGUE

Art of Netting. Published by S. YOUNG. MISTERTON, S.O., SOMERSET'. The Art of Netting booklet is known to have been published in at least seven editions.

Due to this business buying in other manufacturers' products, it is very hard to decide which traps Young's actually made. Obviously, from the previous comments, they made some of the all wire cage traps themselves, as well as the wire and wood ones. On the back cover of the undated poultry booklet of circa 1911, mentioned above, is stated 'sparrows ! rats ! The greatest pest of the poultry keeper. Thousands caught with my Eclipse Sparrow Traps. Always set. Always ready. Price 4/6 each, also for Rats same price. One of each for 9/6. Carriage Paid'. The comment 'one of each for 9/6' suggests that the single model could be made with slightly different sized openings to allow either the sparrow or the larger rat access into the trap. Young's 1937 catalogue shows this trap was made in two lengths, Small 2ft long at 7/- and Large 1 yard (3ft) long at 9/- carriage paid. Larger sizes were made to order. Young's 1962 catalogue states: 'The 2ft size have 2 entrances and the 3ft, 4 entrances'. It also mentions: 'These traps will take starlings if adapted. We will do this free if requested when ordering'. In the 1976 price list, Eclipse Sparrow Traps were priced at £6.50p (2ft) and £7.50p (3ft) to which must be added postage/ carriage and V.A.T. In the price list of 1987, only the 2ft size of trap is advertised for sale, at £16 plus V.A.T. This trap was listed as the Eclipse Rat Trap, with no mention of sparrows. These traps usually have wired on the top of them, a small oblong galvanised metal label with their name and address.

Another bird trap made by Young's is their spring net trap. In their circa 1937 catalogue it is illustrated and advertised under the heading 'Naturalists bird traps for taking birds for marking or ringing', along with other types of bird traps. The catalogue states: 'The 'Catch All' Self-acting takes every kind of bird alive uninjured, without attention. Goldfinch, Bullfinch, and Sparrow size 1/9; larger for Rooks, Pigeons, Thrushes, and Blackbirds, 2/9. Sent carriage paid.' The same illustration is shown in their 1968 catalogue where it is described as being made 'On wood frame. Sparrow size, 12/6; larger for Rooks, pigeons, etc., 17/6. Carriage paid.' The 'Catch All' bird trap is not illustrated or mentioned in the 1972 catalogue. The smaller sized trap was made out of two long pieces of wood, side by side, nailed to two smaller pieces going across them at both opposite ends underneath. The spring mechanism is the same as an ordinary breakback mouse trap, but with the addition of netting over it. The bait plate, is a round shallow dish for containing seed etc, with two holes in the middle for water drainage. In the larger version , three boards are nailed, from the end, across the two side rails underneath, and only cover half of the base, whilst the fourth narrower board is nailed across the opposite end to allow the fixing of the trigger. The remaining half of the base is left uncovered so that when the trap is in the set position, the grass or ground shows through and helps camouflage the netting, thereby making it less suspicious. Both sizes of this trap usually have a small oval brass plaque fixed to the top side of the wooden base. These plaques can state either S. Young & Son Enterprise Works Misterton. Som. Eng. or S. Young & Son (Misterton)

Ltd Enterprise Works Somerset. England. and are all in capital letters.

The other bird traps mentioned and illustrated under the heading of Naturalists Bird Traps in the 1937 catalogue are Young's Original Perfection Bird Trap, Young's Famous Improved Net Traps, and Young's Wicker Pheasant, Poultry, Pigeon, or Bird Trap.

Perfection Bird Trap. This trap is stated to be 'Most useful out of sight trap made for Robins, Wagtails, Nightingales. Recommended by Mr John Frostick. Baited with live worms, etc, for Finches of all kinds, also Sparrows, Thrushes, etc. Price 1/9 each, Three for 4/9. Extra Large Size 3/9, Two 7/- Carriage paid. Beware of Imitations of this Genuine Trap.' In Young's 1976 booklet price list the small trap was priced at £1.00, whilst the large size was £2.50, both plus postage/carriage and V.A.T. This trap is not listed in the 1987 price list.

Famous Improved Net Traps. The 1937 catalogue states this trap to be 'One of the most successful traps offered. Can be made to work self acting or by a pull line – Small 3/6, Large 5/6. Carriage paid. The most out of sight trap made for Goldfinches, Bullfinches, Linnets, Sparrows, Blackbirds and Thrushes. The largest will take Pigeons, etc.' In the 1976 price list the Improved Net trap is priced at £3.50 for the large size and £2.50 for the small size, both plus postage/carriage and V.A.T. This trap is also not listed in the 1987 price list.

Wicker Trap. This trap was said to be 'Just the thing for catching up Pheasants, Fowls, Pigeons &c. Just place few peas or corn under the trap. The bird steps on bender and trap falls and secures it uninjured.

Also useful in taking stray cats alive.' Its size was stated to be 3ft 6ins square with a door at the top for removing the birds. However, the illustration shows the trap with sloping sides and a flat top. This trap is advertised in the 1937 & 1940 catalogues but not in the 1956 edition. An earlier illustration of this Wicker Trap, but called The Take-up Trap was used for catching fruit-eating Blackbirds etc. This illustration appears in the book, *The Balance of Nature* by George Abbey, published in 1909, which states 'we commend the Take-up Trap used for catching pheasants required for pens, but of smaller size.' The size stated for catching Blackbirds with the Take-up trap is 'basket 2ft 6in. square, 15in. high, with door at top for removing the birds'.

Young's Hawk Trap Cage. This trap, according to the description in the 1937 catalogue, is basically an identical copy of the hawk trap patented by George Black of Hatton, near Wragby in Lincolnshire. Young's 1937 price, packed and carriage paid, 34/-, and stating 'the above trap can be used for catching other kinds of birds. Any kind of trap made to customers' own design'. This trap was still being advertised in their 1968 catalogue 'price, packed and carriage paid £6.0.0'.

Enterprise mole trap. The 1937 catalogue states 'Steel springs as used in barrel mole traps 4/- dozen, or 21/- per 100. Carriage paid. Patent waterproof trap cord 7/6 per Ib, 4/- per half Ib, 2/3 for 4 ozs, 1/3 per 2 ozs. Post paid. This cord runs about 14 yards to the oz. Steel wire also for sale for customers' making their own traps'. Noting the above comments and also the advert on the same page for the 'Enterprise' spring mole trap, it is probable, but not certain, that Young's made this trap, as well as selling the separate items to anyone wanting to make their own. The description for the Enterprise mole trap states 'Similar to. . . half barrel traps, only with flat wood top, and copper wire loops instead of cord. Hundreds of these traps are supplied to professional mole trappers in all parts every season, and considered by them to be the best traps on the market. Price 12/- per dozen, 6/3 per half dozen, single traps 1/2 each. Carriage paid'. This mole trap is last advertised in Young's 1956 catalogue.

During the period that Young's sold the Enterprise mole trap they also sold the 'Perfection' wooden full barrel, and wooden 'half barrel' mole traps which were made by the National Patent Company Limited of Johnstone, Scotland, who also happened to sell 'the various parts of the mole traps separately'. This Scottish company ceased trading during the middle of 1956. Although Young's are still advertising the 'Perfection' and 'Half Barrel' mole traps in their 1957 catalogue, these traps must be previously bought stock items. It is therefore possible, but again not certain, that this Scottish company may have made the 'Enterprise' mole trap exclusively for Young's, calling it after Young's own Enterprise Works.

'Tophole' and 'Auto' Mouse trap. Almost certainly, due to their ease of construction, just small sections of wood forming a cube with one side made of wire mesh and with a hole in the centre of the wooden top, these mouse traps would have been built by Young's. The Tophole mousetrap was not illustrated or mentioned in their 1937 catalogue but is in their 1940 issue priced at 3/-

each. The illustration boasts 'Licks the Cat. The Famous Tophole Mousetrap'. In the later 1956 catalogue the illustration and caption have changed slightly becoming 'The Famous 'Auto' Mousetrap'. The illustration now shows one wire handle, instead of two metal straps, on the top of the trap. The side is now also made from sheet metal with uniformal rows of small holes. The price is now 6/- each post paid. This illustration remains the same up to and including Young's 1972 catalogue, where it is now priced at 63p each with part post costing 13p. In the 1987 price list, the 'Auto' mouse trap cost £7.00 plus V.A.T. to which 'Postage or Carriage must be added'.

Clausius Tunnel Box Trap. Again this design of trap being of simple wooden construction would most probably have been made by Young's on their own premises. It should be noted though, that this design of live catch trap has been in use in Europe, (probably originating in Germany), and here for centuries. During the 1960s, because of the ban on using gin traps, there was a revival of these cheap humane, live catch traps, and probably many were 'home made'. Young's catalogue of 1937 lists them as single trap 8/-, double trap 14/6d, carriage paid. The price in early 1972 was £1.75 each plus postage, whilst in 1987, the cost was £7.00 each plus V.A.T. plus postage or carriage.

Young's also sold wire cage fish traps, mainly for catching Pike and Eels, but again it is difficult to decide if they made them all or just certain ones. They most likely made the 'Suffolk' Eel and Fish Trap which seems to have sold well. In the 1956 catalogue they were priced at 35/- each, carriage paid. In 1972

THE FULLER 'CONTINUAL CATCH' UNIT
DESIGNED ESPECIALLY FOR USE IN AREAS OF HEAVY INFESTATION
Can be used for quite a number of Small Rodents

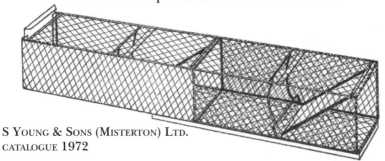

S YOUNG & SONS (MISTERTON) LTD.
CATALOGUE 1972

This is not a trap in the true sense but a catch unit designed to be attached to any conveniently-sized container that could serve to hold the squirrels that have been caught by, and passed through the catch unit. Briefly it will continue to trap all squirrels that may venture inside the unit. Designed for areas of heavy infestation, this catch unit is invaluable wherever a rapid and extensive catch is the prime essential.

An additional advantage of this particualr model is that, with the end sliding door kept closed, the unit becomes a most effective and compeltey self-contained trap suitable for dealing with one or possibly two squirrels.

The holding or retaining compartment used need not necessarily be of wire-netting; any suitable container would serve, as for instance, a five gallon drum with a hole in the side to receive the end of the the catch unit.

The unit is four inches high, four inches wide and 30 inches long. Suspended from the roof inside the trap, are two metal swing doors made to open in one direction only. Beneath the unit is a detachable bait tray in which is placed the whole maize, acorns ot other tempting biat that lures the squirrels into and through the swing doors of the unit.

priced at £5.00 carriage extra, and then in 1987 the individual price had risen to £31.00 plus V.A.T. and postage or carriage costs. Strangely,this trap does not seem to have had a metal label attached. Instead a removable brown card label was tied to it. This label has printed 'Young's Automatic Eel (or Fish) Traps'. Other information states, 'A few trapping hints for eels' and contains such advice as best time, bait to use, and best position for setting the traps. A nice touch to this label is the quote of an old saying which runs 'When the willow comes out in bud, then the eels come out of the mud'. It also has Young's name and address printed across the bottom of the label.

The "Bath" Pigeon Trap

This trap has been designed specially for Town and City Councils who are troubled by the masses of Pigeons, both wild and tame, who throng the buildings with their messy droppings, besides the damage they do to Parks and Gardens.

It is made of Galvanize Mesh with a metal bottom for food or bait, it is always set and as many as 20 can be caught at one time. It is galvanized after being made and is washable and sanitary.

Fitted handles for carrying.

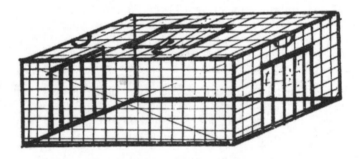

Size 30 ins. long, 17 ins. wide and 11 ins. high.

INSTRUCTIONS

Keep up the bolting wires on each end and feed the birds inside for a day or so then let down the wires and they push their way in. Take out the birds by the large door at top

Price £6·50 each

The weight of this trap is about 11 lbs. It is best to set the trap overnight and take out the catches early in the morning and put the trap away during the day. That is if they are to be used in public places.

S Young & Sons (Misterton) Ltd. catalogue 1972

THE "WINDSOR" PHEASANT CATCHERS
Galvanized after made

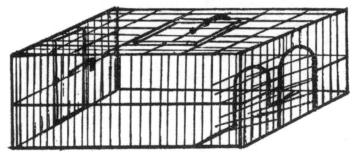

Size 3 ft. long, 2 ft. wide, 12 ins. high. Made from very heavy galvanized wire, weight 14½ lbs. Door in top, also end for taking out birds caught. These traps have been used on one of the largest Estates in England for a great many years. Last a lifetime. Always set and will take as many as 8 birds at a time. £6·75 each.

YOUNG'S 1972 CATALOGUE

BOTH ADVERTS FROM YOUNG'S 1940 CATALOGUE

MOUSE AND RAT TRAPS
THE AUTOMATIC CATCH-ALL

Self-acting and self-setting; will take about 20 rats one after another without attention. The best trap ever invented. Testimonials from all parts. Full instructions and a valuable recipe how to make an irresistable bait, free with every Trap. Rats 4/-, Carraige paid.

AUTOMATIC MOUSE TRAPS.
Similar to rat traps above, only smaller, 2/3 Post `free.

FOLDING PHEASANT CATCHER.

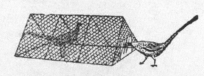

For catching up Birds for Aviary, &c. Requires no watching. Always set. Made of best galvanised wire. Can be left out in all weathers. Simply put corn in and leave door open for a few days, then close. They will then enter very easily, but cannot possibly find way out.
Size : 3ft. long, 2ft. wide, 15in. wide.
Price, **8/6** ; three for **24/-** ; Carriage paid.

Now used on all leading Game Farms.

IMPROVED TRAP FOR BIRDS EXTRA STRONG

A Call cage can be put inside if desired.

Size 19in. x 12in., 3/9, Small Birds.

Size 23in. x 16in., 6/6 Patridges Pigeons, &c.

Size 27in. x 19½in., 11/-, for Pheasants, Grouse, Ducks, Pigeons, &c. Carriage paid.

'IMPROVED BIRD TRAP FROM YOUNG'S 1940 CATALOGUE

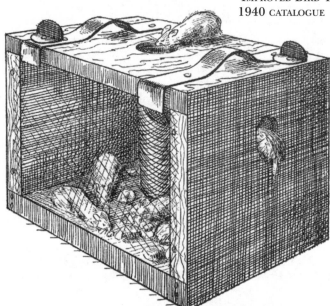

'TOP HOLE' MOUSETRAP FROM YOUNG'S 1940 CATALOGUE

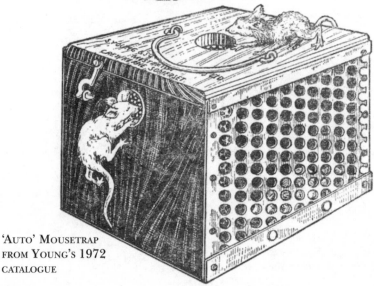

'AUTO' MOUSETRAP FROM YOUNG'S 1972 CATALOGUE

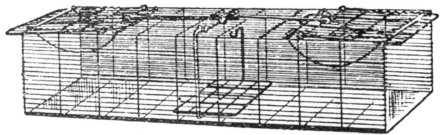

YOUNG'S 1972 CATALOGUE

WIRE BOX TRAPS For catching alive and uninjured

One of the Finest traps ever invented for catching Vermin, Animals and Birds, such as Rats, Stoats, Weasels, cats, Foxes, Squirrels. Also Pheasants, Pigeons, Duck and other Birds.

These traps are used and recommended by the Ministry of Agriculture and are giving the greatest satisfaction in use at several Government Parks and Zoological Gardens.

The Trap, having open doors at each end, allows for a clear straight through entrance from either end, thereby causing no suspicion whatsoever.

THE 'SIMPLEX' WIRE CAGE RAT TRAP.

This trap is a great improvement on the old form of Cage Trap and will catch dozens where the Old Pattern trap was useless. It is offered as a Rat Trap, but is suitable for other Vermin, such as Stoats, Weasels, Squirrels, Cats and Birds. Also, owing to its semi-circle shape, it can easily be fixed over a Rabbit or Rat's Hole, and is useful for fixing over Rabbits' Holes for trapping a laid-up Ferret. It is fitted with Bait Hook, also Treadle Bridge, and when either of these is touched the door is relelased and springs acting on levers close the Door.

YOUNG'S 1940 CATALOGUE

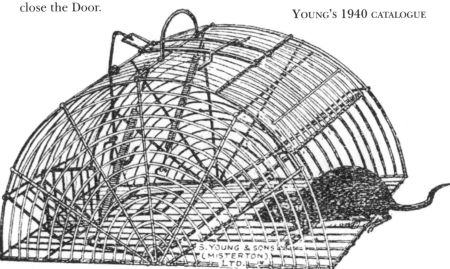

263

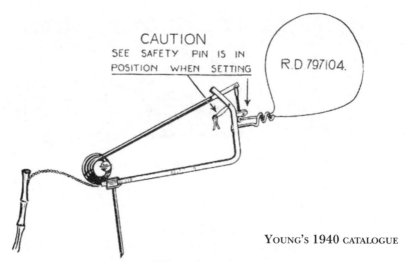

YOUNG'S 1940 CATALOGUE

THE 'MARWOOD' HUMANE RABBIT SNARE.
RECOMMENDED BY THE R.S.P.C.A.

Light and strong. Weight about 10 ozs. New Wires can be fitted in a few seconds. It is certain in action, and death is quick and painless. Can be set at Entrance to Hole or in the Run, and is sprung from either side. The Snare has no equal for simplicity in handling, quickness in setting, efficiency and durability. It is of first-class workmanship and with ordinary use practically indestructible.

YOUNG'S GENUINE AND ORIGINAL ECLIPSE SPARROW TRAPS
Can be used for Rats or Grey Squirrels with great success
State purpose required when ordering

If you are troubled with sparrows send for one of these improved Sparrow Traps. Takes about 50, one after the other, without attention : always set, always ready. As many as 50 have been taken in one day.

These traps will take Starlings as well as Sparrows if adapted. Free if requested when ordering.

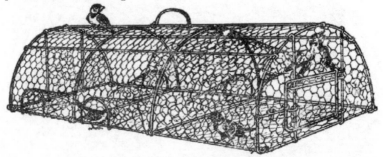

'ECLIPSE' SPARROW TRAP, YOUNG'S 1972 CATALOGUE

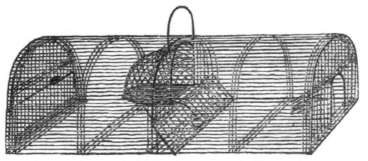

AUTOMATIC 'WONDER' RAT TRAP, YOUNG'S 1940 CATALOGUE

SPARROW TRAPS

Prices—

Wicker, **9 -** ;
Cane, **14 6** each.
Galvanized wire, painted a dark colour (weather and rat-proof).
23 /- each.

Carriage paid.

GILBERTSON & PAGE, LIMITED, HERTFORD, HERTS.

1941 ADVERT

Spratt's Pheasant Catcher.

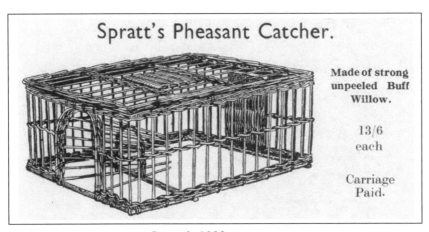

Made of strong unpeeled Buff Willow.

13/6 each

Carriage Paid.

SPRATT'S 1933 CATALOGUE

Pheasant trap illustration from 1885

Young's 1940 catalogue

YOUNG'S WICKER PHEASANT, POULTRY PIGEON, OR BIRD TRAP.

Also useful in taking Stray Cats alive.

YOUNG'S
MISTERTON
SOM.

Just the thing for catching up Pheasants, Fowls, Pigeons, &c. Just place few peas or corn under the Trap. The Bird steps on Bender and Trap falls and secures it uninjured. Last lifetime with care.

Size, 3ft. 6ins. square, ins. high, with Door at top for removing Birds. **11/-.** Cariage paid.

Chapter Five

SOME BETTER KNOWN
MODERN TRAPS

RSPCA SAWYER RABBIT TRAP

Since the Society for the Prevention of Cruelty to Animals was founded on 16th June 1824, the 'Royal' title being granted later in 1840, its aims have been to eliminate all use of any type of traps which cause suffering to any animal. The RSPCA policies on animal welfare (revised 1994) are that 'The RSPCA is opposed to the manufacture and use of all snares and any trap which causes suffering. It approves of live traps only when certain conditions are adhered to.' In further explanatory notes it states 'a) the term 'all snares' includes those using stops, ratchets, etc. b) the Society recognises the necessity for capturing animals on a limited scale for a variety of reasons, and in such cases live traps are adequate and humane provided that they are visited frequently, the frequency varying from 1-12 hours depending upon the species and trap concerned. Those animals taken in a live trap for destruction must be im-

mediately and humanely destroyed.' The RSPCA has organised many competitions over the years to find a humane solution as an alternative to the commonly used gin trap. In 1874 the renowned naturalist Charles Darwin offered, through the RSPCA, a prize of £50 for a humane device. Three more competitions were organised in 1906 (see Tildesley), 1913 and in 1928, all of which again did not produce a satisfactory humane trap. However, in 1946 a rabbit trap was invented by a Mr. Sawyer which proved to be effective and humane. This trap was a little difficult to set, but despite this drawback and having received expert advice, the RSPCA Council decided to award the inventor the £300 prize. According to *The Animal World*, the official magazine of the RSPCA, (August 1947 issue) under the heading, A Notable Invention, the Sawyer trap 'has been tried out extensively during the past twelve months under the supervision of the Society's Humane Slaughtering Department and both Mr. H. Nun, Manager of that department, and Mr. R. Roger, the Society's Humane Trapping expert, declare themselves satisfied that it fulfils its claims. The Society has acquired the sole rights of manufacture of the invention and proposes to place an order for the delivery of 100,000 traps at a price which bears comparison with those now on the market.'

In the Annual Report of the RSPCA Council for 1947 it was stated that 'Progress with the new rabbit trap has been slow owing to the difficulty of obtaining the hundred tons of steel required for manufacture on a large scale, only five tons having been allocated. All possible pressure has been put on the Ministry concerned, but the official attitude is that, before additional steel is granted, the authorities must be satisfied that the trap is all that it is claimed to be. This means that several hundred traps have to be made and passed over to the Ministry of Agriculture for testing before the general public can be supplied. The Ministry has, however, stated that tests already carried out have shown promising results, and it is hoped to start production on the largest possible scale as soon as sufficient material is available. Meantime, orders for the trap have reached headquarters from all parts of the world.'

In a later issue of *The Animal World* (July 1950) there was a reprinted article from the *Illustrated London News* which stated 'At least there is comfort in the fact that 25,000 'Sawyer' traps have been sold in a year, without advertising.' By the end of 1952, according to A.W. Moss's 'Valiant crusade', page 147, a total of 49,373 Sawyer traps were being used in England and Wales.

Frank Edmund Sawyer applied for a patent for this rabbit trap on 21st February 1946 (No 5473/46) and the specification was accepted on 24th September 1947 becoming Patent No 592,658. His address was Choulston, Netheravon, Salisbury, Wiltshire. In the Country Gentlemen's Association Ltd General Price Book of 1951 these traps are priced at 4/6d each, yet in a later edition of 1954 the same trap was priced at 3/9d each, carriage paid on three or over. In Young's of Misterton catalogue of 1957/8 the price was still 3/9d each with the advert stating 'This trap is the winner of a prize of three hundred pounds offered by the Royal Society for the Prevention of Cruelty to Animals.' Unfortunately none of these three adverts have an illustration of the trap.

However, four known types exist. Type (a) has six coils on the spring and the tongue is attached by a 'L' shaped lug to the upright broad jaw. Type (b) has six coils on the spring, but the tongue is attached to the upright broad jaw directly through a hole. Both of these types also have the trap chain attached to the protruding cross member upon which is fixed the supports for the trap plate. Type (c) has nine coils on the spring. The tongue is attached to the upright broad jaw directly through a hole. The narrow jaw has a twist in it just before it goes through the broad jaw. The cross member is broader than in the other two types and is attached to the side of the main frame on the outside. The chain is attached to the rear of the trap between the broad upright jaw and the main frame.

Type (d) is the same as type (c) except that the twist in the arm is now at the bottom next to the base frame.

In the August 1947 RSPCA magazine article are two illustrations showing the Sawyer trap, but it is not known if this version has been produced or not. According to the spring traps approval order 1957, the Sawyer (RSPCA) rabbit trap was not listed as an approved trap by the government for taking any type of animal.

IMBRA

This easier setting trap than the Sawyer rabbit trap was again invented by Frank Edmund Sawyer. The Imbra trap was patented on 27th August 1951 (Patent No 682,427) and was made in Mark I and Mark II models. Both of these traps were made with a safety catch fitted behind the tongue. However, in the Mark II version, type B, this trap has no safety catch. The history of Imbra trap production is rather vague. Seemingly, Mr. Sawyer went into business with Mr. Capjon of Capjon Pressings Co., of Pewsey, Wiltshire to produce his traps. The Imbra trap was named after the Army's Imbra ranges on Salisbury Plain where they were first used experimentally in rabbit trapping trials. A 1954 advert shows the price of the Imbra trap as 10/6d each, carriage paid on 36 or over, but with no mention of the manufacturer. However, an advert in May 1959, seems to indicate that the

1959 ADVERT

Tetra Engineering Co. Ltd. of Wembley, London, were the manufacturers, although this may have been on a sub contract or licensed basis. In a Forestry Commission booklet *Traps for Grey Squirrels* revised 1962, Tetra Engineering was still stated as being the manufacturer with the price remaining at 15/- each, as in 1959. According to this Forestry Commission booklet, only the Mark II Imbra was then available. What is known is that upon Mr. Sawyer retiring and his son having no interest in traps the business of trap production went to Scotland. During the 1960s Mr. D.W. Grassick bought the small business of James Low and Sons Ltd, Atholl Smithy, Atholl Street, Blairgowrie, Perthshire from the two Low brothers. Later on whilst visiting a Game Fair Mr. Grassick heard the rumour that the trap production of the Imbra traps was being offered for sale. Upon contacting Mr. Sawyer, eventually an agreement was reached, and, by the late 1960s the production of Imbra traps was continued from Blairgowrie. The traps were sold through Gilbertson & Page Ltd, but by March 1973 production had ceased. Eventually the business ceased trading completely about 1975.

A prototype 'Imbra' type trap was patented on 27th July 1936 (Patent No 473,718) by Mr. Sawyer and a known trap was produced (possibly by W.H. Tildesley Ltd of Willenhall) as this trap was included with many other types donated to the Walsall Museum, by this company.

SAWYER VERMIN TRAP

This was another trap invented by Frank Edmund Sawyer of Wiltshire, but I have been unable to find out when they were first made or for approximately how long. However, the trap was approved for use, by the Humane Trap Committee in 1966 and it is known that they were first made by Capjon Pressings Co., Pewsey, Wiltshire, and had stamped on the trap plate the words Sawyer Vermin Trap. They are similar in Design to the Fenn trap, but do not seem to have remained on the market for too long, probably due to the success of the rival Fenn trap's popularity. Gilbertson and Page sold this trap according to their illustrated advert in *The Gamekeeper and Countryside Magazine*, December 1967 issue for 10/6 each with carriage extra. Writing in the January 1968 issue of the same magazine 'Warm-Barrels' says: 'the New Sawyer Vermin Trap is now on sale. . . (and) I am grateful to Frank Sawyer for the opportunity to try the first production models, and I have tested them thoroughly under practical gamekeeping conditions. I like the trap very much. It is efficient. It is easy to set. It is robust, and so far as practical requirements go, these are three essentials.' He continues: 'It is strongly and soundly made, as was the gin, and as a result its working life will be equally long. In the trials I carried out I caught with no difficulty whatsoever the following species: rats, grey squirrels, weasels, mice, a stoat, and a hedgehog. In each case the victim was dead.' In an undated list of approved traps, the Sawyer trap is mentioned as being manufactured by or under the authority of James S. Low and Sons Ltd, Atholl Smithy, Atholl Street, Blairgowrie, Perthshire. Sawyer vermin traps are known to have been out of production by March 1973.

JUBY TRAP

The inventor of this trap was Reginald Walter Juby and the patent application date was 17th September 1956 (No 28348/56). The complete specification being dated 24th September 1957 (Patent No 813,066) and was patented by the Ministry of Agriculture, Fisheries and Food, London. It was manufactured by W.&G. Side-

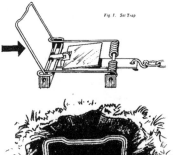

Fig. 1. Set Trap

Fig. 2. Showing Trap in Tunnel

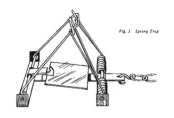

Fig. 3. Sprung Trap

Introducing . . .

THE *NEW* SAWYER
VERMIN TRAP

With Official Approval for :

GREY SQUIRRELS, STOATS, WEASELS, RATS, MICE and other small ground vermin

Suppliers name

---

botham of Wednesfield, with the sole distributor being Gilbertson & Page Ltd. Production of the Juby trap was sporadic and is dealt with further under Sidebotham's. The Juby was produced in two versions. The Mark I has a straight bar and the jaws pivoted on lugs from the bar and has a very 'stiff' look to it. The chain is attached to the 'square' shaped wire projecting from the bar. In the Mark II version the rear bar is curved upwards and the chain is attached to inwardly angled wire joined across by a flat strip of metal at the end. Some are found with this flat strip of metal drilled for the attachment of the chain whilst others are left blank. Alternatively a hollow tube is attached where the flat metal usually is.

An interesting article is to be found

in the December 1958 issue of *The Gamekeeper and Countryside* magazine. Under the headline 'The Redesigned Juby Trap is Now Available. A Better Tool at a Lower Price' it reads: "Since the abolition of the gin trap we have continued to give much thought to the supply of an efficient substitute, and with the co-operation of the Ministry of Agriculture, Fisheries and Food we turned out attention to the approved Juby trap. Our purpose was to make it more workmanlike, more compact and – most important – cheaper to produce and to sell. With this in mind we consulted the well known firms of Castings Ltd., and Carver and Co. (Engineers) Ltd., both of Walsall, from whom we have received much help and

JUBY TRAP MARK II VERSION

advice. A great deal of test work has resulted in the production of a trap which, we feel , is going to meet the requirements of practical keepers and trappers. We are satisfied that it is the most serviceable and economic of those approved by the Ministry which are intended primarily for use against rabbits. The improvements leave the basic design unaltered, as they must do, but the arc of the 'scissors' or arms has been reduced to a minimum (which, of course, simplifies setting and means that less preliminary excavation is required). The trap sits into the ground much more snugly, an important point. The weight of the trap has been reduced to about $2^{1}/_{4}$ lb. A safety catch is incorporated in such a way that it is possible to get the traps ready for setting before going out on the round. It will be remembered that the original Juby was expected to cost about 19/-, and we are very pleased to be able to offer this improved version at the reduced price of 12/9, carriage extra. The use of a very new material called Pearlitic Malleable Iron for the scissors has contributed to the reduction in price. We are now able to take orders for the new Juby trap, having received a licence from the Ministry of Agriculture to make and sell them. Supplies will be coming forward steadily, and we advise all who will require traps to give their orders at once.'

In the Forestry Commission booklet *Traps For Grey Squirrels* revised 1962, the price was 13/6d each whilst in the Forestry Commission's *Grey Squirrel Control* booklet of 1973 they are priced at £2 each.

LLOYD TRAP

The inventor of this trap was Huw Gwynfor Lloyd, and the patent application date is 13th July 1961 (No 25418/61) whilst the complete speci-

THE LLOYD TRAP

British Patent
No. 596735

TWO VARIATIONS OF THE
GLENMOOR TRAP
ABOVE, MK I
BELOW, MK 3

fication is dated 4th October 1962 (Patent No 987,113). This trap is an adaptation of the gin trap mechanism. Huw Lloyd used the wire spring gin trap as a model but replaced the ordinary type jaws with two 'L' shaped wire jaws which faced each other when opened and set. Upon closing, the jaws enclosed the small animal (stoat, rat etc.) with one jaw passing under the other. When in the closed position, the jaws form roughly the letter 'T' shape when viewed from along the stock. The Lloyd trap was manufactured, under the authority of the National Research Development Corporation, who patented it, by W.&G. Sidebotham of Wednesfield. Gilbertson & Page Ltd. sold these traps in 1973 at £1 each, and they were surprisingly still in production in 1979, although seemingly a poor seller.H.G.Lloyd also developed a Spring Loaded Foot Snare. Ministry of Agriculture, Food and Fisheries staff conducted trials of this foot snare at Worplesdon, near Guildford, Surrey during the early 1970s, but the trap failed their stringent tests. Approximately 15 to 20 of these hand made prototype traps were made.

GLENMOOR TRAP

A woman patented three trap designs, of which the first provisional patent applied for was on the 1st August 1945 (Prov. Pat .No 19810/45) which became accepted on the 9th January 1948, becoming Patent Number 596,735. The second provisional pat-

ent's date of application, and also the filing of the complete specification, was 28th July 1949 (Prov. Pat. No 19899/49) and was basically a slight modification to the previous original model's triggering mechanism. The patent specification reads 'It is an advantage of one form of the present trap that the animal brushing against the trap as it moves forward will actuate it. Further, according to the invention, the trigger is operated irrespective of the direction in which the animal goes through the trap, i.e. whether it be from one side or the other.' This modification, being in effect a Mark II version of the original design, became Patent Number 663,126 with the complete specification being published on 19th December 1951. The third patent of Margaret Alice Glen of Little Court, Horton, South Buckinghamshire was applied for on 23rd December 1950 (Prov.Pat.No 15751/50) and the date of filing the complete specification was 24th March 1952, with the complete specification being published on 8th September 1954, being Patent Number 715,264. All of these traps were to become known as the Glenmoor Rabbit Trap and were approved in principle by the RSPCA. The Mk 3 trap (bottom photo) was advertised at 10/6d each carriage paid in catalogues dated 1954 and 1957. It was marketed by Chalwyn (Sales) Ltd of 15 Hanover Square, London and was made of rustproof steel throughout. Although these three trap designs were patented by Margaret A Glen, it is thought that the traps were actually designed and the prototypes made by her partner Mr Moor, hence the trap name of Glenmoor. He was supposedly in the Canadian Air Force during World War I, whilst she is thought to have appeared in 'silent movies'. The reason that M.A.Glen patented the traps in her name, is due supposedly, to Mr Moor being declared a bankrupt.

FULLER GARDEN TRAP
FOR GREY SQUIRRELS

FULLER TRAPS

The Fuller garden trap was tested by the Forestry Commission and ministry of Agriculture of Great Britain and licensed under the Spring Trap Approval Order of 1957 'only for the purpose of killing or taking grey squirrels.' In the Forestry Commission booklet, *Traps for Grey Squirrels* (revised 1962), the maker is stated as being Fuller Industries, Venture, Pondtail Road, Horsham, Sussex with the price being 30/- each ex works. The trap is boxed shaped and measures roughly six inches by four inches by six inches in size. In a later Forestry Commission publication (Booklet 56) of 1973, the supplier is Fuller Engineering Ltd, Three Trees, Loxwood Road, Bucks Green, Rudgwick, Sussex and the price is £3.25 each. The first type of trap was all welded, whilst the last version was bolted together to aid any repairs or maintenance. Fuller also made the wire cage traps called Legg PB (Permanently Baited multi capture trap), Legg Midget (Gilbertson & Page also made a version of this trap) and the Legg single trap. All these traps having been invented by Mr. J.V. Legg, who was a warrener at Queen Elizabeth Forest, in Hampshire. Fuller also made their own single live capture squirrel trap called the 'Bullseye', provisional patent no 35628/68, which sold for £1.30 each according to the March 1973 Forestry Commission leaflet No 56 *Grey Squirrel Control*. This trap consisted of a 100mm diameter PVC pipe, with a vertical drop door at one end. Along the top of the outside of the trap a rigid wire engages a hole in the bottom of the square door when in the set position. This trap was not a success, compared to the wire cages. In Young's of Misterton's catalogue of 1972 the Fuller 'Continual Catch' unit is advertised at £2.50 each. This trap was for catching grey squirrels but 'can be used for quite a number of small rodents.' In a 1992 catalogue, Fuller Engineering Ltd was by then a member of the Rentokil Group with their address being Felcourt, East Grinstead, West Sussex RH19 2JY. This catalogue shows them mainly producing cage type traps and has no mention of the Garden Squirrel trap or the Bullseye trap.

A.B. COUNTRY PRODUCTS, Sambourne. Year 1985 – present.

On 1st April 1985 A Fenn mentioned in a leaflet that they were ceasing their manufacture of F.R. Fox and Rabbit wires (snares). Instead they were to be produced under the A.B. Country Products name located at 8 Dark Lane, Astwood Bank, Redditch. This was a new business being established by Richard Cook, who was previously the works manager at Fenn's. In the 1989 edition of the Game Conservancy's booklet No 16, the A.B. Country Products advert shows that they were now located at the Troy Industrial Estate, Jill Lane, Sambourne, Near Astwood Bank, Redditch, Worcestershire B96 6ES. Telephone Astwood Bank (052789 2320). This advert states that as well as manufacturing the Springer No 6 and No 4, which are Fenn trap copies, they also produce scissor mole traps, fox wires (snares) plus cages for rats, squirrels, mink, fox, rabbit, and feral cats.

FENN, ALAN ALBERT. Redditch. Year 1955 – present

Trap maker, High Street, Astwood Bank, Redditch. Tel: Astwood Bank 281. 1959-1966.

In 1967 the address remains the same but the telephone number changes to 2881. Then between September/October 1978 Fenn's moved to Hoopers Lane, Astwood Bank, Redditch where they remain today.

On 7th January 1955, Alan Albert Fenn of Church Meadow Cottage, Cookhill, Alcester in Warwickshire patented what was to become the successor to the doomed gin trap. Patent

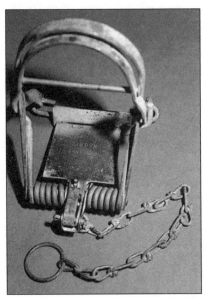

FENN RABBIT TRAP, MARK I

No 763,891 was to be the forerunner to the Mark II, III, IV, and Mark VI improved types of this trap. It is thought that originally only 18 Mark I Fenn traps were produced. These were made and used for the Government trials with regard to the Spring Trap Approval Order. Of these original 18 traps, during a relocation and 'clear out' of office premises,15 are known to have been accidentally thrown out and 'scrapped', leaving just 3 traps which were in a different location at the time. These three remaining traps are now in three separate private trap collections. One is in a collection in The Netherlands, another is in my own collection, whilst the third trap remains in the collection of Mr Fred Courtier in Southern England and from whom the other two traps originated. Mr Courtier was originally involved in testing these traps for efficiency and humaneness. Interestingly, it has been rumoured that Mr Fenn was either going to make, or actually did make, one experimental trap in a smaller version to catch mice. Unfortunately nothing else is known about it, or whether it

For setting in holes or tunnels to kill rabbits, mink and smaller pests.

Trapping hints supplied with trap.

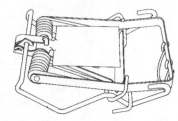

NEW MK6 GENERAL PURPOSE TRAP Jaws 6" Wide When Set

MK4 RAT TRAP Jaws 5" Wide When Set

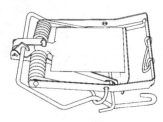

For setting in holes or tunnels to kill rats, grey squirrels, stoats etc.

Trapping hints supplied with trap.

Easier to set in deeper runs.

Trapping hints supplied with trap.

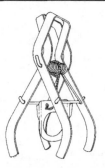

SCISSOR MOLE TRAP

FENN DOUBLE CATCH MOLE TRAP

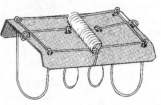

Capable of catching two moles at once.

was actually made or not. The Mark II version however was the first commercial run of traps produced, but for how long again remains unknown. In a 1957 catalogue of Young's of Misterton, the Fenn Vermin Trap (no mark number) is priced at 3/9d each. In the Forestry Commission's booklet *Traps for Grey Squirrels* (revised 1962) it states that only the Mark III is now being made and is priced at 8/6d each with swivel. Between the Mark IV and Mark VI general purpose traps a Mark I rabbit trap was introduced. This trap has the same patent number but was of slightly different design and has stamped on the plate Rabbit Mk I. The Game Conservancy *Rabbit Control* Booklet No 22, first published in Spring 1976 in cooperation with the Ministry of Agriculture, Fisheries and Food, states that the Fenn Rabbit Trap Mark I 'received approval in the middle of 1975.' This trap seems to have had a short period of production and was replaced with the above mentioned Mark VI version for catching rabbits and mink. The Mark I rabbit trap was advertised in *Shooting Times* during 1978 at £3.10 each or ten for £29 by Bryant's of East Molesley, Surrey. This price included both VAT and postage. On 12th July 1960 a further patent, Number 881,931 (Provisional patent No. 24751/59, dated 18th July 1959) was granted to Mr. Fenn, who had recently moved to Cottage Farm, Callow Hill, Redditch in the County of Worcester. No trap seems to have been put into production although two slightly different prototype traps are known to exist. Earlier, undated setting instructions for the Mark III version, show the price as 6/8d each with chain and thumb loop. Swivels were 6d extra. As mentioned under Sidebotham's, in March 1969 Fenn's received from W.&G. Sidebotham of Wednesfield a completion order of 120 dozen 4 link x 10g JAPD chains with rings and small strong 'S' hooks,

without swivels at 3/9d per dozen. Two known versions of the Mark III trap exist. In the just mentioned setting instructions for the MK III, the first trap version has one wire jaw, (the free jaw, which usually has the thumb loop), bent at a right angle on each of its outer edges forming 'corners'. This is the same style of trap as shown in the Forestry Commission's 1962 revised booklet also just mentioned. However, the trap plates are slightly different in both illustrations. In the earlier illustration for the setting instructions, the trap plate is a normal flat plate (Type a), whilst in the 1962 revised booklet the trap plate (Type b) has a turned down front edge which presumably acts as a sort of 'soil guard'. In the second version of the MK III, the wire jaws are straight and do not have the opposing 'corners'. The first has a 6 link elongated figure 8 type chain with ring at the far end, and a swivel attaching it to the two piece 'open' wire base. The trap has a brass tongue and till with a wire 'S' shaped safety catch. The second type also has the same brass tongue and till with the same wire 'S' shaped safety catch. However, the chain consists of a long loop chain with five loops and ring at the far end. The swivel protrudes underneath from a hole in the base plate between the two springs. The base plate being of a triangular shape with the two wire spring arms going through a triangular shaped opening, with both arms turning at right angles, left and right, to join the wire frame. The plate is marked FENN MK III.

Ten years later, in a 1972 catalogue of Young's, the Mark IV version is priced at 69p each and states 'These traps are now galvanised to prevent rust.' Whilst in the Forestry Commission's leaflet No 56 *Grey Squirrel Control* the price, at March 1973, is 87p each and states that 'Only the Mark IV version is available.'

According to Bryant's *Shooting Times* advertisement in November, the price for the Mark IV vermin trap is £2.10 each or £19 for ten, which also included both VAT and postage. The Mark III vermin trap consists of both jaws being made of wire, whilst in the Mark IV version only one jaw is made of wire, the other being made of flat steel. Modifications to the Mark IV trap include:

(a) A long loop chain with five loops, wire safety catch, brass tongue and till.

(b) Small linked chain, wire safety catch, brass tongue and till.

(c) Small linked chain, new type 'flat' safety catch, brass tongue and till.

(d) Small linked chain, 'flat' safety catch, brass tongue and till, vertical plate guard to reduce the risk of earth or small stones accumulating under the plate and so stopping the trap from operating efficiently.

(e) Small linked chain, 'flat' safety catch, vertical plate guard, steel tongue (no brass fittings at all on this version). The till is of a new design being a lip cut out and formed from the actual plate by being bent upwards and back towards the tongue forming a lip to take the end of the tongue.

General copies of the Mark IV and Mark VI include the Springer and the Northwoods. In Young's 1972 catalogue and the *Grey Squirrel Control* leaflet of 1973, both show identical Mark IV traps which consist of a chain with five long loops, wire safety catch, brass tongue and till and have no vertical plate guard, e.g. Type (a) whilst in Fenn's 1985 illustrated list both the Mark IV and Mark VI traps have the 'flat' safety catch and brass till plus the vertical plate guard, presumably the tongue would be of brass also therefore making them type (d).

Other traps produced by A Fenn & Co. in 1985, as well as their established Mark IV and Mark VI traps (which were priced at £4.40 and £5 each respectively and included VAT) were according to their price list and illustrated leaflet, 'live catch' cage traps at £12.55 single gate, £13 double gate run through, triangular folding cage (two sizes) £11.96 and £17.75, weld mesh clap trap side closing £10.25. Mole traps offered were the double catch £1.95 each, and the scissor type £1.85 each, all prices included VAT. Missing from this price list is their live catch metal box tunnel – 23"x5"x4$\frac{1}{2}$". This trap had previously been advertised in the Game Conservancy's paperback booklet No 16 *Predator and Squirrel Control* (1981). The name Fenn is embossed on the top of the metal tunnel. This trap was illustrated though in C.T.F. Field Sports Limited, Sutton, Surrey, catalogue of 1983, where it was described as being 'Safer for the fingers than wire mesh tunnels'. In Gilbertson & Page's 1986 price list they were still offering for sale at £5 each, the 'Fenn double entry galvanised tunnel trap (whilst stocks last)'. Incidently, Fenn's also made a dozen (12) experimental metal tunnel traps, which contained a trip plate and a killer bar. The size of this tunnel trap is 11" long, by approximately 4$\frac{3}{4}$" wide, by 5$\frac{1}{2}$" high. Both ends of the tunnel are open, with one end having a thin metal wire rod inserted from top to bottom. This wire rod being approximately 3" from one of the sides, and behind the axle rod on which the trip plate pivots. At the opposite end, a flat metal lever, which is attached on the left hand side, is lifted up to the inside of the roof of the trap, to set the device. In this position the lever protrudes out from the tunnel in a horizontal position, next to the wire safety catch hanging from the top of the trap.

In the same, 1981, *Predator and Squirrel Control* booklet, Fenn's own advert also mentioned the 'Humane Fox Holder – Metal collar. Safe to set almost anywhere'. This wire snare was illustrated in the C.T.F. Field Sports

Limited catalogue of 1983, where it was called the 'Safety Fox Holder' and was described as being 'Designed to hold without injury. Will not hold dogs, sheep, or deer by the foot. Swivels at the closed loop'. The Safety Fox Snares, as they were listed in the 1983 catalogue price list, were 70p each or £6.50p per 10. From 1st April 1985, A Fenn & Co. ceased to manufacture free running fox and rabbit wires (snares), instead they were produced under the name of A.B. Country Products of 8 Dark Lane, Astwood Bank, Redditch. However, in Fenn's January 1995 price list, free run fox snares with swivel, tie wire and fastener are priced at £10 per 10. Other prices in the same price list are Mark IV rat trap £5.50, Mark VI rabbit/mink trap £6, scissor mole trap with easy set trigger £4. Their live catch cage trap prices

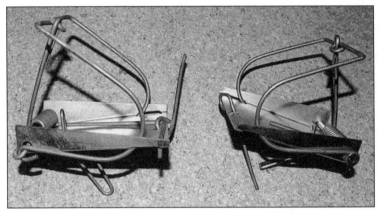

TWO DIFFERENT FENN 'LOOP' TYPE MOLE TRAPS
NOTE LEFT TRAP HAS A WIRE SETTER, RIGHT TRAP
HAS A SOLID STRIP OF METAL FOR A SETTER

THE 'ALL WIRE' SCISSOR TYPE MOLE TRAP

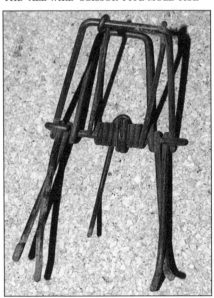

are single entry mink/squirrel/rat cage with bait door £16. The double entry run through version being a pound dearer at £17. The rabbit/feral cat cage (fold flat) single entry with bait door cost £25. All prices quoted are for individual traps and are inclusive of VAT.

Mole Traps

The mole trap illustrated in the 1985 leaflet has a 'cord' attached over the coil spring and down to the setter, which on other makes of this type of trap is usually made of wire. A later version of this mole trap dispenses with the 'cord' and attaches the setter directly to the outer support of the trap legs via one hole only. Thereby when the setter is dislodged by a mole it is retained on the trap and can't get lost as often happens with other types. This is the only type of mole trap now made by Fenn. Previous mole traps include the flat topped (half barrel type) 'Double Catch Mole Trap' which was also in the 1985 leaflet. It was also illustrated in the C.T.F. Field Sports Limited 1983 catalogue. The 'Loop' type mole trap shown in Guy N. Smith's book *Moles and Their Control*, published in 1980, seems to have been just on the market as Smith in his acknowledgements thanks Fenn's for supplying details of their new trap. Both of these mole traps are mentioned in the 1983 catalogue just referred to, but only Fenn's wire 'Loop' type in the 1981 *Predator and Squirrel Control* booklet. However, the 'Double Catch' and 'Loop' mole traps seem to have only been produced for a short time and then disappeared off the market completely. Another earlier type of Fenn scissor or pincher mole trap is also shown in Smith's book but unfortunately nothing is known about it except that the molecatchers didn't like it and it was short-lived also.

According to a January 1990 price list from Rural Trading Co. of Webheath, Redditch they were offering for sale genuine new Fenn traps, but the only listing for a mole trap is the scissor type. Another trap listed is the Fenn 'Venus' corvid catcher priced at £12.95 each, which seems to be a variation of the previously mentioned Weldmesh clap trap.

This company was advertising the new 'Venus' Magpie Trap in a March 1990 issue of The *Shooting News*, still priced at £12.95p, but now 'also live catches rabbit / rats etc'. Their January 1990 price list describes the 'Venus' Corvid Catcher as 'A very versatile catching device suitable for magpies, rabbits, etc. Made with 1"x1"x14G weldmesh. 20"x12"x4½" approx, when closed. To set: Pull sides apart to their fullest extent, then raise treadle till sides are held apart. Keep fingers away from edges after setting. Corvids: Place in position in rough herbage so that entry is made from one end, or from above. Camouflage, then bait with eggs, dead chicks, rabbit, etc. Make sure the trap is firm when set and secure it if thought necessary. Can be set in hedge out of reach of dogs, etc. Rabbits: Can be caught on runs through undergrowth, fences, etc. Camouflage trap well. In some situations carrots can be used as bait. Captives can easily be extracted if one spring is unhooked. Lubricate the spring slides for easy operation. The trap will also catch rats, squirrels, etc.' The *Shooting Times* later carried a short article under the heading, MAFF Warning on Magpie Traps, which stated, 'Owners of 50 magpie traps bought from a company in Worcestershire could be breaking the law, as the trap which uses a spring has not been approved for sale. It is not an offence to own one of these traps, but it is an offence to use one. This trap does not meet the standards of humaneness and efficacy required

THE APPROVED 'FENN' HUMANE TRAP

For use in tunnels and for rats on open runs.

PAT. No.
763,891

MK. 3
VERMIN

TO SET

Hook the loop provided on to bar C.   Place left thumb in loop, and fingers under base D.   Right thumb on bar A. with fingers under spring B.   Squeeze with both hands to fully open jaws, give trap an upward flip with right hand to swing Safety hook E. over bar A.   This prevents jaws closing.   Both hands are now free to adjust brass catches, taking care not to remove safety hook.   Place trap in position with spring coils parallel with run, making sure centre of trap is in centre of run.   If trap is to be covered with soil, rougher material (leaves etc;) can be used round the treadle plate to prevent soil running under.   A larger treadle would reduce the efficiency of the trap.   Remove safety hook.

This trap will fit in any tunnel normally used with a four inch gin.   Entrances should always be twigged to prevent game entering.

A baited wire cage, with trapped wooden tunnel entrances, is safe and effective for Squirrels.

When used in buildings, a piece of thin sacking is useful to conceal the trap.

Handle traps weekly to keep them working freely.
To avoid damaging the traps, do not spring them empty,
Always oil traps when not in use.

6/8 each, with chains & thumb loops. Swivels 6d. extra. Wood box tunnels supplied.

UNDATED SETTING INSTRUCTIONS LEAFLET

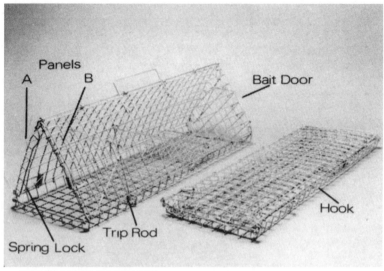

FOLD FLAT LIVE CATCH CAGE

under section eight of the Pests Act 1954. The company has supplied MAAF with the names and addresses of most of the people who bought their Venus Magpie Trap but fifty owners could not be traced.'

Clap Trap. This live catch trap was advertised by Fenn's, in 1981 in the Game Conservancy's paperback book No 16, *Predator & Squirrel Control*, where they described it as being 'Wire mesh, for catching surface rabbits etc'. An undated illustration shows this trap as a type of pointed arch held open by a treadle. The two separate coil springs that operate it are situated at either end of the wire trap and are fixed at the top of the arch-shaped entrances. It is described as being a 'wire mesh clap trap, 1" weld mesh. 20"x 10"x 9".'

Fenn's Weld Mesh Clapper Trap seems to be a modified version of the Clap Trap, and is known to have been advertised in 1985-86, but probably also later. This trap is also a 'Side closing live catch Weld Mesh tunnel' with its size listed as 22"x 9"x

10" , 1"x1"x14 guage Weld Mesh'. This trap was to be 'Set on runs through fences or along netting in plantations. Can also be used in gardens or buildings. Pull panels open until panel 'A' engages trip hook. Rabbits are attracted by fresh earth, so stir soil when possible before positioning trap, taking care panel 'A' is free to close. This also applies if using bait. The trap falls when sprung, locking against the trip mechanism.'

Foldflat Live Catch Cage. This triangular shaped trap was designed

CLAPPER TRAP

to catch mink, rats etc and was made in two sizes. The standard size of trap was 24"x 8"x 7$\frac{1}{2}$" and made out of 1"x 1"x 14 gauge Weld Mesh. The larger size, made to order only, was 34"x 12"x 11". This trap was described as being 'Easy to carry and store. Ready to use in seconds. Unhook and raise panel 'A' then panel 'B'. Withdraw connecting rod, insert eyes on panel 'B' through loops on panel 'A' then rethread rod through eyes to make cage rigid. One method of setting for Mink, is to dig a trap size trench in a suitable position, bait the trap, put it in trench with one end open, then cover to hide.' This trap was being advertised on the same illustrated leaflet as the Clapper Trap.

In Fenn's January 1995 price list were advertised their magpie catcher and magpie holder, both being made of wire mesh.

FENN MAGPIE CATCHER
Size: 30"l x 15"w x 15"h approx.
A walk-in type cage trap for the live capture of crows, magpies, etc.
Consists of 2 catching compartments, each with a side-entry drop door.
The trap folds flat for easy storage and transportation.
Weight: 3.7kg (8lbs) approx.

FENN MAGPIE HOLDER
Available separately. Same size as Catcher.
A single-compartment cage to hold a decoy bird. For use with the catcher. Folds flat.
Wooden perches and roof shelter, supplied and fitted by The Domestic Fowl Trust, are included.
Weight: 3.2kg (7lbs) approx.

Both cages are of heavy duty 1" x 3" x 12 guage galv. weld mesh are manufactured by A. Fenn & Co. and are available from:

The Domestic Fowl Trust,
Honeybourne Pastures,
Honeybourne, nr Evesham, Worcs,
WR11 5QJ Tel. Evesham 833083.

In a letter to me, dated 11th January 2006, Michael Roberts writes: 'I helped design the Fenn magpie trap. As you will see it is made in two halves. The Larsen trap was a cumbersome and bulky affair, difficult to put into some cars and heavy to carry across fields. Also I wanted a trap which would fold down, so it could be easily transported and sent through the post. One half is for the call bird, complete with trap door, perches and wooden weather cover, the other half contains two drop-down hinged doors, operated by a wire treadle. The doors are secured by a bar sliding down the two side rails, an idea we took from the French trap.
'The round French magpie trap (now sold by Solway Feeders) will catch four birds, with the call bird in the centre. There was a larger circular trap made in France which could catch eight birds at a time.'

Mr Michael Roberts originally established the Domestic Fowl Trust in 1975. When he purchased the land it was overrun with foxes and magpies. About 1990, he thought of a folding 'flat pack' Larsen trap with a separate section to hold the decoy magpie. With Mr Fenn's help these were put into production. Mr Roberts eventually started up Gold Cockerel Books.

The workforce in 1999 consisted of Graham Fenn and his sister, plus Mr. Joseph Archer who has made all types of Fenn traps since the beginning of the business until he retired at Christmas 1999. Other temporary workers were employed during very busy periods.

Caught! (1898)

Chapter Six

MANTRAPS AND GAMEKEEPING

THE ENCLOSURES or conversion of the common lands into private property in England began in the fourteenth century with the open land system of farming giving way to enclosed fields. This process became widespread during the fifteenth and sixteenth centuries with the enclosed fields often being used for sheep rearing. The upheaval and distress that was caused to the populace led to serious rebellions in 1536, 1569 and 1607. Government measures introduced during 1489 to 1640 to reduce depopulation of the countryside were seriously hampered by the land owning Justices of the Peace. Further enclosures took place during 1760 to 1820, and effectively reduced the yeomanry to becoming agricultural labourers, or even drove them off the land permanently.

One person to fight on behalf of the poor against the Enclosure Act was the Rector of Birdinbury (1764 to 1791) in Warwickshire. The Reverend Henry Sacheverell Homer issued a pamphlet which showed when and where there had been past uninterrupted usage of the common land by the poor peasants, but all this effort was to no avail. Country estates were now created in place of the old system of open fields with loosely knit villages. The new landowners were now able to protect the animals and birds that dwelt in their newly enclosed fields and woodlands for their own pursuit and sport exclusively.

Previously in a Charter of the Forests of 1217, provision was made that 'None shall lose life or limb' for pursuing the King's game, but the rules were then changed by Richard II in 1389 to allow people to pursue game only if they were the owner of land. Then further new Game Laws were introduced in 1671 by Charles II. To 'qualify' to pursue and kill game, a person had to own land valued at £100 per year or alternatively hold a 99 year lease on land which was worth £150. This effectively narrowed down eligible persons to a very small and elite band of the most rich and influential members of society. Any person who qualified, with the rank of Esquire or other higher honour, was to appoint a gamekeeper who had the authority to seize from

Mr. R. P. Williams had had trouble with constant trespassers and poachers two years previously:

"NOTICE

All qualified Persons are hereby requested to REFRAIN FROM SPORTING over, or trespassing in Pursuit of Game, or Hunting on the Lands belonging to or in the Occupation of MR RICHARD POWELL WILLIAMS, in the Liberty of SWINDON and Parish of Wombourn; and all unqualified Persons found trespassing thereon after this public Notice will be prosecuted according to the Law.
Sept 1, 1829."
—"Wolverhampton Chronicle" of 9 September, 1829.

PUBLIC NOTICE FROM 1829

LICENCES. THE GAME ACT OF 1831 MADE PROVISION, AMONGST OTHER THINGS, TO ALLOW 'PERSONS WHO ARE HOUSEHOLDERS, SHOPKEEPERS, OR KEEPERS OF A STALL' TO BE LICENCED TO DEAL IN GAME PROVIDED THAT 'EVERY PERSON LICENCED TO DEAL IN GAME MUST AFFIX TO SOME PART OF THE OUTSIDE OF THE FRONT OF HIS HOUSE, SHOP, OR STALL, A BOARD HAVING THEREON IN CLEAR, LEGIBLE CHARACTERS, HIS CHRISTIAN NAME AND SURNAME, AND THE WORDS LICENCED TO DEAL IN GAME. LICENCES HAD BEEN PREVIOUSLY INTRODUCED FOR SHOOTING GAME SPECIES, BUT THESE ONLY ALLOWED THE OWNER OF LAND OR HIS GAMEKEEPER ETC TO LEGALLY SHOOT GAME AND DISPOSE OF IT. WITH THE PASSING OF THE GAME LICENCES ACT IN 1860, A GENERAL LICENCE WAS INTRODUCED IN 1861, WHEREBY ANYONE WHO OBTAINED PERMISSION TO SHOOT OVER LAND COULD NOW LEGALLY SHOOT GAME SPECIES AND SELL THEM THROUGH A LICENCED GAME DEALER. HOWEVER, IT WAS NOT UNTIL THE GUN LICENCE ACT OF 1870 THAT A PERSON SHOOTING GAME ACTUALLY NEEDED A LICENCE TO OWN A GUN TO SHOOT THE GAME BIRDS ETC.

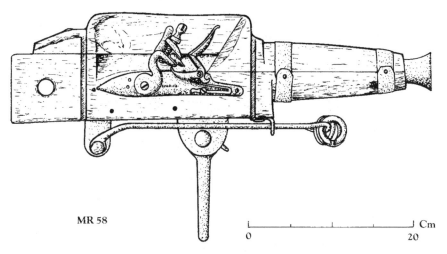

MR 58

0   20   Cm

SPRING GUN IN THE NATIONAL MUSEUM OF ANTIQUITIES OF SCOTLAND

'unqualified persons' any equipment being used for poaching whilst on the estate grounds. Equipment could include snares, guns, dogs, nets and such like.

The new laws of 1671 were very strict about who was allowed to take game. Only the landowners, their eldest sons, and their regular gamekeepers had permission. Other sons of the landowner, or a tenant farmer who rented a large acreage of land was not allowed the privilege of being able to pursue and take game on that land. Poaching was to become increasingly widespread due to the necessity of the poorly provided peasants to feed their families and just to survive.

Punishments for poaching though did not become too severe until 1723 when it then became a capital punishment offence. This Act was initially introduced for a three year period, but became renewed regularly, finally being made permanent in 1758.

Records show that mantraps were being made in 1770, and landowners now also employed these devices throughout their estates to protect their wild game and fruit crops from the hungry peasants. Harsh laws or not, an empty stomach needs filling, but stepping onto one of these carefully concealed mantraps would have caused instant punishment. In an account of 1785 a Hampshire gentleman described the scene in P.B. Munsche's book *Gentlemen and Poachers*, as 'The most shocking I ever beheld.' What he had seen was four poachers caught in mantraps, three of which had their thighs broken, whilst the fourth was dead. If the poacher survived the encounter, often he could later on lose life or limb due to infection caused by rusty teeth on the traps.

Spring guns were also used with devastating effect in an effort to stop the poaching forays. These small, flintlock-operated versions of cannon were first used around the late eighteenth century and seem to have been used extensively in the East Anglian region of England from the earliest times.

When set, a flintlock operated spring gun would be susceptible to any damp or wet weather conditions whilst silently waiting for an unsuspecting victim to enter the wood. Obviously, if the black powder became damp, the sparks from the striking flint would not ignite it, and so render the spring gun useless in doing its deadly duty. The gun makers minimised this problem by putting a metal, usually brass, cover plate over the firing mechanism, and so thereby enclosing it from excessive rain etc. This cover plate fitted into usually either one or two, vertical slots in the wooden stock either side of the flint lock, and was secured firmly in place by a metal pin on a length of chain. This pin was multi functional as it could also be used as a pricker for cleaning out any burned powder residue left in the small touch hole. Another use, as found on my own example, was as a safety pin when inserted underneath the spring gun, thereby locking the trigger mechanism from firing accidentally whilst being attended to. This safety pin would most likely be employed during the daylight hours when the gamekeepers were working in the immediate area of the spring gun – just in case they forgot it was there! The trigger on a spring gun works by being pulled forward, rather than pulled backwards as on a normal gun. The so called 'trip wire' was not intended to break immediately, when an intruder encountered it, but to resist very slightly so that the effect of someone's leg 'pushing through' the taught length of thin wire, actually pulled it slightly in a forward direction and in doing so fired the spring gun in that direction. The trigger forms part of the horizontal bar which is located along the underside of the spring gun. This bar or rod of iron, usually terminates in the shape of a ring. It is from this ring that the 'wire' is stretched out to its secured point across the woodland path. When thin wire was used, as the 'springge', it was normal practice for the gamekeeper to eliminate any shiny reflection off it, by passing it through the smoke of a small fire or candle. Depending on the situation, either a single trip wire would be employed, or possibly two or three stretched out in slightly different directions. It is commonly thought that when more than one trip wire was used, and any of the trip wires were encountered, the spring gun would slowly swivel in the desired direction and ultimately release its deadly charge of shot. However, it is possible that the main reason for multiple trip wires was to fool the poacher.

The gamekeeper Thomas Cank, states in his book (1891) when refering to alarm guns:

> When they are set by a wood side, or in a wood, they are easy

to be found by an old hand; by means of him carrying a little short stick in front of him, which will come in contact with the wire before any part of the body; and when these searches are made for the wires there is a pair of scissors, or wire cutters not far away; the wire is cut, and the gun is thereby disabled; and on they go with their job.

This method would have also been employed years earlier by poachers when trying to locate the trip wire of a spring gun. However, when extra wires were closely stretched across a path, the poacher would detect the first wire and cut it. Rather than trying to 'follow up' the wire to locate the spring gun and deactivate it properly, an action which might cause it to accidently discharge, the trip wire would be left where it fell. Thinking that the spring gun was now non operational and that the path would be clear, he would start to continue his journey. In the darkness of the wood, unaware of the second wire, maybe only a couple of feet or so away, he would unsuspectingly blunder into it with possibly fatal results. The spring gun itself was usually set in a suitable position on a small post, knocked into the ground, or on a convenient tree stump, where a small hole was bored out big enough to accept the metal peg located under the spring gun. Once this peg was set in position, the spring gun could then be angled up or down by the use of a pivoting joint, and locked into whatever position the gamekeeper wanted by the broad headed thumb screw.

Being able to elevate the spring gun's muzzle would have been seen as an advantage when used on uneven ground. The angle of discharge dictated whether the intruder received a charge of shot to the legs or chest. The spring gun would have been first loaded with a measured charge of gunpowder followed by a quantity of small calibre round lead shot, which would have been poured down the muzzle of the barrel, and compacted by the use of a ramrod. All that was left to do would be to cunningly conceal it. This would not be hard to do, as most spring guns are small in size. My own, stamped RIGBY on the lock, has an overall length of 21 inches, an overall height of 10 inches, which includes the $3^{1}/_{2}$" long peg which goes into the tree stump. The overall width is only a maximum of 3 inches. Measurements from two other flintlock operated spring guns that I have closely examined, seem to indicate that this is an average size for this type of weapon. A few examples are known of percussion operated spring guns, but the majority of them are flintlock.

Although spring guns are mainly known as an anti-poaching deterrent, they were also employed occasionally by the richer members of society in churchyards. This was done out of fear, to protect their dearly beloved family member's newly interred body from being illegally exhumed by body snatchers. Body snatchers sold the newly dead to the medical profession for dissection.

Another device set up in woods but to detect poachers without harming them, was known as the alarm gun. Alarm guns in their modern form are still being used by present day gamekeepers in their battle to protect game from the unwanted attention shown them by today's poachers. Like the spring gun, this device is fired by coming into contact with the trip wire, and thereby firing a blank cartridge in the direction of the ground or upwards into the air. The report from the blank cartridge thereby alerts the gamekeeper to the presence of possible poaching activity in the woods.

Gamekeepers had relied on the protection afforded the wild game, by keeping vermin levels down to a minimum and reducing the poaching activities, to produce good sporting results for the estate owner. Then in 1761, Andrew Roe, Rockwell, County Tipperary established on his estate what must be one of the earliest recorded game farms. He states:

> The farming of feathered game is an innovation of mine to
> supply the demesnes of noblemen and gentlemen within this
> Kingdom, and now my game birds go beyond the seas as well.
> In the year 1761, I laid out my game enclosure in a horse
> paddock of three Irish Plantation acres in area, beset and
> surrounded by a pinery and shrubbery. Around the wood belt
> I have an enclosure fence behind and above hurdles fixed to
> the outer tree boles to the height of 10 feet, made of fishing
> nets coated with wood tar to preserve them. This excludes the
> animals of the farm, foxes, and badgers and keeps my wing
> game within bounds. The young of the pheasant, partridge
> and wild duck are hatched out by broody barn door hens in
> huts made of wood, each hut being 30 feet long, by 7 feet
> wide and 6 feet at the front, with a backfall roof made with
> old pine boards with shingle laps to bear off the weather.
> Partridge chicks are hard to rear, but pheasants are much like
> the farmyard broods. Wild ducks are brooded in the same way
> and have a fish pond in the paddock to water upon.
> In the year 1767, I raised more than 500 brace of pheasants
> alone. I can well now cope with the earnest demands of the
> nobility and gentry all over the Kingdom and send breeding
> braces to England and Scotland and my breeds are reported
> as thriving well.

Then twenty years later, the first English hatchery using collected wild eggs was established in 1787 at Blenheim Palace for the rearing of pheasants under broody hens. Now there were more game birds being reared and released, so obviously there were more to be poached. The landowners' answer to this problem was to remove the poachers. This was achieved by the Government introducing in 1816 the Night Poaching Act which allowed for seven years transportation to the Australian continent. Fortunately, this practice ceased in 1868.

Confusion about the Game Laws and their harsh penalties brought public outcry to the notice of the Government. Innocent people were being horribly maimed or killed by the mantraps and spring guns lurking in the undergrowth of woods, where peasants were in the habit of collecting wild growing nuts, mushrooms, and wood for their fires.

Warning notices appeared in the local press, and town and local parish criers repeatedly spread the news of them being set in the area. Although landowners displayed notice boards on the boundaries of their estate, warning the public that 'Mantraps and Spring-guns set here', this was of little help in an era when must people could not read or write.

Debates took place in *The Edinburgh Review* in 1821, regarding the legal and moral issues raised by the use of mantraps and spring-guns. Questions are asked such as:

> If the owner of woods cannot set spring-guns in his woods, the owner of an orchard, or of a field with potatoes or turnips, or any other crop usually the object of plunder, cannot set them in such field. How then are these kinds of property to be protected, at a distance from the residence of the owner, in the night, and in the absence of his servants? It has been said, that the law has provided remedies for any injuries to such things by action. But the offender must be detected before he can be subjected to an action; and the expense of continual watching for this purpose would often exceed the value of the property to be protected. . . My brother *Bayley* has illustrated this case, by the question which he asked, namely, Can you indict a man for putting spring-guns in his enclosed field? I think the question put by Lord C.J. Gibbs, in the case in the Common Pleas, a still better illustration, *viz.* Can you justify entering into enclosed lands, to take away guns so set? If both these questions must be answered in the negative, it cannot be unlawful to set spring-guns in an enclosed field, at a distance from any road, giving such notice that they are set, as to render it in the highest degree probable that all persons in the neighbourhood must know that they are so set. Humanity requires that the fullest notice possible should be given; and the law of England will not sanction what is inconsistent with humanity. . . This case has been argued, as if it appeared in it that the guns were set to preserve game; but that is not so; they were set to prevent trespasses on the lands of the defendant. Without, however, saying in whom the property of game is vested, I say, that a man has a right to keep persons off his lands, in order to preserve the game. Much money is expended in the protection of game; and it would be hard, if, in one night, when the keepers are absent, a gang of poachers might destroy what has been kept at so much cost. If you do not

allow men of landed estates to preserve their game, you will not prevail on them to reside in the country. Their poor neighbours will thus lose their protection and kind offices; and the government the support that it derives from an independent, enlightened, and unpaid magistracy. . . We are thoroughly and honestly convinced, that Mr Justice Best's horror at the destruction of human life for the mere preservation of game, is quite sincere.

It is impossible, indeed, that any human being, of common good nature, could entertain a different feeling upon the subject, when it is earnestly pressed upon him. . . My Brother Best justly observes, that prevention of intrusion upon private property is a right which every proprietor may act upon, and use force to vindicate – the force absolutely necessary for such vindication– (however) If the ultimate object in preventing such intrusions is pleasure in sporting, it is better that pleasure should be rendered more expensive, than that the life of man should be rendered so precarious. Continuing he says, Why may not an intruder be held in a toothless trap till the proprietor arrives ? – such traps as are sold in all the iron shops in this city? We are bound, according to my Brother Best, to inquire if these means have been previously resorted to; for upon his own principle, greater violence must not be used, where less will suffice for the removal of the intruder. He must not make laws (and those very bloody laws) for himself. . . I do not say that the setter of the trap or gun allures the trespasser into it; but I say that the punishment he intends for the man who trespasses after notice, is death. He covers his spring-gun with furze and heath, and gives it the most natural appearance he can; and in that gun he places the slugs by which he means *to kill* the trespasser. This killing of an un-challenged, unresisting person, I really cannot help considering to be as much murder as if the proprietor had shot the trespasser with his gun. The practice has unfortunately become so common, that the first person convicted of such a murder, and acting under the delusion of right, might be a fit object for the Royal mercy. Still, in my opinion, such an act must legally be considered as murder.

All my brother Judges have delivered their opinions as if these guns were often set for the purposes of terror, and not of destruction. To this I can only say, that the moment any man puts a bullet into his spring-gun, he has some other purpose than that of terror; and if he does not put a bullet there, he never can be the subject of argument in this Court. Pointing out that, The victim of the spring-gun may have gone astray, may not be able to read, or may first cross the armed soil in the night time, when he cannot read; – and so he is absolutely without any notice at all... (therefore) ..the slaughtered man may be perfectly innocent in his purpose. . . (so) It is my duty, instead of making

Nᵒ 0 . *s* 18 . *d* 0 each.

Nᵒ 1 . 21 . 0 „

Nᵒ 2 . 38 . 0 „

THE 'HUMANE' MAN TRAP HAD NO TEETH ON THE JAWS
ILLUSTRATION FROM WILLIAM BULLOCK & CO. CATALOGUE

one abuse a reason for another, to recal the law back to its perfect state, and to restrain as much as possible the invention and use of private punishments.

Whatever be the law, the question of humanity is a separate question. I shall not state all I think of that person, who, for the preservation of game, would doom the innocent – or the guilty intruder, to a sudden death. I will not, however, (because I am silent respecting individuals), join in any undeserved panegyric of the humanity of the English law. I cannot say, at the same moment, that the law of England allows such machines to be set after public notice; and that the law of England sanctions nothing but what is humane. If the law sanctions such practices, it sanctions, in my opinion, what is to the last degree odious, unchristian, and inhumane.

To destroy a trespasser with such machines, I think would be murder; to set such uncontrollable machines for the purpose of committing this murder, I think would be indictable; and I am therefore of opinion, that he who suffers from such machines has a fair ground of action, in spite of any notice; for it is not in the power of notice to make them lawful.

The last comments of course presume that the victim survived the encounter with the rusty, germ-infected mantrap or the full charge of shot from the spring-gun, and could afford to take the landowner to court!

In May 1827 Lord Suffield of Gunton Park in Norfolk had passed by Parliament, but only by a modest majority, his Engines of Destruction Bill. This Act 'to prohibit the setting of spring guns, mantraps, and other engines calculated to destroy human life or inflict grievous bodily harm' strangely, only banned these devices from being set in the open, out of doors. The right was reserved however, to set or place 'from sunset to sunrise any spring-gun, mantrap in any dwelling-house for the protection thereof.' A few years later in 1831, a bill was brought before Parliament seeking to give a single Justice of the Peace the power to grant a licence for mantraps to be set in out-buildings also. This bill was not looked upon favourably, and so was not passed into law. Although supposedly banned from use outwith a house they could still be made and sold as is shown in the 1838 Trade Directories which list among others, Richard Bellimore and Mary Hames as mantrap makers. Obviously any non-humane mantraps made would be, or more correctly should be, export items only, whilst humane mantraps sold for use in England, should be for use within a 'dwelling-house for the protection thereof.' However accounts are known of mantraps being used in defiance of the law in 1835 and 1846.

Obviously, many landowners' were under the impression that as long as the mantraps set in their woods were of the humane type and did not 'destroy human life or inflict grevious bodily harm' to the poacher or unfortunate innocent victim, then it was perfectly permissible and within the law. A game lessee, Mr. Villebois, speaking before a committee in 1846 stated that:

'Not a gun can come on the land without my leave. I can preserve all the game I like, 10,000 partridges if I can get them. I can keep a whole regiment of guards if I choose, to pass over any part of the farm by day or night. I set traps, and a man may get into them if he likes.'

Between 1833 and 1843, forty two gamekeepers were killed and many more seriously injured, so maybe certain landowners felt justified in still allowing the use of mantraps on their estates to help their gamekeepers in the battles against violent poachers. A writer in 1851 advised his readers:

'if it be thought necessary to use steel man-traps in the preservation of game, what is called the humane trap should be chosen. This merely holds the thief fast without inflicting injury, which cannot fail to result from the common trap.'

In the Offences Against the Person Act of 1861, mention is again made of the setting of mantraps and spring guns:

'Whosoever shall set or place, or cause to be set or placed, any spring gun or mantrap or other engine calculated to destroy human life or inflict grievous bodily harm, with the intent that the same or whereby the same may destroy or inflict grievous bodily harm upon a trespasser or other person coming in contact therewith, shall be guilty of an offence, and being convicted thereof shall be liable to imprisonment for a term not exceeding five years.'

Although spring guns were banned from being used to 'destroy human life or inflict grievous bodily harm', Idstone writing in 1872 tells us that 'Spring guns or alarm guns may be used still, supposing that they merely make a report, and are not dangerous.' He goes on to mention however that 'They are still set in India for the destruction of wild beasts, and the son of a friend of mine, going down the river, was killed by one on landing from his boat.' Idstone then proceeds to describe two proper alarm guns. The first 'made by the celebrated sword cutter, Wilkinson. He sold a metal plate with a gun metal hammer worked by one strong spring. This could be screwed to a post or tree, and the trigger could be made as sensitive as the keeper desired; whilst the strings or wires could be arranged in all directions, and at any height from the ground. The explosive substance was secured in a 'maroon' of varnished string, absolutely impervious to weather, and the hammer fell upon a tube of detonating powder.'

The second type described, which he thought to be a far better alarm gun, '(was) made by W. Wigg of Barnby Foundry, near Beccles. It consists of a rough, cast iron, short barrel, with such a spring and hammer as that I have described of Wilkinson's metal; a metal projection or shed protects the percussion cap from rain, and it can be lightly or heavily charged, as the situation may require. When the muzzle is placed upwards, the report is much louder than when it is turned downwards.'

Flintlock-operated spring guns also usually had a metal cover which enclosed the powder and trigger mechanism completely, thereby keeping the powder dry and the gun operational during the worst of any rain storm.

During the early 1740s local and county associations were formed by the land owning game preservers who often offered financial rewards to informers in order to prosecute the poachers. Then in 1752 a national association was formed by these landowners from various parts of the country. This association consisted of several hundred game preserving landowners who would, when the need arose, allow the deployment of their own gamekeepers to an estate which they had discovered was going to be poached. Therefore, a larger force of gamekeepers were able to confront the gang of unsuspecting poachers.

Just when gamekeeping, in its recognised form, came into being is hard to determine. However, the gamekeeper, as we know him now, probably originally evolved from the occupation of warrener. The warrener's job was to maintain the structure of the warren, where the conies lived underground, and the surrounding enclosure for keeping them in. At this period in time, *circa* twelfth century, conies (adult rabbits) had only just been introduced into England by the Normans, and so were regarded as valuable livestock. Other duties included making sure that there was enough feeding throughout the year for all the conies and their offspring, the young rabbits. He was also responsible for culling the adult conies for fresh meat for his master's table or for general sale of the meat and fur that they provided. Another important duty was obviously to protect the animals from attack by winged and ground vermin and of course the hungry peasants who lived close by, who might succumb to temptation at the thought of an easy meal.

When in 1671, gamekeepers were to be appointed by a qualified person, due to the abuse of the system by the landowners, who employed large numbers of the so-called gamekeepers, they were in effect becoming landowners' private armies. To stop this abuse, or at least curb it, in 1716, by an Act of Parliament, a landowner was forbidden to appoint a gamekeeper with the authority to kill game unless certain provisions had been strictly met. Then in 1784 the legislation was relaxed, again allowing a landowner to employ more than one gamekeeper, but subject to each gamekeeper being registered with the County Clerk of the Peace.

THE WARRENER (1803)

Obviously, gamekeeping around this time was concerned solely with the preservation of wild game, by the total destruction of vermin and keeping people out of the woods and coverts. The idea of intensively rearing game was not introduced in England until 1787 as previously mentioned. By the 1850s it was reliably estimated that 20,000 gamekeepers and their assistants were employed on game preserving land.

Initially, most poaching was done by individuals, when the opportunity presented itself, and on a small scale. The poacher really did, as has so often been quoted, 'take one for the pot', and with the only intention of feeding his often very large and hungry family. The main method of catching both fur and feather, which also happened to be the quickest and easiest way, was with the wire snare set in a hedgerow. Poachers did use steel traps, but it was not a common method as traps were expensive items to buy and took longer to conceal properly. These traps would have been 'found' and 'aquired' by either, quietly watching a gamekeeper on his beat setting or checking his traps, or else by furtively checking known rabbit warrens. Indeed, Gilbertson & Page's booklet entitled *Poachers versus Keepers*, published in 1894 advises regarding Stolen Traps:

> 'It is never advisable for a keeper to place his vermin traps
> directly where the labourers may see them; for although they
> would not perhaps purchase traps for their own use, yet would
> feel little compunction in appropriating one of his. Should a
> trap be missed at any time, a careful search will generally
> discover it set in some sly place. It is easy for the keeper to put a
> private mark on his traps; even filing a slight notch in some part
> will be amply sufficient, then if it is found in another man's
> possession he may be prosecuted for having stolen property.'

In these early days, before the industrial revolution, most of the population lived in poverty, and worked in the very rural, and sometimes isolated, countryside. Most people lived 'a day to day' existence, and were employed from dawn to dusk in hard back-breaking work as agricultural labourers. Therefore, they had ample opportunity to watch and study the habits of the various creatures that lived around them. When out working the long hours in the fields, this knowledge would be put to good use by the amateur poacher. The booklet *Poachers versus Keepers*, again advises:

> 'No class of poaching is so difficult to cope with as that
> carried on by a sneaking labourer employed on the farm. He
> possesses the right of being on the ground, and the keeper
> cannot always be watching him, so he selects the most
> favourable of times and places to carry on his evil practices.'

The booklet continues advising:

> The keeper will need all his wits to contend successfully with such men; he must be up early and late, and always on the alert. The sneaking labourer seldom poaches in an elaborate manner; he rarely fills a hedge with wires or places down a dozen traps. Such extensive work requires more time than he can devote to it away from his labours without attracting attention. Two or three snares, or perhaps a trap, placed in the likeliest places are quite sufficient, as he seldom disposes of his quarry, preferring to utilise it for his own pot and pantry.'

Two forms of poaching by farm labourers using the ordinary rabbit gin trap to catch partridges and pheasants is described for interest. The labourer would carefully watch a located covey to decide the best place to put his trap. Firstly he would find a bare patch amongst the rows of turnips that partridges like to frequent, and casually place the set trap or traps and cover slightly with soil. He would then sprinkle a few grains of corn on and around it. Whilst going about his work in the field or hedgerow, he would slowly manoeuvre the selected partridge covey to go into the general direction of his awaiting traps. Partridges would rather run down a row of turnips than take to the wing. Whilst continuing his work he would be ever watchful and always listening for the snap of the trap and the fluttering of the caught bird which would immediately send the rest of the covey rising into the air and quickly away. Casually, but determinedly, he would make his way over to the unfortunate bird and in one smooth movement put both bird and trap into his pocket and be on his way.

Another version for pheasants was to use red sealing wax to stick on to the trap plate, so making the droplets look like berries. Grain or raisins, which pheasants especially like, would be scattered on and around the trap plate with one or two actually stuck into the sealing wax. The pheasant would then start pecking at the grain or raisins on the trap plate which was very finely set. Obviously the bird would have to peck harder at the fixed raisins and the red sealing wax 'berries', and in due course the trap would spring and catch the bird by the head or neck. It was a very effective method during the winter months when food was in short supply.

Some unfortunate poachers who were caught using traps are recorded for example, in the *Norfolk Chronicle* newspaper between the dates 1832 and 1859. Appearing before the Magistrates was John Stokes, labourer. 'This individual was charged with illegally using a trap. He was in default of paying his £1 fine and received 14 days hard labour' (1832). James Carr, labourer had taken a pheasant in a rabbit trap and was fined £2 which he paid (1842). Matthias Hardingham, labourer was trapping hares, and paid his fine of

PARTRIDGE POACHING WITH STEEL TRAP (1893)

£1.15 shillings (1854). Henry Sharp and David Sharp, both labourers, were caught using traps for game, Henry being fined 6 shillings and 6 pence, which he paid, whilst David was discharged (1857). Lastly, Henry Wakefield, labourer, was setting rabbit traps and fined £1.16 shillings and 4 pence, which he paid (1859).

It is probable that mantraps started to appear, in their recognisable form, by 1770. To start with, the traps would have just been large single or double flat springed animal traps, which would have been common enough around this period due to the fur trade in North America. They would have been deployed in and around the coverts and fruit orchards with the intention of deterring potential poachers. When it was realised that these traps, although capable of catching their intended victim and causing terrible wounds, were not restraining the poacher, improvements had to be made.

A poacher although caught by the trap and in a great deal of pain would endeavour to get free before the gamekeeper came along and apprehended him. If he was poaching with others, it was a simple matter of them standing on the spring or springs and so releasing the jaws for the unfortunate victim to free himself. Advice regarding the type and quality of mantraps being sold in London is given by the Reverend William B. Daniel in his book *Rural Sports*, Volume III in 1812. He advises against 'large mantraps with a few long spikes' and also because 'not one spring in twenty will throw the jaws of the trap close after remaining on the stretch several nights together.' He recommended that remote coverts should be 'well studded with mantraps. . .

lightly covered with moss and leaves.' The improvement which distinguished between a large animal trap (which may have been used as a mantrap) and a genuine mantrap was simply a locking device that needed a separate key to unlock it. Now if a poacher was caught, even his friends, if they were to stand on the springs could not release him. As the traps were usually firmly secured to a solid object by a length of chain, the poacher would still be there in the morning when the gamekeeper checked his traps. Release from the trap could only be by a key, duly kept by the gamekeeper.

Basically mantraps can be divided into two groups for convenience: humane and non-humane. The older type of non-humane mantraps were probably mostly produced by the local blacksmith or the earlier trap makers of the Black Country. The later, 'humane' square versions seem to have been mostly produced by the Black Country iron founders in the industrial towns. As previously mentioned the non-humane traps were basically of the same design as the large animal traps complete with large spikes or teeth attached to the jaws. Due to the Black Country trapmakers working in a local community which included many key and lock makers it was only natural that the lock makers' expertise would be combined with the trap makers' to produce a simple but effective locking device which the trapmakers could incorporate into their large animal traps. The locking mechanism on the non humane mantrap, in my own collection, consists of a slightly curved bar with a row of notches along one side which is riveted to one jaw. On the other jaw is riveted a 'padlock' shaped lock with an opening at the top, as in a normal padlock. When the jaws close, the curved bar aligns with the hole in the 'padlock'-shaped lock, enters and goes right through as far as is possible. The serrated notches then act as a rachet inside the lock stopping the jaws from being opened again, until a key is used.

A very common mistake of misidentification surrounds the so-called 'mantrap with spikes on its plate'. Many people think that the spikes on the plate are there to attach and keep in place such items as leaves and grass to conceal the trap. This idea is totally wrong. They are in fact large animal traps, and used for catching such animals as badger and fox. Idstone, who obviously enjoyed fox hunting, writing in 1872 clearly describes them as:

> 'fox traps (woe betide the makers of them!) large enough to hold a wolf' and goes on to describe the trap 'with double springs and circular jaws. The spike teeth are on the *outside*; there are nine of them, flat and wedge-shaped. This trap weighs nearly 40lb., and is 4ft. 6in. long. It has a peculiar trigger plate 9in. by 11in., furnished with six large points, like small dog spears, for holding on a bait. An experienced master of foxhounds, who saw it a few days since, pronounced it a fox trap, and told me, as a boy, he had seen many of them in Kent.'

IDSTONE WRITING IN 1872 DESCRIBES THIS AS A FOX TRAP

The earliest known reference to a 'bait spike' on the plate of a trap, is recorded by Mascall in 1590 when he says 'that if any otter, fox, or other, do but tread thereon he shall be soone taken. Or ye must bind a piece of meate in the middell, and put it on the pricke, and so bind it fast. In pulling the baite, the clickets will slippe and the springes will rise, and so it will take him.' It must be remembered that in the early days of trapping fox, badger, and larger animals, that they were usually caught by the neck or upper body, and so therefore a very large jaw size was needed, and so therefore, larger traps were built.

Gerstell, writing in his book *The Steel Trap in North America*, says that James Isham, a Hudson Bay Company official, was in charge of Prince of Wales Fort, at the mouth of Churchill River on the western shore of Hudson Bay. In one of Isham's reports, which was sent to the Hudson Bay Company's Governor and Committee in London in 1743, Isham observed,

> 'There is severall sorts of traps which is made use of in these parts to catch Vermin, as steel or Iron traps, which have a trigger in the midle which Keeps the chaw's Downe catching by a Notch in the midle, by the baite where the baite is fastn'd on, which when the Vermin takes, the plate falls on one side, by which the springs forces the chaws up, by which they are trapp'd, there being teeth in the chaws 2 inches long.'

Accompanying this written, eyewitness record are hand drawings of two types of large double flat spring traps. One has square jaws whilst the other has round or oval jaws. The interesting thing about these drawings is that

SNARES AND TRAPS CONFISCATED FROM AFRICAN POACHERS
(REPRODUCED WITH PERMISSION OF THE AUTHOR FROM *THE SHAMBA
RAIDERS* (1972), BRUCE KINLOCH)

THIS HUMANE
MANTRAP HAS FOUR
FLAT SPRINGS AND NOT
THE NORMAL SINGLE
SPRING ON EITHERSIDE

they both show very large traps catching a fox around the neck or upper body region. These traps are much too large to catch a fox by the foot or leg, as was the later normal practice with smaller 6 inch jawed fox gin traps before they were banned. These drawings seem to indicate that large traps were commonly used to catch foxes etc by the neck or upper body region in these earlier times, otherwise Ishman would have drawn the fox with its foot or leg caught in the jaws. He was simply drawing what he commonly saw and was familiar with in daily life. Therefore it has to be remembered that all large traps are not lion traps, and all large lion traps are not mantraps. From a historical and trap collector's point of view, the only way to define a genuine mantrap is if it has a locking mechanism that needs a separate key.

Before the banning of the mantrap due to the outrage they were causing with the capture of innocent victims, the trap makers turned their attentions to producing a more acceptable version as there was still a demand from estate owners and other land owners to protect their game and fruit crops. As a concession to humaneness, they omitted the rows of teeth. Later models produced included single and double flat-springed 'humane' types with 'off set' jaws. Off set jaws have a small spacing going along the full length of the top of the jaws which allows the jaws to fully close around the leg without supposedly causing too much pain or discomfort to the victim.

The Reverend Mr. Lawson who was the Curate of Nedham Market, near Stowmarket, Suffolk, would most likely disagree though. Whilst strolling through a plantation 'botanising' at Barking Hall, he had the misfortune to step onto a 'humane' mantrap. When he was finally released by the gamekeeper, after an hour and a half of excruciating pain, his leg was found to be 'much lacerated'. It is a wonder the shock of this encounter did not kill the 62 year old clergyman.

A NON-HUMANE MANTRAP –
A LOCKING MECHANISM, SHOWN
ABOVE, WAS INTRODUCED TO
PREVENT ACCOMPLICES
RELEASING THE VICTIM

CLOSE-UP OF THE SAME
LOCKING MECHANISM

The square standard type of humane mantrap came in three sizes and seems to have been produced mainly by the general ironfounder companies around Wolverhampton and West Bromwich. An early directory advert of T.&C. Clark, Wolverhampton in 1849, shows humane mantraps being offered for sale, but unfortunately show no illustrations. Other manufacturers who produced these humane mantraps included William Bullock & Co., Izons Whitehurst & Izon, and Archibald Kenrick & Co, all of West Bromwich, their adverts appearing in *Pigot's Directory* of 1822/3, but again no illustrations.

According to Harry Hopkins in his book *The Long Affray*, in an 1821 catalogue of William Bullock & Co. they announce 'that triumph of the new technology, the humane mantrap.' He also mentions that in an 1818 catalogue of Izons, Whitehurst & Izon they present themselves as 'original patentees and manufacturers of cast kitchen furniture, Empyreal stoves, cast butts, mantraps, and digesters.' Most illustrations that have been found of West Bromwich manufacturers come from catalogues that bear no date but are thought to be from around the 1830 to 1860 period. Illustrations from the undated catalogues of William Bullock & Co, and Izons Whitehurst & Izon, although looking the same at first glance, show a slight variation in their springs, Izons & Co.'s No 3 being a larger size with roller springs, instead of the usual flat springs. In 1807, due to humanitarian agitation from the reformer William Wilberforce MP the slave trade in the British dominions became prohibited, but slave holding was not abolished throughout the British Empire until 1833. After May 1827, presumably for a short while, mantraps would probably still be sold to plantation owners and used as deterrents to stop 'their' slaves from running away. In America, slavery was only declared illegal, after the Civil War, by Lincoln in 1865, so there may still have been a small export market to that country.

According to an article by 'Petrel' in a 1980 issue of *Shooting Times,* Sir Theophilus Biddulph BT, of Birdingbury Hall, Warwickshire was 'the considerate inventor of a humane mantrap for poachers and garden thieves which detained them by means of a chain, without injuring their limbs.' The Baronet was also 'unequalled at every description of trap, net, or other engine for the taking of all kinds of animals, birds or fish.' His lifespan 1757–1841 certainly puts him in the right era of the mantrap but unfortunately, nothing else is known about this unusual 'humane' chain mantrap.

However, two years after the mantrap was prohibited from use outside, on 28th March 1829, 'William Madeley of Yardley, in the County of Worcester, farmer, or of 49 Moor Street, Birmingham, machine maker' patented 'a certain apparatus or machine for catching, detecting, and detaining depredators and trespassers, or any animal, which I denominate the humane snare.' To quote the patent papers:

'The mechanism of the humane snare consists of a box or boxes, spring or springs, made of any materials that may be most suitable; also of a chain or chains made to draw out double or single, of sufficient strength to take and detain men and living animals. Now, I make the outer box of wrought iron, or of any other metal, or of wood, twelve inches square, four inches and an half in deep inside, or any other size I may find more convenient. In the inside is placed what I designate one or more spring barrels, through which is an upright spindle permanently fixed in a square at the top of the box, and also at the bottom of the box. In this box, which is made to turn loose upon the fixed spindle, is one or more spiral springs secured to the spindle and coiled round it, and secured to the barrel inside. Upon the ends of the barrel are two flanges, and at one end is a rotchett wheel, and a lock attached so that the bolt drops into the rotchett wheel. There is also a hook screwed to the outside of the barrel to which the chain is attached. The chain is then coiled round the barrel ready for fixing the snare. To set the snare, the chain must be drawn through the hole of the box until it comes to a round link. The pivot or treddle pin is then put through the round link; you then take out the key, and the snare will be locked and set. I then lay down the box upon two or more pieces of wood to give space for the pin to fall and liberate the springs. To catch the depredator the treddle has two or more springs to support it. The fork of the treddle is attached upon the pin head. I also find it convenient to have a wood frame grooved round to receive the chain and support it until the treddle is down. There is also a swivel in the box to attach a chain, and lock the same to any tree or other object that may be most convenient.'

Could the two references relate to the same trap? I certainly think it is possible. Due to the mantrap being banned from use two years earlier I would also presume that this 'humane snare' would also have been regarded as a mantrap by the authorities and so therefore illegal to use no matter how well meaning. Yardley is only approximately twenty five miles, as the crow flies, from Birdingbury Hall, so maybe it was tried and tested there with the story being passed on from generation to generation and with Sir Theophilus Biddulph getting the credit for inventing it.

Lastly, it is interesting to note the sale by Christie's of London of a famous collection of traps and crime and punishment items. This collection was built up over a period of thirty years by Michael Forman who first bought a Georgian mantrap and then expanded his collection to include other types of traps. This collection then later on diverged into a wider collection of crime and punishment material thereby extending the theme of man's inhumanity to animals to include man's inhumanity to man through the artefacts and ephemera connected with restraint, torture and execution. This sale took place on 29th May 1992 and included some interesting traps, three of which are described below, from the catalogue.

> No. 5 'A large gin type mantrap, the jaws each fitted with bottom spikes (some lacking) and lock mechanism. 55in long (139.2 cm). 19th Century.
>
> No 8. 'A rare large gin type mantrap with plain jaws, double ratchet locking devices. 49½in long (125.7cm). 19th Century.
>
> No 22 'A very rare, possibly unique, massive humane mantrap, the square base decorated scrolls, the plain bar jaws (large gap to allow for shin bone) fitted with four spring locks. 75in long (190.5cm). Late 18th Century. Note chained and padlocked to a tree, to open, keys must remain in locks, and two men required to release massive springs, making escape impossible. (Poaching was a hanging offence). Exhibited in the dungeon of Windsor Castle 1983-1989.

What I find interesting about traps No 5 and No 8 is that, apart from having double flat springs, and a locking device and also being larger, they are of the same design as the ordinary single flat-springed otter trap. This design of trap, square frame with two sides being bent up at right angles, seems to be the only type of trap to have the 'plate stops' as a regular feature. Trap No 22 is also very interesting, although again designed the same as the basic otter trap. The difference, as mentioned above, is that it has four spring locks and wide offset jaws. The strange thing is that the plate is not made in the normal way. Usually the plate is a solid sheet of metal, but in this case is two 'C' scrolls back to back. Could it be that the trap makers knowing that poachers were in the habit of using a long pole to probe the ground in front of them whilst on their poaching foray decided to produce a more 'open' type of plate? Thereby hoping that by so doing, the long stick whilst probing the ground, would 'go through' the plate and give the unsuspecting poacher a false sense of safety. The mantrap would still spring in the same manner, once the poacher stood on the 'C' scroll plate. I would also suggest that this type of trap is not late eighteenth century but immediately preceding the square humane mantraps of the early 1800s, or even possibly being built at the same time. My reasoning for this comment is that both the small square mantrap and the larger one with the double flat springs have offset jaws and both have an 'open' plate. In the smaller square humane mantrap the plate is merely a cross shape holding the jaws open under tension.

It is interesting to note in the book *Experiences of a Game Preserver* by 'Deadfall', published in 1868, how 'Deadfall' tells of his purchase of an estate and how he went about improving its game potential. The estate was of 2,500 acres situated six miles from a market town, and four miles from a railway station in a northern county of England. The wages and conditions he gave to his new, but very experienced, gamekeeper, Thornton, were, '16s. a week, with a cottage and garden' plus vermin money. 'The recompense fixed upon was 6d for cats, polecats, stoats, weasels and hawks; and 3d for carrion crows, magpies, jays and hedgehogs. He was to nail the tails of the 'ground vermin' and the heads of the 'flying' gentry on a board. In this bargain he had to find his own powder and shot. At the end of the quarter Thornton received his money, and the trophies were destroyed.'

A few pages later in the book, 'Deadfall' states,

> 'I ordered by his directions (Thornton's) two score of good
> bowspring rabbit traps – the sort usually sold under this name
> being large enough for every sort of ground vermin; and I
> also directed half a dozen of the round hawk traps to be sent.
> Deadfalls and figure of four traps I told him to get made
> according to his own plans and devices. He suggested that I
> should get a few different priced rabbit traps sent as
> specimens; and three or four kinds of that make having

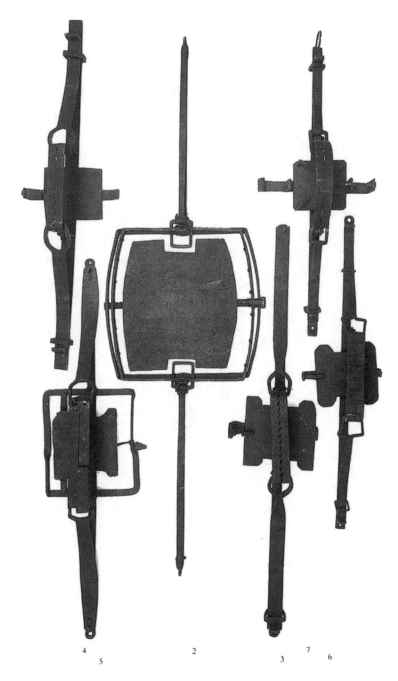

4

2

5

7

3

6

A SALE OF THE FORMAN ARCHIVE OF CRIME & PUNISHMENT AT
CHRISTIE'S IN 1992 DISPLAYED SOME GENUINE MANTRAPS WHICH
WERE ALSO SHOWN AMONGST OTHER VARIOUS LARGE ANIMAL
TRAPS (ON THIS PAGE AND OVERLEAF ONLY NUMBERS 5, 8, 21,
22, ARE GENUINE MANTRAPS, THE REST ARE VARIOUS TYPES OF
LARGE ANIMAL TRAPS)

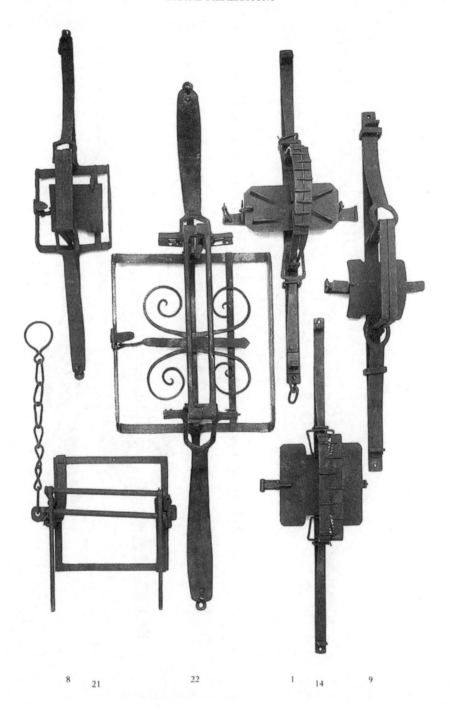

8   21   22   1   14   9

arrived in due course, he selected those with the jaws made very light (stamped out of the bar of iron), and not measuring across the jaws, when closed, more than three quarters of an inch. Some were sent to be looked at which had the catch and corresponding notch piece made of brass, but they were more expensive, and Thornton told me the others were equally durable, with common attention and care. I let him get spikes at the blacksmith's; and as to chains, I got a long piece sent by the same people who furnished the traps, and had it cut into lengths of eighteen inches, and fastened to the traps with 'S' hooks'.

With regard to the 'figure of four' traps, Thornton shot and killed five small birds from a flock because. . .

'these he wanted for baits for the stone traps. I had seen very similar traps set in our garden when a boy and naturally supposed Thornton's to be the same in every particular. The original ones had the principal notch cut in the 'stretcher', and the bait was frequently nibbled off by the mice, but the slate had not fallen. Now, in Thornton's trap the centre support was an inch wide, and the notch was cut in that, and only a shallow one in the 'stretcher'. The consequence was that it fell at once. This made all the difference between a bad trap and a first rate one. On arriving at one of them, Thornton tied a bird to the end of the 'stretcher' and gave it a cut with his knife. This was to cause more scent either with birds or mice.'

Thornton had asked permission to be allowed to make some long 'trough' Deadfall traps 'after a plan of his own'. This being granted, he was allocated a room above the stable for the use as a workshop where the work bench and joiners tools being ready for him, he occupied himself on the Monday morning in making one of the long Deadfall traps, which he finished by noon.

'It was about three feet long by eleven inches deep inside, and three inches wide. A treadle worked in the bottom of the box on two brass pins. One of these came through the side, and had on it a sort of finger about a couple of inches long, terminating in a sharp point. There was a spring fastened to the side of the box, with its end (also pointed) just wrapping over the finger alluded to. A couple of strong screws were fastened into the side of the trap, with a notch in the head of each, into which a short piece of iron would catch. The weight to crush the vermin was a piece of three inch square deal, about an inch shorter than the whole trap. Across the top of the opening, and just in the centre, was a piece of hard wood, with a hole bored and burnt through. The heavy weight was attached by an old boot lace to the small cross piece of iron. To set the trap you had to press the spring down and turn the

treadle, till the finger caught on the end of the spring. The
cross bit was placed in the notch, and the weight then kept
suspended in the trap, evenly balanced. Any small vermin
running through, and passing over the treadle, caused it to tilt
on one side, and the spring being released, it flew out and
knocked the cross piece of iron away, and the weight, of course,
falling, crushed the weasel or stoat, and killed it
instantaneously. The trap seemed wonderfully quick in its
action, going off almost like a gun, it was so rapid. The treadle,
I should have said was a foot long, and the whole trap being
three feet, the vermin could not possibly escape, as whichever
way it entered, that particular end of the treddle must be
pressed, and there was then, of course, two feet of trap to allow
for. Thornton said he always rubbed the spring and finger with
mercurial (or what is commonly called blue) ointment, and the
weather had no effect upon them.'

This trap was then set 'in a dry ditch under one of the hedges leading to
the wood'. On the fourth day a rat had been caught, but the following day
two weasels were caught, one in the morning and another later the same
evening.

'These were both of them 'Jill' or female weasels, and not
weighing much more than good well conditioned field mice,
spoke most favourably of the capabilities of the trap. There
are other traps of apparently the same kind; but in the trap
we used the treadle was independent of the weight, while in
the common ones the weight is always straining on the
treadle, and so renders them liable to remain unsprung if any
light vermin passes through'.

Thornton later on makes another trap, again to his own design, but this
time it is described as a 'live trap'. Deadfall upon meeting him coming down
from the workshop 'with a long narrow box under his arm' asks to inspect it
and proceeds to describe it as:

'being made of deal, and two feet four inches long, five inches
and a half outside depth, and three inches and a half in
outside width. In the centre of the top was a lid about a foot
long, and, on opening the trap, I saw that it was divided
equally across the centre by a division, in which division was a
small hole. On each side, or, as I should express it, in each
compartment, was a treadle playing loosely on the floor, and
fixed in the treadle was an upright wire arm. Another piece of
wire went from the upright in a horizontal direction, and
passed through a small staple in the roof of the compartment.
At each outer end of the box was a falling door, working very
loosely on the two pins. The door being raised with one hand,
the horizontal wire was slipped under the end and propped it
up. Any weasel or stoat running into the trap and pressing, as

it would of course do, on the treadle, must cause it to tilt a little, and the wire being consequently withdrawn the door falls down, and, closing from within renders the escape of the vermin utterly out of the question.'

Deadfall, expressing his desire to see the trap being set, and being asked to bring a spade, the two set off for the rabbit warren.

'Having arrived there the keeper selected a part where the wall passed over a bank of no great elevation. Here he proceeded to dig a trench about a foot wide and three yards long, and having finished it, he placed the trap equidistantly from each end, and then made a rough sort of drain (if one may so call it) from the trap to these points. There was a good deal of stone about, so he had no difficulty in forming it, although he said a 'turf' drain could be made with equal facility. When completed, it certainly presented every appearance of a common field sough. Having set the trap, Thornton placed a stone on the lid and we left it.'

About a week had passed with the trap being regularly inspected each morning, but without any results,

'when one morning, on going to look, and gently raising the lid, the brown back of a stoat was discovered. A very careful investigation showed us that we might proceed to open it wide, for the stoat was quite dead. A very odd thing it is sir, said Henry (Thornton), and I never can account for it; but although I've caught dozens on dozens of weasels and stoats in these traps, yet I never found one of 'em alive, and what it is as kills 'em passes my comprehension. It certainly was very strange. We had looked at this trap the day before; and the stoat was in first rate condition, and had not a mark upon him anywhere. It would appear an anomaly to call it a 'live trap' where the inmate is invariably taken out dead after, at the utmost, only twenty four hours' confinement; but certainly there was nothing about the trap to kill him.'

Another writer, Idstone, writing a few years later in 1872, thought that 'the keeper who kills most vermin makes the least noise about it. He is not continually shooting about the manor, and yet he keeps it down. I need hardly say he does this with traps, and unless he can trap well he is not worth his wages'. Later on he mentions borrowing a trap with double springs and circular jaws, and says,

'The spike teeth are on the outside; there are nine of them, flat and wedge shaped. This trap weighs nearly 40lbs, and is 4ft. 6in. long. It has a peculiar trigger plate 9in. by 11 in., furnished with six large points, like small dog spears, for holding on a bait. An experienced master of foxhounds, who saw it a few days since, pronounced it a fox trap, and told me, as a boy he had seen many of them in Kent.'

Idstone then says that the springs 'on this trap have lost all their vigour, and it would not hold a rat. The jaws are suspended in single studs, and the whole thing is coarsely made'. Next he describes a humane man trap which lies before him as. . .

> 'weighing something less than 20 lbs. It consists of a light yet strong iron frame of about eighteen inches, and two active but not strong springs; the jaws are of the same size as the frame, and run upon an iron jointed rod notched at one end, and self locking at each side. The jaws close to the size of the leg, and there hold the delinquent until the keeper releases him in the morning. Not many years ago there was hardly a village which was not well supplied with these barbarous things. It was common enough to see them placarded in gardens and orchards, and they generally were combined with spring guns . . . I have ascertained that four or five have been beaten into horseshoes by the village vulcans within a radius of ten miles, as have many pieces of iron of rare antiquity no doubt.'

Although it is true to say that mantraps and spring guns were widely distributed throughout the countryside, it is also true that in many places where these signs were displayed there existed no mechanical threat at all lurking in the undergrowth. The signs were simply a psychological deterrent employed by the more humane estate owner in the hope of persuading any potential poacher not to venture onto his land after his game. These signs would also have been a cheaper alternative to any land owner who could not afford to purchase mantraps or spring guns. These 'wooden falsehoods' as they were known, may have deterred the casual poacher to look elsewhere, but didn't really stop the more determined. Obviously the local 'grapevine' would also have helped to establish if actual mantraps or spring guns were deployed throughout the woods. Though banned in 1827, Idstone states, as previously mentioned, that spring guns could still be used as long as they caused no physical harm, thus basically making them into alarm guns. If so used, any poacher setting off one of these devices in a wood at night would still think that it was still being used with grapeshot, and the psychological effect would have been greatly enhanced. Most spring guns were of the flintlock type but percussion examples exist.

Poaching could still be a dangerous activity to indulge in, even if no mantraps or spring guns were being used. Injuries to both gamekeepers and poachers were common occurrences as can be seen in two separate newspaper articles in 1878. The first reported in the *Daily News* in April stated:

> 'Three keepers of the Duke of Westminster, at Eaton, came upon some poachers who at first retreated, but being reinforced formed a rudimentary square and repulsed the

keepers, they were armed with stones and spears. Two of the keepers were felled to the ground, a third was stabbed in the chest. The poachers killed two large mastiffs.'

The second is from the *Hull Express* which reported the Bridlington Petty Sessions of 20th May, and wrote that. . .

'Two poachers were charged with night poaching, and a game watcher named Riby Green with shooting one of them. Stanning the game keeper called to the poachers to stop or he would 'warm' them. He then ordered Green to fire, and Green took deliberate aim at Appleby, who dropped down. He was examined by Dr. Allison who found that he had 48 gun-shot lodged in his thigh, back and the side of his head.'

In Victorian times, a gamekeeper was also known by the alternative name of Velveteen. This was due to the material of his clothing. Velveteen was a cotton or mixed cotton and silk and many Victorian gamekeepers had their own estate 'uniform' comprising their velveteen suit, with livery buttons, plus reinforced bowler hat, and were recognisable instantly as the estate 'keeper. In 1850 the 1st Earl of Leicester had commissioned Mr. Bowler, a milliner at Lock's of St. James's, London to create a suitable hard hat that would protect his keepers' heads when out riding. The gamekeepers soon realised the benefits of Mr. Bowler's hat during poaching affrays. Their modern counterparts, now at Holkham Hall, Norfolk, still carry on their predecessors' tradition and wear their bowler hats on shoot days.

On game shooting estates where the owner also rode to hounds after the fox, the gamekeeper was also obliged to preserve the fox for the local hunt to chase. The gamekeeper wouldn't want the foxes to decimate the stock of pheasants that he would have carefully raised. The solution to this problem would be to keep the foxes well fed with rabbit meat thrown near to the den entrance on a regular daily basis. On this type of estate it was common also for the gamekeeper to use either a 3" or a $3\frac{1}{2}$" jawed gin trap to catch rabbits, rather than a normal 4" jawed gin trap, and so thereby reducing the risk of accidentally catching and holding a fox. Gamekeepers could be instantly dismissed in some cases if their employer discovered that foxes were being trapped or killed by a gamekeeper who thought that there were too many on his beat and a threat to 'his' pheasants.

Vermin money, as previously mentioned, was regularly paid to gamekeepers as an incentive bonus, but this tradition started to cease after World War I, due to financial restraints in a changing world. However, the gamekeeper could still collect extra money, whilst still doing his job, by supplying good prime winter fox pelts, stoat skins, and various feathers etc to such businesses as Horace Friend & Co of Wisbech, who were established

INJURED GAMEKEEPERS,
T. GAMBLES AND T. MORRIS AT
GANTON, SCARBOROUGH

GAMEKEEPER TOM ATKINSON OF
SHERBURN WAS MURDERED IN THE
AFFRAY WITH POACHERS IN 1905

THE GANTON POACHING AFFRAY
THE INJURED AND MURDERED GAMEKEEPERS (ABOVE)
AND THE POACHERS (BELOW)

WILLIAM HOVINGTON
('CURLY BILL')

THOMAS DOBSON
('FEZ')

CHARLES HOVINGTON
(SON)

The Ganton Poaching Affray

This poaching affray is also known as the Sherburn Poaching Affray. The two names refer to the same incident simply because it happened by the railway between Ganton and Sherburn. The land upon which the poaching took place was owned by Sir Algernon Legard, Bart, but Mr Emmerson Pickering of Garforth and Scarborough, had the shooting over the land. According to the local newspapers *The Scarborough Mercury* and *The Scarborough Evening News*, the gamekeepers' involved were Thomas Morris, Thomas Gambles, William Wellburn, and Thomas Atkinson, the unfortunate gamekeeper to be murdered. He was aged about 49 years and lived at Sherburn with his wife.

The poachers who set in motion this fateful tragic event were all Scarborough men, William Hovington (aged 58), otherwise known as 'Curly Bill', his son Charles Hovington (aged 28), and Thomas Dobson (aged 62), who was known as 'Fez'.

According to the evidence of William Wellburn, on Friday evening (25th November 1904), about 8.15, he and Thomas Gambles were on their way to the pheasant cover in Brompton Carr, each having a gun with him. They were joined on the main road by Thomas Morris and the deceased Thomas Atkinson. When about half way between the high road and the cover they heard a shot, and proceeded into the cover and concealed themselves. They heard four more shots, and several pheasants rose. It was a very moonlight night, frosty, and with snow on the ground. Eventually, Wellburn saw two men, whom he recognises as William Hovington and Thomas Dobson. A little later he saw the third man Charles Hovington, who apparently was waiting on the fringe of the wood. The keepers gave chase to the poachers, who ran out of the wood into the open fields beyond where the snow lay three or four inches thick and was crisp with frost causing the footfalls both of pursuers and pursued to ring quite distinctly.

The poachers were chased across two fields by the four gamekeepers. Here the gamekeeper, Albert Card and the railway man Stephen Bell, joined the keepers in the second field, having heard the shooting, and rightly supposing that there was something amiss. There were now six men engaged in the chase after the three poachers, and one of the latter, as the pursuers were climbing the second fence fired. This discharge fortunately had no greater effect than to just graze the forefinger of Card, who along with Gambles was taking a course on the low side of the field, the others being higher up. The third field was one of considerable width, and at the far side of it there was a high fence. The poachers, apparently exhausted by the heavy going, just before reaching this fence stopped on a raised bank alongside a cart road. By this time the pursuers were close upon their heels, and the three men stood in line, raised their guns to their shoulders and as they were about twenty-five or thirty yards distant all three men fired. Only two guns however, discharged.

Atkinson dropped at once, and, the poachers having now fired three shots at them, Card aimed and fired at the poachers. Gambles had also been hit by the fire from the poachers, but he engaged with the others in the final rush for them, one of whom he tackled along with Card. Then a general melee ensued, during which the poachers, standing on the high ground, which the keepers had to reach by crossing the low cartway, used the butts of their guns freely. Gambles and Morris were very badly hit about the head. Wellburn received several blows on the forearm which he raised to protect himself. Bell had made off in the direction of Sherburn for assistance, so that there were only Wellburn and Card left standing. They fought courageously until the poachers, each of whom had also been badly knocked about the head, retired to the fence. Wellburn and Card did not follow them, but remained to render assistance to the wounded men. The poachers held a consultation together in front of the fence, and in consequence of what he heard them say in the distance, Wellburn raised his gun and fired at them. 'I'm shot,' one of the men called out, and this evidently settled them, for they cleared off.

The severity of this hand to hand encounter was obvious as the newspapers recorded. The deceased gamekeeper Atkinson, 'presented a shocking appearance, his chest and face being literally riddled with shot.' Gambles was suffering from numerous shot wounds in the abdomen, and from scalp wounds, but Morris has also been very badly mauled indeed.

The Scarborough Police, once alerted to the incident, immediately stationed police officers at all the roads leading into the borough. The poachers wounded and on foot had also suffered severely in the encounter. About four o' clock the following morning, the three poachers were arrested, without resistance, near the Racecourse gates at Scarborough, and later charged with murder and poaching offences. They were all tried at the York Assizes in March 1905, being found guilty of manslaughter, not murder, and so escaping the hangman's noose. However, the two older men 'Fez' and 'Curly Bill' each received a sentence of ten years apiece whilst 'Curly Bill's' son Charles Hovington was sentenced to seven years.

THE KEEPER'S BRIBE (1891)

in 1860, and E. Veniard of Thornton Heath, Surrey, who were fancy feather dealers. Other businesses that also advertised in *The Gamekeeper and Countryside* magazine included John Lee & Son (Grantham) Ltd, who were furriers and skin merchants (established 1845), and Robert Ramsey & Co Ltd, Glasgow, Scotland, who were wool and skin merchants from 1856.

Other gamekeepers decided that by leaving their profession and starting up on their own in a related business, this would be a better option financially. Two such gamekeepers were Robert Grass and Thomas Cank. Briefly, 'Bob' Grass as he was more commonly known, was born in 1890 on the Tyntesfield Estate in Somerset, where his father was employed as a gamekeeper. Moving first to Alnwick Castle with his parents as a young child, it was here that he spent much of his spare time looking after the many estate gundogs. In 1902, at the age of 12, Bob went into hunt service as a kennel boy, with the North Durham Foxhounds. Here he met and worked with Dick Freeman, who had a vast knowledge of the medicinal properties of herbs and plants. Bob soon took a keen interest and started to try and develop his own homemade herbal remedies to treat dogs etc. Having a gamekeeping background, he left the hunt just before the start of World War I, to take up a gamekeeping position on an estate near Doncaster. It was here that all of his experimenting came to fulfilment, when he produced an ointment that cleared up skin disorders on the various estate dogs and local village dogs that had developed mange. This ointment became so popular because of its effectiveness, and being encouraged by friends and the many satisfied customers, he began producing it commercially. Due to the ointment's success, he decided to concentrate on selling this and the other canine medicines that he had also successfully produced. In September 1933, he resigned his position as gamekeeper. During World War II, Bob temporarily returned to gamekeeping, back on his previous estate, as a favour to his old boss, as his gamekeeper had been called up for war duty. Afters hostilities ceased, in February 1946, Bob again started producing his dog remedies. However, business quickly outgrew his small production, and so he decided that a Lancashire pharmaceutical company should make and dispatch his customers' orders. He lived in the village of Hooton Pagnell, near Doncaster and died aged 92, a wealthy man.

Thomas Cank was born circa 1845, at Grimsall, Shropshire and his father was also a gamekeeper, but in the service of a Baronet of Acton-Wrennall Hall, Shropshire. Thomas was from a large family of nine. He started to earn his own living and contribute to the family income at the age of 10 when he started as a rabbit catcher on local farms. He followed this trade working on the Baronet's estate and estates in the surrounding area until he was aged 22. Most of his rabbit catching was done by using snares, but he also used traps, with which he had to be careful setting as the Baronet was a fox hunting man. According to Cank, the greatest enemy he had was the fox:

> 'As a rule they paid me a visit two or three times a week
> among the ready-catched rabbits, and a very common thing
> to find six and upwards of a dozen rabbits' heads left behind
> for me. . . (and) of course there was no pay in rabbits' heads
> for the rabbit catcher, and to kill a fox was to do a deed that
> the Baronet would not forgive, nor ever allow on no
> consideration.'

He used 'to work fifty or sixty traps along with about two hundred snares'. He commented:

> 'The great art that I always found in setting traps for rabbits
> was well blocking up every hole in the bury, excepting those
> holes to lay the traps in, and shaping the hole so that the trap
> would lie level in it, and well packing the soil on each side of
> the spring, making the ground solid for the rabbit to tread on,
> then covering over the whole of the trap lightly with the damp
> sand or soil. The class of trap I always liked to have was the
> best made ones, running from eighteen to twenty-two shillings
> a dozen, (one dozen of these traps will outlast three dozen of
> those costing about eight or ten shillings per dozen, for you
> are always running to the smithy to have them repaired at
> more than their original cost), three and a half inch jaws, but
> never above four inch; the former I preferred, that size was
> light, and I could carry from thirty to forty at a time. I never
> had a trap with a big plate, or better known as treadle, for this
> reason – if the rabbits happened to tread just on the edge of
> the treadle, sprung the trap and just caught her by the cleaves

or a small portion of the foot; as I found rabbits being in a trap
and got slightly wounded, would die from hunger in their
holes before passing over the trap again.'

He recommended purchasing the Real Dorset Trap with a small plate
because 'when the rabbit treads on it, her foot is bound to be in the centre,
and there the jaw is sure to clasp the leg'. Aged 22, and by now a very
experienced rabbit catcher and vermin destroyer, he now gained employment
as an under-gamekeeper in the Welsh county of Breconshire. This was a
mountainous area and not really to his liking as when he stood at his door he
could see nothing, 'either to my left or right but mountains; with the exception
of a few fields in the valley'. However, he describes using in the open
mountains, 5" inch jaw real Dorset traps to catch foxes.

'I have done upwards of forty foxes in a season, old and
young; but all young cubs, that I could dig out or buy from
adjoining keepers, that were not hurt or disabled in anyway I
used to send them alive into Shropshire, where I had a ready
market for them, at ten bob (ten shillings) each, which paid
me better than killing them.'

He only stayed gamekeeping in the mountains for about fourteen months,
before moving on to another estate about four miles away near Crickhowell
in South Wales. Poaching was a big problem here though:

'For during the time I was there, I never knew a winter pass over,
but what the poachers turned out upwards of twelve nights
during the winter, one place or the other; and never less than
nine, and up to thirty in number, and two out of every three
armed with guns. The keepers and night men never dare
approach them, and when they did approach them, poor old
George King was shot, and lived only an hour afterwards.'

If dealing with a known individual poacher of fairly regular habits, then
Cank waited for him, in his favourite wood that he liked the best.

'I used to like for there to be a pheasant or two up, so that I
could wait very close to nail my gentleman, after he had
emptied his gun at the bird instead of me, or rather, running
the risk of having to compete with a man with a loaded gun. If
there was no pheasants up at roost in the trees of his favourite
track, if I had an idea of his next visit, within a fortnight, I
would pick out an easy tree that I could ascend, and place up
two dummy ones for him, made of ferns, or some other
suitable substance of which I could make them; and after I had
fixed them, it would take a cleaver expert to tell the difference

CATCHING A POACHER (1874)

between my dummy birds, in the moon-light or star-light, from
a gradely bird. When I got tired, and wanted to go home I used
to take my dummies with me, so that if he came afterwards, I
didn't spoil my catch for another time.'

It is interesting to note that Gilbertson & Page's 1913 catalogue lists
'Decoy Pheasants 15/- each Postage Paid' for those gamekeepers not so good
at making their own dummy pheasants. Despite this constant winter danger,
Thomas Cank remained on this estate, as a single-handed keeper for nine
years. His next employment was as a Head Gamekeeper in North Wales,
which lasted only 2 years and 9 months. He then worked on an estate near
Preston, in Lancashire, holding again another position as Head Gamekeeper.

On 15th July 1884, Thomas Cank of Hutton Hall, near Preston,
Lancashire, describing himself as a Gamekeeper, patented 'an improved trap
for capturing animals alive', which was given the Patent Number 10,178.
The patent states:

'a trap for capturing alive rabbits, foxes, badgers, and the like
class of animal being mainly designed for the purpose of
being inserted within the mouth of the holes or burrows in
which such animals have their abode. The sides of the trap
are hinged upon metal bars or rods mounted on a frame
running longitudinally of the trap and are caused to close or
remain open by the employment of spring. A central platform

322

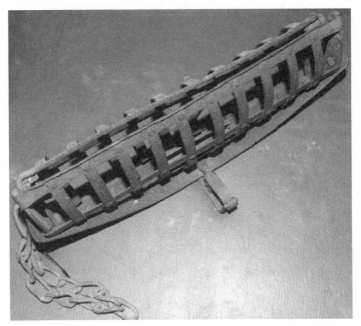

T. CANK'S TRAP

or plate with the ordinary trigger mechanism is arranged. . .
to hold the trap open until the plate is depressed . . . when
the sides will fly up and close in. When closed the trap
assumes an elongated barrel-like appearance the sides of the
trap being suitably curved inwardly or arched over when
brought together so as to afford an inner space for enclosing
the captured animal without injuring it. The sides are formed
of a series of wire ribs or fingers whose upper extremities are
so curved as to overlap or pass beyond the extremities of the
fingers of the opposite side.'

It was whilst employed on this estate, that Thomas Cank decided to go
into the business of rearing pheasants commercially, and selling them to the
various shooting estates that were being created. Therefore in 1884, the
Lancashire Pheasantries at Leyland were established, with 'the old dark breed'
of pheasants, which he had purchased from his former employer as breeding
stock. Later in October 1890, he also patented an 'alarm gun' which he
called by the name of 'Repetitional' guns. Prior to these two inventions, and
whilst on the same estate, he had also at an unknown date, 'invented the
Alleviator, for the successful distribution of the gape powder, which I had
proved its sterling qualities, for over fourteen years'. Then in January 1891,
he published his book, *40 Years Mingled in Game*, where he states that he is a
'Game, Poultry and Dog Food Manufacturer'.

However he was also involved in selling traps and other sundry related

323

items to the gamekeeping fraternity as can be seen in the Preston & District directory for 1892 where he is listed in the Leyland section selling Game Food and Game Requisites from The Lancashire Pheasantries. According to the 1901 census, Thomas Cank and his family were living at Rutters Farm, in Ulnes Walton, which was a rural area just south west of Leyland. Here he is listed as a Game Farmer, whilst his son, also Thomas and aged 20, is recorded as a gamekeeper. The last reference to Thomas Cank that I have found is in a 1933 Spratt's Catalogue, under the heading of Recommended Game Farmers. Strangely, the address is stated to be, The Lancashire Pheasantries, Stockton-on-Forest, near York.

Not many gamekeepers' were as fortunate as Grass or Cank, which was why earlier in 1886 the Keepers Benefit Society was founded to help keepers who had fallen on hard times often through encounters with violent poachers. Ten years after the establishment of the Keepers Benefit Society there appeared the original magazine, *The Gamekeeper*, which was first produced as a monthly magazine in 1896 by the business of Gilbertson & Page of Hertford. Previously Henry Gilbertson, who was a Victorian grocer, had built up a reputation for supplying the many estates of the landed gentry with food essentials throughout the shooting season. Alfred Page, who was Gilbertson's manager at the time, then suggested that the company supply the cereals etc. needed for the successful rearing of the game birds, and by 1884 the business of Gilbertson & Page had expanded, by including the making and supplying of their own dog food, across Hertfordshire.

THE KEEPER'S HUT IN THE WOODS (1885)

THE HATCHING BOXES   THE LAST OF THE HENS.

A CORNER OF THE PHEASANTRY.

THE KEEPER'S MUSEUM.

KEEPER FEEDING THE YOUNG BIRDS.

PERCY R. CRAFT. 1890.

PHEASANT REARING (1890)

With the introduction of *The Gamekeeper* magazine, this further allowed the company the opportunity of combining informative articles on the gamekeeper's profession, whilst at the same time advertising their own and other manufacturers' products. This 'journal devoted to the interests of game preservers' as it was described, advertised for sale everything the gamekeeper needed from boots to, of course, traps. Much later, due to gamekeeping being a restricted profession, the magazine's appeal was limited, so during relatively modern times the magazine changed its title to *The Gamekeeper and Countryside* in a hope to broaden its appeal to the general public whilst remaining loyal to its original customers. This occurred about 1946.

A few years after the appearance of the Gilbertson & Page *Gamekeeper* publication, a Gamekeepers Association was formed. The Association was founded in 1900 and was known as the Gamekeepers Association of the United Kingdom and published a bimonthly paper called *The Gamekeepers' Gazette*. In 1975 this Association became incorporated with the Wildfowlers Association of Great Britain and Ireland (WAGBI), which itself was founded in 1908. Then in 1981 WAGBI decided to change its public image to reflect its growing number of shooting members who were not just wildfowlers. The membership was also concerned with sustainable wildlife conservation, and through discussion the title of British Association for Shooting and Conservation (BASC) was formed. Five years later, yet another association, the Moorland Gamekeepers Association, was established in 1986 by a small group of Gamekeepers with the same feeling that their own branch of the gamekeeping profession did not have a voice of its own. In 1988, at their first AGM there attended over 100 moorland gamekeepers, a number that has been maintained. Dr. David Bellamy, the famous botanist and conservationist is the Association's patron.

All the branches of gamekeeping now have the opportunity to put forward their own point of view through the BASC 'Keepers Committee and there is also the added benefit of the Gamekeepers Welfare Trust in times of great need. The BASC now also produce a magazine called *The Custodian* for their gamekeeper members.

However, since these gamekeeping groups were formed, there has been constant verbal attacks upon the gamekeeping fraternity by certain conservation organisations with regard to alleged illegal poisoning and trapping of birds of prey etc.

Early in 1997 there were also certain television programmes which seemed biased towards an unfair representation of alleged illegal gamekeeping practices. Many gamekeepers were annoyed that their own organisation, BASC, was not challenging these statements. Therefore, a group in the North of Scotland held public meetings to set up a wholly Scottish organisation to properly represent their interests. Unknown to this northern group of gamekeepers, another group, in Tayside, had also got together with the same idea in mind. Once the two separate groups became aware of each other it was obvious that the two groups should amalgamate. This happened on 26th June 1997 at Aviemore and the Scottish Gamekeepers Association, incorporating gamekeepers, stalkers and ghillies, was formed. This Association now also produce their own magazine for their members entitled *Scottish Gamekeeper*. Due to these same television programmes and other related incidents, other gamekeepers throughout Britain had also, more or less, lost faith in the organisation that was supposed to represent and safeguard their interests. In April 1997, a group of twenty gamekeepers met in Staffordshire and discussed the feasibility of setting up a new organisation. The result was the newly formed National Gamekeepers Organisation (NGO). In the words of Mr. Dave Clarke, Head Keeper to Lord Barnard on the Raby Estate, 'The best person to speak up for gamekeepers – is a gamekeeper. The benefits to the countryside from this profession are outstanding. We provide the best game conservation and management in the world.' Since its recent formation, the National Gamekeepers Organisation has now over 2,800 members and produce their own magazine called *Keeping The Balance*.

With the outstanding success of the National Gamekeepers' Organisation in such a short time, Paul Wilby speaking on behalf of the Moorland Gamekeepers Association said, 'The challenges facing gamekeeping mean we need the strongest possible organisation representing our profession. The Moorland Gamekeepers' Association has made huge strides but both organisations believe they will be more effective as a united body – joining forces with the National Gamekeepers' Organisation will enable us to improve the promotion of upland keepering shoulder to shoulder with our lowland colleagues.' Therefore at the Country Landowners' Association's Game Fair, held at Harewood House near Leeds in Yorkshire in 1999, an announcement was made that the two separate organisations were to merge. The two merged organisations would now operate under the name of the National Gamekeepers' Organisation, whilst the Moorland Gamekeepers' Association would become the Moorland Branch within the NGO. The merger of these two groups means that the NGO now had a total membership well in excess of 3,000 members making it the biggest organisation to represent both gamekeepers and their interests. Dr. David Bellamy, who was the patron of the Moorland Gamekeepers' Association, kindly agreed to become the patron of the NGO, thus continuing with his belief that gamekeepers are true conservationists. At the end of 2003, the NGO had 3,300 gamekeeper members and 4,700 supporter and other category members.

GAME CARRIERS!
FROM AN IMPERIAL CHEMICAL INDUSTRIES LTD ADVERT 1936

Chapter Seven
TOOLS OF THE TRADE

Rabbiting Hoe, also known as the **Trapper's Hammer**.

Although many gamekeepers and rabbit trappers used either the heel of their foot or the rounded end of certain types of rabbiting spades to drive the trap stake or peg into the ground, a rabbiting hoe or trapper's hammer was specifically made for this job. The hoe's 'blade' was shaped like an adze and was used for digging out the soil, to bed the trap, whilst the opposite end was the hammer head which was used for knocking in the trap's peg and thereby securing the trap to that one place.

William Hunt & Sons, The Brades, Ltd, near Birmingham produced two types of rabbiting hoe. The normal type has the square hammer head and broad hoe with a notch cut into its side. When ordering this type of hoe the buyer quoted No 487 and the telegraphic word 'Stiffly' from their catalogue. The second type has the same hoe 'blade' with the notch cut into the side but instead of the hammer head this type now has an axe head. When ordering this hoe the buyer quoted the catalogue No 713 and the telegraphic word 'Crocione'.

Other types of hoes can be found, either with a plain 'blade' or with just a single hole instead of the usual notch. Another company known to make rabbiting hoes/trapping hammers was C.T. Skelton of Sheffield. The reason for the notch on the side of the hoe was so that the trapper could insert the chain into it and then pull up the peg out of the soil. The single hole in the hoe was there so that the round metal trap stake or peg, could be pushed through it thereby removing the accumulated soil and so avoiding leaving human scent on the loose soil at the trapping site.

The earliest illustration of a trapping hammer that I have found is in *How to Trap and Snare* by 'Moorman' published in 1908. He commented, 'The trapper's hammer requires to be a handy and well made tool, (as) they are very labour saving, and when properly formed add greatly to the efficiency of the work done.'

Young's of Misterton were still offering a trapping hammer in their 1972 catalogue for £1.50 each posted. The 1972 catalogue cover states, 'Many costs continue to rise, including railway carriage and postage. . .', so it is no surprise to find that later a separate price alteration leaflet, dated 1st July 1972, was issued. Therefore, the price of the 1972 trapping hammer from July onwards had risen to £2.25p plus postage / carriage and 10% V.A.T. On 1st May 1974 the trapping hammer was now priced at £2.50p plus the extra charges, whilst in the 1st September 1976 price list it was now costing £3.00p plus the extra charges to buy a trapping hammer. Unfortunately there is no illustration to show to which type of trapping hammer the price refers.

In a Spratt's catalogue dated 1933, an unusual pair of trapping hammers are illustrated. According to the illustration the 'G.K.' (abbreviation for GameKeeper?) trapping hammers had a patent applied for, and a Registration No. 6541. The unusual thing about these trapping hammers was that they were combined with a spade. The usual wooden T-handle of the spade was now formed into either a hammer and axe head, or a double hammer head. The length overall was 18 inches.

Trap Chains and Pegs

Trap chains come in various styles and lengths due to the fact that both trap makers and the specialist chain makers produced them. Pegs, also known as the stake, were usually made of metal and supplied by the trap makers, but wooden ones were produced commercially and sold by various suppliers or just home-made. Their purpose as mentioned above is to secure the trap, to which it is attached by a chain, to a certain place on the ground. Although the animal is caught by the foot, it still is allowed a bit of movement because of the chain, but can not walk off with the trap attached to its foot, due to the peg being firmly fixed into the ground. This also stops any predator, e.g. a fox, that finds a dead rabbit caught in an approved humane trap from removing the trap along with the dead rabbit.

Sieves

These items are usually circular, wooden and with a wire mesh base. Size is approximately 8 inches diameter by $3^{1}/_{2}$ inches deep. However, other shapes occur, oblong and shield-shaped, which is ideal for use in the mouth of a rabbit burrow. Their use is to sift soil over the trap, once bedded *in situ*, and so blend it in with the surroundings. The small sized wire mesh stops larger debris from falling through which might stop the jaws from operating properly.

Sieves used in trapping situations, as opposed to gardening or mixing egg foods for feeding to pheasant chicks etc, are usually of smaller construction so that they will fit more conveniently into the trapper's pocket. The earliest illustration that I have found of a trapping sieve, with a folding wire handle, is illustrated in *How to Trap and Snare* by 'Moorman' published in 1908. Gilbertson & Page advertised a trapping sieve with a folding wire handle in their 1913 catalogue priced 1/3d each, postage paid, whilst what looks to be

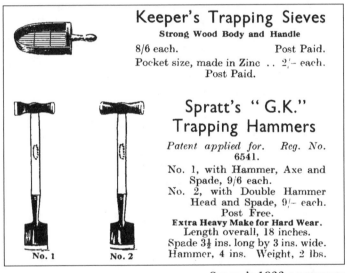

Keeper's Trapping Sieves
Strong Wood Body and Handle
8/6 each.   Post Paid.
Pocket size, made in Zinc .. 2/- each.
Post Paid.

**Spratt's " G.K."
Trapping Hammers**
Patent applied for.   Reg. No. 6541.
No. 1, with Hammer, Axe and Spade, 9/6 each.
No. 2, with Double Hammer Head and Spade, 9/- each.
Post Free.
Extra Heavy Make for Hard Wear.
Length overall, 18 inches.
Spade 3½ ins. long by 3 ins. wide.
Hammer, 4 ins. Weight, 2 lbs.

No. 1   No. 2

SPRATT'S 1933 CATALOGUE

an identical trapping sieve, but minus the wire handle, was advertised in a John White of Birmingham price list for 1938. Both of these sieves appear to be made of metal. The size of the sieve given in White's price list being $5^{1}/_{2}$ x $4^{1}/_{4}$ inches long and priced at 2/6d each, post paid. Spratt's 1933 catalogue, shows a shield-shaped trapping sieve made with a 'strong wood body and handle' priced at 8/6d each, whilst another mentioned, but not shown, was 'Pocket size, made in Zinc, 2/- each'. In 1956, Young's of Misterton were offering for sale two types of trapping sieves. One type 'with folding handle for pocket' had a size of 6 inches x $4^{1}/_{2}$ inches deep. The larger 'round trappers sieve' type was galvanised and was 8 inches in diameter, and $3^{1}/_{2}$ inches deep.

In Young's 1972 catalogue only the larger 8 inch diameter, sieve is listed. However, in their 1987 price list no sieves are listed. Obviously, apart from the commercially made and sold sieves, as they were easily constructed from wood and wiremesh, many would have been home made, especially when employment and money was scarce, as during the depression years.

Two types of egg sieves were also advertised in Spratt's 1933 catalogue. The square pattern being 16 inches by 11 inches in size, whilst the round pattern was 16 inches in diameter. Both types could be 'supplied with coarse, medium and fine mesh'. A more unusual egg sieve is mentioned by Leslie Rawlings in his book *Gamekeeper: Memories of a country childhood* (1977):

> 'In the centre of the rearing field, under a large oak stood the keepers' hut on wheels. Inside it was stacked full with sacks of choice seeds and biscuit meal. Outside were boiling cauldrons full of hens' eggs. They were boiled hard and mashed through fine hair sieves and mixed with biscuit meal to start the chicks off. . . After a day or two the food changes. Wheat, dairyseed, split maize, meat gristle – all cooked and done to a turn are then given.'

The hair used in these sieves was most likely, the long, strong coarse hair taken from a horse's mane or tail.

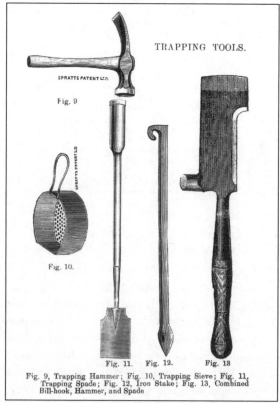

TRAPPING TOOLS.

SPRATTS PATENT LTD.

Fig. 9

Fig. 10.

Fig. 11.   Fig. 12.   Fig. 13.

Fig. 9, Trapping Hammer; Fig. 10, Trapping Sieve; Fig. 11, Trapping Spade; Fig. 12, Iron Stake; Fig. 13, Combined Bill-hook, Hammer, and Spade

1908 ADVERT

Dummy or Sham Eggs

Leslie Rawlings writing about the rearing field says,

> 'another part of the wood was surrounded by tall wire. Inside
> were rows galore of sitting boxes. Each long box had eight
> compartments. Each had a sloping roof and airholes in front.
> Sand was placed inside, hollowed out, and lined with hay. All the
> nearby farms and cottages were scoured for broody hens. . .
> The hens were put on china eggs for a while to let them settle
> down, then each given their clutch of pheasants' eggs. It was a
> wonderful sight each morning when all the old hens came off
> their nests. There were long rows of forked sticks and to each a
> hen was tethered by the leg with a length of fine cord. They all
> had a feed of boiled maize, a pan of water and a small heap of
> sand to bustle in. (Eventually) . . . back they all went, each dusted
> good and proper with Keatings powder first, to prevent fleas.'

Another use for 'sham' eggs was with the Euston system. Basically, a gamekeeper picks up game bird eggs from vulnerable nest sites, such as those located on roadside verges. He replaces the vulnerable eggs with imitation eggs and takes the proper eggs away to be either reared under broody hens or the 'electric hen', the artificial incubator. Once the eggs are nearly ready for hatching, they are replaced in the nest, and the dummy eggs removed. This way the real eggs are not subjected to potential danger from the weather or predators for too long, and once hatched the chicks would be reared naturally by the 'parent birds'. It was usual to mix the eggs from different nest sites, which had been laid on the same day, ensuring that they all hatched out about the same time. The reason for this was to ensure that 'new blood' was introduced into the existing gene pool, and so thereby reduce the chances of the birds inbreeding, and so producing much healthier birds. If 15 partridge eggs were originally laid, it was normal practice to replace with 20 eggs. Thus, more chicks would be reared naturally, and with a better survival rate. The Euston system was invented about 1902, and was first tried out on a large scale, on the Duke of Grafton's estate in Suffolk. Suppliers of artificial pheasant and partridge eggs, around 1910 to 1925, included Mr. G.Malden, Horne, near Horley, Surrey and Mr Edwin Leadbeater, Drewery Place, Longton, Stoke-on-Trent, but it is not know what material they were made of. Spratt's 1933 catalogue shows imitation pheasant and partridge eggs that were made in both wood or clay. Quadtag Limited (who acquired Gilbertson & Page Ltd.) 1995 catalogue states they sold wood, hen, pheasant and partridge dummy eggs and also composite wild duck dummy eggs. In 1999 they were still selling them plus plastic hens' eggs, but in their 2000 catalogue the wild duck composite eggs are no longer listed. Instead, a china hen's egg is listed with the others. In the 2004/5 Gamekeepa Feeds Ltd catalogue, a single pheasant / partridge dummy egg (pottery) was priced at £1 each. Their wooden dummy partridge egg was priced at £1.60p each, whilst their wooden dummy pheasant egg was slightly dearer at £1.95p each. No other type of dummy egg was listed for sale.

An interesting item used by some gamekeepers for the safe carrying of eggs was The Foster Mother Egg Belt, an advert for which was found in the Gilbertson & Page Ltd. book *Game Rearing Illustrated* (1909). In this same book Gilbertson & Page Ltd were also offering for sale their GILPA Incubator, which was made in two sizes. However, although artificial incubators were becoming available, due to the outbreak of World War I, followed by the depression years and then World War II, it was not until the very late 1950s that they really started to be reintroduced. From the early 1960s onwards, the broody hen then started to become redundant.

Spades — 1934 ADVERT

Again, these come in various shapes, e.g. Norfolk and Suffolk patterns, and sizes, from six feet long rabbiting spades used by warreners and rabbit trappers whilst ferreting, to ones with 28 inch handles. Mole catchers used smaller lighter versions. The six feet long rabbiting spades had a hook on the end of the shaft for extracting a rabbit carcass, which had been killed by the ferret, from deep within the rabbit burrow. The spade would be used to dig down to the 'laid up' ferret with its rabbit, and if fairly straight, the hooked end would

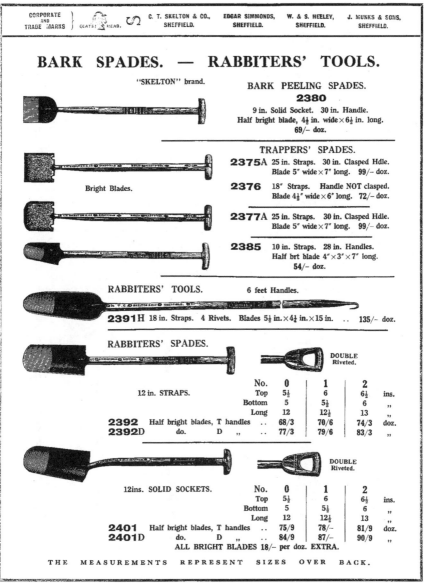

BARK SPADES. — RABBITERS' TOOLS.

"SKELTON" brand.

BARK PEELING SPADES.
2380
9 in. Solid Socket. 30 in. Handle.
Half bright blade, 4½ in. wide × 6½ in. long.
69/– doz.

TRAPPERS' SPADES.

Bright Blades.

2375A 25 in. Straps. 30 in. Clasped Hdle.
Blade 5" wide × 7" long. 99/– doz.

2376 18" Straps. Handle NOT clasped.
Blade 4½" wide × 6" long. 72/– doz.

2377A 25 in. Straps. 30 in. Clasped Hdle.
Blade 5" wide × 7" long. 99/– doz.

2385 10 in. Straps. 28 in. Handles.
Half brt blade 4" × 3" × 7" long.
54/– doz.

RABBITERS' TOOLS.
6 feet Handles.

2391H 18 in. Straps. 4 Rivets. Blades 5½ in. × 4½ in. × 15 in. .. 135/– doz.

RABBITERS' SPADES.

DOUBLE Riveted.

12 in. STRAPS.

No.	0	1	2	
Top	5½	6	6½	ins.
Bottom	5	5½	6	,,
Long	12	12½	13	,,
2392 Half bright blades, T handles ..	68/3	70/6	74/3	doz.
2392D do. D ,, ..	77/3	79/6	83/3	,,

DOUBLE Riveted.

12ins. SOLID SOCKETS.

No.	0	1	2	
Top	5½	6	6½	ins.
Bottom	5	5½	6	,,
Long	12	12½	13	,,
2401 Half bright blades, T handles ..	75/9	78/–	81/9	doz.
2401D do. D ,, ..	84/9	87/–	90/9	,,

ALL BRIGHT BLADES 18/– per doz. EXTRA.

THE MEASUREMENTS REPRESENT SIZES OVER BACK.

Telegraphic Address: "SKELTON, SHEFFIELD."   Telephone No. SHARROW 51001 (2 lines).

A PAGE SHOWING RABBITERS' TOOLS FROM A 1927
CATALOGUE BY C.T. SKELTON & CO. SHEFFIELD

be inserted into the hole and the rabbit carcass secured onto the hook. Upon extracting the carcass it was hoped that either the ferret would refuse to relinquish its hold of the rabbit and be brought to the surface with it, or the ferret thinking that its prey was escaping would follow it up to the surface, where upon emerging it was quickly placed into the ferret box.

Pattern Nos.	
66a	**GRIFFIN'S PATENT C.S. FACED NORFOLK PATTERN RABBITING SPADES,** 5-ft Handles. 5 x 4 x 12" doz
66b	**GRIFFIN'S PATENT C.S. FACED SUFFOLK PATTERN RABBITING SPADES,** 6-ft. Handles $5\frac{1}{4}$ x 4 x 14" doz
66c	**GRIFFIN'S PATENT C.S. FACED MOLE SPADES, 3-ft. 4-in. Handles.** $4\frac{1}{2}$ x $6\frac{1}{2}$" doz
66d	**GRIFFIN'S PATENT C.S. FACED STRAPPED CRUTCH WELDLESS LANGET RABBITING TOOLS, 2-ft. 4-in. Handles.** $6\frac{1}{4}$ x $5\frac{1}{2}$ x $12\frac{1}{2}$" doz
124	**GRIFFIN'S TRAPPING SPADES,** Clasped Crutch Handles 30". Strapped to Hilt, 5 Rivets. All Bright Blades. 5 x 7" doz
125	**GRIFFIN'S TRAPPING SPADES,** Long Handles, 36". Half Bright Blades. 4 x 3 x 7" doz If with Crutch Handles, same price.

RABBITING SPADES FROM ELIZA TINSLEY & CO LTD CATALOGUE MID 1930S

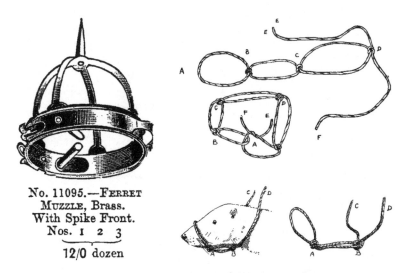

No. 11095.—FERRET
MUZZLE, Brass.
With Spike Front.
Nos. 1 2 3
12/0 dozen

AN UNUSUAL FERRET MUZZLE   TWO TYPES OF MUZZLES MADE OF CORD

Ferret Muzzles

A common practice at one time was to put over the ferret's jaws a device that was designed to stop the ferret from biting its prey and, whilst underground, 'laying up' with its kill and eating it. Unfortunately the ferret had no means of defending itself, due to the restrictions of the muzzle, if it came upon rats. Another problem was if the ferret emerged from the rabbit burrow unnoticed by the rabbit trappers and wandered off. Having no means to catch itself food it would eventually starve to death.

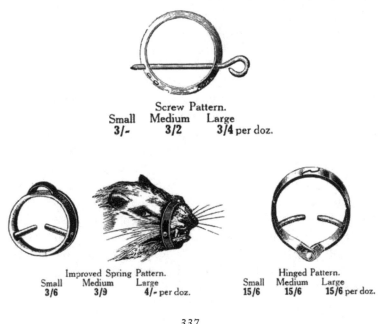

Screw Pattern.
Small   Medium   Large
3/-   3/2   3/4 per doz.

Improved Spring Pattern.   Hinged Pattern.
Small   Medium   Large   Small   Medium   Large
3/6   3/9   4/- per doz.   15/6   15/6   15/6 per doz.

The "Humane."

This muzzle consists of a very light ring of steel wire, nickel plated, being. the lighest ferret muzzle made.

It has practically no projections which are liable to catch in roots, &c. There are a double set of holes for the cross-pin, so that it can be adjusted to a large or small ferret.

Each, 0/7 .... doz 6/0

Leather Muzzles.

Best hand-sewn ....each, 0/8 ; doz 7/0
    „   „   '' The Improved,'' fitted with 6 buckles and straps, thus enabling it to be easily adjusted to fit any sized ferret.................................... each 1/10

Muzzles were made of leather, brass, and occasionally were also nickel plated. The metal muzzles were made in five styles, with four of them being made in three different sizes. The earliest advert that I have found is from the 1907 Army & Navy Stores Catalogue which shows The 'Humane' and states that 'this muzzle consists of a very light ring of steel wire, nickel plated, being the lightest ferret muzzle made.' This muzzle could be 'adjusted to a large or small ferret' according to the advert. Some gamekeepers and ferreters, muzzled their ferrets with thin string and tied it off behind the ferret's ears as is shown in a British Field Sports Society booklet entitled *Rabbiting & Ferreting* (7th edition 1976). This idea was thought to be more humane if the ferret wandered off unnoticed, as the thin string would became loose over time and eventually fall off and so therefore not restricting the ferret from killing to eat or from being able to defend itself from other predators. Parker Hale

FERRET FINDER II

AN UNDERGROUND LOCATION SYSTEM DESIGNED SPECIFICALLY FOR FERRETS OR TERRIERS, WITH A WORKING DEPTH OF UP TO 20FT (6M).

THE LOCATION SYSTEM - The system is a totally new design feature a low profile transmitting collar and a receiver with 'search' and 'locate' LED display which indicates distance from the collar. The LED display and a varying pitch sounder allows rapid location of the transmitting collar. With a 20ft range the system can both be used for ferret and terrier location.

RECEIVER FEATURES:
Varying pitch sounder - for fast location without adjustment.
LED bar graph display to show distance from transmitting collar.
'Search' range up to 20ft (6m)
'Locate' range up to 10ft (3m)
Weather proof - magnetic switches
External PP3 battery compartment
Colours - two tone Graphite or High visibility Orange/Graphite
Batteries included
12 months warranty
CE Approved

High visibility Orange
Varying pitch sound - for fast location without adjustment
Purpose designed ABS moulded case
Weatherproof On/Off switch
Battery compartment
Weatherproof Search/ Locate Switch
10 LED bar graph display indicates distance from transmitting collar

TRANSMITTING COLLAR FEATURES
● Low profile moulded module size - 34x20x10mm
● Powdered by two silver oxide cells (type 393 supplied)
● Sliding battery lid for ease of battery removal
● 16mm nylon collar strap for durability
● Ferret collar length 200mm
● Terrier collar length 400mm
● 12 months warranty

200mm Ferret Collar
400mm Terrier Collar
High profile moulded transmitter module
Slide to turn On/Off
High quality micro circuitry
Two Tone Graphite
Hi-Vis Orange

FERRET FINDER II
Complete set
High Vis. £125.00
TERRIER FINDER II
High vis. £127.00
**8ft MK 1
FERRET FINDER KIT**
Inc. receiver, collar, carry case, batteries, free delivery.
£75.00

the **WOLSELEY RADIO FERRET**

Four times as many rabbits with a minimum of digging.

The Modern Method of Ferreting

Particulars from : Wolseley Sheep Shearing Machine Co., Ltd. Witton, Birmingham, 6.

The above mentioned Radio Ferret may be obtained from Gilbertson & Page Ltd., Hertford, Herts. *Price £17* carriage paid

---

Ltd. were offering for sale in their 1947 catalogue a complete ferreting outfit priced at 13/6d each. The outfit comprised of one ferret collar, one ferret bell, one ferret line with swivel attached, three extra swivels and three pairs of metal muzzles. The muzzles came in three different styles and two different sizes for each style. Young's of Misterton were still offering for sale the three different styles of ferret muzzles in their 1962/3 catalogue. The muzzles' inside measurements were $1\frac{1}{8}$ inch (large) 1 inch (medium) and $\frac{7}{8}$ inch (small). An unusual brass ferret muzzle, which was made in a proper muzzle design, and also came in three different sizes, was made with a spike protruding from the front of it. Presumably this was intended to encourage the rabbit to move along its underground burrow.

Incidentally, the hinged pattern ferret muzzle known as the 'Handy' had its patent applied for on 2nd July 1919 (No 16,564/19) with the patent being accepted on 18th March 1920, becoming Patent No 139,986. The patentee was Alfred Duckworth Melson of Masshouse Lane, Birmingham who described himself as a manufacturer. The muzzle is marked 'Hiatts Improved Handy Patent 139,986 Made in England', around the edge. Hiatts of Birmingham are of course famous for their manufacture of handcuffs.

All the above-mentioned items are now obsolete as modern battery operated locators are mainly used in finding ferrets that have killed and laid up underground. A predecessor of today's commonly used battery operated ferret locator, in use in the early 1950s, was known as the Wolseley Radio Ferret. It sold for £17 in 1952 and was obtainable from Gilbertson & Page Ltd.

Bill Hook

An 18 inch long bill hook known as the 'Gamekeeper's Friend' which sold for 75/- per dozen in 1927 was in regular use in the day to day management of a 'keeper's duties. This handy item was used for such tasks as cutting down small scrub when making a travel route upon which to set a snare, or for opening up a feeding area for the pheasant poults.

The earliest illustration that I have found is in *How to Trap and Snare* by 'Moorman' published in 1908. The latest for sale reference is in Young's of Misterton's 1940 catalogue where they were still advertising for sale: 'The Trapper's and Gamekeeper's Friend. Three useful tools in one. A hammer for driving pegs, &c., a spud for loosening soil, and a hook for cutting bushes. Blade $8\frac{1}{2}$ inch.'

"GAMEKEEPER'S FRIEND" Socketed.   18 inches Overall .. 75/– doz.

BILL HOOK
FROM A 1927 CATALOGUE BY C.T. SKELTON & CO. SHEFFIELD

Swivel Gun

These small cannon type devices have been mentioned earlier.

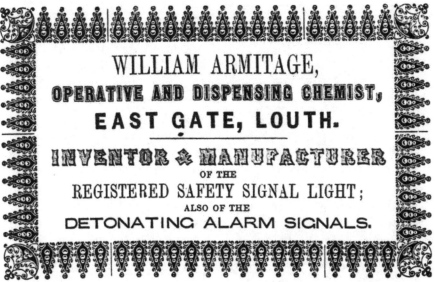

WILLIAM ARMITAGE,

OPERATIVE AND DISPENSING CHEMIST,

EAST GATE, LOUTH.

INVENTOR & MANUFACTURER

OF THE

REGISTERED SAFETY SIGNAL LIGHT;

ALSO OF THE

DETONATING ALARM SIGNALS.

1849 ADVERT

Alarm Guns

These early warning devices come in many styles and are still in use today. Their mode of operation has been described earlier. As well as the usual type of alarm guns being employed throughout the woods, modern technology has introduced electronic detection systems using infra red beams and radio transmitters which send out silent signals of intrusion to the fixed unit installed in the gamekeeper's cottage or a mobile receiver handset carried in his vehicle. With these systems the poacher remains unaware that he has been detected and that the gamekeeper is already on his way to confront him. It would be almost useless for the poacher to run off and hide in the undergrowth and remain silent as before, because the gamekeeper can now locate him easily with the help of one of the many types of military night vision glasses which are readily available.

These night vision glasses work by 'seeing' in the total dark, the body heat generated by a person. Even though a crouching human body outline can not be seen by the human eye in the darkness of night, the unseen 'heat glow' produced by the human body can be readily identified by this type of common military equipment. Mobile telephones are also now being commonly used in the struggle against poachers. These telephones can keep each gamekeeper or river bailiff in constant contact with each other and the police, whilst updating the poachers' whereabouts and activities instantly. Mobile phone photographs can be taken of their car etc, and the poachers themselves and used as evidence in court. During night time poaching activities, mobile telephones can be put on 'vibration mode' so as not to 'ring' in the normal way, which would alert the poachers in the quietness of

FIXING ALARATE GUNS

1883 ILLUSTRATION

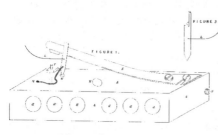

NAYLOR'S ALARM GUN

night time. Text messages can be sent to one another, rather than having to speak in a whispered hushed tone into the telephone. Another way of keeping in touch is through the use of two way radios but these devices are usually limited to use within a two mile radius and are better suited to being used on shoot days. Using these radios during a shoot's drive, the headkeeper can keep the beaters in line better, and has more control instantly, should an unexpected problem arise. It is certainly a better system than the headkeeper trying to keep in control of events by shouting instructions at the top of his voice.

Once the spring gun had been banned in 1827 from being loaded and used with lead shot to deadly effect, some landowners would have instructed their keepers still to use them, but with only a charge of black powder. A poacher, now accidently setting one of these off with the sudden loud noise roaring through the silence of the night, would apart from scaring the hell out of him, cause him no actual harm. Early references to proper alarm guns sometimes still called them 'spring guns', but over time the term 'spring gun' was replaced with the more correct term, alarm gun.

The most common type of alarm gun, which has been in use since early times, and is still in use up to the present day, is the 'gravity or drop' alarm gun, which was also referred to in earlier times as the 'falling' alarm gun. Basically, it is a metal rod, shaped like a walking stick or shepherd's crook, from which an attached weight drops down the length of, ultimately firing the blank cartridge. This shape allowed the alarm gun to be either stuck into the ground in the normal way, or hung up on a low branch near the trunk of a tree, so that it blended in better with its shadowy surroundings on moonlit nights. Most poachers expected a trip wire to be set no more than about knee level height, and so would not expect to encounter a trip wire hung from a low tree branch. This simple-to-operate device either fired its blank cartridge downwards or upwards. Although the upward firing alarm gun made a louder noise, as the charge was fired into the open air, rather than being muffled as it fired downward towards the ground, gamekeepers preferred the downward firing alarm gun. The reason for this was simply that sometimes a mistake was made, perhaps due to cold hands etc, when setting up the device, which often resulted in the weight being dropped when the cartridge would quickly fire in its upward direction. Sometimes the gamekeeper had his face in the line of fire, which might result in singed hair at best or even the loss of an eye at worst. If a mistake was made with the downward firing alarm gun, then generally no harm was done. The gamekeeper, Thomas Cank, noted in his book *40 Years Mingled in Game*, published in 1891:

> Alarm guns are excellent things in their place, against long
> nets, or rather, the game; but there are so many different
> classes of alarm guns. There is a class, that really the setter is
> in danger . . . (and) I could name upwards of a score of
> keepers that have found it as such; for the powder marks in
> their face and neck (prove it). This is caused from the class of
> gun that run down a rod and strikes a plate of iron at the
> bottom, and shoots upwards; and which many a user of the
> same has found out to his sorrow. The guns I used to use
> were not those running down a rod and exploding upwards, I
> can assure you; for I have always held more respect for my
> top-piece, than run the risk of them.

An early unusual alarm gun was patented by a gamekeeper called Isaac Naylor of Stainbrough near Barnsley in Yorkshire on 22nd November 1836, being Patent No 7232. His invention was stated as being 'An alarm gun or reporter and detector' and his invention consisted of 'an alarm gun holding several charges, which are discharged one after the other by means of a fuse which communicates with the whole.'

His patent drawing shows an alarm gun with six charge bores, but other known examples exist which have four and ten charge bores. His reason for more than a single report alarm gun device is that:

> these bores may be of any suitable dimensions, and at any
> distance from each other, according to the loudness of the
> report and the interval of time between each report which may
> be required, one object of my invention being a succession of
> loud reports to wake persons out of sleep, and to draw their
> attention to the place where those reports arise; for, when a
> person is suddenly awoke by one report of a gun, or any loud
> noise, he seldom knows by what means or cause he is so awoke,
> whereas by a succession of reports he becomes thoroughly awoke

and alarmed, and his attention is more effectually called to the place where a thief, depradator, or trespasser, who unintentionally lets off the alarm gun, may be.

'The fuse,' he states, 'may be made of any combustible composition, such as gunpowder and any matter that will ignite gradually, and not cause all the charge bores, which are charged, to go off together, as would be if the fuse bore were filled with gunpowder only.'

Having placed the alarm gun in its intended situation and also having connected the trigger lever to set it, he then extends the trip wire or string and fixes the other end. . .

'to any door post or other fixed point, having first extended them across the room or grounds so that whenever any thief, depradator, or trespasser comes in contact with any of the said wires or strings, . . . the spring will slip from the notch in such trigger and strike the detonating cap, and in about from two to seven seconds (which depends upon the distance of the charge bores from each other and the strength or nature of the fuse composition) cause the first report and the rest in succession, so that the thief or depredator not hearing the report at the time he feels the wire or string will not be aware that he has let off the gun till he has got past the wire.'

At the Great exhibition in 1851, Messrs Charles Osborne and Co, gunmaker's of Birmingham, displayed their percussion firing alarm gun. According to an article which appeared in the *Windsor Magazine*, circa 1900,

'It is a well finished contrivance of brass and steel, and is fired by means of a percussion cap. At the back is a screw, by which the gun may be affixed to a post or tree trunk; . . . A later and plainer form, similar in design, but of iron only . . . (was made).'

The alarm gun that was exhibited, used a bow spring style of striker or trigger which was attached from the underside of the alarm gun and curved over the end of the extended horizontal 'arm'. The later model has a more simple style of trigger, being of a flat spring design, which was riveted to the top of the horizontal 'arm', at its end. Three trip wires could be stretched out from this alarm gun. This alarm gun is known to have C OSBORNE impressed on one side of the horizontal 'arm' and INVENTOR on its reverse side.

Another type of early percussion alarm gun, is stamped with the name Baxter. This device was not screwed into a post etc, like the one just mentioned, but its long iron rod was pushed into the ground just like the 'gravity or drop' alarm gun. This alarm gun also fired harmlessly, downwards.

In Kelly's Directory of Staffordshire, 1880, William Burgess of Malvern

Wells was advertising a wide range of alarm guns. Under the heading BURGESS'S the advert stated,

'Improved Patent Central Fire, Illuminating, Springless, Damp-proof Eclipse Prize. ALARM GUNS are the greatest protection against poachers and their wholesale long nets, and the silent guns they use for pheasant shooting; also fowl stealers and garden and orchard robbers are put a stop to for a few shillings by the use of these Guns.'

Offered for sale were:

No1. Central fire Breech loader, brass plug, 12 gauge 11/6d each. Cartridge cases per 100, 4/0d.
No2.Central fire, with brass cap, 12 gauge 11/6d each. Cartridge cases per 100, 4/0d.
No3. Central fire, 16 gauge, brass cap, 10/6d each.
No 4. Side action, muzzle loader, charged 10 to 12 drams, very simple, 9/6d each.
No 5. Brass Guns, Muzzle loaders, for out or in door use 13/6d each.
No 6. Pin fire Alarm Guns, 5s. each, or 48s. per dozen.
No7. A new Alarm Gun, Central fire, made to shoot up or downwards, very simple and safe to use, 7s.6d. each, including 12 Cartridge Cases.

Unfortunately, there are no illustrations with the advert. This 'new alarm gun, central fire, made to shoot up or downwards' which is listed by Burgess may be the type or 'class' that Thomas Cank referred to previously.

In Cank's book he also refers to an alarm gun that he patented in October 1890, and which he called by the name of 'Repetitional'. He states,

'I call them this name, simply because they can be carried up to any number of guns. . . to explode one after the other, after the first ball is liberated for discharging. If a poacher, or burglar, comes in contact with the wire and liberates the first ball, all the others will follow; and if he cuts the wire he will liberate the first ball, and the others are sure to follow. The most prominent guns that will be before the public, for fields, game preserves, gardens, orchards and inside dwellings, will be No.1 and No.2. The former will be fitted with two barrels, and the latter with three. Nos.3, 4 and 5, and upwards will all depend on the demand.'

Again, there is no illustration showing this type of alarm gun.

In the later Army & Navy Stores catalogue of 1907, listed are Pollard's Patent Falling Alarm Gun, which fires upwards, priced at 9/6d each, Burgess' Improved Patent Pin Fire Gun, priced at 7/6d each and Henson's Patent

Osborne's
Improved Alarm Gun.

THE OSBORNE IMPROVED ALARM GUN.

One of the advantages of this Gun is that the wire becomes detached after firing, so that if it is followed up the Gun is not likely to be found and stolen by poachers as is so frequently done. Several wires can be attached.

Each 9/6

GAMEKEEPERS' IDENTIFIERS.

To order.

Can be used like an ordinary blue light, and have a spike on the end of the handle, by means of which they can be affixed to a tree or post. Each identifier is labelled with printed instructions as to how to use.

The above will burn for a period of 3 to 4 minutes, according to the state of the wind .... doz 12/0

Not less than 1 doz. supplied

ROCKET SIGNAL APPARATUS.
(To order only.)

Consisting of rocket, firing trough, and box of line 60/0

Rockets............................. each extra 10/0

POLLARD'S PATENT FALLING ALARM GUNS.

Instructions for use.—Fix the iron rod firmly in the ground, passing it through the hole in the circular ground plate, remove the breech and place the cartridge in the chamber; replace the breech. The gun is held up by placing the catch to which the wire is attached under the projection on the gun. This falls, and the cartridge is exploded when the wire is pulled.

Each 9/6

Burgess' Improved Patent Pin Fire Gun 7/6

Henson's Patent Falling Alarm Gun, with Rocket Apparatus, 17/3; rockets ... doz 6/6

Muzzle loading Alarm Gun for Shutters or doors............... each 8/0

Do. for Trees or Posts ,, 3/9

Wire extra......... 100 yds 0/9

The price of wire is apt to vary.

Pollard's Patent Falling Alarm Gun.

12 bore cartridges for Alarm Guns, loaded with 3¼ drs. black powder ...... per 100 5/0

Falling Alarm Gun, with Rocket Apparatus priced at 17/3d each. The rockets cost 6/6d per dozen. Other alarm guns offered are Muzzle loading alarm guns for shutters or doors, priced at 8/0d each or if you wanted the same for Trees or Posts they cost 3/9d each. The Osborne Improved Alarm Gun cost 9/6d each, and its advantage was stated to be that 'the wire becomes detached after firing so that if it is followed up the gun is not likely to be found and stolen by poachers as is so frequently done.' Another advantage was that several wires could be attached. This is an unusual alarm gun because, although it works on the gravity principle, nothing slides down the iron rod as in the more common alarm guns. Near the top of the iron rod, which is pushed into the ground in the normal way, there is a slight bend or 'knee', further above which is an 'arm' with a short barrel protruding, for accepting the blank firing cartridge. This assembly is held in an upright position, by a hook. Once the trip wire has been 'tripped', the arm and barrel pivots downwards, under its own weight. The short barrel's firing pin then strikes the bend or 'knee', the force of which detonates the cartridge.

Gilbertson & Page's catalogue of 1913 shows Shaw's Alarm Guns, which either drop and detonate singularly, or could be ordered as a Double Alarm Gun, which 'yields a second report some few moments after the first'. Both variations fired upwards.

Another unusual alarm gun is one made by Thomas Horsley & Son of York. Horsley was born in Doncaster in 1810, and served his apprenticeship with Richard Brunton at Stonegate, York. About 1830, he took over his employer's premises and started his own gun making business in Stonegate, York, moving to 48, Coney Street in 1834. Then in 1856 he moved along the same street to premises located at No. 10, where they stayed until 1915. Their next move was to Blossom Street, with their last address being at 102, Micklegate,

York. The business finally ceased trading in 1959. Thomas Horsley & Son also had premises at 6, Scott Lane, Doncaster, and are first recorded there in the trade directories for 1889, but it is thought that they were trading from this address as early as 1878. They remained at this address until 1899. In 1900, G.J. Smithson (Est,1880) took over the Doncaster premises, moving from his own premises along the street, at No 10 Scot Lane. In an 1893 advert of G.J. Smithson's, it states that he was '25 Years with Messrs. Horsley & Son, and 10 Years manager at Doncaster'.

In Spratt's 1933 catalogue, they were only offering for sale a downward firing alarm gun of slightly different design to the normal gravity 'drop' iron rod, alarm gun. Again, another different style of alarm gun was advertised in the Modern Arms Company Ltd, London, catalogue of *circa* 1933. This AVUM alarm gun being described as 'the smallest, simplest and cheapest alarm gun on the market'. The price was12/6d each. This alarm gun has two screw holes for fixing to a post etc. However, in Parker-Hale's 1939 catalogue, they

THE AVUM ALARM GUN FROM A 1933 CATALOGUE

were selling two different types of alarm guns. The normal gravity 'drop' alarm gun and their own 'spring' alarm gun. Their advert for the 'spring' alarm gun states, 'This Alarm Gun is made from heavy Gunmetal castings (and) is rust and weather-proof'. These two same adverts appear in their 1946 catalogue, but the 'spring' alarm gun is now described as the 'Cannon' type alarm gun. This 'Cannon' type alarm gun was also advertised by Parker-Hale in the October 1947 issue of the *Gamekeeper and Countryside* magazine, priced at 35/- each with postage was 6d. A few years later in their 1950 catalogue, only the gravity 'drop' alarm gun is being offered for sale, at a price of 35/- each, which included the price of the compulsory official proof. This situation remained the same in their later catalogues up to at least 1958.

In a price list dated March 1948, Gilbertson and Page Ltd were offering 'Alarm Guns, for fixing to trees etc. 33/6d each, post paid'. Unfortunately, there is no illustration of it, but the 'fixing to trees etc' suggests a small coil spring type action. In their September 1951 issue of *Gamekeeper and Countryside* magazine, they were still offering their 'tree mounted Gilpa alarm gun, priced at 34/6d each' plus also an 'upright' type at 25/- each. This 'upright' alarm gun most likely refers to the common 'gravity or drop' alarm gun. The Gilpa coil spring-operated tree- or post-mounted alarm gun is known to closely resemble the Parker-Hale 'spring or cannon' type of alarm gun. This close resemblance suggests that Parker-Hale may have made these alarm guns for Gilbertson and Page Ltd and discontinued their own style. This could be due to Gilbertson and Page's business serving the sporting gun and gamekeeping profession, whilst Parker-Hale's business concentrated mainly on the target shooter. Much later, in Gilbertson and Page's Ltd 1986 catalogue/price list, offered were Gilpa spring alarm (parts replaceable) each £14.30, Longstaff alarm mine, each £2.75, flares (for Longstaff alarm), each 0.70p, adaptor for flares, each £1.80p, upright alarm gun, each £11.50, blank cartridges per 100, £16.00. In the Quadtag Limited catalogue of 1989 (aquired from Gilbertson & Page Ltd), the new proprietors were still offering for sale the above range of alarm guns.

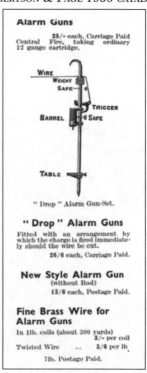

GILBERTSON & PAGE 1935 CATALOGUE

Alarm Guns

25/- each, Carriage Paid
Central Fire, taking ordinary 12 gauge cartridge.

WIRE
WEIGHT
SAFE
TRIGGER
BARREL
SAFE
TABLE

" Drop " Alarm Gun-Set.

" Drop " Alarm Guns
Fitted with an arrangement by which the charge is fired immediately should the wire be cut.
26/6 each, Carriage Paid.

New Style Alarm Gun
(without Rod)
13/6 each, Postage Paid.

Fine Brass Wire for Alarm Guns
In 1lb. coils (about 300 yards)
3/- per coil
Twisted Wire ... 3/6 per lb.
7lb. Postage Paid.

Alarm Gun

Takes the ordinary 12-bore brass or paper case. Can be loaded or unloaded in less than one minute, and set with ease and certainty in the dark. When no alarm is required, they may be blocked at pleasure without removing or unloading.

CAGI—Fires down .. .. single 10/6
       ,,   ,, ... double 21/-
Damp-proof Brass bore .. single 27/6
Brass Wire for above (300 yards coil),
              3/- per Coil.
              Carriage Paid.

Position Finders

These handy little articles are used as a pocket lottery, to determine each Shooter's position.

PF3

PF 3 — Best White Metal Vest - pocket Case, Electro Plate Nickel Silver, with ring to attach to watch chain.

Price, 12/- each. Post Paid.

SPRATT'S 1933 CATALOGUE

PARKER-HALE
SPRING
ALARM GUN.

This Alarm Gun is made from heavy Gunmetal Castings, with the same precision as an ordinary gun. It is rust and weather-proof and will take 12 bore Blank Cartridges up to 3" in length. By law, each Alarm Gun must be proved before sale and the fee for this is included in the price. It may easily be fixed by two screws in any position on a stout stake driven into the ground, or on a gatepost, tree, etc. We recommend however, that it should be mounted for safety, with the muzzle in a downward direction.

INSTRUCTIONS FOR LOADING AND SETTING THE ALARM GUN.

The Alarm Gun being firmly fixed in its firing position, pull the knob on the striker until one is able to insert the Safety Pin in the hole drilled through the striker. The Safety Pin must be pushed **right in.** Then unscrew the Breech Plug from the barrel and insert the cartridge in the Chamber. Making sure that the Safety Pin is correctly in position screw in the Breech Plug. When the Breech Plug is screwed right home **and the Safety Pin is still in position** pull on the striker knob until the groove around the striker is visible. Into this groove place the disc, with the crescent as near central on the striker as possible, then gently lower the striker to grip the disc. When one is satisfied that all is in order, and NOT BEFORE remove the Safety Pin.

NOTE. The Trip Wire is attached to the hole in the disc and NOT to the Safety Pin.

List No. SAG.3.   Price 20/-.   Postage 6d.

For prices of Blank cartridges and wire, see above.

PARKER-HALE 1939 CATALOGUE

However, listed in their 2000 catalogue, the Gilpa alarm gun had been renamed the 'Quadtag brass spring alarm (parts replaceable)' and cost £25.97 each plus postage. Quadtag were also selling the 'Henry Krank alarm gun' at £8.81 each, whilst the 'Upright alarm gun' was priced at £25.85 each, both plus postage.

Thomas Lightwood & Son, was recorded as being a 'Gun implement maker' in the directories for 1864, at 16 1/2 Loveday Street, Birmingham. In 1878 Lightwood, Thomas & Son had premises on Price Street. Whilst in the 1894 directory the business was recorded as being at 2 & 3 New Bldgs, Price Street. In 1951 they are stated to be Lightwood & Son Limited, mfrs of small tools for electrical & allied trades & gun implement mkrs, Price St, 4. T.A. Lightwood, Birmingham; Aston Cross 2622'. In 1969-70 they are still manufacturers of small tools but now their address is 3, Fleet Street. In 1973-74 their telephone number is 021-236-2961. Their last known entry is in a 1983 directory and simply states 'Lightwood & Son Ltd, Partridge Wks, Fleet St. 3, 021-236-2961'. This business, operating from its Price Street address, would have been located in the heart of the Birmingham Gun Quarter and is known to have made a 12 bore central firing 'Gravity or Drop' type of alarm gun. This downward firing alarm gun has a small separate 'cap', containing a centrally located movable firing pin, the whole of which is attached next to the cartridge chamber by a small length of chain. The 'cap' with its integral movable firing pin, sits upon the blank cartridge head, which has been inserted into the breach, and awaits the falling weight to slide down the square metal rod and strike the firing pin and so detonate the blank cartridge. A later version, probably made about the 1950s or 1960s, of this alarm gun, now has the upright metal rod made from flat bar steel instead of the normal square metal rod. Another easily distinguishing feature, is that the cartridge chamber is now welded to the upright metal rod rather than being cast in one piece and attached to the upright rod with two pins. The separate sliding weight is also welded together, rather than being formed out of a single piece of metal. Lastly, the firing pin in the 'cap' is formed out of the 'cap' and therefore is a solid non-moveable striker.

In the August 1981 issue of the *Guns Review* magazine, appeared a test report for a modern made alarm gun. This small, coil spring alarm gun, was being sold by John L. Longstaff of Pudsey, near Leeds in Yorkshire. Describing the new alarm gun, the article stated,

> 'The device is certainly not a gun in that it has no barrel and could not be used to fire live ammunition (as the old alarm guns sometimes were). The device consists of a metal bracket which is screwed to a tree or a suitable stake if used outdoors or to any wooden support if used indoors. At one end is a recess to take the head of a 12 bore blank. Below this is a

spring loaded striker with a loose sear which holds it back until the trip wire is released. The kit is complete with a nylon trip cord, a safety device for use whilst setting up the alarm and even the screws for fixing it. With the device screwed to a suitable surface, the striker is pulled back against the spring until the safety can be inserted in a hole through the striker. A 12 bore blank or capped case is then placed in the shell holder and the detachable sear is slid in, leaving the pin in place. The trip cord is then run out and its free end is attached to something at a suitable height or, if used indoors is attached to the door or window to be protected. When all is set up, the safety pin can be removed leaving the alarm live. Very little pressure in the trip cord results in the blank being fired. We set the alarm up outdoors and found that it was easily set, stable enough for its purpose yet easily tripped. The noise created depends on the type of blank used but a standard 12 bore blank would be more than adequate. This really is a winner. At the modest price of £2.95 each, we can see keepers and others wanting to protect shoots making good use of them. They would also be of value to people like poultry farmers wanting to protect sheds and outbuildings.

The article ended by saying that 'available with the alarms are warning signs which landowners might find useful.' Mark I and Mark 2 versions exist of this alarm gun. In the Mark I version, the top of the spring loaded striker has a right angle in it for the finger to pull it up with. The Mark 2 version has a rounded hook instead. The other difference between the two types, being that the Mark 2 has the spring loaded striker guide formed out of the back of the bracket, by being bent inwards. The Mark I version has a solid bracket. The packaging consists of bold black writing on the small yellow oblong box and simply states on its top, Alarm Signaling Device, whilst on the bottom of the box, and underneath in very small lettering, Made in Italy. The Mark 2 was still being sold around 1987/8.

In an advert in a 1987 *Gun Mart* issue, Henry Krank of 108, Lowtown, Pudsey, were offering for sale an Alarm Mine, the illustration of which, is the same as the Mark I sold by Longstaff. It is possible that by this time the Mark I type had been replaced by the Mark 2 version, but the same illustration was being used as the alarm gun/mine still worked in the same way. The price for this alarm mine being £3.41. In the same advert was 'also available, pressure plate activated ground mine. For use when alarm mine is impractical. To be used with 12g capped cases. £4.51'. In 1994 Henry Krank of 100/102 Lowtown, Pudsey, were selling, for £6.00 each, another type of small spring loaded alarm gun. This operates in exactly the same way, with a spring loaded striker with the right angled finger pull. The solid body though, looks to be die cast. Again the packaging is a small yellow box with bold black writing stating Henry Krank Alarm Mine for use with 12B black powder blanks. The box also states, Manufactured by Henry Krank & Co Ltd.

Another modern manufacturer of a coil spring operated alarm gun is Helston Gunsmiths now of Water-ma-Trout, Helston, Cornwall. Originally, during the 1970s , the company was based at The Clies, Meneage Street, Helston. During their time there, they started to produce The Helston Alarm Gun which was featured in the magazine *Guns Review* which commented that

J LONGSTAFF OF PUDSEY ALARM GUN MARK II VERSION

HENRY KRANK OF PUDSEY PRESSURE PLATE GROUND MINE ALARM GUN

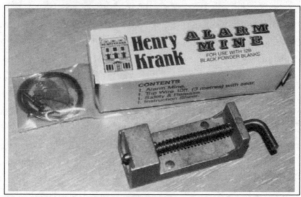

HENRY KRANK OF PUDSEY ALARM MINE

they were 'producing a very robust alarm gun which is reliable in operation and designed to last a lifetime'. Describing it, the article went on to say that,

'A plated striker mechanism of $^7/_{16}$ inch diameter runs through two guides in the heavy metal backing plate. The top has a comfortable round plastic knob and driving power is provided by a good coil spring. The rod is pulled back by hand until a notch cut into its circumference is above the top guide. The 'trigger' is a round plate with three notches which is permanently attached to the device by a chain. A safety pin is similarly attached and can be fitted into a hole above the notch whilst the device is being set up. The cartridge holder is a substantial ring of $^1/_2$ inch metal and the distance between the top of the cartridge holder and the bottom of the striker is such that it is not possible to load a full length cartridge by mistake. The striker itself is machined into the bottom of the rod. Placement of the cartridge is more positive than it is with other makes and the device is much more robust. We tested it and found it very reliable. The alarm gun will retail at about £6.50, including VAT.'

It is stamped with HELSTON in small capital letters on the middle support under the coiled spring striker. A mark II version of this alarm gun was also produced. Basically, they simplified their original idea by utilising one thin strip of metal in its construction, and bending it into a series of right angles. This design allowed for the thick metal ring, and middle support, which were separately welded onto the back plate, being discontinued. Instead, a hole was made in the end section of the metal strip to accommodate the seating of the blank cartridge, the coiled spring striker, going through two of the three bent sections and finally coming to rest upon the head of the blank cartridge. The Mark II version has no name or any other markings.

In a leaflet dated August 1995, a new type of intruder alarm (Patent applied for) was being placed on to the market. The Commando MK I, advertised as, 'the ultimate thief and burglar stopper' used a 9mm blank cartridge instead of the usual type of 12 bore blank cartridge. This portable intruder alarm was made in Great Britain and each one had a serial number. According to the information supplied with this new alarm gun,

This intruder alarm was invented in order to satisfy the demand for protection of outlying buildings, garden space and road vehicles. It is all mechanical – no electronics – and whilst it is similar to types of World War II detonators that were used extensively by the Royal Engineers to deter an advancing enemy, it has now been brought up-to-date and made safer by using 9mm blank cartridges. The Commando MK I is made in brass, so it is suitable for use in all weathers.

HELSTON ALARM GUN MARK I

HELSTON ALARM GUN MARK II

COMMANDO ALARM GUN MARK I

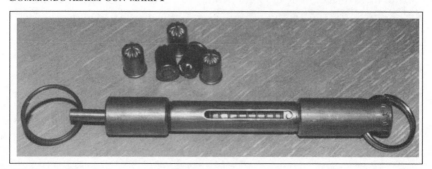

Length app 13.5cm (5.5in); diameter app 2cm (0.8in); weight app 225g (8 ozs).

Continuing with its advantages over other types of alarm guns it states that, 'As a deterrent against intruders, it can be placed behind doors or other openings, or across pathways etc (and its) portability and weight make the Commando MK I also suitable for the kitbag, for use to attract help if needed, as well as to deter unwelcome visitors.' The cost of this intruder alarm was stated to be £29.25 plus 70p P&P, and could be obtained by mail order from W.Roper (Alarms and Accessories), Foxwood, Capel Road, Ruckinge, Kent. TN 26 – 2EJ.

Some of these modern types of alarm devices are still available, and can still be purchased from such outlets as B.A.S.C., The Game Conservancy Trust and some of the larger Sporting Gunshops.

Obviously, as well as the commercially produced alarm guns, some 'home made' ones do appear from

UNMARKED ALARM GUN

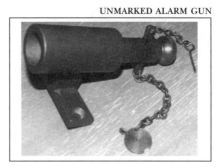

1950s ADVERT

NEW IMPROVED ALARM GUNS.

For Protecting Buildings, Poultry Farms, Orchards, Gardens, Game Preserves, Parks, &c., against Burglars, Trespassers, &c. Works with fine and unbreakable Wire.

PRICE
30/-
Post Paid.

It is a strong, sure, durable, and simple little gun easily handled and easily carried. The main advantage of this alarm gun is that it can be affixed to almost any position desired—tree, hedge, stake, door, wall, or hut, and can therefore be used for the protection of a variety of property or ground.

DIRECTIONS FOR SETTING :—

Press spike of alarm into ground, or reverse spike (point upwards) and screw to timber of buildings or other suitable place—attach your trip wire to bottom of trip latch—swivel safety plate with firing pin away from cartridge chamber—lift striker and suspend same by latch—insert cartridge—swivel safety plate until firing pin rests on cartridge—alarm is then ready for use.

An ordinary 12-bore **blank** cartridge can be used in these Alarms.

32/– per 100. Carriage and Packing 1/9 extra.

Fine Wire for Alarm, 4/4 lb. (About 300 ft.).

time to time. These 'Do It Yourself' alarm guns are usually of the simple 'gravity or drop' type, as they are the easiest to make. They usually consist of a long piece of suitable diameter tubing, down which a heavy weight falls, detonating the blank cartridge, which then fires in a downward direction. Sometimes though, the breach from an old worn-out or badly damaged shotgun barrel is suitably converted into an alarm gun. Years ago, I had an interesting conversation with an old retired gamekeeper who lived near Sheffield, Yorkshire, regarding the unofficial use of the 'gravity or drop' alarm gun. He stressed that it had to be one of the type that had been 'officially proofed' and fired downwards for obvious reasons. Due to having serious poaching problems from the local miners in the area, he decided to teach them a lesson. He set up in a wood, a 'gravity or drop' alarm gun. He then took a solid metal plate from an old cooker and placed it, at an angle, stuck into the ground, well below the short barrel of the alarm gun. He then loaded it with a live cartridge containing small shot, and suitably concealed it. He then stretched out and affixed some fine fishing line and removed the safety catch, the idea being, when the alarm gun was 'tripped' and the cartridge fired, the small shot hitting the metal plate would ricochet across the path, causing the poacher 'to dance a bit'.

Swingle/Life Preserver

The Swingle and Life Preserver as they are known, are really nothing more than a gamekeeper's truncheon and were used for self defence against violent poachers who resisted apprehension. Some gamekeepers though preferred a more aggressive approach to catching poachers. Thomas Cank recalled in his book, published in 1890,

> My way and instructions to every man on these occasions was this – Get your sticks ready and don't move until they come close to us, and ask no questions, but knock the first man down you come across, and we will ask all questions after all is over; for if you come across a poacher in the night, and you don't knock him down first, in nine cases out of ten he will you.

Earlier nineteenth century swingles were usually made of hard wood such as beech, and were of a more ornate design, consisiting of a 'turned' wooden handle with an attached wooden 'ball' or egg shape made from the same material. To some extent these swingles are reminiscent of the old medieval knights' ball and chain mace. They had become obsolete by 1900, when life preservers had already started to replace them.

In 1909 and 1913, life preservers could be bought from Gilbertson and Page at 2/6d each. Spratt's 1933 catalogue has illustrated two life preservers. One is the usual normal 'Braided cord on cane, stiff, Post Paid 3/6', but the

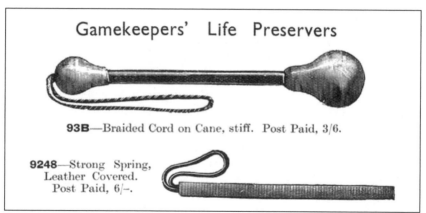

Gamekeepers' Life Preservers

93B—Braided Cord on Cane, stiff. Post Paid, 3/6.

9248—Strong Spring, Leather Covered. Post Paid, 6/-.

SPRATT'S 1933 CATALOGUE

PARKER-HALE'S 1939 CATALOGUE

GAMEKEEPER'S SWINGLE

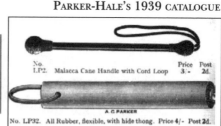

No.		Price	Post
LP2. Malacca Cane Handle with Cord Loop		3/-	2d.

A. C. PARKER

No. LP32. All Rubber, flexible, with hide thong. Price 4/- Post 2d.

second is described as being a 'Strong spring, Leather covered, Post Paid. 6/-'.

Two types of life preservers were advertised in a 1936 Midland Gun catalogue. The first was the usual type, made of cane with netted cord head and priced at 2/6d each, whilst a new type was made of special rubber and priced at 3/9d each. This new line was not illustrated though. Three years later in Parker-Hale's 1939 catalogue, they were advertising the usual 'Malacca Cane Handle with Cord Loop' life preserver priced at 3/- each plus 2d postage. However, also illustrated was the 'All Rubber, flexible, with hide thong' life preserver priced at 4/- each plus 2d postage. Young's of Misterton's September 1940 catalogue was also offering an unknown type of life preserver priced at 5/-. Although these many different types of life preservers were definitely used by gamekeepers, many gamekeepers preferred to use an ordinary police stave, more commonly known as a truncheon. Young's were selling 15 inch long police staves in 1940 for 9/- each, post free. A gamekeeper would either get the trousers of his estate suit made with a long narrow pocket of a suitable length to accommodate the truncheon, or get his wife to alter them accordingly. By doing this, the gamekeeper always had, literately by his side, at all times, a means of protection or a 'priest' for administering the 'last rites' to some unfortunate animal.

Concealable Guns

A very handy gun both for the gamekeeper and especially the poacher was the folding .410 calibre shotgun. This type of shotgun was made in both single and double-barrelled versions and with the choice of either a solid stock or a skeleton stock. The skeleton stock helped to slightly reduce the weight of the shotgun, and because of its ability to fold up upon itself made it easier to hide. This was a distinct advantage when poaching. The report from a .410 shotgun is quite modest, especially if used on a windy or stormy night. Combined with an effective killing range of about 25 yards, and with a maximum range of no more than 30 yards, these handy little shotguns were ideal for close range work at roosting pheasants.

MADE IN ENGLAND.

·410 Single Collectors' Gun   Folding Pattern
OUR OWN MANUFACTURE.

HALF PISTOL
GRIP STOCK GIVES
THE GUN A FINE
APPEARANCE.

Length of Barrel 28".   Weight 3¼ lbs.
Length Overall, 41".
No. **8251**. Side Lever Action, neatly balanced, Steel Barrel, spring stop. For 2-in. and 2½-in. Cartridges.

Skeleton Stock .. **£**   Solid Stock .. **£**
Half Pistol Grip Stock   extra.

·410 Bore Double Folding Gun

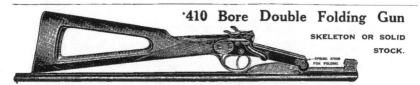

SKELETON OR SOLID
STOCK.

Weight 4¼ lbs.   Length of Barrel 28".
Length Overall 43½-in.
No. **8245**. Steel Barrels, proved for 2-in. and 2½-in. Cases.

Skeleton Stock .. **£**   Solid Stock .. **£**
For Cartridges see Special Slip—.410 bore 2-in.   .410 bore 2½-in.   .410 3-in. Magnum.

These interesting, handy little weapons can be put to innumerable uses. For the Garden, the Orchard and the Farm they will be found invaluable. Everybody can use them, from the juvenile to the sportsman of experience. They are well made guns built for hard work, taking both the 2-in. and 2½-in. cartridges. First-class British manufacture.
SPECIAL. These guns can be chambered and proved for 3-in. cartridges.   extra.

Walking Stick Guns (Foreign.)

PERFECT FINISH.

No. **5504** — STICK GUN, steel barrel, Rosewood covered with fancy black horn handle and concealed trigger, shooting .410 walking stick Cartridges, sliding breech, secret trigger. Length of Barrel 28"

No Firearms Certificate

Required

For 2 in. cartridges.

in Great Britain.

.410—2-in. W.S. Cartridges, Paper Case   per 100.

CONCEALABLE GUNS FROM THE MIDLAND GUN COMPANY CATALOGUE 1939

Walking stick shotguns were made in a variety of small calibre sizes and were mainly used for specimen collecting by the wealthier gentleman. The small calibre used would not cause too much damage to the plumage etc. of the unfortunate quarry, often a rare or unusual species. However, they would also be employed when the occasional poaching opportunity presented itself, to the more 'sporting gentleman' whilst out for an evening or early morning stroll.

Although two different types of shotgun have been mentioned above, any small, quiet, concealable firearm which could be taken apart easily would be pressed into service when required.

An old and a modern example will illustrate the point. The American-made Steven's Model 44 'Ideal' rifle, in the .22 Rimfire version, which was first made about 1893/4 and dismantled into two separate halves would indeed live up to its name. A modern type of concealable .22 Rimfire rifle suitable for use in poaching, especially if equipped with a sound moderator is the American-made AR7 Survival Rifle, which when not in use can be dismantled and completely stored in its own waterproof stock.

Game Carriers

As their name implies these items were used by gamekeepers and 'pickers up' at shoots for carrying the shot game in groups, rather than trying to carry a large number of birds etc. individually. These items are made in various styles.

The illustrations shown overleaf are from Gilbertson & Page's 1913 catalogue, but they were in use over a very long period of time. In Spratt's 1933 catalogue, the 'Marwood' Game Carrier Regd. No. 220860 was stated to be able to 'carry 10 Partridges or Grouse (2 on each string), also suitable for Pheasants and Rabbits. Keeps the game clean and cool. Will go into pocket or Gun Case. Post Paid, 3/9'. They were also selling their own Pocket Game Carrier, which consisted of '12 Leather Loops with wooden handle. Strong and convenient. 4/6 each. Postage Paid'. Two wooden ones were also still being sold, priced at single 7/6, double 10/6, postage paid. A similar type made of 'Polished oak, leather handle and cords 9/-. Postage paid', was also available. By 1948 Gilbertson & Page's prices for the single wooden game carrier was 9/6d, whilst a double cost 13/6d each. The Marwood being priced at only 5/6d each. These prices remained the same during 1951.

The Sussex Game Carrier

★ Carry your birds easily and comfortably, without crushing.

★ No more messy game bags and spoilt birds.

★ Up to 14 pheasants or 30 pigeons carried easily in two neck irons hung over the shoulder.

★ Strongly made in washable nylon-coated steel and best leather connecting straps.

★ Will never rust.

★ A must for all keepers, rough-shooters and pickers-up.

★ Price 27/6 plus 2/6 postage and packing from :—

SEA STAR FORGE · SELSEY CHICHESTER

1970 ADVERT

The "Marwood" Game Carrier.

Price 2/3 each, *postage paid.*

Suitable for all kinds of game, hares & rabbits.

Wood Game Carriers.

With Brass Trap, double .. **9/–** each, *postage paid.*
   „   „   ·, single. .. **5/6** „   „ „

Badger Tongs

This sturdy calliper type tool known as badger tongs were employed by both badger diggers and badger baiters and were still sold up to 1972 by Young's of Misterton at £5 each. The overall length of a pair of Badger tongs is approximately 36 inches. This consists of a handle length of approximately 24 inches, whilst the distance from the bottom of the handles to the end of the jaws is approximately 12 inches. The jaws have squared-off blunt ends, as the purpose is to hold the badger, usually by its neck skin, and not cut into the skin, which would happen if the jaw's ends tapered to a narrow edge. The jaw's diameter when shut, is approximately 3 inches across, but when opened out, $4^5/_8$ inches. Confusion surrounds badger digging and badger baiting, with the two generally being linked together as the same thing, which they certainly were not. Baiting was the digging out of badgers from their sett and capturing them alive and then transferring them to a pit where they were forced to fight for their lives against a team of dogs. Heavy gambling on the outcome was also involved. This practice of badger baiting has been prohibited in Britain since 1850. Badger digging however only became illegal in Britain in 1972. Digging was regarded as a service to the farmers as the badger is known to carry an infectious disease called Bovine TB which can be passed on to cattle and then by the cattle to the general public. Where outbreaks of Bovine TB have occurred, it has been found that 20% of the culled badgers were infected. Due to the badger diggers' use of terriers and digging out of the badgers from their sett, the general public linked the two activities together. However, in badger digging once the terriers had located the badger and kept it at bay in the underground sett, the digger dug

BADGER TONGS

SPRATT'S 1933 CATALOGUE

Spratt's Pocket Game Carrier

12 Leather Loops with wooden handle.
Strong and convenient   ..   4/6 each.
Postage Paid.

Game Basses or Fish Mats

Made in three sizes.
65/- per gross assorted. Carriage Paid.

down to the badger and used the tongs to grip the large and powerful animal by the neck to restrain it before it could be humanely dispatched.

Otter Boards

The poaching devices known as otter boards are usually made from a single wooden board with a weight affixed, to make sure the board floated in the correct way, like the keel of a sailboat. Double keeled otter boards, resembling a catamaran shape, are also known. A metal rod on one side had attached to it a length of fishing line, with attached to that separately, 6-10 artificial flies. A long, slightly heavier line was also attached securely to this rod, so that the poacher could control the 'otter board' from the water's edge. When not in use the heavier line is wound around a wooden 'flat reel', known as a twister, so that it doesn't get tangled up. The poacher used the otter board mainly on lochs, but this method could also be used on wide rivers. With the wind on his back, the poacher would push the otter board out towards the centre of the loch, unwinding the line off the twister, as the wind and water currents took hold of it. By holding on to the long heavier line the poacher would remain in control of it and could also pull it into shore at short notice if need be. With the action of the gentle wind and slightly choppy water, the flies would act as normal 'wet flies' that a legal fisherman uses. Used correctly this could be a very effective way of catching fish whilst remaining concealed. It has been illegal to use otter boards since 1861.

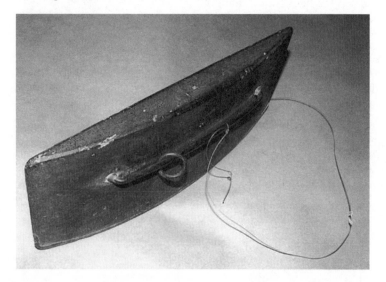

Dog Spikes

These were made of metal in the form of an arch, like a croquet hoop, with a single horizontal spike attached to the top pointing in both directions. The dog spike was then set into the ground across a known hare run at a height which allowed the hare to pass through it in either direction unhindered, whilst the pursuing poacher's dog, running at full stretch with its head down, ran into the spike with disastrous results for the dog.

Whistle

A small handy tool for the game-keeper was a whistle. This device had many functions. It was useful during the night, when he was on patrol for poachers, for signalling when to apprehend the offenders, or for summoning assistance from other gamekeepers. Another obvious use was for dog training. A whistle was also useful on shoot days, for the beginning and ending of the drives etc. This was signified by the different number or length of blasts produced by the whistle. Whistles were produced in various styles and included a folding whistle with a 12 bore cartridge extractor attached.

1910 ADVERT

Gamekeeper.

A nicely shaped 'best quality nickel plated whistle', simply known as the 'Gamekeeper' was sold by Hiatts of Birmingham and was illustrated in their catalogue at 14/6d per dozen in 1910. This whistle was made by B. Lilley & Co of 19 Barr Street, Birmingham and was made in three sizes, with and without the notch in the sound window. Production of the 'Gamekeeper' whistle ceased in 1905. In a Gilbertson & Page Ltd, unillustrated price list for September 1951, the 'Gamekeeper' whistle was priced at 4/6d each. Nothing is known regarding this later Gamekeeper whistle.

Game Despatch Boxes

Once the shot game had been collected up, they would then be taken by the game cart to be sorted out in the estate's game larder. From there it would be an easy task to deliver to the local game dealer. If though, the shot game had to travel many miles, such as the traditional first grouse shot on the 12th August, which usually ended up being sent to one of London's top class restaurants, then the birds were usually sent in some form of hamper. Gilbertson & Page were advertising in their 1913 catalogue 'Folding Game Despatch Boxes, complete with string and label . . . (which) . . . Fold up flat when not in use.' In their 1975 November price list, they were still selling

'Game Boxes, Despatch, Folding, with label. (13" x 7" x $4^{1}/_{2}$") per 10', for £2.00p.

It is interesting to note that in the 1896 edition of 'The Country Gentlemen's Catalogue' an advert mentioned 'Thos.P.Bethell, Plain & Fancy Cardboard Box Maker. Patentee & Sole Manufacturer of The 'Unique' Folding Postal Box. 115, Islington, corner of Soho St. Liverpool.' Not only did he sell postal boxes for 'Fruit, cut flowers, eggs, bottles etc' but he also advertised 'Unique Folding Boxes for the transit of Game' in six various sizes.

Folding Game Despatch Boxes.

Complete with string and label. May be forwarded by post or rail. Great saving of time and temper. Fold up flat when not in use.

To hold 1 brace Grouse or Partridges, 2/6 per doz.
,, 2 ,, ,, ,, 3/- ,,
,, 1 ,, Pheasants ,, 3/6 ,,
Post free.

Telegrams:—
"UNIQUE BOXES, LIVERPOOL."
Telephone No. 5238.

LONDON, 1865.

LONDON, 1887.

"Unique" Folding Boxes for the Transit of Game.

Length	Breadth	Depth	Per doz. nett.	Postage Extra.	Per 100 nett Free by Rail.		
No. 1 ... 7	... 5	... 3	... 2s 4d ...	6d	... 17s 6d	to hold	Small Game
,, 2 ... 9	... 7	... 3½	... 3s 0d ...	1s 0d	... 23s 6d	,,	1 Brace Grouse / 1 Leash Partridges
,, 3 ... 14	... 7	... 3½	... 3s 9d ...	1s 4½d	... 29s 3d	,,	2 Brace Grouse / 3 Brace Partridges
,, 4 ... 11	... 8	... 6	... 4s 3d ...	1s 6d	... 33s 3d	,,	3 Brace Grouse / 1 Brace Pheasants
,, 5 ... 14	... 7½	... 7½	... 4s 9d ...	1s 9d	... 37s 3d	,,	4 Brace Grouse
,, 6 ... 16	... 8	... 4½	... 5s 3d ...	2s 0d	... 41s 0d	,,	1 Leash Pheasants

Orders over 20s. Free by Rail to nearest station.

Kohler Signal Horn

In Gilbertson and Page's catalogues, dated 1909 and 1913, there appears exactly the same advert for the Kohler signal horn. Part of the advert states that 'Sportsmen will find the horn preferable to a whistle as its sound will carry considerably further.' Some gamekeepers signalled the start of the 'drive' by sounding a whistle, to let the guests know that the beaters would be starting to head their way, steadily moving the birds towards them. At the end of the 'drive' a horn would be sounded, to stop the guests from further shooting. Due to the loud noise created by the many guests firing their shotguns constantly at the steady stream of overhead pheasants etc, a louder and different sound, signifying the end, would be used. The Kohler horn was ideal for making this distinction. In 1935 Gilbertson & Page were listing in their catalogue Kohler horns, single note, 5in long 5/6d each, double note polished brass 12/6d each, double note imitation silver 12/6d each all post paid. In 1937 the price had risen to 6/- each for the single note and 13/6d each for the double note, postage paid. In February 1951 Gilbertson & Page were advertising 'Horns, (Signal) Single note, 6in. nickel plate, each 8/-, Single note 6in. brass 10/6 each, Single note $8^1/_2$in. nickel plate 15/6 each.' There was no illustration with the price list, so it is not known if these horns listed are Kohler horns. Kohler horns are known to be marked on the horn with Kohler & Son, Bromley, Kent. Above the maker's name there are two small marks, bearing the dates 1851 and 1852. Later models are known to have the words stamped 'Swaine & Adeney, 185, Piccadilly, London. Proprietor of Kohler & Son'. Again the dates are above the writing. The wording, The Kohler Signal Horn is also stamped on the opposite side of the horn to the maker's name and address.

Eel Spears/Gaffs

Both of these items were used for legal purposes and of course when the opportunity arose, illegal purposes as their owner desired. In 1972, in Young's catalogue, eel spear heads were being sold at £1.50 with three prongs, £1.75 with four prongs and £2.00 with five prongs. Wooden shafts were added with lengths ranging from approximately five feet up to about 20 feet. Gaffs with telescopic shafts, which could be easily concealed in large inside pockets sewn into coats, were a favourite with casual poachers who knew where to find a fish lying in shallow water. In 1883 a Mr. Henry Ffennell exhibited his extensive collection of salmon poaching equipment, which consisted of several hundred implements, at the International Fisheries Exhibition. The collection contained no models and all the implements shown were actually seized by water bailiffs from poachers who were caught whilst in the act. Many exhibits had labels attached to them telling of the fate of their previous owners. One example was a seven pronged spear that was taken from a poacher on the River Wye near Builth. The man was tried and found guilty 'of using lights and spears and killing three salmon during close season.' He was fined £11 and costs. Reproduced on page 373 is the article that accompanied the illustrations.

EEL SPEARS

The Prongs are about ⅜in. wide, having small sharp points about ¼in. along both edges of prong. Well made, with iron socket for fixing a pole or handle. With 3 prongs, £1·50 ; 4 prongs, £1·75 ; 5 prongs, £2·00

Nets

As well as the nets used in fish poaching, various other types of nets were used on land. These ranged in size from the purse nets, that were placed in front of the rabbit burrow when the rabbit was being evicted by the ferret, to the long nets which could be up to 100 yards in length, used to intercept the rabbits when they were chased back from their feeding ground to their burrows by the gamekeeper's or poacher's dog.

BOULTON & PAUL ADVERT (1908)

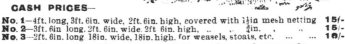

THE 'DOUGLAS' DEVICE
(IN CIRCLE SHOWS DEVICE IN DROPPED POSITION)
YOUNG'S 1940 CATALOGUE

'DOUGLAS' RABBIT NET DEVICE
FOR LONG RABBIT NETS

The supports, 4ft. 2ins. long, are of Ash, and the arms of beech – the former with steel ferrules at top for driving with a mallet.

The fittings are of brass so as to avoid rust and the whole light in weight and easily portable.

The operation is similar to that of the 'Collington', as one pull of the release line drops the arms on which the net is placed in the raised position and allows the net to fall to form a perfect rabbit-catching barrier.

The illustration shows the general construction and method of dropping the net.

Prices: 10 supports with arms and release pins for 100 yards run, together with 2 ground pegs and 150 yards of release line, **£1/15/9**.

165 yards tanned and lined 4ft. 4-ply net to set the above. **£3/0/0**.

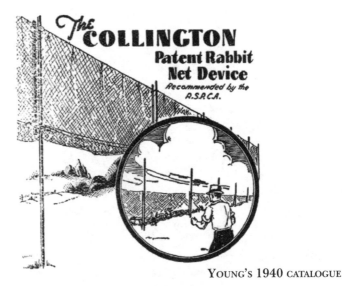

The COLLINGTON
Patent Rabbit Net Device
Recommended by the R.S.P.C.A.

COLLINGTON'S PATENT NET SUPPORTS
FOR LONG RABBIT NETS

With these Supports the Nets can be set up at any time. The Net is run out in the ordinary way, and is then pushed up on these supports and kept up on the pole with a small pin, so that the Rabbits pass out under the Net. The small pins keeping the Net up in position are connected to a line, the end of which can be carried back out of sight. When it is desired to catch the Rabbits one sharp pull of the line will allow the Net to drop into position to catch all rabbits that are out feeding. If this is done during the night the net can be slipped up the poles and dropped again in the early morning. The Appliance can be left standing as long as is required or until all Rabbits are cleared.

HINTS TO OPERATOR

The appliance can be set on most types of ground, but is especially suitable for burrows, woodsides and hedges. Where the ground is uneven, small weights can be attached to the net to ensure that no space is left between the ground and net when dropped.

The operator should avoid, if possible, getting to the windward of rabbits when about to drop net. Strict silence should be observed before net is dropped.

After the drive is over, the operator should run along the net and despatch the rabbits at once. They are usually found hopelessly entangled (though quite unhurt), and in order to kill them, grasp the head firmly in one hand and the shoulders in the other, and force the hands together, thus causing death instantaneously.

WILDFOWL NETTING IN LINCOLNSHIRE (1888)

RABBIT NETTING IN EPPING FOREST (1847)

THE "SUFFOLK" EEL AND FISH TRAPS

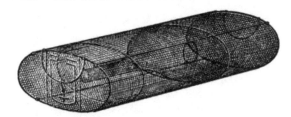

One of the most successful traps on the market, self-acting, will catch large numbers without attention, strongly made with heavy gauge ½in. mesh galvanised wire netting, on strong framework. The traps are 30ins. long, and 14ins. wide.

Trapping hints sent with each trap, price **£5·00.**

The following testimonials give excellent proof of their efficiency :—

Mr. W. J. S. Moore, 1 Oswald Cotts, Bridge Road, Oulton Broad, writes :—
"Received Traps safely, very pleased with them, they are fishing very well indeed, and I wish you to send me another 20 Traps. I shall be sending another order later, when you have supplied this lot."

Mr. R. W. Beney, 6 Stanley Road, Oulton Broad, Lowestoft, writes :—
"Traps working well, I enclose cheque to cover cost of 40 Eel Traps, please send soon as possible."

Mr. W. Victor Gee, The Old House, Eye, Peterborough, writes :—
"I have tried one of your Eel Traps in a river with a few worms in a tobacco tin inside it and left it for 24 hours. When I pulled it out I was amazed ; it was crammed full of eels. I have never seen so many eels in one trap."

YOUNG'S ORIGINAL EEL TRAPS, with Double Entry

The Trap is very effective. Automatically catches any quantity of Eels without attention. Always set, always ready. Made from Fine Galvanised Wire Netting. Last a life-time. 1yd. long, **£3·50**; 3 for **£10·00** ; 4ft. long, **£4·00** ; 3 for **£11·50**

With trapping hints, best times, baits, best position for traps, etc.

FISH TRAPS

Similar to Eel Trap. Also same price.

MINNOW TRAP

Celluloid, collapsing telescopic. **£1·35** each.

MINNOW TRAPS

Similar to Eel Traps above, only made in Best Fine Mesh. Also 2ft. long, **£2·50**; 3 for **£7·00**

STRONG ROPE

⅜in. diameter, **40p** lb. Also size ⅛—³⁄₁₆ and ¼ inch diameter at **45p** per lb. (The ⅜in. rope, runs about 7yds. to the lb.).

CORKS AND LEADS

For Fishing Nets. Corks, **£1·00** doz. 4oz. Leads, **£1·75** doz.

SEE FRONT COVER FOR INCREASED POSTAL RATES

S Young & Sons (Misterton) Ltd. catalogue 1972

Aug. 18, 1883

THE INTERNATIONAL FISHERIES EXHIBITION.
SALMON POACHING IMPLEMENTS.

Mr. Henry Ffennell's collection of salmon poaching
implements at the International Fisheries Exhibition is
unique; nothing of the kind has been attempted before.
This collection, which is displayed on the walls and counter
of the first division in the East Quadrant, numbers several
hundreds of implements. It will be a revelation to many of
the ingenuity which is applied to the craft of the salmon
poacher. The number of names of rivers that appear in the
exhibit show that it is completely representative of the
subject. The collection contains no models. All the
implements shown are actual weapons of war seized by
water-bailiffs from marauders caught red-handed, *in
flagrante delicto,* harrying the salmon on the breeding beds
and elsewhere, along the rivers and streams of England and
Wales. It is interesting to note that some of the implements
were taken within a few weeks of the opening of the
Exhibition. To many of the captured implements are
attached labels, telling the exact penalty inflicted upon the
man caught with that particular instrument of salmon
destruction. Some of these penalties, by-the-way, appear to
be pretty stiff. As an example of this, we may cite the seven-
pronged spear delineated among our illustrations, which
was taken from a poacher on the River Wye, near Builth.
The man was tried and found guilty 'of using lights and
spears and killing three salmon during close season.' The
penalty inflicted was £11 and costs. The blacksmiths who
manufacture such spears for the poachers have, of course,
to do so in secrecy.

It is curious to note the differences there are in the rude
designs which characterise the poaching salmon-spears of
various districts. The Wye poaching spear, which we have
just alluded to, is not formed on at all the same principle as
the salmon-spear used by poachers on the River Dovey. The
salmon leister, with its nine barbed prongs, used in the
Cumberland and Westmoreland rivers, is very dissimilar
from the unbarbed four-pronged salmon-spear of the Usk
and Ebbw. The spear from the River Seiont, with its three
prongs, only two of which are pronged, differs also from the
three pronged spear of the River Lune. Both these,
however, bear a certain amount of resemblance in their
form to the wooden and bone spears used by the Eskimos
and various tribes of North American Indians. Another
variety of salmon-spear is that we have drawn with four
slanting unbarbed prongs. This is remarkable as a pattern

of the implement alluded by Sir Walter Scott in *Red Gauntlet*, where he tells of the salmon spearing on horseback in the shallow waters of the Solway Firth. In the same engraving is shown a very curious salmon snatch, taken from a poacher on the River Wear. The man was fined £1 for having the implement in his possession. We have given two groups of gaffs or click-hooks, seized in the Usk and Ebbw district. In Mr. Ffennell's collection there are no fewer than 240 of these instruments, which were all seized along the Usk and Ebbw; and the Inspector of Salmon Fisheries' reports indicate that this is the favourite weapon of the poacher on those particular rivers. From the River Eden and the West Cumberland rivers we give several examples of various kinds of deadly snatches and click-hooks. Some of these are drawn through the water with a cord. Others, as will be seen, are furnished with a metal funnel, attached to the iron hook. These are generally carried in the poacher's pocket, as he walks along the banks of the river and watches his opportunity, when the coast is clear, to pull a stake out of the fence or cut a long rod from a tree; and then, knowing well where the salmon lies, with this long-handled gaff he makes short work of the fish. The drag shown from the Derwent river, with an oyster-shell at the end to attract the fish, is worked by a rope between two men, one on each bank of the river.

The poaching nets, of which we give a representation, are the shackle or double-armoured nets. This style of fishing for salmon, supposing the mesh to be of suitable dimensions, is not illegal in all districts, but is very deadly in its capturing power; and, of course, becomes a poaching implement on those rivers where its use has not been specially legalised. The standing net, from the Usk and Ebbw, is used by the poacher who knows the lie of the fish, and dips his net into the hole where the salmon rests under the bank. Along with the nets, we give drawing of two anti-poacher implements, invented by Mr. Mostyn Owen. These are wonderfully simple and effectual contrivances, calculated to lie concealed in the water. They tear the poacher's nets to pieces, making it impossible for him to carry on his operations, and destroying his gear. Our remaining illustration shows the rude form of dark lantern affected by the salmon poacher; and the more elaborate naphtha torch which can be flared up in a moment, and as quickly extinguished or darkened by returning it into the metal case.

Anyone who wishes to understand the deadly injury inflicted upon the salmon fisheries by poachers may consult the official reports presented every year to Parliament; from these we learn that there have been during the last three years 1512 men convicted for salmon poaching.

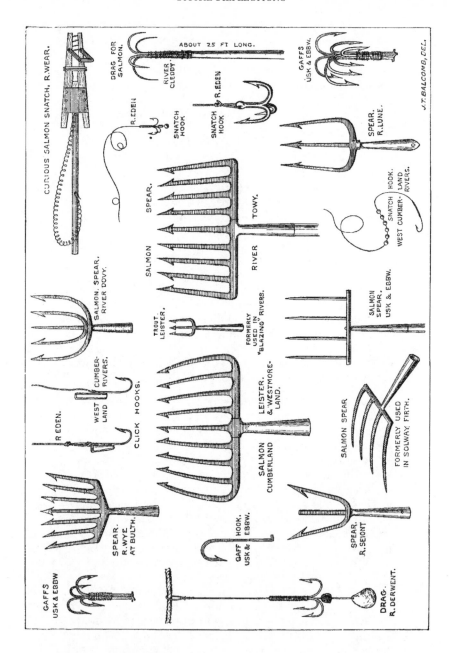

A PRESENTATION OF SALMON
POACHING IMPLEMENTS AND THE
RIVERS IN WHICH THEY ARE
COMMONLY USED AT THE
INTERNATIONAL FISHERIES
EXHIBITION OF 1883

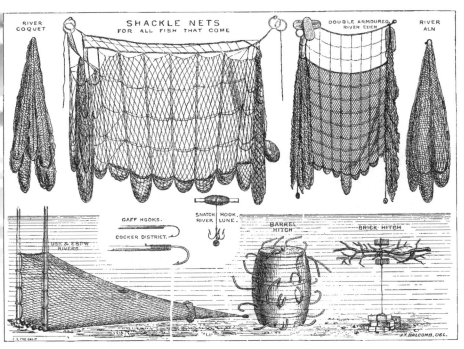

A PRESENTATION AT THE INTERNATIONAL FISHERIES EXHIBITION OF
1883 OF SHACKLE NETS USED FOR SALMON POACHING

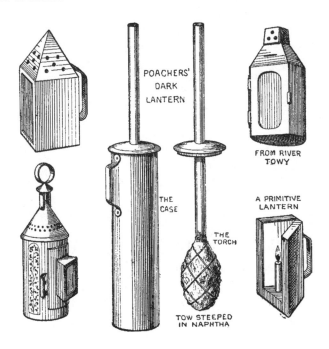

SALMON POACHER'S LANTERNS

THE BENT HAZEL STICK AND NOOSE MOLE TRAP (1904)

Chapter Eight

MOLE AND RAT CONTROL

ALTHOUGH mole traps were commercially produced by such companies as National Patent Company of Johnstone, Renfrewshire, Scotland most early wooden types of traps would have been made by the mole catcher himself, or the component parts purchased separately and assembled at his leisure. During the 1890s and early 1900s articles appeared in Work – the Illustrated Weekly Journal for Mechanics showing how to make your own mole traps as well as 'useful mouse traps'. In the 15th April 1899 issue these mouse traps consist of The Block trap, more often referred to as the Deadfall, a live catch single slide down door trap, made from wood and metal wires, and the wooden parts that form the figure 4 in a brick deadfall trap. In a later issue, 7th January 1911, a more elaborate 'house shaped' live cage trap, again made from wood and metal wire is described and illustrated. It is said to be 'of rather original form, and has stood the test of many years as a first rate trapper of mice'. Instructions such as these would be easily understood by anyone, which would result in the same design of trap being produced throughout Britain by various amateur makers.

Indeed, a reply featured on 5th December 1891, states regarding flat topped wooden mole traps,

WOOD BARREL MOLE TRAP
Full Barrel

WOOD BARREL MOLE TRAP
Half Barrel

No. 115. Sudden Death Mouse Trap.

THIS is the most certain trap ever invented for the destruction of mice, they simply run into it for shelter, and none escape.

Cash Price - 2/6 each

Place trap against the wall, and the mice will run into it for shelter.
If there is a mouse in the house this trap will catch it.

BOULTON & PAUL, NORWICH CATALOGUE 1902

E.R.D. (Sherborne) sends the following method of making mole traps in reply to J.J. (Cumberland).

This reference alone, complete with illustrations, shows how a simple design can quickly spread from the south coast of England to the northern limits of England and beyond.

Another correspondent, this time replying in the 17th October 1903 issue, describes how to make the wooden full barrel mole trap, with the 'spring made of stout steel wire', again complete with detailed illustrations. He comments that 'the principle of this trap is similar to a very old form of trap that is still in use in some parts of the country'. He then goes on to describe the wooden flat-topped mole trap. His accompanying illustration shows both types of mole trap. In the book *The Balance of Nature* published in 1909 are two illustrations of 'The Common Wood Mole Traps', the first showing both the 'tube trap' and the 'board top' trap, now known as the wooden full barrel and the wooden flat topped mole traps. The second illustration, again shows the same two traps, but this time because they have a flat metal spring to operate them they are called 'The Kent Garden Tube' and 'Board-Top Mole Traps'.

An unusual copy of a wooden full barrel mole trap was made out of baked clay. This type of trap is basically a modification of an ordinary terracotta field drain, with the bottom middle section and holes cut out before it was 'fired' in the potter's kiln. In the late Victorian period, a mole catcher, Thomas Turner of Tingewick, Buckinghamshire, is known to have had his initials TT, permanently put onto his clay mole traps.

Obviously, metal mole traps were also being used, but the wooden types had the advantage of being cheaper and were easily repaired. Young's of Misterton were advertising in their September 1940 catalogue several different types of mole traps. Included were the common metal 'pincher' type with the 'two flat steel springs', the Anglo-Impassable, the wooden half-barrel

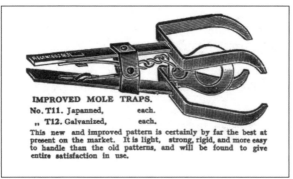

IMPROVED MOLE TRAP AS DISPLAYED IN THE CATALOGUE OF
THE MIDLAND GUN COMPANY, 1937

'with best coppered red steel spring', and surprisingly 'The Enterprise' spring mole trap. The 'Enterprise' mole trap was described as 'similar to the above Half-Barrel traps, only with flat wood top, and copper wire loops instead of cord. Hundreds of these traps are supplied to professional mole trappers in all parts every season, and considered by them to be the best on the market. Price 13/- per dozen, 7/- per half dozen, single traps 1/4d each. Carriage paid.'

One type of metal mole trap not favoured by the professional mole catcher was the guillotine spear type patented in 1888 and known variously as the Anglo-Impassable or the Slayer. The reason for this dislike was because the trap's spikes, upon impaling the mole, totally ruined the mole skin, therefore rendering it useless for selling to the furrier.

This creature's pelt was the origin of the original material for moleskin trousers, waistcoats, hats etc. 'Moleskin' is now made of a fine piled cotton fustian which has had its surface shaved before dying a dark dull colour to resemble the true product.

The mole catching season usually lasted from 1st November through to the end of June the following year, according to Arthur Randell in his book *Fenland Molecatcher* (1970). If purely trapping moles for their pelts though, Guy N. Smith in *Moles and Their Control* (1980) states, 'The mole trapping season lasts approximately from November to March, but it is during the first ten weeks that the pelts will fetch the best prices. After the December moult it is barely worth the trouble of skinning your catches.'

These good quality pelts were known as best winter clears. After the good quality pelts had been trapped and only inferior pelts left, the mole trapper would hang from a farmer's fence a row of freshly caught moles to let him know that he was still doing his job around the fields.

Some farmers suspected that the old mole catcher was only catching

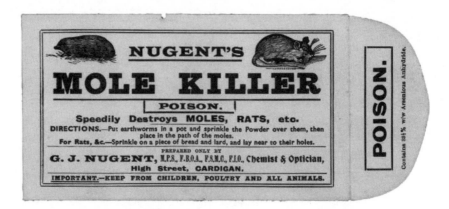

enough moles off their farms to sell to the furrier, and therefore leaving a breeding stock, for next year. These farmers preferred a mole catcher not to use traps but to poison them. Moles that had been poisoned by strychnine etc were unfit for sale to the furrier. Nowadays, a permit is needed to control moles by the use of strychnine poison. This permit only allows the strychnine poison to be used for the underground control of moles, and only for moles. Anyone using strychnine for anything other than mole control is breaking the law. Indeed, a letter by Dr Sue Popple, Director of Policy, at the Pesticides Safety Directorate, appeared in the 17th March 2005 issue of *The Countryman's Weekly*.

> In the UK strychnine hydrochloride can only be used legally to control moles. This is laid down in the *Animal (Cruel Poisons) Act 1962*, and the resulting *Animals (Cruel Poisons) Regulations 1963*. The conditions of approval for the use of strychnine hydrochloride for mole control are strictly regulated by the *Poisons Rules (1982)*, and *Control of Pesticides Regulations 1986* (COPR) (as amended), made under the *Food and Environment Protection Act 1985* (FEPA). To suggest that strychnine hydrochloride can be used to control other common pests is dangerous and misleading.

Farmers didn't want moles in their fields because livestock could break a leg, if their foot sank into a mole hole or run. Gamekeepers also dislike moles because their constant burrowing can get them under the protective wire of a release pen and thereby allow a weasel later access to slaughter the confined and immature poults.

No. 236 Round

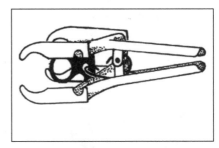

GALVANISED MOLETRAP WITH HALF
ROUND SECTION HANDLES
(1952 CATALOGUE)

NO 236R MOLE SPADE; ALL BRIGHT,
T HANDLE P& R FLEMING & CO
GLASGOW 1953 CATALOGUE

1903 SCOTTISH BILL FOR MOLE CATCHING

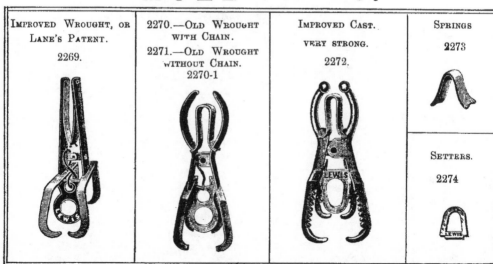

AN UNKNOWN MAKE OF HALF BARREL MOLE TRAP

MOLE TRAPS.

IMPROVED WROUGHT, OR LANE'S PATENT. 2269.	2270.—OLD WROUGHT WITH CHAIN. 2271.—OLD WROUGHT WITHOUT CHAIN. 2270-1	IMPROVED CAST. VERY STRONG. 2272.	SPRINGS 2273
			SETTERS. 2274

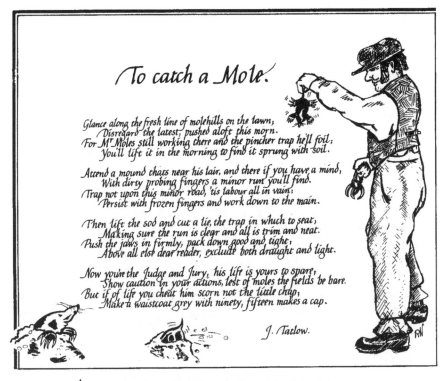

To catch a Mole.

Glance along the fresh line of molehills on the lawn,
   Disregard the latest, pushed aloft this morn.
For Mr Moles still working there and the pincher trap he'll foil;
   You'll lift it in the morning to find it sprung with soil.

Attend a mound thats near his lair, and there if you have a mind;
   With dirty probing fingers a minor run you'll find.
Trap not upon this minor road, 'tis labour all in vain;
   Persist with frozen fingers and work down to the main.

Then lift the sod and cut a lie, the trap in which to seat;
   Making sure the run is clear and all is trim and neat.
Push the jaws in firmly, pack down good and tight;
   Above all else dear reader, exclude both draught and light.

Now you're the Judge and Jury, his life is yours to spare;
   Show caution in your actions, lest of moles the fields be bare.
But if of life you cheat him scorn not the little chap;
   Make a waistcoat grey with ninety, fifteen makes a cap.

                                        J. Tatlow.

**AN AGE OLD PROBLEM GIVEN POETICAL TREATMENT IN A
1980 ISSUE OF SHOOTING TIMES & COUNTRY MAGAZINE**

MOLE TRAPS.

PRICE PER DOZEN JAPANNED.

No. 166.   No. 167.

FLAT SPRING.   SPIRAL SPRING.

4/6   4/6

**IN A 1938 GENERAL CATALOGUE, SPIRAL SPRING MOLE TRAPS
WERE PRICED AT 4/6 PER DOZEN**

Official Ratcatcher to Her Majesty

As a note of interest, during the reign of Queen Victoria (1837-1901) there was a man living in London called 'Jack' Black who was employed as the Official Ratcatcher to Her Majesty. His hand bills were headed 'V.R.Rat and Mole Destroyer to Her Majesty'. His costume or uniform consisted of white leather breeches, a green coat with scarlet waistcoat, and a gold band round his hat with a belt across his shoulder. His belts were painted with four white rats by Mr. Bailey, an animal painter, but later he decided to have the rats cast in metal and fixed onto his belt for more effect. His cart also had rats painted around it. When he was first employed by the Government, under the Superintendent of Parks, he was to have been paid six pounds a year, but after that it was altered to three pence a head. Not only did he exterminate rats but he also bred them. In his own words 'I've bred the finest collection of pied rats which has ever been knowed in the world. I had about eleven hundred of them – all wariegated rats, and of a different specie and colour, and all of them in the first instance breed from the Norwegian and the white rat, and

afterwards crossed with other specie. I have 'em fawn and white, black and white, brown and white, red and white, blue-black and white, black-white and red. When I sold 'em off, 300 of them went to France.' The descendants of these rats bred by 'Jack' Black are held in high regard by Britain's National Fancy Rats Society members.

The last royal rat catcher was Mr Edward Pritchard of Twickenham, London. He had a ratting dog which was a mixture of spaniel and bull terrier. This dog, Punch, as he was known, was so efficient at killing rats that in Queen Victoria's jubilee year of 1887, the local shopkeepers of Twickenham, bought him a

JACK BLACK, HER MAJESTY'S RATCATCHER

handsome collar and had it engraved 'The Royal Rat-catcher'. The royal rat catcher's office was abolished in 1908. However, local county councils still employed ratcatchers and even today Environmental Health Departments of local councils employ Pest Control Officers part of whose duties is controlling any rat infestation.

According to the book written by another Victorian Ratcatcher *Full Revelations of a Professional Ratcatcher, After 25 Years Experience*, Ike Matthews, not only were rat catchers employed to eradicate rats from farms, town buildings etc., they were also paid by country gentlemen and other people of a sporting nature to capture live rats for rat coursing and for pitting dogs, usually terriers, against the rats in rat pits. Ike Matthews states,

> 'The rat pit is of circular construction, say ten feet diameter, and about four feet six inches deep, the sides being perfectly smooth to prevent the rats climbing up and making their escape. A certain number of rats are placed in the pit according to the arrangements made with the owner of the dog. Then the dog is put in the pit with the rats to kill them, which a good dog does very quickly. The reason the pit is built circular is so that the rats will keep running round, for if it were square they would all run in a corner, one on the other, and the dog would have no difficulty in killing them. It is better to have the pit fairly deep; if not, the rats might escape.'

He also mentions that 'It was a common thing for a rat catcher to receive an order for 100 rats' and he even 'supplied 400 rats in one week, all to be killed in rat pits.' Rats were also caught alive to be used in training terriers to 'course' and catch rats out in the open. These sporting activities, like cock fighting, also involved heavy gambling and were eventually made illegal. Rat infestations also commonly occurred aboard sailing ships and obviously had to be dealt with. In the January 1857 issue of the *Quarterly Review* (No. 201) it is reported that 'The rat catcher to the East India Company has often destroyed as many as five hundred (rats) in a ship newly arrived from Calcutta.'

Social life and values had changed after World War I and people in the intervening years before World War II were trying to adjust accordingly. The 'Great Depression' years of the late 1920s and 30s caused further hardships with again war looking imminent. World War II came as expected, bringing with it devastation and destruction. The ruined bombed out shells of buildings and insanitary conditions caused by the war created ideal breeding areas for rats. To help bring this situation under control, under a Government scheme, 850 rat catchers were employed in the eradication of rat infestations on farms and in shops. As many as 200 of these rat catchers were members of the Women's Land Army. It was estimated that during 1942 the value of food and feeding stuffs for livestock eaten or spoiled by rats amounted to £25 million per year and cost the farmer six shillings a year for every rat on his farm.

Although rat catching is part of general vermin control done by gamekeepers, it has always been a specialist job for others. Already, previously mentioned, was 'Jack' Black, the rat catcher to her Majesty Queen Victoria, and today's modern pest control operator. In fact though, since man has sown, harvested and stored grain and other food items for his own benefit, he has waged continual war upon the rat. The first serious attempt at co-ordinated rat control occurred when the Rats and Mice Destruction Act was introduced in 1919. This act also encouraged people to control their own rat problems. Occasionally, before World War II, the Government would announce a National Rat Week, in order to encourage the general public to try to control the expanding rat population through out the country. One such week occurred from 2nd – 7th November 1936, and such businesses that produced rat poisons would obviously take advantage of this occasion to heavily advertise their deadly products and boost their sales.

In later years the County Boroughs of Northampton, Leicestershire and Rutland joined together in a rat control campaign. One such campaign was started by these co-operating local authorities on Monday 26th November 1973, who also requested that all farmers and anyone else who had an interest in the countryside and its wildlife should help to try and exterminate the rat in their immediate area.

The tools used against the rat basically amount to, traps of various types, poisons and a good ratting dog, usually some sort of terrier. Small white ferrets were also used to bolt the rats from their underground stronghold. Pure white ferrets would only be used, because in the excitement of trying to kill anything that emerged from a hole, a white shape appearing would be instantly recognised from that of a dark-shaped rat. Ratting dogs were usually kept in close proximity to the ferrets, so that the dogs were used to seeing them about and could hopefully recognise them in the heat of battle. The very alert terrier would be waiting to pounce on the rat, once it emerged and tried to escape, resulting in a quick grab and a shake of the terrier's head, leaving another dead rat on the floor. Sometimes though, the terrier misjudged its killer strike, and would end up being severely bitten by a very angry rat hanging from its face.

If a ferret was not available to flush the rats from their home, then an artificial aid could be used. Young's of Misterton were supplying from their 1972 catalogue a 'Grand Invention – Bolting Fuse'. This could be used, 'for bolting Rats and Rabbits' and was 'a good cure for a ferret if it lies up, will make him bolt as well'. If neither a ferret nor a Bolting Fuse was available at the time, then you could always dig the rats out for your terrier, using a special ratting spade. Mark Hovell, writing in his book *Rats and How to Destroy Them*, published in 1924, describes the qualities needed in a ratting spade and is reproduced overleaf in full.

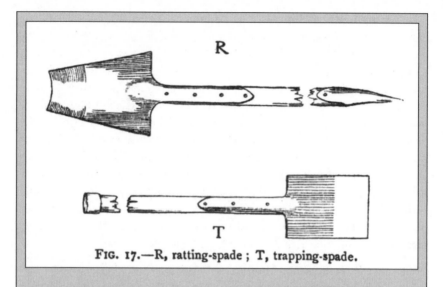

FIG. 17.—R, ratting-spade ; T, trapping-spade.

A ratting spade must be light, but yet strong, the handle therefore should be made of a good piece of ash, and the other parts of well-tempered steel, and the bottom edge of the blade must be sharp enough to cut quickly through roots. The ideal spade is about 4ft in length, the handle immediately above the blade being not more than $1\frac{1}{4}$ inch in diameter, and the blade, which should be as light as possible, consistent with the necessary strength, about 8 inches long, 5 to $5\frac{1}{2}$ inches wide across the top and 3 to $3\frac{1}{2}$ inches wide across the bottom. The blade, although shorter, is in shape somewhat similar to a Norfolk rabbiting-spade, which is smaller, and slightly hollowed at the bottom, and tapers to the square-shouldered top. The handle, instead of having a hook at the upper end, as in the case of a rabbiting-spade, is attenuated for several inches to a sharp point, and cased in iron just as a dibble is cased. The sharp end is required to feel for a lost hole; a long dig and much time will frequently be saved by finding it.

A trapping-spade is usually about 3 feet in length, and its blade, which should be the same width at the top and bottom, about 6 inches long and $4\frac{1}{4}$ inches wide. But instead of being furnished with a spike at the other end, the handle should be cut off at a right angle, so as to make the end flat, and this should be shod with a band of iron to prevent its edges getting broken when it is used to drive into the ground the pegs to which the traps are fastened.

A ratting-blade will do for a trapping spade, but a trapping - blade is not suitable for a ratting-spade. If retail dealers do not wish to stock both patterns, it would be better for them to stock ratting-spades, and to affix a spike or iron band to the top of the handle as required.

from *Rats and How to Destrouy Them* Mark Hovell (1924)

Poisons

Many and varied were the poisons used against rats and vermin generally, and I couldn't possibly list them all. However, I will mention a few interesting ones.

Sheared Lip Bottles

The earliest type of bottle, and the simplest in form, are known collectively, as sheared lip. The shear lips, as they are more commonly known by bottle collectors, were produced by the glass blower allowing his finished blown bottle to cool sufficiently hard enough to be snapped or sheared off from the end of his iron blowpipe. The finished bottle would then be allowed to cool slowly on a shelf in the furnace flue, where it would gradually become hardened due to the process of the glass annealing. Where the bottle was sheared off, a jagged edge around the neck would be left. This proved ideal for creating a secure seal, as the jagged edge would bite into the cork when it was pushed into the neck. Shear Lips can be found on the neck of Victorian glass fly traps as well as poison bottles. It would take time for an old method of production to finally fade away, but certainly by 1910 it would have been obsolete. This would be due to the more efficient Rolled Lips, as found on beer bottles for example, and the mass produced moulded type of glass. Due to the introduction of hinged mould's during the nineteenth century, it became possible to have embossed lettering or a simple design put onto a bottle. Some early sheared lip bottles only have the name of the contents, or the vendor, embossed on them. One poison bottle has both, plus a pictorial design.

Farmer's Rat Paste

This rat paste poison, came in four different sized bottles. All the bottle sizes quoted are approximate, as it depended upon where the shear lip neck actually snapped off. Surprisingly though, the sizes don't vary by very much. The largest size being 4 inches (10cm) high, medium size, $2^3/_4$ inches (7cm) high, small size 2 inches (5cm) high. The smallest size of bottle, is just under 2 inches tall, but is only $1^1/_8$ inch in diameter, compared to a diameter of very nearly $1^1/_2$ inches for the normal small sized bottle. The bottles are known to be found in colours ranging from clear glass, pale green also known as green aqua, pale blue or blue aqua, but which is usually known as columbine blue, and a rich dark blue known as cobolt blue. There is also an amber coloured bottle. The embossed wording FARMERS RAT PASTE and pictorial rat are to be found in various combinations on the different bottles.

Large Bottle: On the base, a pictorial rat in the centre of the base, facing to the right, surrounded around the edge with the words in capital letters FARMERS RAT PASTE.

Medium Bottle: (Type a) Pictorial Rat in the centre of the base, surrounding the edge with the words in capital letters FARMERS RAT PASTE.

Medium Bottle: (Type b) Pictorial Rat only on the base, with FARMERS RAT PASTE, again in capital letters, around the shoulder of the bottle, below the neck.

Small Bottle: This bottle is the same design as the Medium (Type a) bottle.

Very Small Bottle: On the base, a Pictorial Rat, only. The pictorial rat faces the same way on all the bottles.

Another type exists that has no pictorial rat on it. The base simply has FARMERS around one edge and directly opposite on the other edge the word PASTE. Across the centre in between the two words is the word RAT. All the wording is in capital letters.

It is most likely, but not definitely established, that the manufacturer of Farmer's Rat Paste was Frederick Farmer & Co, who was located in the east end of London. Frederick Farmer first appears in the 1904 London directory described as a 'vermin destroyer', his address being given as 17, Poole Road, Hackney. There is no mention of him in Kelly's directory for Hackney and Homerton in 1907, but he is listed in the 1909 edition at 1a, College Lane, Homerton. In 1924, an advert states that 'For the speedy destruction of Rats, Mice & Beetles use RATMOUSINE (which) dries up the carcase'. In this advert the business is described as '& Co'. The last mention of this company is in Kelly's directory for 1951. It is reasonable to suggest that Frederick Farmer, first used his Farmer's Rat Paste poison in shear lip bottles. However, when this type of bottle became obsolete, he took advantage of the situation and changed the poison's image with his new type of containers. Therefore, it is possible that Farmer's Rat Paste then became 'Ratmousine' which according to the 1924 advert was 'Sold everywhere in Tubes and Jars. $7\frac{1}{2}$d & 1/3 each'.

Cheeseman's Rat Poison

Mystery surrounds this product, because the trade directories only list Cheesman's as an Oyster Room from 1877 to about 1934 when the building became a hairdressers' wholesaler. The building was demolished about 1940 in preparation for a new town hall and police station. According to a surviving 'pot lid', off a pottery jar, the lid states 'Cheesman's new Rat Poison. 19 Little East St. Brighton. Telephone. Brighton-1717'. In the centre of the pot lid is a drawing of Cheesman's building. Unfortunately, nothing else is known about this rat poison.

Rodine Rat Poison

This world famous product was invented by Thomas Harley who first appears in the trade directories for Perth, Scotland in 1891/92. Here he is listed as being a chemist and druggist at 21 High Street. Around about 1902, T. Harley seriously started marketing his rat poison, 'from a small room', as is recorded in *The Perthshire Advertiser*, dated 19th September 1928. Under the heading of The Pied Piper of Perth, the paper also reported that 'Rodine was put on the market some twenty six years ago by Mr Harley, and the demand for this efficient vermin destructor increased with such rapidity as to necessitate the resale of the poison by other chemists and an extention of the premises in which the business was carried on. A new factory was equipped in the immediate vicinity of his retail shop at 29 High Street, but in recent years it had become increasingly apparent that if Mr Harley's enterprise was not to be cramped, more suitable accommodation would have to be aquired. Mr Harley was fortunate to be able to take over the factory formerly occupied by Messrs Garvie & Deas, spinners and weavers, situated between South Methven Street and New Row. In the short period of three months, these premises were reported to have undergone a transformation and Rodine would henceforth be manufactured in premises which were the last word in equipment and convenience.

'There are four floors. The ground floor is utilised for storage purposes, while there is also a tin blocking plant which turns out tins for the reception of the poison at the rate of 1,000 an hour. An electric hoist conveys the tins to the second floor, where Rodine is manufactured, and the tins are filled for conveyance to the despatch room on the first floor. Printing plant is also installed, and it is significant of the extent of the business that stock with literature in three languages is seen on the shelves.

'Young women are engaged on one floor filling tins of Rodine at the rate of 1200 an hour, and to protect the health of those workers every precaution is taken. Then in the manufacturing room the same care is taken, four fans being continually in motion clearing away the fumes. Tins for the reception of the poison are produced by machinery in the factory at the rate of 10 gross per hour, while another machine trims and finishes off from 1000 to 1200 boxes each hour. The establishment has also an extensive printing room, where show cards, circulars, etc, advertising Rodine are produced.'

The best evidence of the quality of Rodine and its ability to do what it purported to do, lay in the fact that it was used extensively throughout the world.

With the opening of his new factory in September 1928, Thomas Harley retired from being a retail chemist

to concentrate on the Rodine Works. A few years later in December 1932, he died. The business continued on after his death, by being converted into a Limited Company, with Sir Stanley Norie-Miller, Baronet, as the Chairman of the Board of Directors, and Mr.A.F.McIntosh as Managing Director. An article published in 1946, in *The Industries of Perthshire*, states that 'Notwithstanding the success attained in the past, Messrs.Thomas Harley Limited, have recently established Research Laboratories, fitted with up-to-date equipment, under the charge of trained and qualified personnel, licensed under the Home Office, whose business it is to test the raw materials which are used in the manufacture of RODINE. Each manufacture is tested for its toxic chemical content and also bio-assayed. For this purpose a colony of rats is kept, all being carefully selected animals of healthy strain. They are bred and maintained in the Laboratory, and only male rats are used in the test with Red Squill, as they are much more resistant to this poison than females. The average lethal dose of each consignment of Red Squill is determined by biological tests. Further, the tests are made on the compounded preparations for toxicity and attractiveness. Besides this routine checking and control, research goes on into new methods of control and the use of synthetic poisons. The prepared baits destined for export are subjected to a special test, having regard to the climatic conditions in which they are to be used. From this small but yet important industry of Perth there arise products which not only pass stringent Laboratory tests, but which in practice have proved themselves for nearly 50 years.'

In 1960 the company celebrated its Diamond Jubilee. Whilst, in the 22nd June 1960 issue of *The Perthshire Advertiser*, it was reported that Rodine products were being sold in 47 countries. The products being Rodine, Rodine Red Squill and Rodine Warfarin. The total sales of rat poisons during the firm's 60 years of existence amounted to 5,554,760 lbs. A few years later, in 1962, Rentokil Laboratories took over the company, and then closed the factory in 1964.

There were 4 different sizes of tins produced for the original Rodine Phosphoros rat poison. In 1928 the individual prices were 7½d, 1/3d, 2/6d and 5 shillings. These prices seem to have remained the same for a considerable time, as they are the same in *The Gamekeeper and Countryside* magazine issue of January 1948. However, in the February 1948 issue, the prices had increased to 1/6d, 3/-, 6/-. In neither issue was the price of the smallest size of tin mentioned, probably as this size of tin was a sample tin. Packaging, denoting the price transition, can be found stamped with '1/3 now 1/6' for example. In the November 1949 issue of *The Gamekeeper and Countryside* the smallest size of tin was quoted as being 9d, whilst the others were still 1/6d, 3/- and 6/- and so presumably the price of the 7½d tin had increased to 9d in February 1948 as well. A further price increase is noticed, again in *The Gamekeeper and Countryside* magazine, in May 1951 where the four individual prices are now 1/-, 2/-, 4/- and 8/-.

In a general letter, dated April 1936,

to all their retailers, a memo was sent that stated:
'PHARMACY and POISONS ACT — MAY 1936. This is to remind you that under this Act the sale of the Original RODINE Rat Poison on and after 1st May, 1936, will be restricted to qualified chemists. The Original RODINE Rat Poison cannot be sold by listed sellers as it contains Phosphorus. We are pleased, however, to enclose herewith particulars concerning RODINE (Red Squill) Rat Poison which can be sold without any restrictions, no sales licence being necessary. This RODINE (Red Squill) Rat Poison is a guaranteed toxic raticide and one which you can sell freely with the same confidence as you did the Original RODINE Rat Poison.'

Originally in 1936, it seems that Rodine 'Red Squill' was being sold at the same prices as the Original Rodine, and in the 'same' four different sized tins. Presumably, any later price increase would be the same for both product sizes, as the February 1948 advert, just mentioned, does not make any distinction between either product.

In *The Gamekeeper and Countryside* magazine, March 1954 issue, an advert for RODINE Warfarin Powder, Rat and Mouse Killer, appears, the prices being 3/-, 7/-, and 15/-

In late 2004, I purchased from a local hardware shop, Rentokil's Rodine Mouse & Rat Killer. Contained in the box were, 3x50g sachets of poison and 3 bait trays, 'for home and garden use'.

Chapter Nine

MISCELLANEOUS TRAPS

& ADVERTS

The Lewis Rabbit Snare

The patent application date for this trap was 18th January 1924 (No 1503/24) with the complete specification being accepted on 24th December 1924 becoming Patent No 226,382, the patentee being Edwin George Lewis of Basingstoke, Hampshire. The patent reads,

> 'According to the present invention a noose is employed which is set in the run and is attached to a clockwork or equivalent device which is so arranged that as soon as the animal is caught in the noose, said clockwork or the like operates to draw the noose tight, instantly strangling the animal. The snare or trap comprises a spring barrel adapted to be placed on the ground and an arm in the form of a tube is attached thereto, the draw string of the noose passing through the tube and being secured to the spring barrel.'

In *The Game and Gun and The Angler's Monthly* magazine, August 1938 issue, it was reported that

> 'We have recently tried a Humane Rat Snare sent us by Mr.E.G.Lewis, of 21, London Street, Basingstoke, which certainly has much to commend it. It is all metal and proved most effective for catching and killing rats in a variety of sites. We found that it can be adjusted to operate successfully on a floor or on the side of a rat-infested stack. The snare is neatly made and very easy to set – a most important point. Rats are killed instantaneously through the pressure of the spring. After

393

a thorough trial we can recommend this snare with every confidence. We understand that the patent rights for rabbit snares of this description have been bought by R.S.P.C.A., but that Mr Lewis still has a number of rat snares for disposal.'

The Lewis Rabbit Snare was still being advertised for sale at a cost of 2/9d each in a 1939-40 Army and Navy Stores catalogue but there was no mention of the Rat Snare.

The 'Balloon' Fly Trap

This American made trap, which was patented in USA on the 22nd June 1875, was sold extensively here in Britain. It is most probable, that eventually this trap was made in Britain by Joseph Dyson who described himself as a 'manufacturer and agent'.

These traps were advertised from 1900 to 1940. Although advertised in June 1900, George Archibald Cartwright of Glyngarth, Sandown Road Leicester, and Limehurst, Loughborough, who described himself as a merchant, didn't apply for a patent until 19th August 1901. His patent was accepted on 19th June 1902, becoming Patent No 16,616. However, the trade marks journal shows that on 8th October 1900 the word 'Balloon' was registered and related to 'a wire trap of ordinary metal for destroying beetles, flies and insects' by Joseph Loveday Dyson of 17 Leman Street, London E, who described himself as a manufacturer and agent.

BALLOON
FLY TRAP.

No. 1093.
Large ... 6/4½ doz.
Small ... 4/6 „

Glass Fly Traps

As far as is known, these traps were made during the mid-Victorian and Edwardian period, *circa* 1850-1910. They average about 7 inches high and stand on three feet, with their width varying according to their shape. They are made of clear glass and can either have a cork or glass stopper in the

neck. They were intended to sit on a
sideboard or table containing a sweet
smelling sticky liquid substance, e.g.
honey diluted with water, to attract the
wasps or flies. Once they had found
their way in, by entering from
underneath between the three feet,
and having fed upon the liquid they
would then try to fly away. Being
contained by the glass they would
quickly tire and fall down into the
sticky substance, where they would be
held.

THE "LITTLE WONDER."
Brass Tray, Glass Trap.
1 doz. in Box, with Showcard.

A dual purpose decorated glass fly trap, with both three feet and a screw
top lid complete with a hanging hook instead of the usual cork or glass stopper
was advertised in *The Ironmonger* in June 1900, and could be used in the
normal way or else hung up. This trap was called the 'Little Wonder'. Prior to
this date, the normal type of glass fly trap was being advertised by
Zimmermann & Co. of London, who were stated to be 'importers of foreign
goods, manufacturers of bronzes and lamps' with works at Hanau, Prussia.
In this March 1879 issue of Martineau & Smith's hardware trade journal
under the advert's heading of lamps, it says, '. . . and other foreign glass
goods,' and the advert shows an illustration of an 'intoxicating fly catcher.'
Presumably what is thought to be a British glass fly trap may in actual fact be
foreign imports. The same shaped glass flytraps are now being sold new and
are made in Hungary, according to the sellers. These glass flytraps are
produced in clear glass, and also in light green, pale blue and pink. All these
coloured glass flytraps have three clear glass feet below the coloured body.

NEW FLY TRAP, SQUARE.

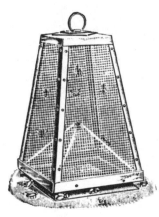

Made of
Tinned Gauze
with
Wood Bottoms.

No. 1129.

5/3 doz.

3 doz. lots, 57/- gross.

Case containing
1 gross lot, 54/- gross.

1909 CATALOGUE

Fish Traps

Allcocks of Redditch were advertising various fish traps in their 1938-9 fishing tackle catalogue, but it is not known if they actually made any of them. One minnow trap (top) is made of 'strong celluloid' with a length of $5^{1}/_{2}$ inches. Another (bottom) is called The Marvel and is made from very small wire mesh. This is a combined fish trap and bait carrier, with a length of 6 inches and a diameter of 4 inches. A willow basket type of eel trap, with a length of 3 feet 10 inches is also advertised, as are two galvanised wire fish traps. The first being a single entry trap with a length of 2 feet 3 inches which is 'also an efficient rat trap', whilst the second, illustrated below, comes as a double entry version and in two sizes of 2 feet 6 inches and 3 feet long.

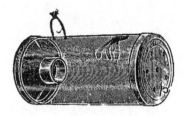

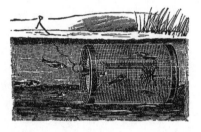

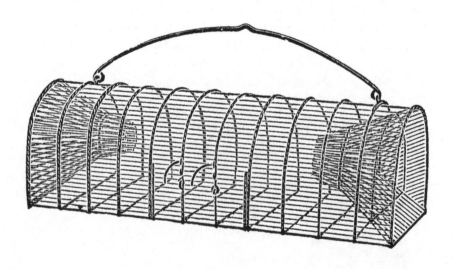

Young's catalogue 1972

FISH AND PIKE TRAPS

Strongly made in galvanised Wire Netting of $^3/_4$in. mesh, on strong galvanised framework, fitted 2 fine funnel shape traps or entrances. These entrances are almost invisible in use, works automatic, always ready, catches large numbers, one after another without attention. A good setting place is between the long grasses or reeds that cross the width of the river, just letting the entrance end come a little way outside the edge of the reeds and grasses, and pikes coming along and seeing the opening will naturally make for it and pass into the trap.

Traps 7ft. long and 3ft. wide by 2tft. high at the entrance end, the other end and the main body of the trap, being 15ins. wide and 15ins. high. **Price £13.00.**

Smaller size traps also made, 4ft. long by 24ins. wide and 15ins. high at the entrance end, the other end and body of the trap, size 10ins. wide and 9ins. high. This trap made in $^3/_4$in. mesh netting. **Price £9.75.**

These traps are suitable for all other kinds of fish, also eels, if $^1/_2$in, mesh wire is used.

Extra price is $^1/_2$in. is required, £4.00 for 7ft. size, and £3.00 for 4ft. size.

No. 503 —THE "DEMON" RAT TRAP.

This Trap is by far the best Trap at present in the market, and frequently as many as from 12 to 15 rats have been caught at one setting.
Galvanized, 14 in. diameter .. .. .. **3/9** each.

GIN BIRD OR MOUSE TRAP.

The "Safe Setter." Bright Steel
3 doz. in a box, 8/ per doz.

The Non Plus Ultra Beetle Trap.

TOP, 1903 ADVERT
MIDDLE 1908 ADVERT
BOTTOM ARMY & NAVY STORES CATALOGUE 1907, PRICE 1/4 EACH

1909 ADVERT

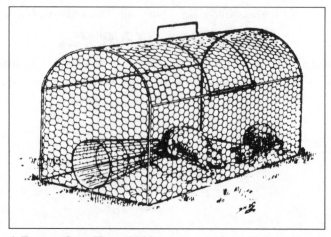

"KLEERUN"

MASTER RAT TRAPS (T)

INSTANTLY AND EASILY SET.
NO SPRINGS.   SAFE.
CANNOT HARM CHICKENS
OR PETS.
SIZE   18 in. × 6 in. × 5 in.

STOVE FINISH.   13/6 each
                       Carriage Paid.

1954 ADVERT

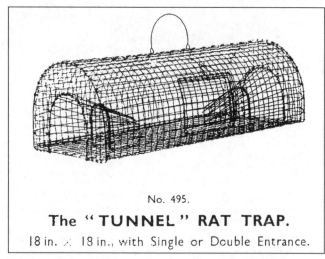

No. 495.

The "TUNNEL" RAT TRAP.

18 in. × 18 in., with Single or Double Entrance.

PROCTOR BROS 1940 CATALOGUE

A FUNNEL CAGE TRAP (1908)

THE 'CLAUSIUS TUNNEL' TRAP

This trap consists of a wooden tunnel fitted with a pivoted floor, attached to the lower side of which is a small metal sprag.

When the floor is overbalanced by the weight of the animal it closes the entrance of the trap and is kept in postion in the sprag.

For catching stoats and weasels set the trap as horizontally as possible in the run through hedges, bushes etc.

No bait is necessary as the natural curiousity leads them to investigate every passage they come across. Seeing the light through the trap they are induced to try and pass through.

Price £1.75
YOUNG'S 1972 CATALOGUE

1963 ADVERT

1962 ADVERT

POTTERY BEETLE TRAP

DEAD CERT RAT AND MOUSE TRAPS

A patented trap which works on the see-saw principle. The rodent has only to exert the slightest weight on the lethal half of the trap to release

the jaw. The trap does not require fine setting and is extremely simple in action. Immediately the trap is "see-sawed" the lever comes into play and pulls down the bait holder, releasing the spring.

1953 ADVERT

1953 ADVERT

KLIK MOUSE TRAP

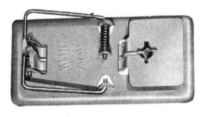

An all-metal mouse trap, of entirely original design, with large treadle. It has an extremely fine, self-setting action, is manufactured from anodized aluminium, and fitted with first-grade copper-coated springs.

UNUSUAL ROUND DEADFALL TRAP

SPRATT'S 1933 CATALOGUE

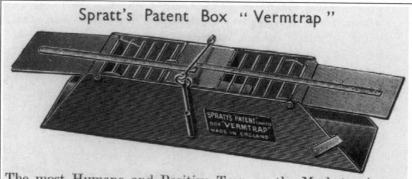

Spratt's Patent Box "Vermtrap"

The most Humane and Positive Trap on the Market. A sure and certain Trap for all kinds of Vermin, and ideal for Specimen collecting, where it is necessary the animal should be unhurt. Made of heavy-gauge sheet tin and iron-plate. Painted Green.
Made in Three Sizes.

No. 1.—23 in. by 5 in. by 5 in. .. .. .. each 25/-
No. 2.—27 in. by 7 in. by 7 in. .. .. .. ,, 30/-
No. 3.—31 in. by 9 in. by 9 in. .. .. .. ,, 35/-
Carriage Paid.

Chapter Ten

MISCELLANEOUS

COLLECTABLES

Stamps

Only two British stamps that I know of have been issued with traps, both as part of a set. The full set of stamps can be purchased on first day covers, or individual stamps can be obtained if preferred. The first set is simply called Fishing, which is slightly misleading as the stamps refer to deep sea commercial fishing. The stamp of interest to a trap collector is the 22p denomination which shows a lobster creel. This set of stamps were issued on 23rd September 1981.

The second set of stamps are called Swans, and the stamp of interest to the trap collector is the one priced at 24p, which shows a duck decoy. This set of stamps were issued on 19th January 1993.

Postcards

Postcards showing traps are hard to find, but postcards of the above mentioned stamps, Fishing and Swans, which basically shows a stamp enlarged to postcard size can be obtained, either in a full set or individually as required. These types of postcards are known as PHQ cards. Two well known producers of postcards, which occasionally show

traps on their products, are Jas. Bamforth Ltd of Holmfirth and J. Salmon Ltd of Sevenoaks.

Bamforth's produced a real photographic postcard entitled 'Caught at last' which shows a rectangular four hole choker mousetrap with a mouse caught in each of the holes. You can see from the picture that the photograph was 'posed' as the spring choker loops are set too high to have caught any mouse for real.

J. Salmon Ltd. produced a comical postcard for the proprietor of Potter's Museum, Bramber, near Steyning in Sussex, entitled 'A friend in Need is a Friend Indeed', which shows two mice freeing another from a wooden live catch box trap.

Comical postcards referring to gamekeepers, poachers etc. can be more easily found. However, the real photographic postcards showing gamekeepers in situations such as in the rearing fields etc. are harder to find, but obviously more worthwhile as they show the keeper at work in his natural environment.

Badges

Various badges have been produced by either gamekeeper organisations or by a country organisation which has a gamekeeping section.

The Gamekeeper's Association of the United Kingdom:

One type known. A round badge with a blue outer ring with the words GAMEKEEPERS' ASSOCIATION in gold lettering. The blue initials GA are entwined in the centre of the badge on a gold background. On the four cardinal points (N.S.E.W.) around the edge of the badge, in a gold colour, is a shaped projection with a single fleur-de-lys in each.

Wildfowlers Association of Great Britain and Ireland:

A round badge, with below it a curved protruding edge, all being a white colour. The gold lettering on the top of the round badge says WAGBI and at its bottom Founded 1908. The white protruding edge, below Founded 1908, has the word Gamekeeper also in gold lettering. The centre of the round badge is in red with a goose flying from right to left across it, which is in gold.

British Association for Shooting and Conservation:

Type (1a) Square. White background. 3 sided green line border, with GAMEKEEPER in silver capital letters across the bottom joining the border together. Inside the border in the top left corner is a square with the letters BA above SC. Below the letters and above the word GAMEKEEPER is the outline of a dog, duck and pheasant head superimposed on each other.

Type (1b) Square. White background. A green edged border with within it, in the top left corner in a square shape, the letters BA above SC. Below this is the outline of a dog, duck and pheasant head superimposed on each other. Below the bottom edge of the green border line is the word GAMEKEEPER in green capital letters.

Type (2a) round, with a scroll obscuring the bottom edge. Colours as above badge white and green. Across the bottom of the badge is the word GAMEKEEPER, now in a scroll, above which in the centre is the previous BASC and superimposed animals heads in a square with various game surrounding it.

Type (2b) same design as previous badge type (b) except the scroll is more cut out and the colours are in green and gold.

Type 3. A partly oblong badge, with a green background and BASC in gold coloured capital letters across it, above which is the original Gamekeepers' Association design of badge. The Words GAMEKEEPERS' ASSOCIATION, are in capital letters and are in gold lettering on a green background. The centre initials of the entwined GA are green on a gold background.

The Game Conservancy:

Type (a) round badge with green outer ring with the words in gold lettering THE GAME CONSERVANCY. In the centre a green and gold partridge on a white background. Below this round badge is a white scroll with the words KEEPER MEMBER in gold lettering.

Type (b) same as previous badge design type (a) but now with the word TRUST added after Conservancy.

Moorland Gamekeepers' Association:

A round badge with MOORLAND GAMEKEEPERS ASSOCIATION written around the edge in gold. A pale blue sky with pale green and dark green landscape. In the foreground a gold coloured grouse butt with seven grouse flying over it.

The National Gamekeepers' Organisation:

Type (1) A square badge with a gold edge. The words THE NATIONAL GAMEKEEPERS' ORGANISATION in white lettering on a green background.

Type (2) A small oblong badge with a gold edge. The capital letters N.G.O. are also in a gold colour. There are 3 different coloured backgrounds to these badges, green, red, and a dark gold colour. These badges were given to any member who raised monetary funds for the organisation. The amounts that had to be raised to receive a Green badge (type 2a) were from £10.00 to £50.00, Red badge (type 2b) £50.00 to £100.00, whilst to receive a Gold badge (type 2c) a donation of £100.00 plus had to be made. These badges were introduced in late 1998.

Type 3. An oval badge with a green background. Horizontally across the centre is a gold stripe with the words SHOOTING TIMES in red capital letters. Below this gold stripe are the initials N.G.O. in gold capital letters. Above the gold stripe is a white bird with out stretched wings facing to the right, all edged in a gold colour. This badge was produced in conjunction with *The Shooting Times,* for the National

Gamekeepers Organisation, Woodpigeon & Corvid Control Day, which took place on Saturday 12th February 2000. This event caused a lot of controversy and unwanted media attention.

The Scottish Gamekeepers Association:

This badge is rectangular in shape and has as its background the Scottish flag (which has a blue background with a white Saint Andrew's Saltire on it). In the centre of the flag is a round logo with the words THE SCOTTISH GAMEKEEPERS ASSOCIATION around its edge, in green, on a white background. The centre logo shows the silhouette of a dog's head in white, on a man's head in pale green, on a darker green background.

The Gamekeepers' Club:

This badge was produced by the publication, *Gamekeeper and Sporting Dog*. The badge is slightly oblong in shape and has a green background with a gold edge. The gold lettering says THE GAMEKEEPERS' CLUB, then under a gold line is also the word SUPPORTER in gold lettering.

National Organisation of Beaters and Pickers Up

This organisation was formed from an idea of Mark Elliott of Amesbury, Wiltshire. It is a register of people who are available to offer their services to a gamekeeping estate during the shooting season. Sometimes an estate's regular beaters are unable to attend for various reasons. If this happens at short notice, the gamekeeper can contact NOBS and request names and telephone numbers of interested people in his area, and so fill those vacant spaces in the beating line on the shoot day. This simple idea puts the supply of beaters where the demand is. Surprisingly, none of the shooting organisations or the Gamekeeping organisations thought that the idea was workable when Mr Elliott initially approached them with his idea! How wrong could they be? The organisation was officially launched in *The Shooting Times*, 26th May 2005 edition, and within 8 weeks of its launch 1,500 people had registered, and the organisation's website had received 5,359 'hits'. The website address is www.nobs.org.uk

The badge is round, with a green border. On the top half of the green border, is the wording, in white lettering, National Organisation of, whilst the lower half continues with, Beaters and Pickers Up. The centre section of the badge is white with a black silhouette of a man with an outstretched arm holding a 'crook', with a dog sitting in front. Both the man and dog are facing to the right.

Mug
The newspaper *The Countryman's Weekly* produced a mug with the logo from their incorporated publication *Gamekeeper and Sporting Dog*. The mug, which is $3^3/_4$ inches high and with a $3^1/_4$ inches diameter approximately, has a white background with The Countryman's Weekly in red lettering, whilst the remaining writing and Gamekeeper/ Dog logo plus the spaniel dog's head on the other side of the mug are in black.

Medal
Reported in *The Shooting Times & Country Magazine*, issue dated 22nd June 1962, under the heading of, 'Silver Medals for Gamekeepers' it

was stated that 'A long service award scheme for gamekeepers is announced by the Council of the Country Landowners' Association. The qualifying period is 40 years' continuous service as gamekeeper, whether as under-keeper, head keeper or as a combination of both. Included in the scheme are warreners and vermin destroyers on estates. Silver medals will be awarded to those with 40 years' service, with a bar for 50 years. The qualifying period is limited to service with not more than two employers or estates and intervening war service counts as qualifying service. The scheme is deemed to have started on February 1, 1962, and keepers must be employed on February 1 of the year in which they qualify. The scheme applies to England and Wales only, and employers need not be members of the C.L.A., or gamekeepers members of the Gamekeepers' Association. The medals will be presented at the Game Fair at Longleat, Wiltshire, July 27-28, and those wishing to enter gamekeepers for the scheme should apply to the C.L.A. headquarters at 24 St. James's Street, S.W.1.'

Prattware Pot Lid
In 1850 F&R Pratt started their pottery business in Fenton, Stoke on Trent. Felix Edward Pratt (1813-1894) saw the potential of producing pot lids and bases, as containers, for the many products which were then starting to appear commercially. The firm exhibited their multicoloured pot lids and bases at The Great Exhibition in 1851. Their pot lids were produced in 3 sizes, approximately 3inch, 4inch and 5inch diameter. Early pieces of Prattware are classed as being from 1850-1890, whilst the

later pieces are dated from 1890-1930. Eventually, Coalport owned the business.

The game bag. A medium sized pot lid of about $4^1/_4$ inches in diameter. This pot lid can be found either without the title or with the title The Game Bag around the foot of the lid. These lids were made around the 1890s.

Royal Doulton Figures

Several figures made by this famous factory are of interest to the collector of gamekeeping items and traps:

The Gamekeeper: Ref. No. HN 2879, Designer E J Griffiths, issued 1984-1992.

The Poacher: Ref. No. HN 2043, Designer L Harradine, issued 1949-1959.

The Lobster Man: Two types exist. Ref. No. HN 2317, Designer M Nicoll, issued 1964-1994, series: Sea Characters. This figure has a dark blue jumper.

Ref. No. HN 2323, Designer M Nicoll, issued 1987-1995, series: Sea Characters. This figure has a cream coloured jumper.

1953 ADVERT

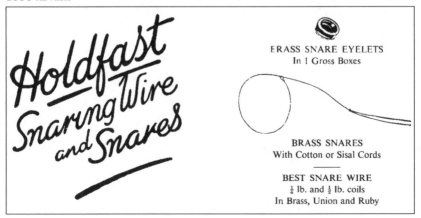

BIBLIOGRAPHY

Books referred to in this text (from which material has been used or quoted)

1576 *Englishe Dogges* (translation by Abraham Fleming) original author, Caius Johannes

1584 *Book of Information* compiled by Robert Legge by order of Sir John Perrott

1590 *A Book of Fishing with Hooke & Line. . . Another of Sundrie Engines and Trappes to take Polecats, Buzardes etc. . .* Leonard Mascall

1660 *Les Ruses Innocents, Dans Lesquelles So Voit Comment on Prend Bêtes A Quarte Pieds* Francois Fortin (French trapping manual)

1686 *The Gentleman's Recreation* Richard Blome

1768 *The Universal Directory for Taking Alive and Destroying Rats, and all other kinds of four footed and Winged Vermin, etc.* Robert Smith (Rat Catcher to the Princess Amelia)

1812 *Rural Sports* Vol.III Rev. William B. Daniel

1838 *The Penny Magazine*

1851 *Mayhew's London* edited by Peter Quennell being selections from 'London Labour and the London Poor'

1857 *The Quarterly Review* No.201, January

1868 *The Experiences of a Game Preserver* 'Deadfall'

1872 *The Idstone Papers* 'Idstone' (Rev. Thomas Pearce)

1884 *Practical Trapping of Vermin and Birds* W. Carnegie ('Moorman')

1890s/1900s *Work – Illustrated Weekly Journal*

1893 *The Partridge* (Fur and Feathers Series) A. Stuart-Wortley *et. al.*

1897 *A History of Fowling* Rev. H.A. MacPherson

1898 *Full Revelations of a Professional Ratcatcher* Ike Matthews

1899 *Smiths' Work* Paul N. Hasluck

1900 *Nature in Downland* W. H. Hudson

1904 *The Keeper's Book* Walker and Mackie

1906 *Practical Gamepreserving* W. Carnegie (Moorman)

1908 *How to Trap and Snare* W. Carnegie (Moorman)

1909 *The Balance of Nature* George Abbey

1909 *The Rat Problem* W.R. Boelter

1924 *Rats and How to Destroy Them* Mark Hovell

1926 *Pheasant Rearing and Preservation* Gilbertson & Page Ltd

1931 *The Grey Squirrel* A.D. Middleton

1962 *Traps for Grey Squirrels* Forestry Commission booklet

1967 *Early to Rise a Suffolk Morning* Hugh Barrett

1969 *The Blackcountryman* Vol.2, No.1

1970 *Fenland Molecatcher* Arthur Randell

1971 *Animal Traps and Trapping* James A Bateman

1973 *Grey Squirrel Control* Forestry Commission Booklet No.56

1976 *Rabbiting and Ferreting* E. Samuel & J. Ivester Lloyd (BFSS booklet)

1976 *Rabbit Control Booklet* No.22 The Game Conservancy

1978 *Wednesfield – the Field of Woden* John L. Smallshire

1980 *Moles and their Control* Guy N. Smith

1980 *Peasants and Poachers* Michael J. Carter

1981 *Gentlemen and Poachers* P.B. Munsche

1982 *The Black Countryman* Vol.15, no.3

1982 *Scottish Poaching Equipment* Colin Hendry

1985 The *Long Affray* Harry Hopkins

1985 *The Steel Trap in North America* Richard Gerstell

1990 *More Black Country Folk at Werk* Ned Williams

1993 *More Tales of the Old Gamekeepers* Brian Martin

1994 *A Short History of the Wolf in Britain* James Edmund Harting (originally published in 1880 as *British Animals Extinct Within Historic Times*)

2001 *Duck Decoys* Andrew Heaton

INDEX

mole trap 20, 35, 42, 84, 90, 95,
103, 133, 150, 152, 153, 154,
155, 159, 162, 163, 168, 192,
193, 196, 201, 204, 205, 206,
210, 211, 215, 217, 218, 219,
220, 227, 234, 235, 237, 242,
243, 244, 245, 246, 255, 257,
258, 275, 276, 278, 279, 280,
376, 377, 378, 379, 382, 383
Moorland Gamekeepers Association 326, 327
mouse trap 123, 168, 207, 208,
214, 220, 226, 227, 232, 255,
261, 262, 398, 403
muskrat 17, 32, 58, 59, 94, 140
myxomatosis 38, 90

N

National Gamekeepers Organisation 327, 407
nets 20, 21, 24, 42, 199, 252, 254,
287, 290, 343, 345, 366, 373,
375
North West Company 28

O

Oneida Jump Trap 62
otter 30, 40, 57, 60, 62, 63, 66, 68,
71, 94, 117, 131, 132, 153,
156, 157, 167, 226, 229, 230,
302, 308
otter boards 362

P

partridge 73, 290, 295, 299, 300,
333, 334, 359, 406
pheasant 14, 17, 18, 254, 257,
261–266, 290, 299, 315, 317,
321–325, 331, 333, 334, 340,
345, 358, 359, 365, 406
pigeon 260
poaching 16, 27, 74, 75, 287, 288,
289, 290, 298, 299, 300, 307,
308, 314, 315, 316, 317, 318,
321, 341, 356, 358, 359, 362,
366, 372, 373, 374, 375, 411

poisons 389–392
pole trap 9, 35, 48, 59, 60, 66, 73,
74, 77, 134, 150, 169, 198, 231

Q

quality marks 79, 81
Queensbury trap 224, 225

R

rabbits 10, 14, 15, 16, 32, 37, 38,
40, 57, 69, 90, 94, 119, 120,
146, 147, 152, 154, 156, 166,
169, 180–184, 187, 188, 194,
195, 200, 203, 204, 209, 212,
226, 229–231, 241, 244, 245,
247, 250, 254, 263, 264, 272,
276, 277, 280, 282, 296, 315,
320, 321, 322, 359, 366, 369,
387
rabbit nets 368, 369, 371
rabbiting spades 335, 336
rat 9, 10, 12, 21, 26, 27, 29, 35, 38,
40, 42, 45, 47, 55, 56, 61, 66,
68, 70, 71, 77, 78, 79, 82, 88,
90, 93, 94, 96, 100, 101, 120,
123, 142, 143, 149, 150, 151,
152, 153, 154, 156, 157, 160,
164, 167, 168, 169, 174, 175,
176, 177, 178, 185, 187, 188,
189, 191, 192, 193, 194, 195,
196, 200, 203, 204, 207, 209,
210, 211, 212, 214, 219, 220,
221, 222, 224, 225, 226, 228,
229, 230, 231, 232, 234, 236,
239, 241, 242, 243, 244, 245,
246, 248, 249, 250, 251, 252,
254, 255, 256, 259, 261, 263,
264, 265, 267, 269, 270, 271,
273, 275, 276, 279, 280, 283,
288, 289, 299, 307, 311, 312,
313, 314, 315, 321, 333, 337,
342, 343, 350, 359, 377–396,
398, 399, 400, 403, 404, 410,
411
ratcatcher 384–387
rat coursing 386